Media Occupations and Professions:
A Reader

Media Occupations and Professions:

A Reader

Edited by
Jeremy Tunstall

OXFORD
UNIVERSITY PRESS

*This book has been printed digitally and produced in a standard specification
in order to ensure its continuing availability*

OXFORD
UNIVERSITY PRESS

Great Clarendon Street, Oxford OX2 6DP

Oxford University Press is a department of the University of Oxford.
It furthers the University's objective of excellence in research, scholarship,
and education by publishing worldwide in

Oxford New York

Auckland Cape Town Dar es Salaam Hong Kong Karachi
Kuala Lumpur Madrid Melbourne Mexico City Nairobi
New Delhi Shanghai Taipei Toronto
With offices in
Argentina Austria Brazil Chile Czech Republic France Greece
Guatemala Hungary Italy Japan South Korea Poland Portugal
Singapore Switzerland Thailand Turkey Ukraine Vietnam

Oxford is a registered trade mark of Oxford University Press
in the UK and in certain other countries

Published in the United States
by Oxford University Press Inc., New York

Oxford is a registered trade mark of Oxford University Press
in the UK and in certain other countries

Published in the United States
by Oxford University Press Inc., New York

Introduction, editorial arrangement and selection © Jeremy Tunstall 2001

The moral rights of the author have been asserted

Database right Oxford University Press (maker)

Reprinted 2005

ISBN 0-19-874246-0

Contents

Introduction   1

Part I: Origins   **23**

1. Political Journalists   25
   MAX WEBER

2. The Profession of Journalism in England, 1855–1914   28
   ALAN J. LEE

3. Journalists   37
   A. M. CARR-SAUNDERS AND P. A. WILSON

4. The Washington Correspondents   42
   LEO C. ROSTEN

5. New Media Occupations in New York   49
   JEREMY TUNSTALL

6. Writers in the Hollywood Dream Factory   55
   HORTENSE POWDERMAKER

Part II: Moguls and Barons   **63**

7. Media Moguls in Europe   65
   JEREMY TUNSTALL AND MICHAEL PALMER

8. Newspaper Tigers   71
   NICHOLAS COLERIDGE

9. Hugenberg: Hitler's Media Mogul   79
   JEREMY TUNSTALL

10. The Soviet Union's Broadcasting Baron   83
    REINO PAASILINNA

Part III: Stars   **91**

11. Hollywood Stars and Actors   93
    LEO C. ROSTEN

12. Cinema Stars in South India   99
    SARA DICKEY

13. Political Talkers on Radio   107
    RICHARD DAVIS AND DIANA OWEN

14. Entrepreneurial Editors of National Newspapers   116
    JEREMY TUNSTALL

Part IV: Professionalizing Media Occupations **125**

15. News Agency Foreign Correspondents 127
     OLIVER BOYD-BARRETT AND TERHI RANTANEN

16. Correspondents and Individual News Sources 144
     JEREMY TUNSTALL

17. The Changing Role of TV Network News Correspondents 153
     JOE S. FOOTE

18. The Culture of Foreign Correspondence 162
     STEPHEN HESS

19. Foreign Correspondents: A Team, B Team 170
     MARK PEDELTY

20. The Hollywood TV Producer 179
     MURIEL G. CANTOR

21. BBC Trade Unions 189
     TOM BURNS

22. Television Producers 194
     JEREMY TUNSTALL

23. The Television Labour Market in Britain 203
     RICHARD PATERSON

24. New Technologies and Changing Work Practices in
     Irish Broadcasting 214
     ELLEN HAZELKORN

**Part V: National and Regional Overviews of
Media Occupations** **227**

25. Media Occupations in Sub-Saharan Africa 229
     GRAHAM MYTTON

26. Servants of the State or the Market? Media and Journalists
     in China 240
     CHIN-CHUAN LEE

27. Australian Media Occupations 253
     RODNEY TIFFEN

28. Journalists and Media Professionals in France 263
     MICHAEL PALMER

29. Media Professionals in the Former Soviet Union 273
     BRIAN McNAIR

30. The Contradictions of Journalism in Germany 283
     HANS J. KLEINSTEUBER AND SIEGFRIED WEISCHENBERG

     Select Bibliography 293
     Index 299

Introduction

As the mass media have expanded, so also the media occupations have expanded and become more central within modern societies. Across the world hundreds of thousands of fresh university graduates want to become journalists, television producers, actors, photographers, radio disc-jockeys, film-makers, and advertising agency people. New media occupations are emerging from the Internet and other new digital services.

However, the media industries and their constituent occupations are also extremely variegated, fragmented, and unstandardized. This fragmentation exists between separate occupations; for example, journalists tend to believe that they have little in common with advertising people, let alone with radio disc-jockeys, actors, or TV camerapersons. There is huge variety also *within* any of these 'occupations'; and there are big differences between separate countries.

There are also sharp contrasts between the core elite of a media occupation and the total full-time and part-time followers of that activity. For instance, in a European country the national elite in journalism might consist of a few hundred, or perhaps a thousand, people; but the total number of full-time, freelance, and part-time journalists might be many thousands. So also with radio and TV producers, advertising people, actors, artists, and others. Media occupations tend to sprawl and go fuzzy at their peripheries.

Consequently we see within the media world and media industries a large number of occupational fragments—many different sub-categories of journalist, of TV production workers, of advertising personnel, and so on. Within this fragmented occupational world there are 'horizontal' attempts of similar workers to combine together as fellow 'professionals', or as fellow 'craft' members or as fellow trade union members. However, there are opposing 'vertical' forces coming from the market and emphasizing very steep hierarchies in terms of financial reward and general status or prestige. A familiar and significant example of a *vertical* occupation is acting, in which the successful stars may be paid one hundred times as much as are less successful actors. A familiar example of a *horizontal* occupation would be traditional skilled print workers employed by a national newspaper with standard rates of pay at the local (or company) level for all fellow craft workers.

From Journalism and Acting: Hierarchy and Occupational Community

Newer media tend to grow from, or expand out of, older media; television drew heavily upon radio and film. Perhaps the most radical upsurge in new media occurred in the late nineteenth and early twentieth century—silent film, recorded music, and then radio. In terms of occupational inheritance, three long-established occupations upon which the twentieth-century media could depend were *journalism* (and writing), *acting* (and other related forms of entertainment), and *music* of various kinds.

These occupations remain central to the present-day mass media. All of these traditional (and subsequently media) occupations can be traced back hundreds of years prior to 1900. All three also had strong traditions of *hierarchy* (and inequality) as well as traditions of collegiality and occupational community.

Journalism, especially daily journalism, was beginning by 1750 to emerge as a separate line of business activity in Europe and North America. It was already hierarchical; the press businessmen were printer-booksellers who were expanding into the newspaper business. Their small numbers of employees included printers and writers (mostly part-time). The 'hyphenate' bookseller-printer-newspaper owner might be receiving several revenue streams (including sales revenue, advertising revenue, and political subsidy), while the 'journalist' might be receiving very little. In the eighteenth (and nineteenth) century the theatre was also a business and there were already star actors receiving premium rates of pay.

In addition to the financial hierarchy and the general division of labour, there was also a 'moral division of labour'.[1] This was perhaps especially salient in the Victorian period. By 1900 there were sharp distinctions in the theatre between the respectable drama performance and various less respectable, more bawdy, more working-class, and more 'adult' types of entertainment. This moral division of labour was also found in the press. A journalist could work for an extremely respectable daily newspaper devoted to politics, finance, and foreign news; but a journalist might work for a blood-and-thunder newspaper which focused on sexy court cases, scandal in high society, crime, and sport. This moral division of labour was also quickly evident in the new film business in the years after 1896. Some film workers were making respectable family entertainment; but the 'flicks' quickly became notorious for what-the-butler-saw nudity and what respectable people defined as pornography. The moral division of labour still continues in present-day media occupations, where it is complicated by an overlay of artistic, political, gender, and ethnic elements.

Also well established by 1900 was the tendency towards an occupational community; this is experienced when the relevant workers find a substantial overlap between their working lives and their non-working lives. Larger cities already had their distinctive theatre and newspaper districts, whose employees typically worked at unusual times (especially the evening) and tended to intermix socially; in these fairly insecure and irregular types of employment, social life also became a network for finding work.

---

1 Everett Hughes, *Men and their Work* (New York: Free Press, 1958) and *The Sociological Eye*, Chicago: Aldine, 1971.

Workers in film, radio, recorded music, and television subsequently established strong occupational communities and sub-occupational social networks. A leading example of the occupational community was already developing in Hollywood by 1920. The first film-making arrivals in Los Angeles came by train; the origins of Hollywood as movie capital were closely entwined with the expansion of California in general and the coming into fashion of the balmy winter climate of the south-western USA. Stars dominated early Hollywood imagery and the first superstars— Douglas Fairbanks, Mary Pickford, Charlie Chaplin—all lived in Beverly Hills, then a raw new suburb just west of Hollywood. They were pioneers in shaping the casual southern California way of life—planting trees and grass, building swimming pools and tennis courts, having picnics on the beach, and taking winter trips over the mountains to the desert.

Subsequent waves of aspiring stars and ready-made (Broadway) stars embraced the idea of working *and living* in Hollywood. Entertainers and actors who wanted to be stars also wanted to live in Los Angeles. A more recent wave of new stars were the rock stars—Elvis Presley wanted to be a movie star as well as a music star; to do this, he lived for lengthy periods in Hollywood.

Los Angeles offers creature comforts; it seemed a good place for a family. Above all you had to live there in order to get on in movies, then in network radio, then in TV. Many participants have described how social life can turn into a series of auditions. As Hollywood became more fragmented industrially, the occupational community became yet more important. Hollywood was obsessed by gossip and negotiation on new projects. Community gossip and industrial news were provided and stimulated by two daily trade papers—*Daily Variety* and the *Hollywood Reporter*.

Hollywood was a better place to live than New York if you were an unemployed actor. Anne Peters studied aspiring actresses and found that they took other employment, but they also attended acting lessons, badgered potential agents, and went to casting 'cattle calls'.[2] For at least a while, this apparently was not too bad a life; and even such few chances of success as existed there would not be available if you did not live in Los Angeles.

The occupational community can provide all kinds of support. Parents, siblings-in-law, ex-spouses, neighbours, hairdressers, tennis partners—any or all of these may assist your career. There are famous acting dynasties and producer dynasties. Hollywood was also built on technical crafts, which, like crafts everywhere, had strong family (especially father-to-son) elements.

Other film (and then TV) occupational communities grew up in other cities around the world; some of these film communities were partly modelled on Hollywood, but all were also responding to basic characteristics of the film business. The Indian movie community in north-west Bombay (Mumbai) was partly modelled on the one in north-west Los Angeles. The Hollywood and Bollywood occupational communities subsequently also embraced television. West London provided an example of a TV-oriented

---

2 Anne Peters, 'Acting and Aspiring Actresses in Hollywood' (Ph.D. dissertation, University of California, Los Angeles, 1971).

occupational community focused on the BBC's scattered buildings (some of which were old film studios) in Shepherd's Bush. The surrounding suburbs (on both sides of the river Thames) were conveniently close and pleasant places in which to live; these same west London suburbs were also heavily used for filming police shows, comedies, and street interviews.

Media people are not only dwellers in an occupational community, they are also the people of the word—the written as well as the spoken word. Both the newspaper and the stage play were written; quite early in the development of the film the *script* became the master document, the blueprint, of what was about to be filmed. Subsequently radio and television became heavily scripted media; so also advertising, and so also the Internet. But media people are also the people of the *spoken* word. It is not only TV producers and directors who are story-tellers; journalists are forever in pursuit of the 'good' story. Journalists, as an occupation, are the professionals of the anecdote. Journalists, producers, and directors are all professionally articulate. They tend to be the people who at school were good at writing, speaking up in class, orating, and acting; with some exceptions, such as financial journalists, they were probably bad at maths and science.

Careers: Youth, Gender, Ethnicity, and Insecurity

The media occupations are not unique in their emphasis on youth. But the young and aspiring media worker is aware of a strong youth emphasis, an emphasis that has at least some rational foundation. Advertisers seek young audiences because young people are more likely to buy new consumer products. A newspaper with an elderly readership can see its circulation dying off with its readers. Young people (research indicates) are more likely to buy a new newspaper or a new magazine or to follow a new television series. Many of the new TV and cable-and-satellite channels which appeared after 1980 were successful at attracting young audience profiles; movies also depend for their success on the initial theatrical audience, which is a young, 'going out' audience. Recorded music is similarly geared to youth and youth purchase patterns; so also the Internet.

Print employers taking on new journalists, or TV acquisition executives commissioning new series, are always looking for young talents who will appeal to young audiences. The theatre and opera have always been youth-oriented; Mozart and other classical musicians were child prodigies. In the Victorian period editors were often very youthful. John Delane was aged 23 when in 1841 he became editor of *The Times*, then London's leading newspaper. C. P. Scott, the *Manchester Guardian*'s most famous editor, was appointed in 1873, also at the age of 23. At the end of the nineteenth century Hearst and Harmsworth were owners of leading New York and London dailies while still in their thirties. All of the new media of film, radio and TV, cable, and the Internet were mainly pioneered by youngish people.

In 1900, like a century later, media workers could see, simply by looking around the office, that this was in truth a young man's (and, by 2000, a young woman's) business. Many careers peak in their thirties or early forties. One of the rewards of having reached a senior position in your forties is that in your fifties you may be given a lighter (but pleasanter) job; ex-editors can become columnists, ex-heads of TV channels or production studios may return to executive producer work. Even ageing acting stars may find work.

But at the start of one's career there is the difficulty that employers really want youth-with-experience. So where does one obtain the initial experience? In recent decades one answer has increasingly become the vocational university course—acting school, journalism school, or film school. Another answer: take a low-level media job for little or no pay.

Nevertheless some established career ladders may get clogged with aspirants, while an obscure new offering can become a rapidly rising career escalator. A new technology, a new publication, a new genre, or a new channel can quickly launch a batch of spectacular career successes. The talkie movies did this in the 1930s. Hollywood has seen a long succession of small independent companies (in both film and TV) which have become big independents with big individual career successes. MTV, as the first music video channel, launched numerous successful careers both for musicians and for executives in movies, TV, and cable.

In some media areas there is a fast track which stays in place for a long time. 'News and Current Affairs' has been the BBC's fast career track. Numerous BBC channel bosses (both in TV and radio) were broadcast journalists; for most of the years since 1944 the BBC's boss (Director-General) has been a journalist. Journalists (with political experience) are thought best suited to run a BBC which is dependent on multi-party political support for its finances and its survival.

Every year a lot of new people are sucked into the media occupations, while at the same time a lot of people leave. Many young people aspire to work in these areas; many do achieve some employment as junior reporters, do get to appear in a few TV episodes, do act in a few commercials, or do work on the lower slopes of advertising. Many of these aspirants persist and find regular work, while others leave. There also appears to be another substantial outflow in mid-career, of people in their thirties or forties. Where do they go? They go to quite a wide range of other occupations. Some are already pursuing a second job; many journalists are already doing some public relations or consultancy work. Many media workers do bits of teaching at a local college; because of the media tradition of learning on the job, many experienced media people in practice have hands-on teaching experience. Many specialists, who for example have made programming or done written journalism—about tourism, chemical engineering, or food retailing—cross over to work in those industries. Popular career destinations for former media people in recent decades have been charities and the cultural industries; many cultural organizations (such as art galleries or museums) want to employ people with media experience. A broad range of media workers spy into numerous obscure corners of the economy and society; some spy what they see as a niche for themselves as self-employed businesspeople.

What about media career prospects for women and members of ethnic minorities? There is huge variation between countries but broadly the proportion of women in media employment has improved in recent decades more than has the position of ethnic minorities (relative to numbers in the overall national population). For example David Weaver, reporting women's employment data from 19 separate national studies, found that about *one third* of journalists were women. All but one of the countries had a figure between 24 per cent and 49 per cent. Women made up between 33 per cent and 35 per cent of the journalist workforce in countries as different as China, Hong Kong, Australia, Hungary, and the USA. The same study found much lower proportions of ethnic minority journalists—for example 8 per cent in both the USA and Brazil, 3 per cent in Canada, and 2 per cent in the UK. Most of the country studies, moreover, did not even report any data on ethnic minorities.[3]

In the past, most media occupations overwhelmingly employed males; both the 'craft' and the more gentlemanly or 'professional' ends of the occupation emphasized the male, the macho, and (in all western societies) the 'white' male. Actresses were one high-profile and traditional exception and the requirements of acting, such as night work and travel, gave actresses a suspect position in the Victorian moral division of labour.

Additional macho elements were perhaps injected into both radio and television, because both employed their first big batches of personnel shortly after a world war. Thus radio in the 1920s employed many survivors of one world war, while television in the 1950s had distinctly ex-military elements in its occupational atmosphere.

When this editor studied British national newspapers in the late 1960s there were very few women (and no ethnic minorities) even in middle-ranking positions, apart from fashion correspondents and editors of the 'women's page'. The picture was similar in broadcasting, especially in television. There have been substantial changes since that time. Several specific media factors have operated in favour of women; advertisers continue to be more interested in women than in men. Much of the newer consumer and lifestyle material is oriented towards women. Nevertheless other recent developments unintentionally operate against women; the trend towards a more 24-hour continuous flow of material, the boom in low-budget television programming, and irregular hours generally—all of these tend to operate against mothers of small children. Successful women media workers are less likely to have young children than are their male opposite numbers.

While women and minorities have made two steps forward, they may have effectively taken one step backwards as a consequence of increased freelance and casual employment. In the past, when a newspaper or a radio/TV network employed most of its people on a semi-permanent basis, it may have seemed easier to introduce, and to pursue, a long-term policy of employing more women and more ethnic minorities.

However, as many media organizations in the 1980s became more committed to employing women and minorities, these same media organizations also slimmed down by transferring catering, cleaning, and then other services to outside specialist companies. In addition media activities which previously had been regarded as core, internal, and staff were 'put out'. It

---

3 David Weaver (ed.), *The Global Journalist* (Cresskill, NJ: Hampton Press, 1998), 457–8.

was not only the most commercial and profit-oriented organizations which did this. For example, in the 1970s the BBC—in keeping with its tradition of excellence in costume design—employed over two hundred costume designers on a 'staff' basis. Subsequently this activity was radically cut back, with most of the (predominantly women) costume designers going freelance and working through agents. These costume specialists, of course, were highly employable people and some left the TV industry at this point.

Similar things have happened within many of the previously macho crafts, including the studio, film-and-tape, and post-production and editing areas of television and film. This has a big impact in terms of career expectations. People who were previously within the hierarchy of a large specialized department or skill are now bobbing about as freelance individuals or belong to groups and teams of a few people. Rather than seeking to ascend through a specific bureaucracy (located on certain floors of a specific building), more individuals see their careers as depending upon the patronage and career trajectory of a key editor or an insurgent 'independent' entrepreneurial executive.

Individuals: Media Moguls

The middle levels of the media are inhabited by 'professionalizing' and 'craft' occupations. But before going on to discuss these, let us look at three categories of powerful and highly paid individuals. None of these three categories is unique to the media. The *mogul* is simply the owner-operator, the entrepreneur, the 'self-made' businessman. Secondly, the *baron* is the top manager; the baron typically is a chief executive either of an entire media company or of a major division such as the movie studio or a television network. Thirdly, the *star* is the performer—the movie or TV star, the famous editor, the celebrity comedian or singer.

All three categories, then—moguls, barons, and stars—existed before such modern mass media as film and radio; all three categories also exist more widely in business and other spheres. However, these three categories of media individuals have certain features which reflect the unusual characteristics of the media business. These smallish numbers of individuals exercise a particular type of power, simply because the media business is unique in taking up the daily attention of billions of people. These individuals uniquely exercise the power of news and publicity, the power to confer (and to deny) celebrity on a national and international scale.

Compared with a broad range of other industries, media businesses may be unusual in the extent to which power and discretion are available to be exercised by people or one person at the very top. A media mogul can buy or sell major subsidiary companies; a media baron can re-schedule and re-organize a television network; a media star can decide whether to appear in that movie or whether to continue with this TV series. Media organizations—and especially daily newspapers and other daily output—lend themselves to being rapidly re-programmed and re-directed from above; decisions to attack this politician or to investigate that company or that scandal can be carried out immediately.

These top individuals in the media, of course, enjoy unique publicity resources. Current stars are among the most highly publicised and most recognised of all people. Some of this publicity washes over onto the media barons and media moguls, who in turn receive more publicity than the mere financial scale of their businesses would seem to justify. These leading media individuals are unique not only in terms of publicity, but also in terms of secrecy and of 'hype', or false information. Much of what is written and broadcast about these people leans heavily on what their publicists choose to reveal, and fails to report what the top individuals wanted to keep secret.

Media moguls are the first of the three individual media categories. Media moguls are owner-operators; the purest case is the media mogul who is the chief owner (or who commands an effective majority of voting shares) and is also the hands-on chief executive. This owner-operator media mogul is an entrepreneur who tends to build his media empire through acquisition; he is a take-over and 'turn-around' specialist, who also launches new media enterprises. Finally, the media mogul has an eccentric personal management style (which matches his ownership control); this eccentric style usually includes a distinctive political stance, which in turn tends to involve populist-conservative positions plus close (and sometimes tense) relationships with incumbent governments and leading individual politicians.

Successful media moguls have tended to start young (they have had a lot of acquisitions ahead of them). The apprentice media mogul may acquire his first significant media property from his father; both William R. Hearst and Rupert Murdoch had an early career boost of this kind.

The first wave of significant media moguls emerged with the mass popular newspaper around the 1890s. William R. Hearst remains a classic example, not least because he went beyond his chain of American big-city newspapers into magazines, a Hollywood independent movie production company, and a major news agency (INS). Other pioneer media moguls began in newspapers. Contemporary with Hearst was Alfred Harmsworth (Lord Northcliffe), who launched the London *Daily Mail* in 1896 and eventually owned a large stable of national and local newspapers, magazines, and children's publications. An important (Hitler-era) German media mogul was Alfred Hugenberg, whose business interests moved from steel to newspapers, news agencies, advertising, and film production. Robert Hersant was perhaps France's leading post-1945 media mogul; he began in provincial newspapers and built a press chain, which included *Le Figaro*, before entering other media fields including television.

The United States, with its large number of commercially successful media outlets, has had, and still has, more authentic media moguls than any other country. Following the early press moguls came the 'founding father' movie moguls. Commercial radio also had its crop of owner-operator moguls. A leading radio example was William Paley, who from 1928 built up the CBS radio network and group of owned stations; Paley subsequently controlled the CBS television network, the CBS local TV station group, and other media activities.

William Paley eventually exemplified a problem which faces other media moguls in their sixties—the question of a successor. Some media moguls hand over to one of their children, usually a son who has been groomed for the post, but who does less well than his dynamic father. The main alternative is to seek out a successor baronial executive. By 1972, William Paley had completed more than four decades as a radio and TV network owner-operator. For most of the next decade Paley hired and fired a succession of CBS chief executives; other media moguls of advanced age have followed this same pattern, which typically marks the relative decline of a once-great media empire.

Whenever press (or radio or film) ownerships have been allowed into commercial television ownership, the situation has been favourable to the emergence of media moguls. In addition to the United States, other early favourable locations were Australia, Mexico, and Brazil. Australia produced a classic example in Rupert Murdoch, with Kerry Packer not far behind. In both Brazil and Mexico dominant mogul-led commercial television companies developed. Emilio Azcarraga inherited a Mexican radio-into-television business from his father in 1964; for the next 33 years Azcarraga controlled the bulk of Mexican television (networks and stations) and he also owned radio stations, newspapers, magazines, music companies, football teams, and the Aztec Stadium in Mexico City. Throughout his 33 years of media moguldom he supported, and was supported by, the PRI as the governing political party in Mexico.

Media moguldom was held back in many countries by state control of broadcasting and by the public service model, as found in western Europe. The deregulatory policies of the 1980s, and the world-wide trend towards more commercial networks, provided golden opportunities for rising media moguls. One of the most remarkable was Silvio Berlusconi in Italy, who in the 1980s came to dominate Italian commercial television. The media mogul pattern spread across western Europe and in the 1990s into Russia and other formerly Communist eastern and central European countries. The spread of commercial television, and of satellite-to-cable, in India and elsewhere in Asia and Africa also led to the emergence of many new media moguls.

Media Barons   The term *media baron*, as used here, relates to a person who is a top manager, who may be a dominating manager of a big media enterprise, but who (unlike the mogul) is not in ownership control. In fact the chief executives of most large media organizations around the world are not moguls but barons. The media baron is often just the familiar case of the chief executive of a public company who is not also the controlling owner; the media baron, like other chief executives, can be voted out by shareholders and/or by a board or executive committee. The media baron can also be one of several media barons working under a media mogul; a mogul might employ several barons each to run one major division, such as the television network, the movie studio, the cable-and-satellite operations, or the newspaper-and-magazine division.

Around the world the most common example of the media baron is probably the chief executive of the provincial city media enterprise. This baron may preside over a newspaper group which has two city dailies and/or two or three commercial radio stations. The baron's job involves working with editors, producers, or other creative people and with finance, advertising, marketing, and technology executives.

In the very largest media conglomerates there might be as many as ten barons. In the merged and converged Hollywood-and-network companies of recent times one of the baronial movie jobs with the highest profile is 'president of production'; this person is in charge of the studio's high-risk annual output of new movies. One of the most publicized incumbents of this occupational role in the 1990s was Michael De Luca, who became Production President at New Line in 1993, at the age of 29. Like many of his predecessors, De Luca came to Beverly Hills via Brooklyn. Most appointees to such baronial jobs in the 1990s were a few years older; even so, a substantial proportion had already been fired by their fortieth birthday.

Performance in baronial positions such as these is of course measured against financial targets and profit within the relevant division. Stress levels are said to be high, as are salaries and other fringe benefits. Producers and other creative people complain about the presence of more and more businesspeople (MBAs, consultants, and accountants), but one consequence has been to escalate still further salary levels and stock options.

Some of the media baronial pattern—high profile, high stress, high pay, and youngish exit—seems to have spread from the USA to Europe. During the 1990s the 'remuneration package' of media barons across Europe rose steeply, although they did not all match the £6.8 million ($11 million) in salary and bonuses earned by Sam Chisholm in 1996/7, his seventh and last year as chief executive of Rupert Murdoch's BSkyB satellite TV operation in Britain.[4]

There is one other sub-category of media baron, namely the not-for-profit baron. The most obvious example is the chief executive of a public, or public service, broadcasting operation. Another key example is the boss of the big, but co-operatively owned, news agency like the Associated Press. Yet another possible example would be the chief executive of a university press, with its scholarly and educational prestige—rather than profit—goals.

The BBC's Director-General is perhaps the best-known example of a not-for-profit media baron; but there have long been similar posts in most other similar countries. Although no comprehensive study has been conducted either of news agency or public broadcasting chief executives these two—apparently quite different—baronial roles seem to have a number of common characteristics:

- The barons in executive charge of these organizations are mostly journalists by professional background.
- These not-for-profit media barons see themselves as 'strong' executives, not just passive consensus-seekers.
- Typically they are in office for quite lengthy periods; recent BBC Director-Generals have lasted an average of seven years. In six

4 Jeremy Tunstall and David Machin, *The Anglo-American Media Connection* (Oxford: Oxford University Press, 1999), 181.

decades up to 1984 the US Associated Press had only four General Managers. Kent Cooper (1925–48) set the pattern for the AP boss,[5] who is perhaps the most powerful single journalist not only in the USA but also in the world. Reuters in its not-for-profit era (up to the late 1980s) also had a run of long-serving General Managers, including Roderick Jones (1915–41), whom even the approved history describes as an 'autocrat'. Another extremely forceful Reuters General Manager was Gerald Long, who made Reuters the strongest of the world agencies again and then led it out of not-for-profit status and into spectacular commercial profit.[6]

■ Public barons of this kind have to engage in much 'political diplomacy'. The BBC baron must consult with both government and opposition politicians; the AP baron must consult frequently with domestic customers and news services and with politicians and media people around the world.

■ The not-for-profit media baron is also involved in complex technological decisions. A news agency like AP (or Reuters) has to be at the forefront of current distribution and news-gathering technologies. The history of news agencies is quite largely a history of technology. Two of the BBC's most effective bosses (John Reith, 1922–38 and John Birt, 1993–2000) had engineering backgrounds and were technological innovators.

■ These public barons must also wrestle with financial problems; the licence fees allowed by governments, like the prices which media customers are willing to pay for agency services, always seem to be inadequate. These chief executives are thus always looking for savings, for cutbacks, and for fresh revenue.

■ Typically the people who appoint the public media baron—and to whom he reports—recognize the complexity of the problems handled by their chief executive. These board members (with some exceptions) seem to recognize their own relatively 'amateur' status. They have appointed an expert who rapidly becomes even more expert in the political, diplomatic, financial, creative, and technological aspects of the baronial task. Compared with a commercial chief executive, or a baron working under a mogul, not-for-profit media barons are often allowed to 'get on with the job' and to exercise a commanding position.

Around the world there are, of course, many not-for-profit media barons who are government appointees. Especially in the recent times of media deregulation and 'democratization', there are many examples of public media barons who are striving to distance themselves (and the public broadcaster or the national news agency or the previously government-controlled newspaper) from political direction and government interference. Along with other varieties of media baron, these 'striving-for-distance' public barons need to be studied.

5 Kent Cooper, *Barriers Down* (New York: Farrar and Rinehart, 1942).

6 Donald Read, *The Power of the News: The History of Reuters, 1849–1989*, 2nd edn. (Oxford: Oxford University Press, 1999).

Media Stars   Our third main category of important individuals are the *stars*. They can be defined in terms of audience appeal; a 'successful' star is someone whose previous performances have had a noticeable (often measurable) audience appeal. This appeal is especially obvious in recorded music, but it extends across a range of film, TV, and print and may also include, for example, the celebrity film director—whose name 'above the title' will add to the film's commercial appeal.

Media stardom, like the media generally, exists at the local, the national, and the international levels. A local disc-jockey or press columnist can be famous in Little Rock, Lyon, or Lima but unknown outside that city. Probably the most prevalent type of stardom is national; the biggest stars in India are overwhelmingly Indian movie and music stars. But there are also international stars—especially music stars and Hollywood TV or movie stars.

The United States, with both its more than two hundred local TV markets and its strong national media, is the greatest single star-producing nation. US stardom is not confined to Hollywood, but is found also in, for instance, the newspaper cartoonist, astrologer, comic strip author, or columnist. There are obvious differences between newspaper columnists (most of whom had a previous career in print journalism) and Hollywood stars (most of whom had an early start in some kind of live performance, if only in high school). There are, however, several marked similarities:

- National distribution and syndication spreads Hollywood star performances across the US. But newspapers also syndicate the work of columnists, cartoonists, and comic strip artists; some leading columns appear in 300 or 400 separate US dailies, while columns, cartoons, and strips (like Hollywood performances) are also syndicated internationally.
- Stars have their support teams. Already by the late 1930s a major movie star would employ an agent, a business manager, and a personal secretary (to answer fan mail); subsequently stars added lawyers, personal publicists, and security guards. The star columnist is also often the front man or front woman of a supporting team of researchers and assistants.
- Stars can be further defined as successful performers who cross over between media. Singing stars and TV stars cross over into films; most performance stars seek print, radio, and TV publicity when their next greatest, latest thing is due for release. American newspaper columnists—even those who specialize in politics—also cross over into other media; many columnists appear regularly on radio and television. Some columnists write additional magazine pieces, make speeches, wrap up old columns into books, and also develop insider newsletters or other specialist output.
- Performance stars are encouraged by their agents and managers to milk their success while it lasts. This does not merely mean 'negotiating up' for larger financial slices in the next movie or the next TV season; it may also generate major additional revenue streams from advertising, sponsorship, or promotional activity. Columnists may

not be in demand as clothing sponsors, but some columnists make a nice living out of after-dinner speaking or conference chairing.

- Many columnists and many performance stars have political connections. A substantial fraction of Washington political columnists worked previously as Presidential speechwriters or congressional aides;[7] there seems to be some affinity between the 800-word column and the six-minute political speech. Many Hollywood stars have also delivered twenty-second sound bites on political platforms.

Are there any similarities in the career trajectories of columnists and Hollywood performance stars? There is a tendency for columnists' popularity (in terms of numbers of syndicated outlets) to peak in late middle age; but some columnists continue into their seventies and eighties. The careers of movie and TV stars tend to peak earlier; most Hollywood stars only enjoy about one decade of major success—consisting typically of about five or six movies, or one successful television series running for perhaps seven years (and thus generating enough episodes for eternal re-run heaven). Apart from a few superstar exceptions, most star careers seem to get stuck somewhere along the way, with the star's now-high price finding no takers. Many stars become typecast into a genre which then goes out of fashion, just as the TV cowboy series did long ago. However, many stars—after perhaps a lengthy period of 'resting'—accept their changed circumstances and develop a less stellar, but still well-paid, second career. Thus former big movie stars who would never have considered TV do decide to take on the potentially long haul of a TV series. A lot of Hollywood stars have pursued later careers in Las Vegas, where they can still attract their old fans and which is only a one-hour flight from Los Angeles.

One final point about performance stars and their crossover activities. Bing Crosby, who crossed over between movies, radio, recording, and television, was also a successful businessman. Moreover, long before Crosby, two actors, one actress, and a director (Charlie Chaplin, Douglas Fairbanks, Mary Pickford, and D. W. Griffith) set themselves up in 1919 as United Artists. In recent times many performers in many countries have developed their own production companies and become mini-moguls.

Thus the three individual categories—mogul, baron, star—are not always pure and simple. Not only stars but also barons seek to become moguls; the media baron who owns a large slice of (but not a controlling interest in) the big media company already exists and may be more important in the future.

Horizontal (Professional and Craft) Occupations versus Vertical/ Market Forces

As suggested above, the members of some media occupations have tried to pursue *horizontal* strategies; one common horizontal strategy is professionalization and another is craft unionisation. These strategies typically focus on controlling one particular line of work; professionalizing strategies focus on 'higher'-level creative, conceptual, or production leadership roles. Craft strategies typically focus on control of the work involved in

7 Sam G. Riley, *The American Newspaper Columnist* (Westport, Conn.: Praeger, 1998), 98–131.

operating a particular piece of technology in, for example, newspaper printing or film or TV production.

With this kind of perspective in mind, it is possible to think of the media industries (much like other industries) as made up of several occupational layers. Fig. 1 shows five levels of media occupation:

1 Top individuals
2 Professionalizing occupations
3 Craft technical occupation
4 White collar
5 Unskilled

Such a classification has some obvious general validity. It loosely matches the social class hierarchy of industrial society; and it also loosely matches the kind of hierarchy which millions of people experience within large employing organizations.

Five layers of horizontal media occupations	Vertical medial occupations
1. *Top individuals* (moguls, barons, stars)	
2. *Professionalizing occupations*	
3. *Craft and technical occupations*	
4. *White collar*	
5. *Unskilled*	

The vertical occupations (read top-to-bottom) are: Journalist · Actors · Musician · Advertising · Camera Photography · Art Design Costume · IT Computing

Fig. 1
Horizontal and vertical media occupations

This perspective of five layers of horizontal media occupations had some validity in many countries in the first half of the twentieth century. This perspective—and the broad professionalizing and craft strategies within it—was most valid and most successful in the third quarter of the twentieth century (1950–75). This success depended quite significantly on the strength of trade unions and the tactics which these trade unions pursued within both the craft and professionalizing layers during this time period.

Trade unions had long been strong within the newspaper industry. This strength was especially evident in cities such as Paris, London, and New York, where there was strong competition between big daily newspapers.[8]

8 See J. W. Freiberg, *The French Press* (New York: Praeger, 1981); Seymour Martin Lipset, Martin Trow, and James Coleman, *Union Democracy* (New York: Free Press, 1956); Graham Cleverley, *The Fleet Street Disaster* (London: Constable; Beverly Hills, Calif.: Sage, 1976); Cynthia Cockburn, *Brothers* (London: Pluto Press, 1983).

These daily newspapers were extremely vulnerable to quickie strikes shortly before printing time, and the competitive situation gave added salience. The strength and legal position of trade unions varied between countries but in the Roosevelt years (1933–45) American unions obtained a favourable legislative climate; and after 1945 the legislative climate for unions was very favourable in Britain, France, and other European countries. Also in Europe, public broadcasting in practice incorporated trade unions into the management system. After 1945 there was a huge media expansion, not least in television; this assisted trade unions, and the television industry in London, Paris, New York, and also Los Angeles became strongly unionized. This unionization strengthened the craft and technical occupations in particular. But the 'professionalizing' occupations were also strengthened by trade union action, although in Hollywood these unions were called 'guilds'.

Within each nation the overall media trade union picture was complex. Typically each major industry such as the press or broadcasting had a number of specific specialized and professional unions, and one or two broad 'industrial' unions. Often yet other unions—notably for electricians, but also for drivers and others—were involved. Overall, however, these complex constellations of trade unions could claim that they had obtained major benefits for their members—especially, they claimed, good pay, substantial security, and some control over entry to the occupation.

But the broad successes of professionalization, crafts, and trade unions in the century's third quarter did not continue into the years after 1975. Computerization and other forms of new technology played a large part in this; trade unions typically resisted computerization in both press and broadcasting and the successful management introduction of new technology substantially weakened the unions. But in retrospect the main union strength could be seen to have focused on the biggest units in the biggest cities—especially major daily newspapers, national television networks, and the national film industry. Outside these major media centres media workers typically received much lower pay and the trade unions were also weaker.

The arrival of additional cable and satellite TV networks weakened broadcasting unions. Some of these new networks were based outside the traditional locations (e.g. CNN in Atlanta) and these new networks also had radically lower budgets for both production and outside acquisition of programming.

From around 1980 (the election of President Reagan) the legislative climate in the US and then in western Europe shifted against trade unions and in favour of deregulation and privatization; it also moved against traditional European public service broadcasting. These large shifts towards commercialization, competition, and market forces worked against both professionalizing and craft strategies. Most media occupations and their members now found it more difficult to obtain security of employment, to influence entry patterns, to achieve stable work careers, and to control or shape their collective occupational destiny.

Weak Media Occupations, but Strong Media-occupational Fragments

We have already noted that journalism and acting were two occupations which existed before the arrival of the modern mass media. Moreover, these two occupations have always tended towards the vertical, with people at the top earning many times as much as people at the bottom of the same line of work. What is true of payment may also be true of prestige.

Elite journalists have traditionally earned twenty to fifty times as much as the lowliest penny-a-line freelance hacks. These huge differences in pay (and prestige) have been found, not only in acting and journalism, but also in other occupations indicated in Fig. 1. Music is another vertical occupation, which has had its stars and lowly practitioners both before and since the arrival of recording and radio technologies. Advertising is another vertical occupation and is, of course, especially closely tied to the commercial market. Yet another vertical line of work is to be found in photography and camera operation; a top fashion photographer or a movie's director of photography is often a highly paid star, but the opposite is true of the photographer on the local newspaper. Art/design/costume and related fields also exhibit strongly vertical characteristics. In recent times information technology/computing work has also exhibited huge internal differences in pay and prestige.

Acting has always been extreme in vertical terms. During 1950–75 most other media occupations became less like acting; but since 1975 most media occupations have become more like acting.

Does this mean that media occupations have been enfeebled by the market-led and technology-led changes of recent decades? While it is widely believed that media occupations have become more powerful and more central to modern society, can it really be the case that media occupations have become weaker? An explanation for this paradox can be given, as follows. Yes, media occupations overall have become weaker, or at least they have been unsuccessful at pursuing their broad occupation-wide strategies of professionalization or craft. However, small fragments of occupations—specific groups of journalists, of TV producers, of film-makers, of technicians—have become more powerful within their occupational niche, their specific target market.

What we see in front of us, it is suggested here, is an audio-visual landscape characterized by weak media-occupations but strong media-occupational fragments. Indeed this was probably always the case up to 1950. The really powerful (and well-paid) people within the media industries were quite small numbers of leading journalists and star actors. Radio, when it appeared, quickly became a fairly top-down medium and, where allowed, star systems developed.

The salience of small occupational fragments was somewhat reduced during 1950–75 by the strength of trade unions (and Hollywood guilds) which followed the obvious trade union path of raising basic and average pay and work conditions. But as television grew and competition between media steadily increased, these occupation-wide strategies weakened. Increased competition and expansion, as well as technology and legal changes, meant that industrial conditions, especially from the 1970s, increasingly favoured small groups (or occupational fragments) who performed key occupational roles, who pioneered new technologies and media outputs, and who could attract large audiences and important advertisers.

Since the 1970s, trade unions and their powers to control occupational entry have declined. Occupations which were recognizable as 'crafts'—strong trade union, all-male workforce, dominance over a specific key technology—have changed radically; in many cases the union has declined, the workforce has been feminized to a greater or lesser extent, and the key technology has been replaced by a radically different technology or competing technologies.

Media occupations increasingly lack firm definitions and sharp boundaries. Even quite specific-sounding jobs such as 'producer' or 'director' are very different between film, TV, and TV commercials. There are big constellations of loosely linked occupations within a specific medium; but these occupational constellations differ sharply between different media such as film and TV and also according to genre within one mass medium. Even within the single medium of network television, for example, there are huge differences between the production team required for news, situation comedy, and game shows. Film and some kinds of television usually use just one camera; live and 'as live' studio shows usually use several cameras; a sports broadcast may use fifteen or twenty cameras.

Media workers increasingly have multiple memberships. For example, a 30-year-old London media person may have worked for the last two or three years on BBC programming; she has worked previously as a print and radio journalist and still thinks of herself as a journalist. Her immediate employment on a specialist travel series (aimed at young people) is as a researcher/director; the employer who pays her is a small independent production company contracted to make the series for BBC television. However, her longer-term employer is the series executive producer (for whom she has worked previously), who is effectively a freelance. Incidentally this television journalist/researcher/director also writes regularly for both a travel magazine and the travel section of a newspaper; she is writing a travel book and she may return from TV to radio in the future.

Media 'professions' do not exist in a form comparable to medicine or law (which have a long period of training, formally controlled entry, a high degree of autonomy, and a recognized, and expanding, body of expert knowledge). However, the media do have 'professional' people in the much broader and looser senses of someone who is 'experienced', 'senior', and 'respected' both inside and outside the occupation. But even this latter assertion is somewhat uncertain and ambiguous for several reasons. Most obviously perhaps, the *commercial* basis of most media means that someone who is financially successful (perhaps as a game show host, or as a tabloid newspaper columnist) may have a less elevated position in the moral division of labour.

Much 'professional' skill actually depends on very 'personal' qualities. There are no media equivalents to the professional ranking system and detached-but-sympathetic 'bedside manner' behind which all medical doctors can operate. The television producer or newspaper executive needs to use his or her personal resources of authority, enthusiasm, diplomacy, and determination in order to lead the team, to meet the deadline, to deliver a good product. Indeed the senior media professional increasingly needs to be ever more multi-skilled. The television producer needs to be a modern Renaissance man or woman with a range of technical as well as creative skills; ideally the TV producer needs writing skills, a strong visual sense, knowledge of the relevant law, and an ability to get on in both formal and informal meetings. The TV producer also needs to understand the major technical skills including camera, lighting, sound, graphics, and post-production. Newspaper editors increasingly require well-developed computer and related technical skills. Thus in both press and TV the most senior 'professionals' also require much 'craft' expertise.

Some of the most effective professionalizing fragments are the American Writers' Guild and the Directors' Guild in their Hollywood manifestations. The Writers' Guild of America, West (WGAW) has a turbulent history. Its writers were the Hollywood group most directly involved in the anti-Communist purges in the late 1940s and early 1950s. In 1988 a WGAW strike effectively delayed the start of the new autumn television season. But the WGAW has long been in conflict with the WGA East (in New York). One of the issues in a 1997 conflict concerned the looser entry requirements in New York. The entrant to WGAE needed only to have signed an option agreement on a TV or film script. But to join the elite band of WGAW members, the aspiring Hollywood writer needed to have sold a full-length movie script or several TV episode scripts. Much of the WGA's Hollywood strength lies in its power to decide conflicts over screen-writing credits (which in turn determine TV 'residuals' and earnings for other subsequent uses). Significantly, most of Hollywood's working writers earn more than half and less than twice the median earnings; this strongly supports their sense of a common 'professional' destiny.[9]

'Craft' versus craft disputes are extremely common. These disputes often focus on particular technologies. The introduction of the computerized television newsroom began in both the US and UK in the 1970s; it was not just one technological innovation, but a long sequence of small advances, and small retreats, over first one decade and then another. Some of the struggles were indeed battles to the death, because a major attraction (to management) of TV news automation was that it promised to remove more and more skills and skilled personnel.[10] Outside the TV newsroom, the traditional camera crew (often consisting of several hulking men with a lot of weighty equipment) could eventually be replaced by one young woman (with lightweight camera-and-sound equipment). Computerization, of course, has had a huge impact on the generation of on-screen images, which in turn has had a big impact on more traditional animation and other skills.

Technological changes, which seem to impact equally on broad swathes of media 'professions' and 'crafts', also impact on the traditional film and

---

9 William T. Bielby and Denise D. Bielby, 'Organizational Mediation of Project-based Labor Markets: Talent Agencies and the Careers of Screen Writers', *American Sociological Review*, 64 (1999), 64–85.

10 Phillip O. Keirstead and S.-K. Keirstead, *Automating Television News: A Generation of Change* (Tallahassee, Fla.: Castle Garden Press, 1999).

TV roles of producer, director, writer, and leading actor. A traditional inhibition to profession-wide discussion is that these terms can mean such different things. As a broad generalization, feature films are a director's medium or a director-writer medium; but television is a producer's medium, or a producer-writer medium. (However, the more film-like TV becomes, especially in the made-for-TV movie, or in the drama mini-series, the more the role of the director becomes salient.)

Is the movie director the film-maker or the subordinate of the producer and the studio production boss? Clearly most of the publicity and the shelves full of books on directing are focused on the celebrity director (who, as a sort of star, is a focus of much secrecy as well as much publicity). Some of these directors do seem to justify the term 'auteur' and the 'Un film de . . .' credit. This latter is known in Hollywood as the 'possessory credit' and was once argued for by David Lean in the case of *Doctor Zhivago* as follows:

> I worked one year with the writer. Unlike him I directed not only the actors but the cameraman, set designer, costume designer, sound men, editor, composer and even the laboratory in their final print. Unlike him I chose the actors, the technicians, the subject and him to write it. I staged it. I filmed it. It was my film of his script which I shot when he was not there. If a director, writer or producer cannot claim such overall responsibility it should not be called his film. If he can, it truly is his film.

Some people argue that today's established movie director, once he or she has received the financial green light, is more autonomous than ever before and especially more autonomous than was ever the case in Hollywood's past. One piece of evidence cited in support is that many Hollywood films are now excessively long; this, it is claimed, is because producers and studios have lost the power to control the director-at-work or to insist on tighter editing.

However, one book which covers a broad range of (mainly) Hollywood movie directors suggests that a more representative middling director, working with middle-sized movie budgets, is far from being a dominant figure.[11] Very few directors made as many as seven or eight films in the 1990s. More common was to direct perhaps three movies in the decade; most Hollywood directors spent more time 'in development' and in negotiation than they actually spent filming and editing movies.

In television everything is different because an hour of television is normally made so very much more quickly, simply, and cheaply than a feature movie. Especially in *series* (the dominant form in TV) the leading figure is the series producer or executive producer. In much television the producer's main co-worker is the chief writer, while the director or directors are of less significance.

---

11 Michael Singer, *A Cut Above: 50 Film Directors Talk about their Craft* (Los Angeles: Lone Eagle Publishing, 1998).

Powerful Occupational Fragments

Such media-occupational power as exists appears to be exercised first by *individuals* (moguls, barons, stars) and secondly by occupational fragments.

Occupational fragments—for instance executive producers of television fiction and comedy—play a key role in shaping and selecting popular entertainment: its stars, its themes, its values. Within journalism there are many small fragments of correspondents, reporters, critics, and columnists (and of course editors) who exercise significant influence within a particular narrow target area.

But the bulk of the national journalist labour force do not belong to these relatively elevated levels. David Weaver's *The Global Journalist* indicates that in a wide range of countries most journalists are located well down the national occupational pyramid. Journalists overall are younger than the total national workforce. Most working journalists are under 45. There are strong suggestions from the USA and elsewhere that because journalism dazzles and attracts so many eager young people, publishers and editors are also able to underpay them. Many journalists, having been frustrated in terms of pay and promotion, leave the occupation in their middle years.

Much attention is directed towards the leading national group of political journalists, and this is obviously a key occupational fragment in any country. Political journalists may spend more time with the politicians than in their own employer's office; these journalists' most important interactions may be with their sources and their 'competitor colleagues', fellow political journalists working for competing media.

The same tends to be true of other small groups of specialist journalists. In Britain, for example, much of the national reporting of a major semi-political field (such as education) is in the hands of at most a few dozen journalists. By balancing pressures from news sources, from competitor colleagues, and from their employing news organizations, these reporters can achieve a fair degree of autonomy and targeted power.[12]

In many specialized fields—such as particular industries, or consumer/leisure interest areas—a small number of relevant TV producers and magazine editors may wield a large amount of influence. This is also true of newspaper critics who cover the arts, films, music, and books. Within their employing newspapers they may play only a fairly peripheral role; but within the specific arts area they cover, these critics are collectively a potent media-occupational fragment. James Curran has studied one such fragment in the form of relevant 'literary editors' in charge of book reviewing on British national newspapers and leading weekly periodicals. He describes a small group of competitor colleagues who come from similar elite educational backgrounds and give precedence to much the same literary genres (biography, literary fiction, history, 'general humanities'). As in other fields of national journalism, a very few people (well known to each

---

12 Jeremy Tunstall, *Journalists at Work* (London: Constable; Beverly Hills: Sage, 1971).

other) decide which items (in this case books) will and will not get publicity in the main relevant national media.[13]

In some journalistic 'criticism' fields the numbers are slightly larger. For example, some 80 members of the Hollywood Foreign Press Association annually choose the Golden Globes winners and provide much of the world-wide reporting and criticism of Hollywood. In other cases a single critic (on the *New York Times*) or two critics (on *Le Monde* and *Libération*) are said to wield an excessive amount of critical dynamite.

New technologies and services—not least Internet companies—are generating fresh occupational fragments with significant focused power. Another example, from advertising, is provided by the newly salient specialized media-buying subsidiary agencies; these media-buying outfits are designed to increase bulk advertising buying power and thus to maximize bulk discounts. By 1999 ten individuals presided over ten media-buying enterprises which together purchased over $90 billion of advertising.[14]

Powerful and specialized occupational fragments of this kind remain, however, very different from a broad traditional profession such as law or medicine. Each of these specialized media-occupational fragments tends to have its own distinctive atmosphere, problems, and values. But this high degree of specialization and distinctiveness is normally driven by the market and/or by technology. The specialized fragment is not linked to a body of formal professional knowledge; it does not have fixed entry requirements; and it has no legislative mandate for self-governance and special legal status.

Meanwhile the media deregulation and work casualization of recent years has affected many, probably most, media workers across the world. One consequence seems to have been a merging of previously separate occupations and a tendency for what were previously seen as either 'professions' or 'crafts' in the media to take on common characteristics. Increasingly many media workers find themselves involved in a mixture of 'professional', 'craft', and performance activities.

Across all media occupations there is now *less* 'staff status' and employment security; fewer media workers are involved in trade unions, or in professional associations, or in bodies offering combined trade union/professional benefits and goals. Definitions of distinct technology-related skills, such as 'sound recordist' or 'linotype operator', are less sharp; there is less male dominance of specific work functions (such as the old doctrine that only men can operate cameras, read the television news, or be football reporters). In particular there are far fewer people and specific crafts in television post-production and 'behind the camera' generally; in the press there are far fewer people who handle the printed text after the journalist's on-screen page make-up phase.

In recent years the media occupations have seen *more* of the following:

13 James Curran, 'Literary Editors, Social Networks and Cultural Tradition', in James Curran (ed.), *Media Organisations in Society* (London: Arnold, 2000), 215–39.

14 'Star Turn', *The Economist*, 11 Mar. 2000, 91–2; Jeremy Tunstall and David Machin, *The Anglo-American Media Connection* (Oxford: Oxford University Press, 1999), 121–4.

- More short-term and casual employment.
- More use of informal, kinship, nepotistic, and colleague networks in obtaining work (although such ties were often previously important in gaining initial entry).
- More multi-skilling and less specific single skilling. Increasingly one individual may exercise two separate skills such as news reporter and photographer, or television actor and TV writer.
- More media individuals find employment in two separate jobs or a day job plus an evening job. (In some Latin American and other countries this tradition has continued uninterrupted since the nineteenth century.)
- More women are employed, with an increasing proportion of lower-level and middle-level media jobs now employing a female majority.

In some respects media work is now more complex, more specialized, and faster-changing; but in other respects all media work has become more similar and also more similar to office work in general. Across the media and across the world, media workers mainly work with bums on seats, talking on the phone, and staring into a computer screen. These people of the word have now joined the people of the on-screen word and picture.

1

PART ONE

Origins

1

Political Journalists

Max Weber

MAX WEBER (1864–1920) WAS a founding father of sociology and social science. This extract is from a much longer piece—originally a speech in 1918—on 'Politics as a Vocation'. Weber points to the multiple uncertainties which surround political journalism and journalists. The job makes big demands on the intellect, and the political journalist must work at high speed, while remaining on the fringes of high politics and high society. Even the most honourable journalists may be blamed for the sins of the least honourable. Weber was a German patriot and, speaking in 1918, his notion of 'honourable' journalism certainly involved loyalty to the Kaiser's regime. Weber mentions several relevant trends in journalism, such as the rise of popular ('boulevard') newspapers, the emergence of the press mogul, and the tendency of journalists to lean to the political left (the orientation of the German Social Democrats).

Within the limits of this lecture, it is quite impossible even to sketch the sociology of modern political journalism, which in every respect constitutes a chapter in itself. Certainly, only a few things concerning it are in place here. In common with all demagogues and, by the way, with the lawyer (and the artist), the journalist shares the fate of lacking a fixed social classification. At least, this is the case on the Continent, in contrast to the English, and, by the way, also to former conditions in Prussia. The journalist belongs to a sort of pariah caste, which is always estimated by 'society' in terms of its ethically lowest representative. Hence, the strangest notions about journalists and their work are abroad. Not everybody realizes that a really good journalistic accomplishment requires at least as much 'genius' as any scholarly accomplishment, especially because of the necessity of producing at once and 'on order,' and because of the necessity of being effective, to be sure, under quite different conditions of production. It is almost never acknowledged that the responsibility of the journalist is far greater, and that the sense of responsibility of every honorable journalist is, on the average, not a bit lower than that of the scholar, but rather, as the war has shown, higher. This is because, in the very nature of the case,

Source: H. H. Gerth and C. Wright Mills (trs. and eds.), *From Max Weber: Essays in Sociology* (London: Routledge and Kegan Paul, 1948), 96–9.

irresponsible journalistic accomplishments and their often terrible effects are remembered.

Nobody believes that the discretion of any able journalist ranks above the average of other people, and yet that is the case. The quite incomparably graver temptations, and the other conditions that accompany journalistic work at the present time, produce those results which have conditioned the public to regard the press with a mixture of disdain and pitiful cowardice. Today we cannot discuss what is to be done. Here we are interested in the question of the occupational destiny of the political journalist and of his chance to attain a position of political leadership. Thus far, the journalist has had favorable chances only in the Social Democratic party. Within the party, editorial positions have been predominantly in the nature of official positions, but editorial positions have not been the basis for positions of leadership.

In the bourgeois parties, on the whole, the chances for ascent to political power along this avenue have rather become worse, as compared with those of the previous generation. Naturally every politician of consequence has needed influence over the press and hence has needed relations with the press. But that party leaders would emerge from the ranks of the press has been an absolute exception and one should not have expected it. The reason for this lies in the strongly increased 'indispensability' of the journalist, above all, of the propertyless and hence professionally bound journalist, an indispensability which is determined by the tremendously increased intensity and tempo of journalistic operations. The necessity of gaining one's livelihood by the writing of daily or at least weekly articles is like lead on the feet of the politicians. I know of cases in which natural leaders have been permanently paralyzed in their ascent to power, externally and above all internally, by this compulsion. The relations of the press to the ruling powers in the state and in the parties, under the old regime [of the Kaiser], were as detrimental as they could be to the level of journalism; but that is a chapter in itself. These conditions were different in the countries of our opponents [the Allies]. But there also, and for all modern states, apparently the journalist worker gains less and less as the capitalist lord of the press, of the sort of 'Lord' Northcliffe, for instance, gains more and more political influence.

Thus far, however, our great capitalist newspaper concerns, which attained control, especially over the 'chain newspaper,' with 'want ads,' have been regularly and typically the breeders of political indifference. For no profits could be made in an independent policy; especially no profitable benevolence of the politically dominant powers could be obtained. The advertising business is also the avenue along which, during the war, the attempt was made to influence the press politically in a grand style—an attempt which apparently it is regarded as desirable to continue now. Although one may expect the great papers to escape this pressure, the situation of the small ones will be far more difficult. In any case, for the time being, the journalist career is not among us, a normal avenue for the ascent of political leaders, whatever attraction journalism may otherwise have and whatever measure of influence, range of activity, and especially political responsibility it may yield. One has to wait and see.

Perhaps journalism does not have this function any longer, or perhaps journalism does not yet have it. Whether the renunciation of the principle of anonymity would mean a change in this is difficult to say. Some journalists—not all—believe in dropping principled anonymity. What we have experienced during the war in the German press, and in the 'management' of newspapers by especially hired personages and talented writers who always expressly figured under their names, has unfortunately shown, in some of the better known cases, that an increased awareness of responsibility is not so certain to be bred as might be believed. Some of the papers were, without regard to party, precisely the notoriously worst boulevard sheets; by dropping anonymity they strove for and attained greater sales. The publishers as well as the journalists of sensationalism have gained fortunes but certainly not honor. Nothing is here being said against the principle of promoting sales; the question is indeed an intricate one, and the phenomenon of irresponsible sensationalism does not hold in general. But thus far, sensationalism has not been the road to genuine leadership or to the responsible management of politics. How conditions will further develop remains to be seen. Yet the journalist career remains under all circumstances one of the most important avenues of professional political activity. It is not a road for everybody, least of all for weak characters, especially for people who can maintain their inner balance only with a secure status position. If the life of a young scholar is a gamble, still he is walled in by firm status conventions, which prevent him from slipping. But the journalist's life is an absolute gamble in every respect and under conditions that test one's inner security in a way that scarcely occurs in any other situation. The often bitter experiences in occupational life are perhaps not even the worst. The inner demands that are directed precisely at the successful journalist are especially difficult. It is, indeed, no small matter to frequent the salons of the powerful on this earth on a seemingly equal footing and often to be flattered by all because one is feared, yet knowing all the time that having hardly closed the door the host has perhaps to justify before his guests his association with the 'scavengers from the press.' Moreover, it is no small matter that one must express oneself promptly and convincingly about this and that, on all conceivable problems of life—whatever the 'market' happens to demand—and this without becoming absolutely shallow and above all without losing one's dignity by baring oneself, a thing which has merciless results. It is not astonishing that there are many journalists who have become human failures and worthless men. Rather, it is astonishing that, despite all this, this very stratum includes such a great number of valuable and quite genuine men, a fact that outsiders would not so easily guess.

2

The Profession of Journalism in England, 1855–1914

Alan J. Lee

THIS EXTRACT FROM Alan Lee's *The Origins of the Popular Press, 1855–1914* covers a period in which English daily newspaper sales multiplied by more than one hundred times. London journalism around 1855 was still closely linked to the legal profession, and during the 1860s some journalists hoped to model their occupation on the legal profession. There were only 43 daily newspapers outside London in 1868; most newspapers were still highly serious, highly political, and targeted at affluent males. The 1860s were later mythologized as a golden period of serious, professional journalism. However, the huge boom in newspaper sales from the 1890s onwards led to a more consumer-oriented and advertising-driven 'new journalism' aimed at men and women in white-collar, and other manual, occupations. Commercialization also turned journalism into an increasingly vertical occupation; many lowly and insecure journalists earned less than £100 a year, while editors could be paid ten, or even fifty, times as much.

The occupational goal of a law-like profession seemed at odds with occupational reality to most journalists. The professionally oriented Institute of Journalists attracted fewer members than did the National Union of Journalists (Founded in 1907). The NUJ had white-collar trade union goals; its focus was on establishing minimum rates of pay and improving the often appalling working conditions experienced by journalists.

Men of great ability and high character (who) gave their best to what they conceived to be a public service without seeking recognition or reward beyond a very moderate emolument for their labour,' was how J.A. Spender described the mid-Victorian journalist. A change was evident in the profession by the end of the century, although there still were men of the type that Spender described, himself amongst them. The change was put

Source: Alan J. Lee, *The Origins of the Popular Press, 1855–1914* (London: Croom, Helm; Totowa, NJ: Rowman and Littlefield, 1976), 104–17.

succinctly by Harmsworth's associate in the *Evening News*. Kennedy Jones, who claimed to have remarked to that model of the old journalism, John Morley, 'you left journalism a profession, we have made it a branch of commerce.' Both observations referred back to what has come to be seen as the 'golden age' of the 1860s and 1870s. If the changing social and political role of the press in the last half of the century is to be understood, it is necessary first to examine the development of the economic position and status of the journalist.

It has been argued by L. O'Boyle that for the first half of the century journalists were rescued from the political patronage of the aristocracy and Old Corruption largely by the demands of commerce, and journalism became less corrupt as it grew to be more businesslike. After a brief, and perhaps illusory period of independence, it is argued, it succumbed to the equally demanding patronage of those commercial men who had liberated it from the old patronage, the men who now ran it, more or less, as a business. Thus the swords of one generation became the fetters of the next. This is, moreover, a thesis which fits not only Britain, but France, Germany, and, it might be added, the United States. The process varied in detail and in pace from country to country, roughly according to the extent of industrialisation, but it seems to have been a process common to most sooner or later. Thus, what its critics regarded as a disastrous betrayal of the cause of the press in the 1880s and 1890s in England, may be seen, in larger perspective, as part of a quite 'normal' development in the history of the newspaper in the industrial revolution, and not as an unfortunate aberration. This is not to deny that 'normal' development might be totally undesirable to the critics, but it is to emphasize that there were deeper and stronger forces determining the path of development than the critics often allowed for. For them the 'golden age' tended to perform the function of a myth to enable them to ignore the unpleasant realities which followed. [. . .]

There was, as has been noted, a certain distrust of men whose job it was to disclose unpalatable and often embarrassing facts. The journalist 'is associated with the general fear of espionage and feeling of insecurity which the custom of anonymous writing necessarily produces', wrote Lord Lytton in 1833. Taking stock in 1851 William Johnston wrote

> The profession of a journalist gives no social distinction, and the occupation is not even avowed, except to intimate friends . . . the feeling of society towards journalists is more that of fear or curiosity than that of respect or esteem.

Johnston, however, seems to have had in mind in this passage those who 'contributed' to the press, rather than those who made their living from it. As to that, H.B. Thompson, as he set about guiding the aspiring sons of the middle classes towards the professions in 1857, warned them that journalism is not a profession 'a man would willingly enter when a competence is open to him'. By his criteria journalism, if a profession at all, was certainly a lowly one, for it was completely open to anyone who cared to enter, and provided little if any security. Thompson put it on a level with the architect, the sculptor, the civil engineer, the educator, the parliamentary agent and the actuary, and he was almost certainly speaking here of only the higher

echelons of the profession. This was demonstrated by the case of E.C.G.
Murray, who in 1857 had been disciplined by the Foreign Office for having
written for the press. Murray wrote a long, anonymous tract attacking this
attitude, and one of his reasons for anger was that 'after the age of thirty all
the liberal professions, all honorable means of obtaining a respectable livelihood, are virtually closed to a man. The option of going into full-time
journalism obviously held little appeal for him.

It was true that journalism, even into the 1880s, could claim few of the
generally accepted qualifications of a profession. It could provide little
stability, no great remuneration, was hardly recognised by the state, and
had no position of monopoly privilege. It sought instead to emphasise the
only asset which it was accredited with, influence. [. . .]

[. . .] It was often argued that influence was a result, in part, of the
English tradition of anonymous journalism. While this may have been true
for the profession as a whole, or for particular papers, however, anonymity
laid the individual journalist open to unlimited competition, and made it
impossible for him to improve his worth by selling his name. The arguments over anonymity went on into the twentieth century. Most of the
literature on the subject was predictably critical, and related mostly to the
difficulty of controlling the abuses to which it was open, such as the difficulty of bringing a newspaper rather than a person to book for libel, or
the power without responsibility which was consistently attributed to *The
Times*. As John Morley put it, the worst aspect of the practice was the
entrusting of 'the most important social influences at this moment to what
is, as far as the public is concerned, a secret society'. [. . .]

[. . .] Those who defended the practice, particularly for leaders, argued
that these might in any case be the work of a number of hands, and
constituted the identity of the paper. It was also claimed that anonymous
writing provided an entry for young journalists into the profession, but this
was a thin case. Usually it meant merely depressing the price they could get
for their work, and it was this that eventually drove increasing numbers of
journalists towards the end of the century to refuse to write anonymously,
except for leaders.

If influence, and the acquisition of an identity, were positive aspects in
the struggle for professionalisation, remuneration and life-style were the
major debit items.

At the top journalists could earn a comfortable living. In the 1830s an
editor of a London daily could expect between £600 and £1,000 a year, with
The Times, the *Courier*, the *Globe* and *Lloyds Weekly News* all paying the
£1,000. Until the 1870s, however, he was unlikely to have got more. Charles
Dickens managed to extract £2,000 from the *Daily News* in 1846, but he
lasted only a few weeks. The editor of the *Morning Star*, on the other hand,
received only 10 guineas a week in the 1860s. By the 1870s £1,000 was
probably the average London morning rate, with Chenery of *The Times* at
£5,000, and the new editor of the *Morning Advertiser* in 1876 at £500.
Arthur Arnold, editor of the *Echo* from 1868 to 1874, and his counterpart
on the *Pall Mall Gazette*, Frederick Greenwood, each received £1,000, while
the editor of the *Globe* managed only £600. Papers which relied less on
editorial than on sub-editorial skills had no need to match these rates. The

Weekly Dispatch, for example, paid only £4 a week in the early 1870s. Rates improved in the 1870s, so that John Morley was getting £2,000 at the *Pall Mall Gazette* at the end of the decade, and the editor of the Morning Advertiser £1,500. Harmsworth seems to have paid the top rate of £5,000 to the editor of the *Daily Mail*, perhaps by the end of the century, and in the next decade there were substantial increases on the more successful papers, so that with bonuses, dividends, and other additions the most successful editors may have obtained more than £10,000 before the First World War.

In the provinces the profession was less lucrative, but it could still afford comfort. The successful provincial editor of the 1830s could have got from £400 to £600, but more usually from £100 to £250. Rarely could country editors, often still their own masters and, therefore, paying themselves no salary, expect to earn more than £150 before the 1870s, and some £300 to £500 after this. When W.T. Stead took over the *Northern Echo* in 1872, for example, his salary was £200, which seems to have been about average. By then only in Edinburgh, Glasgow, Birmingham, Manchester and Leeds were the provincial rates on leading dailies up to London levels, at about £1,000. Generally speaking of course, the smaller the paper the smaller the salary, so that in the 1890s an editor of a small weekly or bi-weekly might get no more than £70 or £80, although this would have been supplemented by other work. [. . .]

Beneath the editor there came the sub-editor, 'generally between forty and fifty years of age . . . not ordinarily one of your press Bohemians, but quiet, severe and respectable'. On a London daily in the 1860s he would have got about a quarter to a third of the editor's salary, say about £250, but this varied greatly with the paper. By the end of the century the leading London dailies were paying £400 to £500, the rest £250 to £300. Provincial rates were about two-thirds of those in London, from £150 to £300 in the 1870s and 1880s, up to £400 in the 1890s. Again there were variations. The chief sub-editor of a popular London daily could get up to £2,000 a year at the turn of the century, while in the provinces even some of the large dailies paid only £75 in the 1900s. The average rates, however, in the 1870s put the sub-editor on a level with the experienced bank or insurance clerk, and at the top of the scale with the coroner or an average medical man. The majority, employed on small papers, had to combine their duties with many others, often unpaid. They had probably been first introduced to control the penny-a-liners, but it was the telegraph which made them indispensable, with their scissors and paste-pots.

Between the editor and the sub-editor in terms of pay and status came the leader writer, and probably also the parliamentary reporters on large, and the foreign correspondents on the largest papers. Leader writers, when not occasional or free-lance, as they often were, could by the 1870s get about £1,000 a year in London. The Rev. Mozeley of *The Times* received £1,800 in the 1850s and 1860s, and C.E. Montague actually extracted the coveted £1,000 from the exiguous *Manchester Guardian* in 1899, but most had to be content with less. It was reckoned that a good provincial daily in 1885 paid up to £400. They usually enjoyed a very high status. Many were recruited directly from Oxbridge, and were duly isolated from the rest of the staff. In the 1860s they constituted a small group of about a hundred educated, comfortably off men, barristers waiting for briefs, unattached clergymen and government officials. This class distinction caused some tension in the offices, so that by the 1880s Harold Spender recalled, 'Fleet Street hated the Universities. They despised our degrees; scorned our knowledge: mocked at our modest river prides,' an attitude which T.E. Kebbel thought had begun in the 1850s. No less of an elite were the parliamentary reporters. Arrangements in the House of Commons were such that there could only physically be a small number of them, and they too were usually recruited from the lower ranks of the bar, the Church and the services. Their privileged position and habitual association with each other made 'the Gallery' a tight self-conscious clique, expanded only a little, and grudgingly, by the emergence in the 1870s of 'the Lobby'. In 1830 it was said they could get £200 to £300 a year. By the end of the century this had only risen to £250 to £400, but there were then ample opportunities of working for more than one paper. The latter rate, which had obtained from about 1894, persisted until 1906, but by then journalistic and political changes had made the job much more precarious, with four London morning papers having discharged their parliamentary men in 1904–5, preferring for financial reasons to use agency reports instead.

Of the reporters the foreign and war correspondents were probably superior to the others in status, the latter having appeared since the Crimean and Franco-Prussian wars. They were both paid as a rule on a piecework basis, or on short-term contracts, and little is known about their average earnings. Even at the turn of the century they seem to have been rather poorly rewarded, a war correspondent getting some £80 a month during a war, and £25 a month in peace, plus a £300 a year pension for the widows of those killed in action. The ordinary reporter in London appears to have got about £200 a year in the late 1860s, up to £500 or £600 in the 1890s, and between £500 and £1,000 in 1912. In the provinces the larger papers paid between thirty shillings and £2 a week in the 1830s, and the *Leeds Mercury* offered F.R. Spark £80 a year in 1855. The smaller journals, however, paid only £1 a week in the 1890s, and lower rates prevailed for so-called apprentices and junior reporters, less than ten shillings in the middle of the century. In 1901 it was said that a junior reporter in London and a senior man in the provinces could get £150 to £200 a year on the best papers, but there were probably not many such jobs. For the posts of reporter and sub-editor on the *Southampton Southern Echo* in 1889 the paper received 'eager petitioning . . . from honours men at the Universities, as well as from middle-aged men with families, and asking for salaries ranging from as little as seventeen shillings a week'. At the upper level a reporter's wage was comparable with a top-grade clerk or better, but the average man in terms of income could match only the low grade, or young clerk, or schoolmaster. In the 1870s Thomas Frost had complained that the country journalist could earn only three-quarters of the wage of a bricklayer. It was long accepted that reporters, and even the editors of some country weeklies, would be much more poorly paid than the printers who produced their papers. In 1913, 2,100 of the National Union of Journalists' 3,600 members were insured under the National Insurance Act, and were earning less than £160 a year, whilst the majority of the worst paid were not even members of the union. One of the leading journalists in the country, the editor of the *Daily Chronicle*, Robert Donald, told his colleagues in 1913 that this situation was discreditable to the profession. A proprietor had noted in 1910 that he had applications for jobs at twenty-five shillings a week from competent reporters of forty and fifty years of age with families. At this level things were slow to change, and the 'golden age' had always been an inappropriate epithet. The only improvement, perhaps, had been the virtual extinction of the old 'penny-a-liner', 'a very inferior race of reporters', who had been superseded by the combination of the telegraph and the sub-editor. Earning upwards of three-halfpence a line, they had constituted the casual labour force of journalism before the appearance of the penny dailies. They had had no contracts, were frequently driven to dishonesty and corruption, and were even more frequently the worse for drink, the source of 'copy furnished by the most ignorant of scavengers'. By working many papers it was claimed that they could earn £30 or £40 a week, but this seems implausible and certainly exceptional. They were correctly seen as having got the profession a bad name, and their disappearance was much to the advantage of the other journalists.

The poor remuneration of the rank and file was compensated in part by a 'middle-class' status. In late nineteenth-century Lancashire 'young men sometimes of good education though generally self-taught, who had dreaded the atmosphere of mill or factory . . . had sought to become what came to be called "black-coated workers", mostly respectable but inevitably poor'. As F.H. Rose, one of the prime movers of union organisation amongst journalists, remarked in 1906, they had the status of receiving a 'salary' instead of 'wages', and of accepting an 'engagement' rather than a 'job'. Yet in terms of respectability and security the journalist held a low position amongst the professional men of whom he claimed to be one. Most lived on the fringe of the intelligentsia, but were not a part of it, a fact which had led Lord Lytton to explain the radicalism of newspapermen in terms of their further separation from the aristocracy than was usual in the rest of the middle classes. This was an image repeated in the mid-century picture of the journalist as Bohemian, chiefly metropolitan, but also of the pubs and clubs of the provinces. Edward Dicey recalled of his contemporaries of the 1860s, men like Henry Mayhew, George Sala and Thornton Hunt, that while they had had little formal education, they could write lucidly and rapidly, that they belonged not to the 'swell' West End Clubs, but instead haunted the City taverns, the Cheshire Cheese, the Cock, the Edinburgh Castle, which used to remain especially open for them far into the night, and, finally, that they were men of little social ambition. Some such pattern of life was dictated by the necessarily nocturnal habits of the daily journalist, but it was undoubtedly a pattern which attracted the rootless product of an expanding society, and men seeking the upward social mobility of the burgeoning professions in far greater numbers than the professions could provide places for them. It was a profession which also provided an important niche for the many Irish and Scottish exiles who came to lend England the benefit of their wit and intellect. With an expansiveness perhaps indicating pride rather than prejudice it was claimed by a Scottish magazine in 1849 that three-quarters of London reporters were Irish or Scottish. Certainly no fictional newspaper story of the Victorian period was complete without its Irishman. [. . .]

The insecure and erratic nature of the employment was a contributory cause of the traditional and widespread addiction of journalists to alcohol. This received a great deal of attention at a time when temperance was a militant movement. H.B. Thompson noted defensively in 1857 that 'at present the reporters are as quiet and as punctual as any other class of professional men, even though their late hours oblige them to seek refreshment and employment in places of public entertainment'. By 1904, however, Edward Robbins, President of the Press Association, assured aspiring journalists that there was not one-twentieth of the drinking that there used to be. The life of the journalist was not, indeed, confined to the billiard hall and the tap room. Towards the end of the century even London journalists were becoming suburbanised, and had taken to living in Clapham and Brixton. In 1891 most authors and journalists in London were to be found in the north and south-west of the city.

More important, however, than life-style in securing a higher status for the journalist was the need to obtain some form of state recognition, as the major professions had done. The proprietors had organised, and successfully put pressure upon the state, but the journalists lagged far behind. At first the only provision made for 'decayed or distressed' journalists was the Newspaper Benevolent Fund, set up by the proprietors in 1864. Next came the National Association of Journalists in 1886, again a proprietors' organisation. There had been Press Clubs in the provinces since the 1860s, but they were in no sense professional organisations. This was what the National Association, started in Birmingham, was intended to supply. It began with a membership of 221, which rose to 830 in 1888. Its avowed aim was respectability, and in only four years it had been achieved, with the granting of a charter in 1890, making it the Institute of Journalists. By 1894 there were 3,556 members. From the start there was tension between the proprietors and the working journalists, initially over the control of the Newspaper Press Fund, and then over wages. [. . .]

[. . .] In 1905 and 1906 many local branches of the Institute resolved to exclude the proprietors, and in the latter year F.H. Rose began a campaign in the *Clarion* to get journalists to accept the status of an ordinary working man, and to come closer to the printers. Eventually in 1907, on the groundwork of the Manchester journalist W.N. Watts, the National Union of Journalists was founded as the profession's first effective labour organisation.

The Institute had also been of little use in another and as important a field of organisation, the control of entry into the profession. Other professions and trades attempted to do this by requiring qualifications and providing training. In journalism this was done in a very informal way by the 'apprenticing' of young journalists to small local papers, from which, if they were exceptionally fortunate and persistent, they might move to Fleet Street, or to one of the major provincial dailies. The system, however, provided little if any control on entry. The job had always been populated with amateurs, free-lances and casuals, a truly rootless semi-intelligentsia. It had always been a popular system of out-relief for the unemployed of every other profession, including the notoriously insecure and unremunerative one of politics. It is doubtful whether either the Irish Nationalists or the Labour Party could have provided any MPs had it not been for the opportunity which journalism provided for them to support themselves. Understandably this caused some resentment amongst ordinary journalists against Labour MPs who took advantage of the situation, without joining an appropriate organisation. There had been isolated attempts to provide training. In 1869 John Wisker had made a specific plea for the proper training of journalists, in order to prevent the profession becoming a trade, but the first School of Journalism seems to have been established in 1879 at Crewe, a short-lived private venture. The difficulty was, what training should be provided? The only specialist skill, and this was not widespread until the end of the century, was shorthand. Pressure for training built up in the 1880s, and in 1889 the Birmingham and Midland Counties District of the Institute demanded an examination system for young journalists. Why, it was asked, could not 'the gates that limit entrance to other professions . . . be adapted to limit entrance to journalism'? The Institute, in response, tried to establish certain standards of competence at the lower levels, but on a very informal basis. The difficulty was twofold. There were few skills that could not be picked up in a short spell in a newspaper office, and to demand more than these, such as academic qualifications, or language skills, would have meant raising wage rates to a level unacceptable to the proprietors. Inside the Institute there was no way in which to bring pressure to bear upon the proprietors to raise wages.

Journalism had traditionally, except at the higher literary levels, been a male preserve. By the 1880s, however, there were quite a number of women in the profession and the Association reluctantly admitted them as members. In 1895 they formed the Society of Women Journalists, which sought to improve the status of the woman journalist, rather than challenge the men on their own terms. In 1897 it was reported that the Society 'have contended against poverty, against considerable discouragement', but that it had, none the less, grown slowly. They demanded to be taken seriously. 'We do not welcome the crowd, or endeavour to encourage the amateur,' and they were indignant when some mistook them for 'a sort of Ladies Employment Society'. In other words, they were shrewdly aware of the dangers of overpopulation which constantly beset the men. For some time they seem to have functioned more as a women's press club than as a professional society, but with the support of radical journalists like William Archer, H.W. Massingham and Bernard Shaw, they managed to maintain a small benevolent fund, and by 1901 boasted about 200 members in London.

We may now return to Kennedy Jones' remark quoted at the beginning of this section. Had the 'profession' become a 'trade'? In so far as journalism had ever become a profession, it had been a long and incomplete process, the trappings of professionalisation which it did manage to obtain proving much less effective in protecting its members than was the case with other professions. When told that journalism was a profession, Sir Marmaduke Rowley protested, 'but a barrister's profession is recognised as a profession among gentlemen, Mr. Stanbury,' in Trollope's *He Knew He Was Right*. Yet what came to be thought of as the norm of the 'golden age' in journalism, and persisted amongst the elite even when the 'new journalism' had overtaken them, was very like the norm of what have been called the 'new professions', which 'brought one scale of values—the gentleman's—to bear upon the other—the tradesman's—and produced a specialised variety of business morality, which came to be known as "professional ethics" or "etiquette"'. This, of course, was closely related to the proprietorial ethic, or *capitaliste oblige*, noted above. The same forces pushed both towards a resolution of their delicately balanced positions in favour of business and trade respectively. These changes were at the heart of the debate on the 'new journalism'. When critics of the latter referred to the commercialisation of journalism, the turning of it into a trade, they were not referring as Jones seems to have been, to the replacement of the amateur by the professional, the unskilled by the skilled, the casual labourer by the craftsman, but to the increasing subjection of the journalist to the uncontrollable laws of the market. The changing status of the journalist reflected the growing absorption of the press by the economy as a whole, and its dedication to the pursuit of profit, which was necessarily inimical to the old style of principled journalism. It had become more difficult, without private means, to perform the functions of the 'clerk', in the old sense, or of the 'intellectual', unimpeded by the demands of business. By the turn of the century, if not before, the profession had, indeed, all but succumbed to its new capitalist patrons.

3

Journalists

A. M. Carr-Saunders and P. A. Wilson

THIS EXTRACT, FROM a classic work on The Professions (1933) by Carr-Saunders and Wilson, sees British journalism as an exception; in 1933 many British occupations were moving in a professional direction, but journalism was not. In several other west European countries journalism was coming under the sway of right-wing and fascist governments. In Britain the National Union of Journalists successfully pursued its minimum pay strategy; but the NUJ also remained awkwardly positioned between a semi-professional approach and full-blooded involvement with a craft (printing) trade union orientation. The near impossibility of obtaining societal sanction for professional self-regulation and entry barriers is illustrated both by the tone and the substance of this piece. As members of Britain's academic/intellectual elite, Carr-Saunders and Wilson criticize both the owners and the journalists for a press which they see as too commercial, too sensational and perhaps too oriented towards a new working-class readership.

It has often proved difficult to describe the whole range of activities falling within the scope of a profession; more often than not they are many and various. But a connecting link can usually be found between them because it appears on analysis that these activities take the form of applying a particular technique in different spheres of practice. This cannot be said of journalists. They are employed in reporting, writing up, interviewing, sub-editing, and though these are not jobs which any one can do without a considerable amount of experience, no specialized intellectual training is an indispensable preliminary. Moreover the modern newspaper is the joint product of many persons specializing in different directions; several crafts are brought into play before each item gets into a paper, and so many hands are concerned with any single item, collecting it, writing it up, finding a headline, arranging where it is to go, that the impression made upon the newspaper reader is not to be attributed to any one person.

This division of labour and consequential factory production of newspapers are not in themselves either good or bad. The controlling and co-ordinating power will determine their character; but that power is to-day,

Source: A. M. Carr-Saunders and P. A. Wilson, *The Professions* (Oxford: Clarendon Press, 1933), 265–70.

in the case of the great majority of newspapers, in the hands of the business editors. They work for the proprietors, and the latter regard their papers much as the proprietors of great retail stores regard their shops. They provide what they suppose the public to want. 'They live for the world as it is and serve it on the principle of its essential gullibility; but above all they think of it as customers. Therefore they introduce it in the popular daily to just such a display of materials as may be seen in any great shop window in Oxford Street. They may be good enough for human nature's average food but they are common. They proclaim to "all the sensual world" the pleasures of snobbery, curiosity and amusement.'[1] Thus it comes about that foreign news, apart from 'sensations' in foreign countries, finds increasingly little space, since such news is not thought to be what the public wants. Moreover the whole product is sold at a price that is only a fraction of the cost, and the balance is made up out of advertisement revenue. Therefore the paper must not offend advertisers; in fact it must offend none and must try to please all. It is the function of the modern journalist to serve behind the counter and to contribute to the sales by the performance of some specialized task.

It was not always so. At the beginning of the last century the reputation of the full-time journalist was low, though the occasional journalistic activities of literary men did something to dignify the vocation. Cobbett demonstrated the power of the independent journalist; but it was the founding of periodicals, the *Edinburgh Review* in 1802, the *Quarterly Review* in 1809, and the *Westminster Review* in 1824, with such men as Jeffrey, Lockhart, and Mill as editors, which produced the first responsible, informed, and independent journalists. In those days the periodicals guided opinion; later they were superseded in this function by the dailies, and they came to be organs of comment. The daily may be said to owe its origin to the passing of the Reform Bill and to the invention of steam printing. The great epoch of the daily began with the appointment of Delane to edit *The Times* in 1841. That story is well known. Delane had no newspaper rivals and therefore no need to fear offending his readers; he never had to consider advertisers, financial interests, or millionaire proprietors, and he recognized that power implied responsibility. A passage in a letter from Reeve, one of Delane's leader writers, shows to what heights the conception of professional duty had risen.

> 'The responsibility of journalists is in proportion to the liberty they enjoy. No moral obligation can be graver. But their duties are not the same, I think, as those of statesmen. To find out the true state of affairs, to report them with fidelity, to apply to them fixed and true principles of justice, humanity, and law, to inform, so far as possible, the very conscience of nations, and to call down the judgement of the world on what is false, base or tyrannical, appear to me to be the first duties of those who write.'[2]

In the third quarter of the last century there was thus a group of men in

1 H. J. Massingham, 'The Independent Editor', in *Sells World Press*, 1921.

2 Quoted by B. Kingsley Martin, *The Triumph of Lord Palmerston* (1924), p. 89.

responsible positions, mostly editors and foreign correspondents, who took a high and serious view of their duties. This group was always small in number; its members were scattered, many being abroad. Though united by a sense of common responsibility, no question arose of the testing by examination of new entrants to their ranks, and therefore it is not surprising that no professional association was founded by them. Not more than four dailies now maintain foreign correspondents.

At the time when the great epoch of the daily was passing away and the new journalism was in the making, the first professional association was founded. The National Association of Journalists dates from 1884, and out of it arose the Institute of Journalists which was incorporated by Royal Charter in 1890. It would seem that the impulse towards association was rather a desire to copy the organization of established professions than any spontaneous movement towards coalescence. The circumstances of the time are to be seen in an inspection of the objects of the Institute as set forth in its charter. The hitherto unformulated idea of a profession of journalism takes shape in clauses which assume what was then becoming common form. The Institute is to secure the 'advancement of journalism in all its branches' and to obtain 'for journalists as such formal and definite professional standing'. Foremost among the objects is the promotion 'of whatever may tend to the elevation of the status and the improvement of the qualifications of all members of the journalistic profession'. This is to be achieved by devising 'measures for testing the qualifications of candidates for admission to professional membership of the Institute by examination in theory and practice or by any other actual and practical tests'. It is also an object of the Institute to promote 'by all reasonable means the interests of journalists'.

The Institute was founded at a time when, under the pressure of circumstances, there were increasingly few men whose position evoked a sense of responsibility. The story of the journalists in this respect runs counter to that of every profession that we have so far examined, and in consequence the situation was unpropitious for the adoption of any but trade-union objectives. But though these objectives formed the one bond which was powerful enough to unite the members of the vocation, and though organization in self-defence by the less well paid intellectual workers was at that time coming to be thought respectable, only a small place was allotted to them. In the words of its secretary the Institute 'failed' to satisfy the desire of the mass of journalists for a protective association, and there was a break-away among the younger men. They formed the National Union of Journalists in 1907. Newspaper proprietors, managers, and directors, though they are admitted by the Institute provided that they can qualify as journalists, are not eligible for membership of the Union. 'The Union began mainly, if not wholly, first of all, as a wages movement.' It was organized as a fighting machine and campaigned with unparalleled success. Whereas in 1913 the average weekly pay of provincial reporters and sub-editors was less than £2., the minimum weekly pay is now over £4. Its chief concern at the moment is to obtain compensation when posts are lost owing to amalgamation. By adopting the legal status of a trade union, by concentrating upon a single issue, and by confining membership to working journalists, it has achieved that kind of success at which trade unions aim.

In 1916 the suggestion that the two bodies should amalgamate was put forward by the Institute, and the Union replied to the effect that the Institute was a creature of the proprietors. In 1919 the Union took a step to the left and affiliated with the Printing and Kindred Trades Federation. This created another obstacle to amalgamation, and it is not surprising that, when negotiations were re-opened between the two bodies in 1921, nothing resulted. The Institute was perhaps condescending, and the Union certainly suspicious. In 1926 there was a crisis in the affairs of the Union. Owing to the affiliation mentioned above, the members found themselves called upon to cease work during the General Strike. There was a revolt against the advanced tendencies of the leaders and many resignations; after the strike a ballot was taken, and it was decided to continue affiliation. Nevertheless, when the question of amalgamation was again raised, the Union entered into negotiations in a more accommodating spirit. Amalgamation being found impossible, a scheme for mutual membership and delimitation of functions was drawn up; the Institute was to concern itself with professional and educational matters, while the Union was to deal with salaries. It was finally discovered, however, that the charter of the Institute would not permit of such a scheme, and negotiations were dropped. 'We have to face the fact', said the President of the Institute in 1930, 'that any fusion of the Institute and the Union is, at the moment, quite out of the question. . . . The Institute and the Union must go their own ways. They are, very largely, parallel ways and they must overlap in places.[3] The Union with a membership of over 5,000 is chiefly but not solely concerned with salaries, as may be seen from the fact that it has given an exhibition worth £200 a year in connexion with the course for journalism at the University of London. On the other hand the Institute with its membership of over 2,000 is not uninterested in the salary problem, and it has an economic section of which newspaper proprietors and editors may not be members; its main work, however, lies in what may be called the professional field.

It is not surprising that journalists, whether through the Institute or any other association, should have failed to stem the invasion of journalism by commercialism; it was wholly beyond their power to erect any effective barrier. Even if they had been fully organized and united, they could have achieved nothing by refusing to associate themselves with the new journalism. They have no monopoly of a technique indispensable to the proprietors who are in a position to go their own ways, whether or not the existing journalists are willing to work for them. It is noteworthy that the University of London grants a diploma *for* journalism and not *in* journalism.[4] There are also establishments, such as the London School of Journalism, but they are largely concerned with such technical matters as the correction of printers' proofs.

---

3 *The Journal of the Institute of Journalists*, June 1930, p. 109.

4 The syllabus is widely drawn and is roughly as follows: A. English Composition; B. One of the following subjects: Principles of Criticism, History of Political Ideals, History of Science; C. Two of the following subjects: English Literature, History, Modern Languages, Political Science, Economics, Philosophy, and Ethics.

While this onerous and responsible task of ascertaining the truth about current events, and of commenting upon them in the light of 'the fixed and true principles of justice, humanity and law', has fallen under the sway of men with the manners and morals of vendors of quack medicines, it might well be asked whether journalists, unable to influence the main course of events, have brought influence to bear upon lesser issues. There have been beneficent reforms; the legal restrictions upon reporting of divorce cases is an instance. The part played by organizations of journalists, however, in initiating and pressing such proposals has been small. Among reforms of a similar nature, much to be desired at the present day, are restrictions upon comment on murder cases and upon the writing of articles for other persons to sign. When wives of convicted murderers communicate their memoirs to the Press while their husbands are awaiting execution, disgust is widespread; but the professional organizations of journalists do not seem to concern themselves to find whether such deplorable exhibitions could be prevented. There is no such widespread disgust at the common practice of placing articles before persons of some degree of temporary notoriety for them to sign, because the public is not aware of what is going on. Nevertheless this is a practice closely affecting the honour of journalists, and it is disappointing not to find any organized protest against it.

So little activity is manifested by journalists in these directions that it might be thought that desire for reform was altogether lacking. But any one acquainted with the world of journalism knows that it is not so. It seems that somehow or other the regard for the honour of the profession has never found effective means of expression through associations. Perhaps the impossibility of controlling the main lines of development makes journalists feel so much at the mercy of powers beyond their reach that they have never taken up problems where their influence might be of some effect.

4

The Washington Correspondents

Leo C. Rosten

N 1935-6 LEO ROSTEN collected interview and questionnaire data from some 60 per cent of all Washington-based newspaper and news agency political correspondents. We see here many features of subsequent political journalism, such as both fierce competition and eager co-operation between 'rival' correspondents. We see also a group of journalists who are highly experienced and competent. Yet this total band of some 200 national political journalists also included a sharp internal hierarchy, with the highest-paid of Rosten's correspondents earning fifteen times as much as the lowest-paid. Within this elevated occupational fragment the majority attitude towards the trade union, the American Newspaper Guild (launched in 1933), was broadly positive, but somewhat distant. Some correspondents were close to their employers, while others resented the fierce anti-Roosevelt partisanship of many newspaper owners in 1936.

Max Weber has said, in *Politics as a Vocation*, that journalists, like lawyers and artists, have no clear-cut social classification. The social origins and allegiances of most journalists are, by and large, middle class. Their antagonism to big business is acute. Their discontent with the status quo is greater than their agreement upon alternatives to it or methods for re-casting it. They reflect the indecision of the larger social stratum from which they come. [. . .]

Most of the correspondents believe in democracy. But having seen it operate at close quarters, with its cargo of demagogues, pressure agents, political careerists, and red tape, they are both bitter about the uses to which democracy is put and confused about legitimate controls over it. They are unsentimental about the persons who occupy democratic posts but sentimental in their conception of the kind of persons who could, ideally, occupy them. In this they are no different from most intellectuals.

The correspondents are intellectuals insofar as their primary function is to handle ideas and interpret social events. But their thinking rotates around the concrete rather than the abstract. Their adjustment may be said

Source: Leo C. Rosten, *The Washington Correspondents* (New York: Harcourt, Brace, 1937), 239–42, 244–53, 269–70.

to be that of persons to persons, rather than persons to ideas. In interpreting current affairs they analyze them in the context of contemporary trends rather than against the configuration of historical movements or within a frame of depersonalized reference. This makes for greater 'realism' in their dispatches but less depth in their evaluations. [. . .]

Most correspondents are 'liberal' in their antagonism to authoritarianism, whether from the left or the right. They have a sincere and deep conviction about the license of free speech. And, like liberal groups, they become confused when free speech is used to threaten the structure of the state or to articulate political aims incompatible with democratic society. Hence their theoretical defense of the right of Communists to have access to the soap boxes and the radio, and their personal antagonism to 'agitators' when the privileges are exercised too energetically.

The Washington correspondent lives in a twenty-four-hour cycle of time. He must make 'snap decisions.' This tyranny of the immediate makes it difficult to achieve perspective, or apply what Vincent Sheean has eloquently described as 'the long view.' Each day the newspaperman is faced with new challenges and fresh sensations. Each day presents a deadline which must be met. This telescoping of crises into a daily cycle stamps tension and obsession into the behavior pattern of the journalist.

There is a curious sequence in the day of a Washington correspondent. The morning papers greet him with half a dozen promising stories for investigation. Messages from his home office demand answers to questions of fact or urge him to cover stories of particular interest 'back home.' There are press conferences to attend, committee hearings to visit, 'visiting firemen' to corral. There is lunch at the Press Club with other reporters on the alert for a 'story,' or at the Cosmos Club with voluntary or involuntary news-sources. There are telephone calls to make and illuminati to interview. There may be a debate in Congress which he should witness, a tea at an embassy, or a formal reception by a cabinet member. Above and around all, there is the iron moment of the deadline. No matter how lackadaisical the reporter, how dull the day, how complete the co-operation of his colleagues or the comprehensiveness of his Blacksheets, the meeting of a deadline involves the crisis of an internalized drama. The concentrated fury with which reporters pound out their dispatches is best described as the rape of the typewriter. After the catharsis, there is relaxation in the bar of the Press Club or the coffee shop of the Willard.

Journalists are caught in the remorseless vitality of the moment. They are hyperactive persons. In the exhilarating chase after the Now there is refuge from the restraining past and the disturbing future. [. . .]

The Washington correspondent outstays Presidents and cabinets. He is, as it were, self-sufficient in the small world of his newspaper organization. His first vested interest is his status as a privileged observer. He can attack Senators at their most vulnerable point—the reading public. Not even the President can claim immunity from his pen. One member of the press corps told this writer: 'I watch Congress wrangle over labor unions and old age pensions—and I'll still be paid to watch them when the shooting's over. I see the politicians worrying about whether the Republicans will be elected—and I know there will be reporters to cover a Republican administration too. I'd hate to see a war—but if the suckers stand for it . . . they've got to have war correspondents at the front, too—reporters, not soldiers.' There is consoling security in such a position.

The withdrawal from participation means not merely a uniquely privileged identity but also a stifling of periodic urges to act, advise or take a hand in political affairs. The renunciation of personal action creates tension despite the preferences of the ego (the calculating, rational part of the personality), and, in a time of crisis, precipitates guilt. There is a strong drive to jump into the fight. Some newspapermen contribute to weekly or monthly magazines where they find an outlet for the animus outlawed from their dispatches; others turn to press agentry; others begin to advise Congressmen, officials, or lobbyists. [. . .]

The press corps became conscious of its political power during the battle over the entry of the United States into the League of Nations. Ray Tucker asserts that it was a small group of correspondents, working with Alice Longworth, who:

> conspired hourly with the 'irreconcilables' and performed service
> far beyond the call of newspaper duty. They tipped off most of the
> Congressmen to Wilsonian statements and maneuvers, and started
> Senatorial counterattacks before the War president could unlimber his
> orators. They wrote philippics for the Borahs, Johnsons, and Reeds,
> cooked up interviews . . . carried on independent research into the
> League's implications, dug up secret material. Their dispatches bristled
> with personal hostility to the League, and the carbon copies which they
> distributed to pro-Wilson writers affected even the latter's supposedly
> favorable articles. The Covenant was defeated by the Senate press gallery
> long before it was finally rejected by the Senate.

The role of reporters for the Hearst newspapers in defeating our entry into the World Court is a case of more recent relevance. It was several correspondents who resuscitated Teapot Dome, and supplied Thomas J. Walsh with the more devastating questions in the Senate Committee hearings.

Ruth Finney of the Scripps-Howard Newspaper Alliance, an expert on the subject of power, played an important and continuous role in the fight for the construction of Boulder Dam. She published a damaging report of the 'teller vote' taken in the House of Representatives on the Utility Holding Company Bill. A Washington correspondent revealed the amount of the Vare 'slush fund' in the 1926 Pennsylvania Senatorial campaign, which led to an exposé of the methods of a powerful political machine. Paul Mallon and Raymond Clapper, then reporters for the United Press, published a secret Senate roll call on the confirmation of a Presidential appointment and forced a change in the practice, so that committees began to conduct their public duties publicly. M. Farmer Murphy, then of the Baltimore *Sun*, wrote memorable stories on the trading and chicanery which accompanied the 1930 Tariff Bill through the Senate.

It was a group of Washington correspondents who initiated the historic attack on the confirmation of Charles E. Hughes's nomination for Chief Justice of the Supreme Court. Richard V. Oulahan suggested that certain Senators agreed to take up the newspapermen's campaign in consideration of front-page stories which would benefit their political fortunes. When the Supreme Court declared the AAA unconstitutional, two young newspapermen, J. R. Wiggins of the St. Paul *Pioneer Press* and Felix Belair, Jr., of the New York *Times*, suggested to Secretary of Agriculture Wallace and Chester A. Davis that the purposes of the AAA could be achieved under the Soil Conservation Act, if that measure were slightly revised. The Department of Agriculture gave full credit to these men for pointing out the potentialities of the statute. [. . .]

But many Washington correspondents are cynical, if not disappointed, over the lack of public response to their work: several have remarked to this writer that the public reads the comic strips and the sport pages but scarcely pays any attention to their dispatches. Many have spoken ironically about the fact that their importance is exaggerated. One of the most aggressive members of the press corps remarked, with irritation, that although his articles had been appearing on the front page of his paper regularly, under a 'by-line,' friends would greet him with the annoying question: 'Say, are you still with the *Clarion*? I haven't seen any of your stuff for ages.' These same friends were quite conscious of the fact that the *Clarion* carried the daily wisdom of Beatrice Fairfax or the cultural homilies of Dick Tracy.

One of the most seductive phases of the reporter's life is the sanction which his calling receives from society. He is above the law, in a sense; he flashes police and fire passes; he is admitted to official hearings; he is given a box seat at trials and investigations; he is granted the immunity of priests and lawyers, in some states, with regard to information obtained confidentially; his minor transgressions against speeding laws, his presence in gambling joints, etc., are excused.

Silas Bent tells of the time he signed the name of another person in order to get a telegram which would give him an exclusive story. He experienced no anxiety about this hardly moral act:

> As the child of God-fearing parents . . . I had a strict sense of private property. I would not have pilfered ten cents or ten dollars. But my conscience was wholly untroubled about the message, because I had done the conventional thing. I was living up to the standards of my fellows . . . I was exultant, not ashamed.

It was not merely the exultance of having scored a journalistic triumph; it also contained the pleasure of breaking a taboo serene in the knowledge that society forgives reporters much 'in the line of their duty.'

The reporter's business is often to get secrets and tell them. Any vestigial guilt about this practice is defended by the statement 'that's the job of a newspaperman.' Sometimes there is a direct conflict between the newspaperman's professional and private motivations: as a reporter he should tell; as a friend he should not. Professional guilt is created by withholding facts which private conscience inhibits him from divulging; private guilt is produced by his revealing facts which his professional conscience demands. Hence defenses are required to support either the telling or the suppressing: 'I *had* to write that story, Pete. It was my duty;' or (to his editor) 'I didn't see any reason to put Pete on the spot.' The ideal reporter would have no friends who could be damaged by newspaper dispatches; but since the most valuable information is often obtained from friends in the thick of events, there is a contradiction of relationships which makes the ideal condition impossible in fact.

It is interesting that so many newspapermen react negatively to 'gossip columnists.' Actually, the gossip column, whether in Washington or New York, merely extends the journalistic license, by exploiting rumor, inference, and innuendo. It is journalism pushed to the marginal area. Why, then, should the press corps, like other newspapermen, regard gossip columns with distaste? Partly because 'the key-hole boys' are permitted freedom from the caution required in orthodox reporting, but also because their practices reactivate feelings of moral culpability in other newspapermen. In this context, the antipathy of reporters for gossip columnists may be said to be an over-reaction against murmurs of personal guilt: It is significant that newspapermen, whose trade requires a good deal of prying, were hostile to the activities of prohibition agents and are not captivated by the high-handed performances of the G-men.

The cynicism of newspapermen with regard to politics and politicians is a self-protective device. There is a saying that every cub reporter is an idealist and every veteran is hard-boiled. The 'hard-boiled' eidolon is a kind of professional stereotype, a cherished *persona*, in Jung's meaning. Actually it is a compensatory idealization. Truly 'hard-boiled' gentlemen do not crowd their walls with pictures of ex-Presidents, Vice-Presidents, and Senators, inscribed 'To Charley—a real friend.' The anatomy of many correspondents' glorification of President Roosevelt in 1933 and 1934, their disillusionment in 1935, and their active iconoclasm in 1936 illustrates a significant affective process. [. . .]

The technique of newspaper writing necessitates overstatement. *Competition, in journalism, has been raised from the plane of speed in transmission to the plane of originality in interpretation.* This competition, concentrated upon the interpretation of a common body of subject matter, places a premium upon spectacular judgments and bold 'angles.' In Washington this is particularly true: mass press conferences, handouts, departmental information services, and the excellent overall coverage of the press associations—these drive correspondents into an emphasis upon original insights and interpretive acrobatics. Real 'scoops' in Washington are uncommon. The struggle for the front page revolves around different 'angles' extracted from the same general body of information, or the utilization of private news sources. The necessity of writing a story a day, even in the dullest periods, has pernicious consequences.

Competitive journalism, like competitive advertising, ends in the asseveration of impossible claims. But journalists, unlike copy-writers, are preoccupied with persons, not commodities; they are directly exposed to the influence of their subject matter. Reporters often come to believe in the fictional qualities which they assign to public figures during that professional delirium which characterizes the daily meeting of deadlines. Newspapermen are driven to overstatement because they are competing against overstatements. And men who operate in the realm of words unconsciously assign to the words they use a reality which transcends their intentions. In this context it was not Mr. Roosevelt who hypnotized the Washington correspondents: it was the Washington correspondents who hypnotized themselves.

The one measure of value which most newspapermen possess is the rod of success. Ashmun Brown has stated that, for the Washington correspondent, 'The man who gets away with it is a good politician.' This empirical standard does not create analytic judgments which have validity beyond the immediate day and the successes thereof. The press corps vested a great deal of emotional faith in Mr. Roosevelt; as long as he was a politician 'getting away with it' that faith was justified. But when he began to meet formidable opposition from the Supreme Court, Congress, the Republicans, the elders of the Democratic Party, and the wide front of private groups who fought the President tooth and nail, when he began to meet with a series of defeats or temporary setbacks, some of the Washington correspondents began to falter. The corps had greeted Mr. Roosevelt with frenzy in 1933; in it there was a will-to-believe which, because it ignored future possibilities and past experience, would end by tearing down the myth it was creating.

The 'disillusionment' with the President by newspapermen represented an externalization of guilt. For the Washington correspondents were naive, rather than hard-boiled, in the adulation which, upon their own initiative, they showered upon Mr. Roosevelt. Having 'betrayed' the objective function which they felt they must observe, the conscience of the correspondents acted with doubled vigor. Newspapermen added to a situation for which they held the President responsible, those discontents which might more legitimately have been directed against themselves. [. . .]

The Washington correspondent brings to his work at the capital a long and thorough training in the arts of the police reporter. He brings to it the skills and perspective of one who has written for editors concerned exclusively with the spectacular value of stories. His dispatches from Washington compete for newspaper space and placing with stories from all corners of the world. He must describe the events of his artificial city so that they may compete with the robust news of industrial warfare and Balkan conspiracies.

Newspapermen do not have the time to pursue careful research. They do not have the space to present more than a swift, colorful account of the happenings of the day. In a larger sense it is improper to blame the Washington newspapermen for interpreting events in personalized, melodramatic stereotypes. They operate with a system of values which is natural and inherent in a competitive society. Capitalism, with its strident emphasis upon individual achievement and pecuniary estimations, has created normative images which reporters, no less than other citizens, accept uncritically. It has created a cult of the Big Man, the business and financial Hero. It has applauded opportunism. It has nourished a materialistic scale of appraisal which De Tocqueville long ago recognized as confusing individual successes with social welfare. These brittle norms are part of the world in which Americans are raised and in which they have learned to interpret their universe. They are incorporated into the whole weird structure of tastes which is encompassed by the word 'news.' The Washington correspondents are children of their society and they interpret it in the grammar which that society has offered them with an iron hand.

5

New Media Occupations in New York

Jeremy Tunstall

AROUND THE YEAR 1900, New York City played a key part, not only in generating the modern mass media, but in developing a new occupational structure for these media. New York City was especially suitable because it was not a political capital and because the media occupations could converge with, and emerge from, each other within a single urban location. Just as these new occupations of the mass press-film-pop music businesses were developed on Manhattan Island, so also around 1950 the new commercial television industry and its occupational structure were emerging in New York City. So also by 2000, the same lower Manhattan area was already called Silicon Alley and was giving birth to many new Internet companies and to related new occupations and new versions of old media occupations.

In New York around 1900 the media were for the first time shaped into a comprehensive media industry. The New York media became especially oriented towards poor immigrants from Europe, because New York at the time was packed with poor Europeans. The subsequent enormous appeal of the same media back in Europe is thus no great mystery.

While Paris before the First World War saw a unique flowering of the serious arts, New York saw a unique flowering of the new popular media arts. The press, advertising, popular music and films were all battered into their modern industrial shape in New York City in these years. All of those developments were closely connected with earlier New York traditions in just two fields—the newspaper and the popular live theatre (the Minstrel Show, Vaudeville and Broadway).

Pulitzer's *World* and Hearst's *Journal* fought out in the 1890s the epic sales war of the New York press. But more weighty newspapers in New York were already developing a new American model which was to modify the European notion of a prestige newspaper. New York was also the most important single centre for news agencies, magazines, comics, syndication.

Advertising agencies existed in a simple form in London before any-

Source: Jeremy Tunstall, *The Media are American* (London: Constable; New York: Columbia University Press, 1977), 64–9, 71–3.

where in the USA. But the modern form of the advertising agency was knocked into shape especially in New York City. In the 1890s agencies still usually sold advertising only for particular newspapers or magazines; but the comprehensive agency, handling all media, and including such new trades as the copywriter, was well established by 1910.

Popular music also became an industry for the first time in New York in the 1890s. Tin Pan Alley was some streets on the fringes of the then Broadway Theatre area; song entrepreneurs got songs written, plugged them to singers, published them and hoped to sell them to the public.

The film industry also was based in New York more than in any other single city. D. W. Griffith directed Mary Pickford films in New York—for long the Biograph studio was a brownstone house on East Fourteenth Street. And the greatest single market for the movies was also in lower Manhattan, swarming with immigrants. [. . .]

Both the early film industry and Tin Pan Alley were especially heavily populated with recent Jewish immigrants from the Lower East Side of New York City. Their poor recent immigrant status was at least as important as their being Jewish. The waves of Jewish immigration resulting from persecutions especially in Russia, and eastern Europe, brought these people into the poor areas of New York just in time to get mixed up with the disreputable gutter trades of song plugging and nickelodeon management. Isaac Goldberg, an early historian of Tin Pan Alley, wrote in 1930:

> Tin Pan Alley is forty years old. Beginning as a musical zone of New York City it blazed a trail along Broadway in close pursuit of the theater. The moving picture did not destroy it; the radio poured new life into its veins; the talkies adopted it, until they found that the child was endangering its foster parents; the coming of television can have no adverse effect upon this singing fool; if anything the contrary. . . .
>
> . . . the Alley . . . manages, stammeringly yet at times inimitably, to speak the yearnings, the sorrows and the joys of a new, an emergent folk, different from any other people in the world; and it is most gratefully accepted by that folk in the one true way that song may be accepted: it is sung. Tin Pan Alley, in brief, has cradled a new folk song, a song of the city. . . .[1]

The movies also were cheap entertainment especially welcomed by immigrants, the poor and the lonely. Tin Pan Alley provided the song of the city, the movies provided its art, while Hearst and his competitors provided the literature.

All of these media lived off, and were influenced by, each other. Song writers and film makers alike devoured the popular newspapers in search of dramatic phrases and stories. The silent movies were not silent but throbbed with piano noise (to drown the projector), pop Chopin, ragtime—and while the reels were being changed singers plugged their latest Alley songs. Another sound in the nickelodeons was the murmur of immigrant voices translating aloud the titles into the languages of Europe. In New York City at the turn of the century there was no question of

---

1 Isaac Goldberg, *Tin Pan Alley* (New York: John Day, 1930), 320.

Americans not being good at European languages. At least half of the New Yorkers were at least half-European themselves. As the media expanded, the idea of selling films and songs and comics in Europe was as natural as selling them in the midwest.

Above all, these New York media were to do with selling. Of all the New York media booms of the 1890s, the advertising boom was perhaps the most spectacular.

The industry whose products were to be sold around the world was industrialized in New York City. But the characteristic production pattern was not, and is not, mass production of the car assembly kind. The similarity to car production is only to the very early pattern of cars when a few were built at a time in a small garage or workshop. Tin Pan Alley especially was in many ways a variant of the tailor's business or clothing sweatshop. The boss sat downstairs in a shop dealing with the customers; upstairs instead of a few people leaning over sewing-machines were a few people leaning over pianos. While for sweatshop operatives the task was divided up by parts of the garment, for songshop operatives songs were divided up into words and music and song styles. Songs were turned out in batches of a dozen a week, or if business was brisk perhaps a dozen a day. The early film studios were also in small batch production. A common pattern was one short film a day, six films a week. In well-managed establishments wordsmiths sat up all night writing the next day's script. Often the plot was taken from a newspaper story and often it was written by an ex-newspaper man.

The newspaper was the original small batch production shop. The typical newspaper office in New York in 1890 was still only a small printing shop, with a sweatshop upstairs for reporters and a delivery problem akin to that of a rather successful city bakery. When Pulitzer in 1890 built himself a twenty-storey building for the *World* he was widely thought to be over-reaching himself (which he was); even then most of the storeys were taken up with a gilded dome and offices leased out to other businesses.

But while the production process was, and largely remains, of the small batch variety—the marketing and distribution process was reaching national, and would soon reach international, proportions. Newspapers could be run from small shops because sales were local and much of the news came in from the great news agencies, the precursors of the electronic revolution. But the prime means of *national* distribution was still in 1900 the US Post Office. Advertising agencies based in New York sent their advertisements to papers across the US by mail. Later, electronic distribution was to become more important—radio and television networking. 'Exchanges' of film gave way to circuits of cinemas linked to production studios. New devices like the juke-box enabled enormously large total audiences to be combined with some individual choice.

This combination of large-scale marketing arrangements with quite small-scale batch production reaped scale economies, it provided a high average standard of quality and also flexibility in response to current market demand. At the local level very small and very local output was possible, still linked in various ways to the national market.

Film studios moved on from employing a few dozen to employing by the

1920s a few hundred people; but each studio by now made only a smallish number of features per year. Similar production arrangements still persist in Hollywood today, where television series episodes are produced in small batches. Advertising agencies also developed on this kind of scale—claiming to offer national advertisers individual attention plus wider experience and scale economies.

When a new phenomenon like the animated film appeared, it merely adapted the small batch industrial methods of the film studio and the advertising agency 'creative' department. Walt Disney had—like many media innovators—worked in advertising; he introduced division of labour, with drawing tasks divided up between the more and less skilled. He also developed some star artists whose names he was able for years to keep secret—in the tradition of the early acting stars and their low-paying employers. Disney, however, retained much flexibility and variety—between formats and media—and, like most successful media tycoons, he was first, last and always a salesman.

[...] Both the early production and the most voracious consumption of films occurred only a few city-blocks away from the great popular newspapers of America in Chicago, New York and Philadelphia. Since the period up to 1914 saw the height of 'muckraking' journalism, the many ex-journalist screen-writers probably helped to provide a dose of informed social criticism which appealed to movie audiences.

The American film industry developed an enormous supporting barrage of publicity—both paid advertising and fan material supplied free to newspapers and magazines. The impact of these publicity practices was all the greater in Europe because American press agentry was there less familiar. By 1910–12 superior American publicity was an important aspect of the British film industry's decreasing ability to compete in its home market.

The famous serial movies such as *The Adventures of Kathlyn, Lucile Love* and *Perils of Pauline* all resulted from a Chicago newspaper circulation war in 1913–14, the serials ran both as weekly film episodes and as newspaper serials (in the *Chicago Tribune*, the *Chicago Herald* and the Hearst chain respectively). These film and newspaper serials were forerunners of soap operas for both radio and television. [...]

Many of the myths of huge salaries, outlandish behaviour and the inevitable 'romance' (between two stars who just happened to be appearing together in a new film) were invented, or at least exaggerated, by studio press agents. By 1940 there were 400 journalists assigned to cover Hollywood full-time. [...]

[...] The selling origins of American media tycoons have often been remarked upon. Why should men whose previous experience was in selling, say, furs, do so well in constructing a media industry? Various explanations can be given. Furs are dreams, too, just like the movies. Furs are volatile, luxurious, insecure things, of uncertain origin and uncertain value—experience enough for the movies, motivation enough for wanting some cartel security.

There certainly is a remarkable similarity between the early movie magnates and the early Tin Pan Alley entrepreneurs:

> Louis B. Mayer was a movie-theater owner, the Warners were a butcher's sons, Samuel Goldwyn was a glove salesman, the Schenks were drug store owners. . . . Adolph Zukor and Marcus Loew began as furriers, Colonel William Selig was an upholsterer, William Fox and Carl Laemmle were clothing merchants, Lewis J. Selznick was a jeweler.

Many of the early Alley managers had similar backgrounds. Isadore Witmark, Leo Feist, Joe Stern and Ed Marks had selling experience respectively with water filters, corsets, neck-ties and buttons.

There is, however, an even simpler explanation for these selling backgrounds—both Alley men and nickelodeon operators set up in small shops. Once in the song or movie business, they had no option but to be very close to their audiences. The movie exhibitor was close enough to hear what the audience said, doubtless to smell them also, and survival came to depend upon anticipating their tastes. In the song business the difficult task was to get the song sung—and many early song entrepreneurs plugged their own songs, singing them free to movie audiences, in bars and in cheap vaudeville shows. Irving Berlin, later perhaps the most productive and successful pop song writer of all time, had worked as a singing waiter. Harry Cohn—later the head of Columbia Pictures—had worked in vaudeville and as a song plugger.

Only the newspaper entrepreneurs lacked such selling experience. This suggests that it was simply proximity to, and familiarity with, the audience which was crucial. For newspaper reporters were out among the people looking for the urban melodramas of the day; circulation wars were a crash course in popular psychology and selling, sometimes also in organized violence.

The selling and marketing orientation of the whole media were evident in the dominant position in 1900 of the popular newspaper and its advertising. The requirements of press publicity and advertising were built into the basic commercial practices of the newer media; for example the movie release pattern—starting in the centre of the larger cities and moving outwards—was designed to maximize editorial and advertising, plus word of mouth, publicity. The typical media tycoon had as his right hand man either an ex-journalist or an ex-advertising man.

The American media arrived at the stage of an industrial pattern—comprehensive, nationally spread and still flexible—earlier than did those of Europe; in Europe the media stayed closely linked to political machines for longer. The consequent early specialization in America led to an industrially elaborated division of labour. The occupational role of 'journalist' in the US threw off the overlaps with printer, politician or man-of-letters earlier and more decisively than in Europe. A few basic occupational types emerged—journalist, advertising man, film director—to add to the traditional actor/singer.

These occupational divisions carried basic assumptions about how the media worked. For example the sharp division between journalist and advertising man reflected the ideology of a sharp division between those sections of a newspaper which were for sale to commercial advertisers and those sections which were not. Such ideological divisions, plus simple occupational specialization led to notions of 'professionalism' which were subsequently extremely influential in media occupations in Europe and beyond.

The American film industry quite early developed some distinctive subject matter, and the peculiar mixture of savagery and sentimentality for which Hollywood became famous. Its relatively weak theatrical, high culture or capital city connections enabled the American industry to search more vigorously for material suitable to the new medium. Cowboy films were popular well before the industry moved to Hollywood.

Most of the early actors had some theatrical experience—indeed the American theatrical touring tradition was a major contributor to Hollywood; but few of the earliest actors had been successful in the theatre and few returned to it. In Europe the more volatile film industry conditions meant that actors, producers and directors moved back and forth between films and theatre. Not only did Hollywood go further and faster in developing continuous employment, it also went further in establishing a constellation of new occupational roles and providing them with an ideology of 'professionalism'.

The American advertising agency pioneered a new specialized occupational role—the 'advertising man' who claims to be independent of the media and functionally separate from the advertiser whose advertising is being placed. This role was quickly subdivided into copywriter, artist, account manager, media buyer and so on. Related to the advertising man role a number of other more specialized ones emerged—of which the public relations man and the market researcher are especially important. The development of public relations is connected with advertising in many ways. Once newspaper editorial space was free of political party control, it became possible for outsiders to try to influence it; the larger the number of advertising pages carried, the more space there was to be filled 'to keep the advertisements apart'.

The market research role was given a major boost by the establishment in America of an Audit Bureau of Circulations in 1914. When circulations became more or less known it also became worth while to look at the composition of the audience in a more sophisticated way. Market research grew up mainly in and around advertising agencies and also in and around the major advertising companies in such fields as soap, packaged foods and patent medicines.

6

Writers in the Hollywood Dream Factory

Hortense Powdermaker

HORTENSE POWDERMAKER SUBTITLED her book (based on field research in 1946–47) 'An Anthropologist Looks at the Movie-makers'. This extract focuses on the movie writers, one of the small but vital sub-occupations within Hollywood. There were just over a thousand members of the Screen Writers' Guild, a body which continues today as the Writers' Guild of America, West (WGAW). In the late 1940s the movie writer was subordinate to a particular studio producer. Even under the supposedly secure employment arrangements of the studio system, we again see, within screen writing, a steep hierarchy. The most financially successful writers earned as much in one week as the least successful earned in a year. The Writers' Guild did not negotiate rates of pay; but the Guild was (and is) important on some questions of professional practice and in running a self-regulation and arbitration scheme on the vexed issue of writer 'credit' within a multi-writer system.

[. . .] The best way to understand writers, or any other people, is through their motivations. The primary one for Hollywood writers is the same as it is for everyone else there, namely, the inflated salaries for which the industry is famous. Mediocre writers with no particular ability swarm there with the expectation of earning up to a thousand or more dollars a week. Gifted and talented writers come when they are broke, or are attracted by the idea of getting rich quickly. Usually they do not plan to remain, but many stay and are sucked into the system. [. . .]

Most of them before coming to Hollywood made only a precarious living. They were newspaper reporters, sold an occasional radio script, did play reading in the offices of Broadway producers, read manuscripts or proof in publishing houses, or wrote advertising copy. Some had won a one-act play writing contest in college or the local Y. A number had written unproduced plays which an agent or producer said showed promise. Others were white-collar workers, salesmen, or businessmen. A few were established novelists and playwrights.

Source: Hortense Powdermaker, *Hollywood, the Dream Factory: An Anthropologist Looks at the Movie-makers* (London: Secker and Warburg, 1951), 131–8, 140–1, 143–5, 152–5.

Some writers came 'on their own' to take their chances in getting Hollywood 'gold.' Others arrived at the suggestion of a friend or relative who promised to help them. Many were brought out by producers on a contract with the usual six months' option clause, often given little or nothing to do, and then dropped at the end of the six months. But the writers stayed on hoping to get a break. Some became successful; others are still waiting for their chance.

Of the slightly more than a thousand members of the Screen Writers' Guild, which includes practically all the writers, only a relatively small proportion achieve their goal of big money. Probably not more than two hundred earn their living by writing exclusively for the movies, and even in a period of prosperity less than half are employed at any one time. During unemployment periods in script writing, many of them go back to their former occupations of writing for radio, newspapers or magazines.

Their salaries range from $187.50 to $4500 or more a week. In what was considered the last relatively prosperous year, from November 1, 1945, to October 31, 1946, 57 per cent of the members of the Screen Writers' Guild earned more than $5000 in the industry and 22 per cent less than $5000. The remaining 21 per cent were not employed in movie writing that year. In the first half of the same year, 150, or slightly more than 25 per cent, worked full-time. During the same half-year, weekly earnings were:

Less than $500 a week	248 writers
$500–$1000 a week	163 writers
$1000–$2500 a week	124 writers
Over $2500 a week	12 writers

[. . .] But the salaries of all writers, with and without talent, competent and incompetent, far exceed what they could earn elsewhere. This situation is not unique to the writers, but applies to everyone concerned with the production of movies. There is no other field, except radio, where a writer or anyone else on the lower rungs of the success ladder earns $500 a week and where such a salary is described as 'peanuts.'

It is for this reason that many writers (and others) are willing to sit it out and wait for the breaks. The stakes for which they play are high.

While waiting, they have lower expenses than if they were living in New York or Chicago, since it is not necessary to buy winter clothing and, in the past, rent and food have been less than in Eastern cities. Another advantage is that since there are so many other writers in the 'same boat' they do not feel lonely. [. . .]

[. . .] [T]ypical of a successful writer's party is one with a dozen or more people present when conversation opens on the latest bit of Hollywood scandal, with each one vying with the other to say something clever about it. Then there may be some superficial talk about a new book or movie or politics. After this the men may separate for gin rummy or poker, leaving the women alone to their gossip. Or if they all remain together, the discussion turns to their troubles with a producer or the MPAA office which enforces the Code and to boasting about how much money they are making. Rarely is there serious discussion about writing or movies.

For only a few writers is participation in Guild affairs and politics a major activity. But—whether they play the 'game' or politics, give small unostentatious parties or big lavish ones—the lives of most writers, like everyone else in Hollywood, are limited to the movie world.

The general atmosphere tends to make people soft. Most of the writers, good and bad, have never previously known financial security. Now for the first time, if they have any success, they have money. Instead of living in dingy apartments, they have homes, gardens, a servant and enough money in the bank to pay the doctor's bills, and those in the higher salary brackets have luxury. The much-heralded Southern California climate contributes to the softening process. There is a natural temptation to spend a considerable amount of time out of doors; and for many writers, as well as for other people, one of the major advantages is the ease with which children can be brought up in Los Angeles.

The perpetuation of this pleasant, comfortable life, therefore, becomes the goal for which writers—gifted and ungifted—are willing to be a producer's 'lead pencil.' [. . .]

Mr. Hopeful, in his late twenties, is one of those waiting for the breaks. Back East he had written four or five plays, none of which had been produced. A New York producer who thought he had promise went to Hollywood and took him along on the usual six months' option contract. Mr. Hopeful thought 'heaven had opened' and was sure that his days of poverty were over. During the six months at the studio he was given the opportunity to do only a few small bits on different scripts, not enough to earn a screen credit or to give any indication of whether he had ability. At the end of the six months his option was not taken up. The producer who had sponsored his coming had gone to another studio and no one was particularly interested in Mr. Hopeful. He now began working on original scripts. After several years of no success in selling them, he is working with a more successful collaborator, who, he feels, has no more ability, but whose name is better known. Mr. Hopeful has also begun to write a novel.

After a couple of years in Hollywood he does not seem particularly worried. He feels that any moment his luck will change, and that he will sell a screen play and be made as a writer. He and his wife, who is employed, live very modestly in a one-room furnished apartment. Although he has no screen credit and has been unemployed except for the first six months, he thinks of himself as a movie writer and part of the motion picture industry. He is an active member of the Screen Writers' Guild and is in constant social contact with a large number of other movie writers, some in the same class as himself and others more successful. His life is a pleasant contrast to the lonely one in New York, where he was simply an unsuccessful playwright with little or no contact with other playwrights. Although he talks a great deal about the play and novel he wants to do after he has hit the jack pot in Hollywood, he nevertheless gives the impression that he could settle quite comfortably for becoming a movie writer in the $750-a-week class.

Hollywood is filled with young people (writers, actors and others) who in their home communities stood out as being different from the average. The very desire to write or act set them apart from their neighbors. Success on an amateur level encouraged them to think of this difference as talent. Every big city is filled with them. Outside of Hollywood they tend to come to terms with reality more often and settle for less. But in the movie world they see other mediocre people in prestige jobs, earning big money. So they too wait for the breaks.

Miss Sanguine is one of these. In college she won a prize in a playwriting competition and after graduation came to Hollywood 'cold,' that is, completely on her own. For two years she wrote screen originals, which she took around to story editors and producers, without the help of an agent. At the end of two years a producer who had read some of her originals and with whom she was friendly, had a story he could not lick and gave Miss Sanguine a job. She was employed by the studio for twenty weeks at $150 a week, writing the treatment and then the screen play. On the latter she had a collaborator with a prominent name, and with whom she shared the credit. When the picture was finished Miss Sanguine was not given another job. Everyone, according to Miss Sanguine, thought the 'name' writer was responsible for the screen play. She went back to writing original stories in the hope of selling one of them and getting a chance to do a screen play from it, but this has not yet happened. She is now thirty years old and has been in Hollywood three and a half years. She feels successful, since she has succeeded in getting one credit, and she is optimistically waiting for the chance to get more. [. . .]

Mr. Cynic is one of the many who once hoped to write the great American novel. He started as a newspaperman in the East and came to Hollywood, when a friend, well-established in the movie industry, secured him a writer's job at two and a half times his newspaper salary. Today he is a successful writer of B pictures and over the last five years he has earned from the movie industry approximately $100,000, or an average of $20,000 a year. He considers this very good, and much in advance of what he would have earned if he had stayed in the newspaper world.

Now he is in his early forties, has an attractive home, and is seemingly content with his life. However, he opened a conversation with the statement, 'I am a hack writer,' in a rather bitter tone, and then mentioned that he had no respect for anything that he had written in Hollywood. He never goes to see any of the movies on which he has worked, because, he says, all the original meaning has been taken out and he cannot stand looking at them. He has likewise no respect for any of the producers for whom he has worked and very little for other writers. He seems to have accepted the limitations of the medium, but his acceptance is bitter. He tells a number of funny stories which always show the producers as inferior to the writers. He enjoys the fact that the producers, who are his bosses, are also employees who might be fired tomorrow, and that they are more insecure than he is, because it would be more difficult for them to get another job. Mr. Cynic disparages his own work, jeers at his employers, but enjoys his comfortable home and a substantial bank account.

Not all successful writers are frustrated. Mr. Acquiesce has been in Hollywood about fifteen years and before that he, too, was a newspaperman doing publicity also, and advertising, but he never succeeded in making a good living for his family. Today he is in a high-salary bracket—over $1200 a week—owns a very attractive home, has steady work and a large number of screen credits. He thoroughly enjoys the medium and seems to feel no frustration about working on someone else's ideas or having other people follow him on his script. He appears to have completely accepted all the limitations of writing in Hollywood, and says that these are the conditions which writers must expect and that he is prepared to take them in his stride. He feels the same way about the censorship Code, most of which he considers 'rather silly,' but he obeys it without getting upset and indignant. He stresses the large movie audience as one of the major compensations and talks about getting a message across. Since his pictures are all the most conventional stock melodramas and mysteries devoid of any message, this appears to be wishful thinking or rationalization. It is interesting, however, that Mr. Acquiesce has to have that, in spite of all his talk about accepting the limitations of the medium and enjoying his work and his life.[. . .]

Mr. Gifted has [a] distinguished literary reputation. Before coming to Hollywood he was well known for several novels and short stories, and a play. None of them, however, had been sufficiently popular to enable him to support his family in even modest comfort. After a protracted period of family illness he was broke, and a writer friend in Hollywood suggested that he come there. Mr. Gifted traveled on a bus because it was cheaper than the train, and left his family with relatives, until he could earn sufficient money to send for them. When he arrived his friend talked to the story editor about him, and it so happened that at this studio a producer had read some of Mr. Gifted's short stories, and thought highly of them. Because of this combination Mr. Gifted was employed on a contract basis. But he was assigned not to the producer who had appreciated his writings, but to another one who made only fast-action B pictures and Westerns. Mr. Gifted was known through his novels for subtle insight and understanding delineation of characters and their motivations. Westerns obviously did not call for these qualities. Nor did he have the particular abilities or training required for these action pictures. His work was not successful. The producer was displeased and Mr. Gifted was unhappy. The studio was about to drop him. The first producer, who had known his work and his potentialities, saved him by having him loaned to another studio.

Here he was given a chance to work on a good script, more in line with his particular ability, on which he could use his knowledge of people and his skill in dialogue. The movie was successful, and he went on to another script of the same type; again the picture was successful. Now he was made as an A writer in the upper-salary brackets and in great demand. As soon as his reputation was established he refused to work on a contractual basis and became a freelance writer at over $3000 a week. He has enough prestige to make his own terms and to exercise a certain amount of choice on the scripts he works on. He does a sufficient number to give him the financial backlog necessary for taking time to write novels. He regards himself primarily as a novelist, and his creative satisfaction comes in functioning as such. He and his family live modestly, but comfortably, in an unfashionable neighborhood. He saves a considerable portion of his income from movie writing and for at least six months out of a year works on a novel.

He plays none of the usual Hollywood games. He has, however, a very good relationship with most of the producers and directors with whom he works. He uses the same understanding of people which comes out in his novels and stories in his working relationships. Instead of giving the producers fulsome flattery, he is aware of their little foibles in an understanding way. He also has confidence in his own taste and judgment and says 'no' rather frequently to producers. This increases their respect and confidence in his judgment.

Mr. Gifted is exceptional in a number of ways. He has continued his writing of novels and at the same time become a movie writer in the top-salary bracket, so sought after by studios that he can work whenever he wants to. He lives in the present rather than in some mythical future, has the satisfactions of doing his own creative work and at the same time being regarded as one of the top movie writers. Unlike most writers, he has almost no bitterness, but is tolerantly amused by Hollywood and defends it if necessary.

Writing in Hollywood frequently begins with talking. Going back to prehistoric times, before the invention of writing, all story-telling was oral. In Hollywood many producers seem very much more at home on the verbal level than on the written one. In assembling the script at least as much time, and frequently more, is spent in talking as in writing. At the end of a day a writer and producer may be quite exhausted from talking.

The producer may start by outlining his ideas of the kind of movie he wants. Perhaps his idea comes from a sensational newspaper story, a radio skit, or another movie. He may become quite histrionic in the telling, walking up and down the room acting out his ideas. The writer later transcribes them to paper in a 'treatment.' This is limited to the 'story line,' ranging from twenty to eighty pages, and done for the inspection of the producer to see if he likes it. If it is accepted, it forms the basis for a script. The story line consists of a series of events which have a logical relationship to each other, but often little to the characters, who may be merely pegs on which to string the incidents. The logic of the story line usually takes precedence over the logic of the characters, or of life.

Sometimes it is the writer who, in the beginning, does the talking, selling his idea to the producer. There are some writers whose only ability lies in being able to talk dramatically about their ideas and who have never written a screen play. Gifted writers, too, may become talking salesmen for their ideas. One had an original idea for a movie which a producer thought so highly of that he called together several of the studio's top men, an executive, a director, a story editor, to listen to the writer describe his idea. The writer, quite verbal, was carried away by his own eloquence as he dramatized his recital for an hour and a half to this group. He was so effective that he fired their imagination and at the end they sat with their mouths open, convinced that this was a 'great' story. Having a sense of humor and suddenly seeing the whole performance objectively, the writer, when leaving, said ironically, 'Now get someone to write it.'

The original source may be a novel or play the studio has purchased, and the writer is employed to do an adaptation from it. He makes the changes necessary for dramatic effect in another medium, those required to conform to the producer's personal fantasies and his notions of what the public wants, and to meet the taboos of the Production Code, and tailors it all to the screen personalities of the actors who will play the star roles. Sometimes only the title of the original novel or play is left.

This 'adaptation' then becomes the source for the 'screen play'—probably done by another writer.

It is part of Hollywood movies for the writer to give the pages he has written each week to the producer. There are long story conferences in which the producer suggests, criticizes, and argues with him. He then tries to implement the producer's suggestions. When he is finished, if the script is still not to the liking of the producer, or the front office, or the star, or the director, another writer is called in. Rarely is the previous one called back. The general idea seems to be that he has given his all, and so if the script is not right another one is put on. If the producer is inarticulate the new writer may be told only that the script is no good or that it stinks and that he should make it better. He will go to the producer's secretary and ask to see some scripts which her boss considers successful and he may then ask for a showing of some of his pictures. All this is to try to find out what the producer wants, what will please him. The demands of the story are secondary.

There is a highly developed specialization in the writing. If a more articulate producer decides that the script needs humor, a gag writer is put on. If the plot needs tighter construction, or romantic touches are required, or the characters must be made more human, or the dialogue polished—there is an expert for each need.

The script continues down the line as the gag man, the dialogue polisher, or just another writer make their contribution and pass on to another picture, another studio, or to unemployment. Even if the writer remains at the same studio, at this point it is customary for his contact with the picture to be finished.

At the end the producer decides to whom the screen credits go and, following the rules of the Screen Writers' Guild, he is under obligation to notify each writer who has worked on the picture. Any one of them has the right to object to the studio's award of credit, and in that case the Screen Writers' Guild, or rather a committee of three members chosen from a rotating panel, acts as arbitrator and its decision is accepted by studio and writers as final. Of the approximately 500 pictures produced a year, about 50 are arbitrated for writers' credits; these are the important movies for which credit brings high prestige. The studio awarding of credits is changed by the arbitration committee on about two thirds of the cases.

The arbitration of credits is a highly technical and not an easy problem for the committee. It reads first the final script, then all the preceding ones, and any communications from the writers involved and from any other studio person concerned with the matter. There are no oral hearings. To receive major credit for the screen play, an individual writer must have contributed at least 33⅓per cent; a team of two, 40 per cent; and a writer-producer 50 per cent. The number of writers who can be included in the screen credits are three individuals or two writing teams.

2

Moguls and Barons

7

Media Moguls in Europe

Jeremy Tunstall and Michael Palmer

SINCE THIS PIECE was originally published in 1991 fresh crops of media moguls have appeared in eastern and central Europe and around the world. This piece considers a number of media moguls from Britain, France, Germany, and Italy. The media mogul is defined here as a politically eccentric media owner-operator and risk-taker. This definition restricts 'media moguls' to countries which allow private and commercial media ownership.

A 'media mogul' we define as a person who owns and operates major media companies, who takes entrepreneurial risks, and who conducts these media businesses in a personal or eccentric style.

Given this last characteristic—personal or eccentric style—any two media moguls must differ from each other. We have in mind such proto-types as Hearst, Murdoch and Berlusconi; but even these rather extreme examples do not possess all of the media mogul characteristics in full.

Our use of the term media mogul indicates a person who largely built up his own media empire; this entrepreneurial element can include the launching of new media enterprises, but in practice often consists largely of buying up, and taking over, existing media companies. This entrepreneurial and growth aspect distinguishes the mogul from the 'crown prince'. The crown prince is the second-generation media entrepreneur, who typically inherits major media properties from his pioneering father. The inheritor in some cases is not a son, but a widow, nephew, or other relative.

Thus the initial media mogul is distinguished from his heir, typically a crown prince. Separate, also, by our definition, is the 'baron'. The mogul may be supported by several barons, who normally manage divisions or companies within the mogul's larger interests. The baron can be a chief executive, he may also take entrepreneurial risks, but he is not the ultimate owner or controller of the overall enterprises.

The pure or classic example of the media mogul confines his business activities largely to the media. Most media moguls, of course, own some non-media businesses. There are also examples of entrepreneurs who are primarily captains in some other industrial field, but in addition own and operate major media interests. The captain of industry who also had major

Source: Jeremy Tunstall and Michael Palmer, *Media Moguls*, (London: Routledge, 1991), ch. 5.

media interests became a common pattern in 1980s Italy. We are interested in this latter model—the industrialist/media mogul—although our main concern is with the 'pure' media mogul.

Another basic problem—for definition and analysis—is the media mogul's unusual relationship to publicity. As the owner-and-operator of media enterprises, the mogul can command personal publicity on a massive scale; he is also of special interest to his fellow and rival media moguls and managers. The mogul exercises a special fascination for all journalists and publicists—for whom he may be a past, or potentially future, employer. Moreover the mogul's distinctive personal style often involves a highly distinctive personal publicity stance.

Some media moguls are self-publicists on a grand scale, but other moguls seek to minimize publicity, seldom give interviews and avoid photographers. Most moguls, it seems, pursue some combination of high and low publicity profile—for example carefully limiting their public appearances while talking profusely and 'not for attribution' to selected journalists.

Great public concern and major controversy focus on media moguls in general and certain individuals in particular. We must remember, however, that relatively few people both read and understand the media mogul's annual report—indeed some moguls operate private companies or control public companies through private trusts. Few people—even academic content analysts—attempt to inspect or assess the full range of media output from even a single mogul's media enterprises. Public debate and controversy inevitably relies quite heavily on the media coverage of relevant moguls. Thus the mogul's media image—contrived both by himself and his employees as well as by rival moguls and their employees—is a formidable barrier to objective understanding.

In 1980s France, for example, media moguls such as Robert Hersant were commonly referred to with the prefix 'citizen'—imagery which derives from the French love affair with *Citizen Kane* and Orson Welles. Yet this movie itself involves layer upon layer of myth and fiction. Leaving aside the question of how much Orson Welles contributed to the script, *Citizen Kane* told a story which departed in numerous major and minor respects from the reality of William Randolph Hearst's career as a media mogul. Hearst's influence outside the US was minimal. Even within the US in 1935—at the height of Hearst's political and media importance—his twenty-six daily newspapers had only 13.6 per cent of the national daily circulation. Hearst certainly conducted his aggressive tabloid papers in a highly dictatorial manner but his well documented personal and social life, and his relationship with Marion Davies, bore little resemblance to the startling images of *Citizen Kane*.

With television, of course, the whole business of constructing media images has changed. In recent times Silvio Berlusconi, who has produced perhaps the most remarkable of all media mogul business careers, has also proved himself the most astute and the most *bravura* personal image builder.

But it is the media moguls' political connections and electoral support which lead to the greatest public controversy, the greatest anxiety among politicians and the greatest disputation as to the relevant facts. Hearst's newspapers were concentrated in large cities (such as New York, Chicago, San Francisco, Pittsburgh and Boston); Hearst's belligerent opposition to President Roosevelt and other Democrats had little electoral success but he was accused of delaying US entry into World War II. In Australia Keith Murdoch and his son Rupert Murdoch played an actively involved, sometimes leading, role in nearly every national election between 1931 and 1987. Rupert Murdoch's newspapers were also highly partisan and belligerent in British national elections of the 1970s and 1980s; and Murdoch was no less partisan in city, state and national elections in the US. Axel Springer in West Germany and Robert Hersant in France were also belligerent rightwing partisans of the mass circulation Press in a succession of elections.

In addition to delivering partisan support at national elections, media moguls may actively influence the evolving national political agenda through their ownership of prestige newspapers. Axel Springer (*Die Welt*), Robert Hersant (*Le Figaro*) and Rupert Murdoch (*The Times* of London) all by the 1980s controlled prestige dailies; and all of the leading Italian dailies came to be controlled either by industrialist media moguls or by Berlusconi. Such prestige dailies have a tendency to lapse into financial loss which makes them vulnerable to mogul takeover.

Media moguls also tend to be politically involved in yet another way. The moguls seek favours from their political friends—in return for electoral and agenda-setting support. There is also the implied threat that if a business favour is not granted, then a less friendly editorial stance could result. In their business activities, and especially in their attempts to buy new properties and to enter new media fields, media moguls come into political conflict with media law and regulation on several fronts. Most obviously in entering new fields, media moguls tread on uncertain legal ground; this typically leads to court cases. Moguls come into conflict with independent, or quasi-autonomous, regulatory agencies; but moguls may also face regulatory decisions which lie within the direct power of politicians in office. Finally moguls face the threat or promise of friendly or damaging new legislation.

In Italy this political/business bargaining and deal-making is especially prevalent and especially potent in terms of its business consequences. Silvio Berlusconi in the 1980s became the only individual in any nation outside Latin America to acquire effective personal control over three national television channels; but he did not achieve this without political opposition—or support. Indeed in all the areas just mentioned Berlusconi and his Fininvest company had a cliff-hanger existence, well worthy of serial fiction tradition. Berlusconi faced a long succession of court, regulatory, administrative and legislative threats. Berlusconi's dubious legal position was partially regularized by (1985) national legislation introduced by the then Prime Minister Bettino Craxi who was also Berlusconi's long-time personal friend and political ally. Berlusconi was also friendly with other Italian Prime Ministers, such as the Christian Democrat Giulio Andreotti.

There are other examples of regulatory/political decisions which are not merely helpful to the media mogul but which largely determine his business success or failure. Robert Hersant's 1975 purchase of *Le Figaro*, which established him as a major French media mogul, depended heavily on his own political influence in general and upon acceptance by the then President Giscard d'Estaing and Prime Minister Chirac in particular. The crucial event in the massive growth of the Thomson interests was Roy Thomson's move into North Sea Oil—a move facilitated by his friendly political connections. Murdoch's purchase of *The Times*, the *Sunday Times* and *Today* in Britain all depended on favourable Thatcher interpretations of ambiguously worded monopoly law. Successive Australian governments were even more indulgent of Murdoch (and his belligerently partisan Australian papers) in a series of decisions, which ultimately allowed Murdoch—despite acquiring US citizenship—to control some two thirds of all Australian daily newspaper circulation.

These regulatory and legislative favours, in return for partisan mogul support, are especially transparent in two areas. One is in the body of law and regulation which governs press diversification into commercial television; the second area is monopoly law and regulation within the press itself. Even the United States has monopoly legislation which provides certain special exemptions and favours to newspaper owners. All of the four largest population countries of western Europe have since 1945 evolved bodies of specific press monopoly legislation. In Italy such legislation limits one owner to a maximum 20 per cent of press sales. In both West Germany and France lengthy press monopoly debates have focused on Axel Springer and Robert Hersant. The legislative results in both cases were deliberately weak and full of loopholes; similar weaknesses were evident in Britain.

Are moguls, then, party political loyalists? The answer seems to be no. While usually favouring the political right, mogul political allegiance tends to be opportunistic. Rupert Murdoch has on occasions in Australia, Britain and the US supported the more leftward party. Berlusconi in Italy has inclined to the left. And even the low-profile and balance-seeking Bertelsmann in West Germany has found itself more friendly with the Social Democrats. But moguls are not always loyal and certainly not to a party. Mogul political alliances tend to be with individual leading politicians, not with parties. Berlusconi in the 1980s was a Craxi-ite, not a Socialist; Murdoch's outspoken loyalty was to Thatcher, not to the British Conservatives.

This personal approach to politics is in line with the highly personal style, typical of the classical media mogul. As an own-and-operate entrepreneur the mogul is a risk-taker who, to a greater or lesser extent, follows his personal inclinations. We, of course, are primarily concerned with successful media moguls. Too much eccentricity in personal business style may have contributed to many individual inabilities to make a success of the media mogul role. But looking at broadly successful moguls, we are dealing with people who have not only indulged their personal hunches and played to their individual strengths, but have done so with considerable commercial success. They have themselves put together a group of media companies, which they now run, often out of quite a small central office. There may be relatives and long-time friends in senior positions. The mogul's working life tends to spill into his private life and vice versa. Business strategy and personal characteristics tend to merge into a single business/personal image. This merging seems to appeal to both show business and financial journalists; it makes for volatility, not least in terms of image and reputation, but also in terms of business reality and financial performance. The mogul, keenly aware of his larger-than-life image and his previous spectacular record of successful risk-taking, may be inclined to plunge into yet larger risks; business associates and bankers—also dazzled by image and track record—may encourage yet further leaps into the financial unknown.

Media moguls with track records of successful profit-making are of considerable interest to the financial services and banking industry. The media in the 1970s and 1980s were seen as a growth industry; advertising expenditure increased, while new technologies led to new markets for media outputs—cable, VCR and audio. The New York and London stock markets each have a lengthy list of media companies. This led not only to an active market in media company shares but also to an active market making loans to media companies. Media moguls such as Murdoch and Hersant, moreover, had a strong interest in bank-borrowing, which enabled them to avoid issuing new shares and thus reducing their own control. Hence media moguls became significant figures also in the financial world, beyond the scale warranted by the size and strength of their companies. The large bank loans fuelled additional growth and purchases, additional regulatory decisions, additional celebrity and notoriety. Under radically changed financial conditions in 1989–91, heavy bank debt found Rupert Murdoch and several prominent media moguls in severe business difficulty.

In the 1980s one media industry trend was the attempt of major companies to bestride the Atlantic. The goal of the transatlantic company was pursued by media moguls in general and by Rupert Murdoch in particular. But the US and Europe have quite different media mogul histories.

The American press grew explosively in the late nineteenth century and produced, in men like Pulitzer and Hearst, the first wave of media moguls. When the American film industry appeared, it quickly produced its founding father owner-operators. The same occurred also in radio and television; and similar figures appeared in advertising.

In Europe the emergence of media moguls took a different form. Various conceptions of state or 'public' broadcasting predominated in Europe; funding was largely by licence fee. European broadcasting quickly produced 'baronial' radio executives (such as Reith in Britain and Bredow in Germany) who operated, but did not own, the public system. Broadcasting moguls only arose in Europe with the much later emergence of commercial television.

Compared to the US, the Press in Europe has remained more closely linked to party politics. If newspapers are owned by parties, trade unions or prominent politicians, there is little room for the emergence of a separate breed of media-based mogul. Just as media have been owned for political reasons, a parallel phenomenon has been ownership by big business. Phrases such as the 'perfume press' (Coty) were proverbial around Europe. In inter-war Germany, Alfred Hugenberg's interests spread from the Ruhr Steel industry into newspapers, magazines, news agencies and advertising, as well as into dominance of the film industry. [. . .]

Europe, of course, has a very long media history. The Albert Bonnier who presided over the Bonnier company, controlling Sweden's two largest daily papers and many other publications until he died in 1989, was the great grandson of the Bonnier who founded the company in 1837. But Sweden is atypical—in the length and strength of its free press tradition and in its (related) resistance to television advertising.

More typical of much of western Europe is France where in 1944–5 everything (in theory at least) began afresh. Broadcasting across Europe was re-established under some combination of state and/or political sponsorship with sheltered financing. In the brave new post-1945 world the media had supposedly been re-established as small-scale, correctly democratic, and protected against any media Napoleons of the future.

In retrospect, however, the post-1945 conditions merely made probable the arrival of a new wave of media moguls. In Germany regional press arrangements left a vacuum at the national level which was partly filled by Axel Springer. In France, also, a very different restoration led to a somewhat similar result—a very strong regional press, with one national press mogul (Robert Hersant) in a dominant position.

8

Newspaper Tigers

Nicholas Coleridge

PERHAPS BECAUSE HE was a magazine manager in London, Nicholas Coleridge was unusually successful in gaining access to owners of major newspapers in the USA, the UK and some ten other countries. This extract from his 1993 book tells us about some general features of newspaper owners, including their habit of acquiring yet more newspapers.

[...] Among newspaper owners, longevity means three or four generations. Barely five major newspaper-owning families have any history at all, and four of these are American: the Sulzbergers, Chandlers, Grahams and Cox Chamberses. Their stories all struck me as curiously alike: an exuberant great-grandfather, very often military and so known as 'The Colonel' or 'The General', who makes his fortune building railroads or steelworks, acquires a small newspaper in a town destined to explode in size, gradually buys out his competitors to achieve a monopoly. So emerges a mighty cash-cow that churns out first millions, then hundreds of millions of dollars in advertising revenues. These old families—the aristocracy of proprietorship—sit on prime franchises, virtually unchallenged, so complete is their strangle-hold on the local community and economy. Their newspaper estates resemble the agricultural estates of European nobility; vast tracts of land are dominated by a Sulzberger paper, or a Chandler or a Cox Chambers. Among their rivals, they attract admiration and envy in almost equal measure. When I asked owners around the world which newspapers they'd most like to own, they invariably replied, 'the Sulzbergers' *New York Times*, the Grahams' *Washington Post* and the Chandler family's *Los Angeles Times*...' And yet the newer, entrepreneurial owners like Ralph Ingersoll and Dean Singleton, who have had to purchase their papers with borrowed money at high interest, could never resist telling me that these inheritors are only coasting, and their comfortable monopolies would be impossible to sabotage, however incompetently they were managed. In that, however, they are mistaken. The Warwick Fairfax episode in Australia demonstrated exactly how simple it is to destroy a fourth-generation family empire if you misread the future. The fall of the house of Fairfax leaves only one other *ancien* newspaper family in the First World: Lord Rothermere and the Harmsworths, owners of the *Daily Mail* in

Source: Nicholas Coleridge, *Paper Tigers* (London: Heinemann, 1993), ch. 1.

London, who themselves only narrowly managed to keep their hold on the greasy pole of proprietorship.

Jostling just behind the aristocrats are the group I came to think of as the Opportunists: the high-profile, first division players who inherited a tranche of capital or a modest newspaper that they've built up in their lifetimes into something much greater. It is no coincidence that most have expanded geographically, acquiring newspapers or launching editions wherever they've had the chance, in whichever city or country, since they didn't start off with a major power base like the Sulzbergers and Grahams. Rupert Murdoch, Conrad Black and Sally Aw Sian—the Tiger Balm heiress of Hong Kong—all fall into this group. So, to some degree, do Samir Jain and Aveek Sarkar. Although they inherited virtual monopolies in Delhi and Calcutta respectively, they have used them as bases from which to make inroads into the entire subcontinent.

The remaining owners fall into four categories, though they mostly qualify for more than one. These are political manipulators, number-crunchers, exhibitionists for whom ownership is only another means of attracting attention and proprietors so private that they are virtually reclusive. Louis Cha, the politically absorbed Chinese proprietor of *Ming Pao* in Hong Kong, Robert Hersant who has *Le Figaro* in Paris, and the Goenka family of the *Indian Express*, all own newspapers that act as vehicles for their political views (though Ramnath Goenka was so tightfisted that he qualified as a number-cruncher too). Ralph Ingersoll, Dean Singleton and Lord Stevens have embraced newspapers as businesses capable of generating ever greater profits if the corporate finance is correctly set. Tony O'Reilly, the chairman of Heinz who privately controls Independent Newspapers in Dublin, and the Canadian property whizz Mortimer Zuckerman, who bought the *New York Daily News* in October 1992, are both covert number-crunchers, but not insensible to the scope newspapers provide for prestige and exhibitionism. Robert Maxwell and Asil Nadir were both seduced by the singular glamour of proprietorship. The Aga Khan, Kamphol Vacharaphol (always known simply as Kamphol, pronounced Kampon) and the Ma brothers, despite owning big-deal newspapers themselves, go to extraordinary lengths to avoid the press. The Aga Khan lives in a high-security château outside Paris at Aiglemont; Kamphol and the Mas behind heavily fortified properties in Bangkok and Taipei. [. . .]

[. . .] The great new media empires spanning the world have subjugated more territory in a decade than Alexander the Great or Genghis Khan in a lifetime and funnelled responsibility for the dissemination of news into fewer and fewer hands. Rupert Murdoch needs to come up with political candidates on four continents for his newspapers to support. Almost every proprietor in this book has played some decisive part, through their newspapers, in the political or social history of their country: Katharine Graham's high-stakes stand-off with President Nixon over the Watergate tapes; Robert Hersant's remorseless advocacy of right-wing politics in France; Ramnath Goenka's decade-long feud with the Gandhis in which he toppled both Indira and her son Rajiv; Roberto Marinho's backing of the civilian regime of Tancredo de Almeida Neves against the military junta of General Joao Figueireda; Asil Nadir's self-serving championship in Turkey of President Turgut Ozal; Kamphol's public reticence over the dodgy Crown Prince of Thailand, which may have reprieved the last South East Asian monarchy; Rupert Murdoch's journalistic drag hunt of the British Royals which was largely responsible for the Queen's decision to pay tax, and accelerated the Prince and Princess of Wales's separation; Lord Rothermere and Rupert Murdoch's resolve, election after election, to get a Conservative government re-elected in Britain by respectively targeting (some would argue brainwashing) the middle and working classes.

The point has already been reached in which the traditional diversity of opinion in newspapers has been seriously eroded. News values are set, explicitly or implicitly, by the ever-smaller, ever-more powerful cabal of press tycoons. Their preferences and prejudices are disseminated down through their editors until they inform the entire corporate culture of their empire; until it becomes second-nature on a Murdoch paper that it will clip away at the foundations of the British Establishment—at its traditions, institutions and monarchy—and that virtually no article can find a place in the paper unless it conforms to that line.

And yet sometimes the proprietors are paper tigers in the Chinese meaning of the phrase: giving the appearance of being powerful, but secretly overborrowed or even broke. Ownership of the news allows proprietors more scope for bluff and bluster than anybody else. Until Maxwell went—literally—belly-up in November 1991, having diverted a billion pounds of other people's money into his private companies, barely a paragraph questioning his finances was published in any newspaper.

One of Asil Nadir's apparent motives in acquiring *Gunes* and *Günaydin*, two of Turkey's biggest dailies, was to deter them from poking their noses into his manufacturing and hotel projects on the turquoise coast. Newspaper moguls are practically unassailable. Their personal press is more indulgent than that of any other tycoon, and there is a reason for this. Proprietors themselves, perhaps feeling that there but for the grace of God go they, discourage serious criticism of their rivals. British newspapers owned by Murdoch, Black or Rothermere have scarcely ever published a rude profile of one another. In 30 years, nothing personally derogatory has been printed about the Sulzbergers, Chandlers or Grahams in a Sulzberger, Chandler or Graham newspaper. And there is another reason too. Newspaper editors don't wish to jeopardise future avenues of employment. They may take Black's shilling now, but who knows when they may need Rothermere's. The newspaper tycoon is, to all intents and purposes, inviolate.

Proprietors continually confided in me that such-and-such a competitor was going bust. 'You want to look at his debt ratio,' they advised me in London, Sydney, Texas and Bombay. But when I asked them why they didn't instruct their own business editor to do this, if it was such a great idea, they rolled their eyes and smiled like a Buddha. [. . .]

Proprietorship encourages self-satisfaction and vanity. Politicians, hoping that their careers or personal coverage might somehow be advanced, invite them to sumptuous dinners. 'Let us be completely frank,' Conrad Black was to tell me. 'The deferences and preferments that this culture bestows upon the owners of great newspapers is satisfying. I mean, I tend to think that they're slightly exaggerated at times, but as the beneficiary—a beneficiary—of that system it would certainly be hypocrisy for me to complain about it.'

Editors are alert to the slightest proprietorial prejudice, which they promptly reflect in their pages to curry favour. If the owner happens to mention that he doesn't care for *moules marinières*, a campaign against the danger of all shellfish is immediately launched. If he lets slip that he had a successful holiday in Spain, or a delayed flight, or believes that South American rain forests are an important issue, then travel writers, industrial editors and columnists are instantly assigned to follow up the story. Newspaper offices are echo chambers for proprietorial Chinese whispers. Suggestions from the owner become louder and louder as they reverberate down the chain of command. [. . .]

What most immediately distinguishes the press baron from everyone else in the building is the reckless amount of space he allocates for himself. The Executive Floor. The Chairman's Floor. The Corporate Floor. The expression varies from newspaper to newspaper and country to country, but always there is a moment when the lift doors open on to the proprietor's specially woven carpet and the corridors double in width. After the mayhem of the packed editorial floors, reeking of cigarette smoke and takeaway food, it is like stepping from Purgatory into Heaven. On the proprietor's floor, nobody speaks other than in hushed whispers. It is the silence of a doctor's waiting room in Harley Street, when the only sound is the ticking of a carriage clock and you are conscious that the furniture arranged against the walls—the davenports and escritoires—are there not because there is any expectation of letter-writing but rather to occupy the space. There are seventeenth-century globes on elaborate gilded bases. There are serpentine mahogany bureaux and marquetry *tables à écrire*. In Houston, on Dean Singleton's floor, there is a million-dollar Chippendale boardroom table which seats 24. The luxurious space is true even of the most number-crunching proprietors. Their own office suites would accommodate 50 accountants on a different floor, or 250 telesales girls in classified advertising.

Often these floors are referred to euphemistically by their numbers. The Fourteenth is the Sulzbergers' floor at *The New York Times*. The Fourteenth was Warwick Fairfax's at Fairfax. The Fifteenth Floor means Conrad Black. The Sixth is Rothermere. The Eighth is Kay Graham. An appointment on the Ninth Floor meant Robert Maxwell.

Notwithstanding their isolation, and the fact that they are chauffeured about in limousines with darkened windows and in private jets, owners kept assuring me that they have a special rapport with normal readers. None satisfactorily explained why this should be, but they felt strongly about it. Lord Rothermere told me that, on his periodic visits to London, he makes a point of taking a stroll along Kensington High Street, as a means of getting a feel for what is going on. Both Rothermere and Punch Sulzberger did a stint in the army serving in the ranks, and feel this had given them a special insight into the lives of ordinary people. Rothermere, who spent four years unpromoted as a private soldier, says now that he is grateful not to have been commissioned. 'I found it extremely helpful in understanding the true nature of society. I think it gave me quite an idea about what the real world is really like for the majority of people.'

Proprietors love to accentuate their street-cred. Ralph Ingersoll told me how as a youth he had sold circulation door to door. 'I got to know all the species of dogs in North America having to walk through the front yards and greet them bare-handed.' Donald Graham, discharged from the military draft in Vietnam, enrolled as a policeman in northeast Washington. Jim Kennedy covered City Hall as a reporter. Punch Sulzberger covered Raleigh, North Carolina, with long hair and a leather jacket on a motorbike. [. . .]

How ought a proprietor fill his day? This single question exercised half the owners I visited. I was repeatedly asked how their rivals deployed their time. Proprietorship comes without a job description. There are no set office hours. Editors and managing directors can theoretically produce the papers for weeks on end while the owner suns himself in Palm Beach or the South of France. The balance between hands-on and hands-off is delicate. If they intervene too much and second-guess every decision, like Maxwell at the Mirror Group, it is difficult to retain good editors. If they intervene too little, and devolve all power, then newspapers can become rather soulless. When Katharine Graham first took over the *Washington Post* after the suicide of her husband, she sat alone in her big office, feeling superfluous. Decisions were being taken all over the building by competent executives, but she didn't know where or when and nobody informed her or encouraged her to join in. How, as the new proprietor, could she infiltrate her own newspaper? She learnt to call journalists into her office and invite them, politely and apologetically, to explain this or that nuance of foreign policy and inquire which candidate the *Post* was proposing to endorse in the election. Eventually her own voice joined—some say dominated—the decision-making process.

Geographical proximity has little to do with control. From his office on the Fox lot in Los Angeles, eight thousand miles from Wapping, Rupert Murdoch not only monitors what appears in his British tabloids but, through his thrice-weekly telephone calls to the editors, plays a decisive part in formulating policy. He told me that, despite his film and television distractions in Hollywood, he still manages to devote two hours a day to his newspapers. 'I guess half of that time is spent managing them and the other half reading them. But my reading of the newspapers these days is more like copy tasting, I go in and out of them.'

I asked him if it were frustrating when he didn't like what he found.

'It kills you. I tell you, it's terrible. You know they're getting it wrong over there and then you find they're persistently getting it wrong. Then it's time to start shaking the bushes a bit.' [. . .]

Many media owners have developed a taste for pandemic theorising. As they become further and further removed from the day-to-day running of their newspapers—dancing on the ceiling of the corporation—they must, for want of detail, depend upon overview. And what is the purpose of a proprietor if it isn't to supply a global perspective, perceive a pattern in the chaos of demography? And so they will talk about cultural shifts in the baby boom generation—'the pig in the python', economic implications of the rise of the Pacific Rim, and environmental pressure groups in California and New Mexico.

When I asked Otis Chandler what is the greatest pleasure in owning a newspaper, he replied without a trace of self-consciousness, 'The opportunity it gives you to do important things to improve this planet Earth. Whether it be in science or helping to solve human issues or improve the environment or economic and educational opportunities for people. In other words, unlike any other business, a newspaper gets into every other business you can think of, and it just gives you that opportunity to try to improve and educate politicians and citizens of all types, to give them some guidelines as to how they can lead a better life and improve the *quality* of their life.' Asil Nadir, at the height of his short-lived newspaper empire, claimed to 'own my newspapers in order to benefit humanity and human culture'.

Generally their priorities are confused, their motives mixed. There is a pull of loyalties between making money and shoring up the reputation of the paper. If a large part of the motivation for buying an important news-paper is the prestige that accompanies ownership, there is little point in starving the thoroughbred until its ribcage shows through its flanks or fitting it up with a tacky bridle. This principle is more readily understood by the newspaper aristocracy—the landed monopolists—than by the heav-ily borrowed newcomers. The editorial budgets of *The New York Times*, the *Washington Post*, the *Los Angeles Times* and—to a slightly lesser extent in Britain—Lord Rothermere's newspapers, are enormous. Scores of journal-ists and columnists are deployed at political conventions, sporting events, wars and natural disasters, all of them billeted at the best hotels with expense accounts that are hardly queried. When the proprietor goes out to dinner at the height of the Bosnian civil war or the Somalian famine, he takes a vicarious pleasure in informing friends that 15 of his best reporters are at the heart of the turmoil, and that he has the inside story on what's going on over there.

But for the highly geared new American owners like Singleton and Ingersoll, the commitment to quality is ambivalent. Both assembled vast empires with record speed: Ralph Ingersoll's 240 newspapers took him less than five years to acquire, Dean Singleton's 71 in eleven states were snapped up in about eight years. The later part of the eighties saw the greatest scramble for newspaper assets ever known, with papers changing hands at unprecedented multiples. It made William Randolph Hearst seem, by comparison, cautious and vacillating.

The impetus for the feeding frenzy was very simple: the new proprietors believed that extraordinary financial returns could be derived from the fact that newspapers were America's last unregulated monopoly. Increasingly, in every city and township across the United States, there was only one paper, typically family-owned. Since there was no competition, pricing was in the hands of the proprietor. If they bought out the families, they could hike the advertising rates, hike the cover prices and turn a modestly profitable operation into a cash-cow. [. . .]

Ralph Ingersoll explained to me how he justified the multiples. 'I've always been more daring than the old family ownerships [who mostly sold him his newspapers] in exploiting the advantages of . . . what's the polite word? Monopoly is the impolite word, the *exclusive market position*. When we bought a new paper we felt we could charge rather more, both for circulation and advertising, than was part of it previously. We did away with the old boy advertising rates; rates that were kept low so as not to anger friends and neighbours. Some of the papers we bought had been operated on something other than the profit principle. They [the sellers] equate what we [then] did with being the sons of bitches they wouldn't be.

'The second thing we would do,' said Ingersoll, 'was rationalise the workforce to some degree. And then we'd fix the printing. Most of these newspapers we bought had already converted to cold type, but the conversions had been botched by the families [I acquired them from]. We'd fix them.'

'Botched how?'

'They weren't disciplined enough—they were too sentimental about the old staff relationships. And we simply *knew* how many productive hours per page it takes to produce a newspaper and we were willing to reduce the staff, buy out the positions. So it was not uncommon for us to be able to *treble* the profitability of a newspaper in two or three years. My concept of a good newspaper is the difference between a 10 per cent profit margin and a 30 per cent profit margin.'

Singleton, meanwhile, was refining what has been called his 'cut and slash' philosophy of newspaper management: the five steps from unprofitability or modest profitability to a business capable of repaying the interest on the corporate finance and posting decent profits for the proprietor.

1. Buy Newspaper
2. Cut Staff
3. Cut Quality
4. Cut Objectivity
5. Hike Advertising Rates

Buying newspapers is sometimes compared to betting at a casino at which the roulette table is in perpetual play, and where enormous wins alternate, almost arbitrarily, with huge losses. In fact, as the new proprietors realised, owning newspapers is like owning the bank. The odds can be reset constantly in the bank's favour, and the variables—editorial costs, advertising revenues, staff numbers, union agreements—manipulated even as the wheel is spinning.

One of the most curious relationships is that between the owner and his journalists. Every proprietor assured me that he valued his writers, but several sounded like they were only paying lip-service and were unable to name anyone in particular. Especially among new owners who made their first fortune doing something else, there is often both fear and contempt for journalists. Among the older proprietors I found ambivalence. They accepted that star writers embellished their papers, and helped sell them, but they seemed vaguely to resent their high salaries and were dubious of their loyalty and values. Partly this was the consequence of peer pressure. Owners are held personally responsible for the opinions of their journalists, over which they normally have little or no control. Punch Sulzberger says that his friends frequently chide him ('you and your goddamn scandal sheet') for some derogatory remark in *The New York Times* about themselves or their businesses. 'The tendency is for people to get pretty exercised when they're upset with a newspaper,' Jim Kennedy, the Cox heir to the *Atlanta Journal* and *Constitution*, told me. 'People [often] say something to me when we're out to dinner, if they don't like what's been written.' The more prominent the proprietor, the worse it becomes. If they move socially among politicians and industrial tycoons, every single fellow guest at a dinner party can take them to task over their treatment by the paper. When Otis Chandler's *Los Angeles Times* hired the radical cartoonist Paul Conrad, Chandler was rung several times a month at breakfast time by the Governor of the State of California, Ronald Reagan, or his wife, complaining about his portrayal in that day's issue. Finally Chandler gave instructions that calls from the Reagans should not be put through.

9

Hugenberg: Hitler's Media Mogul

Jeremy Tunstall

I N GERMANY DURING 1918–33, Alfred Hugenberg was an extreme example of the dominating media mogul with distinctive political views. He was extreme in the vast extent of his media interests—these interests included newspaper chains and UFA (the main German film company), as well as advertising agencies and news agencies. When he came to power in 1933, Hitler, thanks to his alliance with Hugenberg, already had control of about half of all German mass media. After 1945 the American, British, and French occupying forces in West Germany were to establish a newly democratic and de-centralized media structure which was intended to prevent the rise of another such media mogul.

By 1933 the Hugenberg media empire [was] a private enterprise media cartel on a scale which has probably never been surpassed in any major nation; the existence of this Hugenberg media empire greatly facilitated Hitler's rapid seizure of the entire media apparatus in Germany. Hugenberg was a Ruhr industrialist. The motivations behind his private media empire were anti-socialist, anti-Semitic, anti-American and pro-nationalist. Almost certainly, Hugenberg was also inspired by the examples of Hearst, Pulitzer and Northcliffe. The first component of the Hugenberg empire was the old Scherl newspaper group; unlike the Mosse and Ullstein groups, Scherl's was neither Jewish nor under efficient financial management. The Mosse and Ullstein newspaper groups were accused of favouring mid-1920s American policy (such as the Dawes plan) and being in league with American press and film interests.

Hugenberg's antipathy towards cosmopolitan, western, Jewish and socialist elements in German life was shared by many Germans at the time:

> A bitterness towards the West, its political institutions and modes of life had taken root in German thought after the Napoleonic invasion . . . the so-called Westerner among German intellectuals easily passed for a subversive. A very high percentage of the Weimar left-wing intellectuals

Source: Jeremy Tunstall, *The Media are American* (London: Constable; New York: Columbia University Press, 1977), 150–3.

combined all the characteristics repugnant to Germanic ideologists: Francophile, Jewish, Western, rebellious, progressive, democratic, rationalist, socialist, liberal, and cosmopolitan . . .

. . . Jews were responsible for a great part of German culture. The owners of three of Germany's greatest newspaper publishing houses; the editors of *Vossische Zeitung* and the *Berliner Tageblatt*; most book publishers . . . were all Jews. Jews played a major part in theater and in the film industry as producers, directors and actors. Many of Germany's best composers, musicians, artists, sculptors, and architects were Jews. Their participation in literary criticism and in literature was enormous. . . .

The left-wing intellectuals did not simply 'happen to be mostly Jews' as some pious historiography would have us believe. . . . The extraordinary Jewish participation in German culture is to be explained by the peculiarities of the Central European Jewish intellectual tradition and by the Jews' historic exclusion from the more 'respectable' professions [such] as the civil service, the army, the judiciary, or university teaching.[1]

Hugenberg was first called in to help to reorganize the Scherl newspaper, magazine and book interests and by 1916 he had managerial control. In 1914 he launched his Ausland agency to handle German commercial advertising abroad; this agency later turned into ALA, which by 1920 was Mosse's main rival—a financial holding company controlling newspaper interests and advertising agencies. In 1917 Hugenberg launched Vera Verlagsanstalt—which offered advice and finance for industrialists and others who wished to buy newspapers; Vera later also engaged in news, feature and photograph agency services—and seems increasingly to have been used by Hugenberg as an intelligence gathering agency which enabled him to buy, influence, and subsidize more and more newspapers. In 1918 a number of German newspapers were temporarily taken over by socialist journalists, which strengthened Hugenberg's opposition to foreign, socialist and Jewish forces. In 1922 he founded WIPRO a news agency designed to funnel nationalist-slanted news into small provincial newspapers; WIPRO provided moulds ready for casting and ultimately 350 papers relied entirely on this service. It was only after this deep involvement that Hugenberg became interested in rescuing UFA—he acquired a controlling interest in 1927.

In the late 1920s Germany had some 4,000 daily newspapers—most inevitably with negligible sales. Berlin alone had daily newspapers owing allegiance to 50 separate political persuasions. But most of the bigger dailies in the main cities were owned by newspaper groups, which also operated as advertising agents (selling their own and other papers' advertising); Mosse, indeed, was an advertising firm first and a newspaper firm only second. The big press groups also had news agency interests; they operated as public relations agencies (distributing publicity material for a fee); they promoted their own group's other services shamelessly; and they were involved with political party and industrial alliances and subsidies. Within this chaotic jungle there was being fought out a newspaper war to the

1 Istvan Deak, *Weimar Germany's Left-wing Intellectuals* (Berkeley, Calif.: University of California Press, 1968), 23, 28–9.

death—quite literally for some participants. Few Anglo-American niceties were observed—no 'neutral' news, little 'professional objectivity' among journalists, no audited circulation figures, no advertising agents independent of both media and advertisers, no independent news agencies; nor was any single publication, news organization or personality accorded general respect. To any Anglo-American advertising man or to any British or American journalist, the German media in the late 1920s must have looked like a jungle—with no objective facts and where everything was tainted with political and financial corruption.

Anglo-American involvement quickened rather than decreased in the late 1920s. Hollywood, with the coming of sound, became an even bigger force in the badly floundering German film industry. Some American businessmen, appalled by German advertising conditions, favoured familiar Anglo-American advertising agencies. When J. Walter Thompson opened a branch in Berlin in 1927 it joined several other Anglo-American agencies; the American McCann-Erickson, the British Dorland and Unilever's Lintas followed in 1927 and 1928. Such agencies insisted on the Anglo-American level of 15 per cent commission. This Anglo-American invasion may have seemed innocent to some people but hardly to an anti-Semitic, anti-American, German nationalist like Hugenberg. He had already suffered the indignity of employing Jewish journalists and of making unfavourable deals with Hollywood businessmen—indignities, indeed, for the man who became chairman of the German National Party, shortly before he formed his alliance with Hitler in 1929. Now he had to witness American advertising agencies coming to Germany to compete with his own advertising agencies. He probably saw an even more sinister threat in the Anglo-American news agencies. Reuters and the American agencies wanted reliable news of the dramatic course of German politics. Competition between domestic German news agencies inevitably involved competition to obtain the most favourable exchange agreements with the international agencies.

In the late 1920s Hugenberg moved more deeply into news agency activities. His Telegraphen-Union took over the family-owned Dammert Verlag and two other news agencies and became a serious threat to Wolff, the traditional German international agency. Another Hugenberg news agency became increasingly strong in economic news services, enabling him to undermine Wolff's monopoly of official news. The Depression brought many bankruptcies which aided Hugenberg's expansion. By 1932 he controlled Germany's major film company and its nationally exhibited newsreel, and elaborate advertising and press interests:

> A rough estimate would be that Hugenberg enjoyed some form of control or influence over close to one half of the German press by 1930. Almost without exception newspapers which professed a right-wing nationalist political orientation—in 1932 about 1,200 papers—and much of the so-called non-partisan press—2,029 *parteilose* papers existed in 1932—had contracts with one or more of Hugenberg's operations. There were 1,600 papers that subscribed to the TU alone . . .
> . . . Without asserting that Hugenberg's press dominion destroyed the

Weimar Republic, one can say that it presented a major obstacle to the implementation of democratic, republican ideas amongst the German public.[2]

The main press opposition to Hugenberg came from the Mosse and Ullstein groups, and from Sonnemann's *Frankfurter Zeitung*. Ullstein's newspaper, magazine and book combine claimed to be the largest in Europe; about half the Ullstein journalists were Jewish and the company had many Anglo-American overtones—including the joint sponsorship of car and plane races with New York and London papers. There were similar Jewish and Anglo-American overtones in the *Frankfurter Zeitung*, Germany's leading prestige newspaper. Its editor and dominant personality in the 1920s, Bernhard Guttmann, had been the paper's London correspondent before the First World War.

As early as 1930 Hugenberg had shown himself willing to use his media cartel in the Nazi interest. The first German showing of the American-made pacifist film *All Quiet on the Western Front*, on 5th December 1930, led to demonstrators organized by Goebbels preventing the second evening screening of this film in Berlin. Further rioting followed and the subject was debated in the Reichstag. The Scherl Verlag (Hugenberg controlled) film trade paper gave the American film a favourable review on the morning previous to the first rioting; a week later, however, the same paper called for the banning of the film. The film was indeed banned from public exhibition. The *All Quiet on the Western Front* episode is a celebrated event in the decline of Weimar and the rise of Nazism.

---

2 Modris Eksteins, *The Limits of Reason: The German Democratic Press and the Collapse of Weimar Democracy* (London: Oxford University Press, 1975), 79.

10

The Soviet Union's Broadcasting Baron

Reino Paasilinna

UNTIL THE BREAK-UP of the Soviet Union in 1991, the boss of the State Committee for TV and Radio Broadcasting (the chairman of Gosteleradio) was in charge of all radio and television across the eleven time zones of the USSR. This not-for-profit media baron was responsible directly to the top man in the USSR (the General Secretary of the Communist Party) and to at least two other high officials in the Party and the Politburo. Reino Paasilinna was himself the Director-General of the Finnish Broadcasting Company in Helsinki and he tells us that he knew all of the chairmen who ran Gosteleradio during 1964–91. He focuses heavily on Sergei Lapin (chairman, 1970–85), a Soviet radio/TV baron who insisted on bland entertainment programming. Meanwhile bad news, serious debate, critical drama, and even audience research were forbidden. Lapin helped to create the 'Cult of Personality' — the television presentation of the Soviet boss Leonid Brezhnev as the benign father figure of a contented and tranquil Soviet Union.

Several chairmen served during the period of my study: S. V. Kaftanov 1960–62, M. A. Kharlamov 1962–64, N. N. Mesetsev 1964–70, S. G. Lapin 1970–85, A. N. Aksyenov 1985–89, M. F. Nenashev 1989–90, and L. N. Kravchenko 1990–91. All of them were removed for political reasons. Each had an important Party background in the Central Committee apparatus. I have had several discussions with all of them, with the exception of the first two chairmen.

Formally, the chairman of Gosteleradio was nominated by the Supreme Soviet. He was explicitly personally responsible to the Party for the tasks and duties of his organization. The collegium, which corresponded to a board of directors, included the deputies of the chairman and other persons in leadership positions. In questions of disagreement the chairman had the final word.

The most important thing in the election of the chairman was not professional competence in the field, but activity within the Party and a

Source: Reino Paasilinna, *Glasnost and Soviet Television* (Helsinki: YLE (Finnish Broadcasting Company), 1995), 120–8.

sufficiently high status in the political hierarchy. This can be seen in their backgrounds. The platform was usually the propaganda department of the Central Committee or something comparable, a position in which one somehow got a preparation for the task of the chairman.

The chairman has been a loyal assistant of the incumbent General Secretary of the CPSU during his term of office. Usually the chairman has been changed with a change in the Party leader or on his orders. Through their relationship with the chairmen, the General Secretaries have kept a firm grip on all television and radio broadcasting. This relationship can be seen also at the points when chairmen have been changed. Since chairman Lapin's period was the longest and most significant one, we can justly examine his performance more extensively than that of the others.

Chairman Kaftanov served earlier in the Party Central Committee and e.g. as the chairman of the Committee of Science and Technology. By training he was a chemist.

Chairman Kharlamov in turn was a son-in-law of General Secretary Khrushchev, and he had served in the Central Committee and the Ministry of Foreign Affairs. Kharlamov's significance as a reformer was not as great as that of the other son-in-law, Adzhubei.

When Khrushchev was removed, he announced in the Politburo: 'You little brats, I'll go to Kharlamov and appeal to the people'. This was clearly not on, and hence Kharlamov was changed for Mesetsev on the same day Khrushchev was ousted in 1964. Mesetsev hurried to the Gosteleradio office on Pyatnitskaya Street the very same night. The personnel noticed to their surprise in the morning that the nameplate on the chairman's door had been replaced. Already at that stage it was understood that television could have a decisive role in a critical period. This also demonstrated the importance of the chairman's position. Kharlamov was abroad at the time.

During chairman Mesetsev's (formerly secretary of the Communist Youth League (*Komsomol*), an official of the Central Committee and the KGB, and a diplomat) time at the helm from 1964–1970 the television system grew into an important factor in the Soviet Union. Under his leadership the departments for audience research and programme planning were established in Gosteleradio. This can be regarded as a rather daring thing to do, because sociological research was at that time opposed by the conservatives of the Soviet leadership (e.g. Suslov). However, Mesetsev was also able to see through the construction of the large Ostankino television centre. In his time, in 1967, the multichannel television system was introduced.

Longserving chairman Sergei Lapin (1970–1985) had a background in diplomacy and journalism, but above all as a Party official (Party member from 1939; Central Committee member from 1966). He was Suslov's assistant at one point. Lapin served in the control commission in Germany, later as a diplomat in Austria and China, and as Deputy Foreign Minister.

It is said that as Director General of TASS, Lapin frequently used to hurry to the new General Secretary (Brezhnev) to report the main news of the day in brief. This led to chess games between the two, of which Lapin actually showed me photographs, and eventually to his appointment as chairman of Gosteleradio. He loved literature and lived in a modest way. He was very well-read and widely informed. The man was strict, sarcastic and shrewd.

Whilst he appeared humane, in his actual work Lapin was regarded as narrow-minded and reluctant to introduce programming reforms. He was a true and orthodox representative of the Party nomenclature. There was a famous case when he changed the conductor of a non-compliant symphony orchestra for a balalaika band leader who could not read music. All the top musicians of the orchestra had to audition before the band leader in order to get their jobs back. The same conductor later won laurels for his interpretations of Sibelius. And he is still conducting.

The division of television channels was established during Lapin's term. At that time the central television had four channels. *Programme One* was the all-Union basic channel. It transmitted news and current affairs programmes as well as entertainment, drama, and movies intended for large audiences. The programme was also relayed by satellite (total 13.5 hours daily).

Programme Two was directed to Moscow and its environs. Its four-and-a-half-hour broadcasts dealt in particular with documentaries and cultural life.

In *Programme Three* the emphasis was on education and popular science. It was seen on the European side of the country and it had 12.4 hours of daily transmissions.

Programme Four was directed to industrial centres and the six republics on the European side. This channel had plenty of sports and drama, and was on the air an average of 5.5 hours daily. In addition, a total of 104 teleradio committees transmitted their own programmes under the supervision of Moscow in the republics and regions.

Lapin created a system of favouritism inside the organization and ousted the vacillating programme makers. Prohibiting programmes was generally unnecessary, since this was taken care of in advance by the Party, departmental head, or censorship (Glavlit). Lapin made of the political observers a kind of Truth Guard, which explained the essential questions to the people in the right way. [. . .]

Journalists with a tendency to personal expression were replaced by readers of texts approved by the censors and announcers of important political events (I. Kirillov, V. Leonteyeva, etc.). These individuals were rewarded in the same way as the best actors in the country with the title of People's Artist of the Soviet Union. Lapin's aim was to prevent free expression that might occur in live broadcasts. At the time this was called the television of the announcers (*diktorskoye*). A written text could in this way be controlled beforehand. It was said that according to Lapin a carefully prepared and skillfully recited text read by a good actor was all the ignorant people needed. The personnel called his term 'The Ice Age'.

Lapin himself was awarded a high honour on his 70th birthday. It was alleged that after he made a request to Brezhnev the distinction was raised to Hero of Socialist Labour. The change took place so late that the prepared press release had to be altered at night in the composing rooms.

Lapin stopped the scientific research initiated by his predecessor in the organization. In addition he was also effectively able to prevent the release of external, analytical criticism and research material that was independent of the broadcasting institution. Examples of this included the Faculty of Journalism of Moscow State University and even the Institute of Social Sciences in the Academy of Science. Lapin was not slow to make use of his Party connections. Forbidden evaluators included the scientists R. Boretsky, B. Firsov, G. Kuznetsov, S. Muratov, V. Vilchek, and others. These researchers tried to evaluate programmes and also to study the role of television and its development in society. Lapin argued that these questions could be resolved only at the highest level within the Party, in the Central Committee. Independent research in the field did not occur much in those days.

Lapin did not want a journalist: (1) to express his own opinions, (2) to become a TV star, or (3) to do any muckraking, but at the same time he was keen (4) to avoid problematic issues, and he felt (5) that there was no need for audience research.

Lapin developed Soviet television, which had grown in its distribution and amount of programmes, into a huge instrument of escapism. The falsification of history [. . .] was not the only thing, but reality was escaped from and avoided, any reality that did not fit into the objectives that the Party leadership had in mind at the moment.

Harmless entertainment and descriptions of national strength were given additional weight in the programme structure. Speaking to the present author, Lapin justified his preferences with the hardworking laborers' need to enjoy themselves and forget their troubles. The justification is not unfamiliar in Finland either. But in the Soviet Union Lapin was actually able to put it into effect. There the leadership, including Stalin, had always regarded music as an ideologically important matter, and so did Lapin. In his view the work of Gosteleradio was mainly ideological, and in it music was the most ideological of all, although Lenin, as is well-known, had emphasized cinema as the most significant of the arts. At one stage Lapin went so far as to prohibit all films and programmes on Tolstoy and Dostoyevsky as expressions of the decadence that came from the West.

In Soviet television under Sergei Lapin there prevailed the order, optimism and peace maintained by a father figure (Brezhnev), although the world outside was in turmoil. Even facts were not allowed to shatter that comfortable image. Happiness and diligent work towards the lofty goal was to be continued. Soviet television was made into the largest stage set in the world, the Potemkin villages extending over eleven time-zones.

The term of chairman A. Aksyenov (1985–1989) was clearly an intermediate one. The appointment of this ex-Party official, KGB general, member of the Belorussian Council of Ministers and former Ambassador to Poland was as much of a surprise to Aksyenov himself. He was a man of principle, reasonably ably professional, and strict. Aksyenov tried to increase the political attractiveness of the programmes by raising professional standards in content and technique. The changes were remarkable compared with his predecessor's term. Programme time was increased, and new programmes and content were developed. What was most important was that he allowed the changes to happen and did not try to stop them. A cautious small-screen glasnost began.

Post-Lapin television broadcasting developed, however, above all thanks to the programme makers in such a way that in a short time about forty new programmes emerged, especially on social themes. Gradually old ossifications were also brought under criticism, social problems were examined, and risky live broadcasts were made.

Aksyenov relied on 'the Party's road toward the truth' and glasnost, which—understood in a new way—changed the relationship of the journalists to the ongoing development. Through television hundreds of magnificent heroes of perestroika were brought into the limelight. The personality cult was turning into a personalities cult.

Chairman M. F. Nenashev (1989–1990) was in addition to his Party background a former journalist, editor-in-chief (*Sovetskaya Rossiya*) and chairman of the State Committee of Printing. He was considered a cautious but rather reform-minded and humane person. In the stormy years of perestroika and glasnost he endeavoured to develop broadcasting on the lines of the Nordic model and towards parliamentary control. However, the chairman was caught in mediating the disputes between the leadership of the country and journalists who were probing and breaking their limits. Neither side was very happy.

The first deputy of Aksyenov, L. Kravchenko (chairman from 1990–1991), was at that time regarded as active and reformist. New programmes had been introduced, e.g. the popular youth magazine *Vzglyad* (Glance), which the same Mr Kravchenko later suppressed as chairman. Like all his predecessors, Kravchenko's background was based in the Central Committee apparat. As a journalist Kravchenko worked on the *Stroitelnaya gazeta* (Construction Gazette) of the construction trade and as editor-in-chief on the widely circulated *Trud* (Work) of the trade unions. He served as Director General of TASS after his term as deputy chairman of Gosteleradio, and he was elected to the parliament of the USSR in 1989. Kravchenko's two terms in the Gosteleradio leadership demonstrated that during that time glasnost had exceeded on television the tolerance limits of the Party leadership—and his own. As chairman, Kravchenko tried to muzzle glasnost.

The chairman of Gosteleradio was in the final analysis a Party soldier who served the General Secretary in tasks of propaganda in electronic mass communication.

The Personality Cult on Television

The cult was part of the system. It was created in order to maintain dictatorial power. An important prerequisite for the cult from the early days of Stalinism was the severing of contacts with the Western democracies. The acceptance of that was a mistake on the part of the Western countries as well, because the isolation relatively consolidated the position of the forces that were hostile to their own people. Without contacts, other states could not influence the development of the Soviet Union, and critical groups within the country did not get support from abroad. Doors and curtains were closed when abuses began. In this case the doors of an entire, vast country were locked.

Stalin's cult was in principle unlimited; he even saw to the execution of those who did not conform. Khrushchev could no longer have people killed, but he was able to imprison, remove from office, and destroy contemporary dissidents morally and economically. Brezhnev, who used the same methods of punishment, was a weaker person than Khrushchev and he did not have Khrushchev's intelligence. But he was a fair judge of men and he relied on Suslov, who had the real power. The first traces of a personality cult on television were seen at the end of Khrushchev's regime. In this respect the Brezhnev era was in a class of its own. Chairman Lapin played a large role in the presentation and praise of the person of the General Secretary.

Nevertheless, the main ideologist Suslov is considered the brains behind the cult. The harmless and publicity-loving General Secretary Brezhnev was suitable for his use of power. It is said that it was Suslov who developed some forms of the cult, such as the positive father figure, statesman and hero epithets attached to the General Secretary. Expressions were also invented by academician G. Arbatov, columnist A. Bovin, and the deputy department chief of the Central Committee, professor V. Zagladin. On the other hand, Brezhnev was actually afraid of the strict and highly intelligent Suslov and usually he made no decisions without consulting Suslov first. Also the influential assistants of the General Secretary played an important role; their position was more important than that of some members of the Politburo.

Chairman Lapin himself personally directed the creation of the huge Brezhnev cult figure with the help of television. Lapin liked to show photographs of him and Brezhnev together, also to the author of this study, and otherwise to stress their close relationship. While Lapin raised the status of television as a medium, he at the same time used television to idolize the General Secretary.

One of the six telephones on the chairman's desk was a rare one: a direct line to the General Secretary of the CPSU. However, Brezhnev lacked the charisma of Lenin and Stalin. In particular the fumbles of his last ailing years were ridiculed among the public. On a visit to India Brezhnev turned to march in the opposite direction from the side of Prime Minister Indira Gandhi when they were inspecting the guard of honour in a live television broadcast. Also some of his more incoherent speeches had to be interrupted and read to the end by the announcers.

The next trick, the technical reconstruction of the speeches, was almost unbelievable. The recordings of a speech were rushed to Ostankino for treatment by a particularly skillful group of sound technicians. They cut the speech into short fragments and each technical wizard started reconstructing his part. Each unintelligible sound from the original speech was replaced using individual sounds that were edited from earlier intelligibly read speech tapes. It was hectic work, because the speech had to be on the air as the central 'news' item at the latest in the main *Vremya* newscast of the same evening.

A special production group of talented professionals was established in order to build Brezhnev's publicity. It followed the General Secretary everywhere, receiving all necessary privileges. Lapin raised the coverage of Brezhnev's visits abroad to a maximum, in order to give the impression of 'a great world leader abroad'. For instance, for the massive coverage of his visits to India and Cuba many heavy outside broadcast vehicles were shipped from Moscow and direct satellite connections were constructed. Lapin brought old-fashioned court flunkey procedures to the world of television.

3

PART THREE

Stars

11

Hollywood Stars and Actors

Leo C. Rosten

AFTER *The Washington Correspondents* (1937) Leo Rosten went west and completed another classic, *Hollywood: The Movie Colony, The Movie Makers* (1941). This extract focuses on the stars and the huge differences between the earnings of stars and the general run of actors. In the year 1938:

> 14 actors and actresses each earned $250,000 or more.
> 40 actors earned between $100,000 and $250,000.
> The average (median) working actor earned $4,700.
> The average (median) working 'extra' earned $317.

A star actor could be earning fifty or a hundred times as much as a fellow actor in the same film and a thousand times as much as an 'extra'.

Ever since the 1920s the vertical dimension of Hollywood acting salaries has been extreme. By the late 1930s the Screen Actors' Guild (SAG) had most working actors in membership; and SAG was doing a fair amount to establish basic weekly rates and to improve conditions (such as the length of the working day). However, SAG focused mainly on the middle and lower levels of actors, who (as one actor says here) might be working for several hundred dollars a week, but only for a few weeks in the year. The screen extras were not eligible to join SAG (they later established a separate Screen Extras' Guild). The higher-earning actors and the big stars gained little or nothing from SAG; as Rosten notes, the stars were already themselves employers of 'agents, lawyers, business managers, press agents, secretaries, maids, yes-men'.

Hollywood means movies and movies mean stars. No group in Hollywood receives as much attention from the public as the men and women whose personalities are featured in films and around whom entire movie organizations have been geared. Of all the movie makers, it is the actors—publicized, romanticized, idealized—who are most potent in attracting people to the theaters. One of the first questions raised in every-day discussions of a movie is 'Who's in it?'

Source: Leo C. Rosten, *Hollywood: The Movie Colony, the Movie Makers* (New York: Harcourt, Brace, 1941), ch. 15.

The interest of the public in movie actors and actresses was manifested at the very beginning of motion picture history, and has never lost its force and fervor. Long before the names of actors even appeared on the screen, in advertising, or on theater marquees, the movie-goers clamored to pay homage to their favorites. The actress named Gladys Smith (Mary Pickford) who appeared in the early Biograph films was quickly identified by movie patrons as 'Little Mary' or 'the little girl with the curls.' The patrons who liked western pictures asked for 'Bronco Billy.'

The producers did not welcome this at first; they preferred to establish their own names, or the name of the company, in the public mind—but they never succeeded. The public's selection of movie personalities was of great importance in the rise of the motion picture industry; for when the public began to prefer one face to another, they also began to distinguish among the films which competed for their money. The choice of personalities led to the expression of opinion concerning the kind of stories or pictures in which those personalities appeared, and then the public began to patronize those theaters which showed the pictures in which popular actors were featured. By 1915, the movie producers began to offer the theaters groups of films, seven or eight to a lot, which featured one star. By 1919, the system of building stories, productions, and advertising around a few selected personalities was the very heart of the motion picture industry.

Hollywood learned that pictures with stars make money, and that those without stars do not—or do not make as much as they would if they featured popular personalities. Almost every factor in movie making was subordinated to the needs and talents of those actors who had a faithful ticket-buying public. The star system was hailed as the foundation of movie prosperity.

A star [. . .] is a monopoly. A Charles Boyer or a Claudette Colbert has a monopoly on those graces of voice, eyes, manner, attitude which constitute the individual personality. There is only one Clark Gable, only one Bette Davis, and although Hollywood is fond of thinking in typologies and attempts to build up a 'Gable type' or a 'Davis type' the public is not won over to synthetic substitutes. The public makes the stars. (Note the public's apathy for some personalities who were highly touted and widely publicized: Anna Sten, Francis Lederer, Grace Moore, Walter Huston, and others.)

The uniqueness of a personality, it is easy to see, places that personality in an almost unchallengeable bargaining position. The producers' competition for stars whose pictures earn profits has always bordered on the frenetic. The movie magnates paid astronomic sums to the movie stars because they had to. Those who wanted stars had to pay the price for them, and the stars who commanded the highest salaries also made the highest profits for their employers. The producers who paid exorbitant sums for talent prospered; those who did not, or could not, lost out. As motion pictures made greater profits, the stars demanded more money; the producers were able to pay it.

The competition of producers for movie stars was scarcely voluntary: the dazzling salaries which the producers paid out were not evidence of insanity, poor business judgment, or recklessness. This was demonstrated in the thirties when Paramount and Universal, under reorganization, tried a partial abandonment of the star system in the effort to cut costs. The 'sensible' businessmen did cut their movie costs by letting the high-priced stars go—but they cut their profits (or increased their lack of profits) even more. And the stars which Paramount and Universal dropped—or who were lured away by Warner Brothers or MGM—kept bringing the big money into the coffers of the studios for which they worked.

The salient importance and profitability of stars can be seen in such cases as Shirley Temple, Sonja Henie, or Deanna Durbin. Shirley Temple is reported to have earned over $20,000,000 for Twentieth Century-Fox in the bright years of her pre-adolescence. Miss Henie, an ice-skater with no film experience, made many millions for the same studio overnight. Deanna Durbin is said to have saved Universal from disaster in 1938–39. Every Durbin picture has earned huge sums; none has made a net profit of less than a quarter of a million dollars. An executive of Universal told this writer that Durbin's box-office power was so powerful and her future value so great that the company would not take $10,000,000 for her contract.

One final example: when David Selznick prepared to make *Gone with the Wind* he discovered that Clark Gable was not only the perfect personality to play Rhett Butler but that the popular demand for Gable in that role was so great that any other choice might prove detrimental to the film's success. Selznick was forced to make extraordinary concessions to MGM in order to obtain Mr. Gable's services: the picture had to be distributed and released through MGM (instead of United Artists, which had released earlier Selznick-International films) and MGM leased the film to the movie theaters for seventy percent of the box-office intake (the highest percentage ever received). MGM's share of the profits from *Gone with the Wind* will probably be as great as Selznick's. Selznick could not get Gable for the role unless he met MGM's terms; the terms were very high; but Selznick found it profitable—and necessary—to meet them. *Gone with the Wind* will gross over $25,000,000; some reports credit it with having passed the $30,000,000 mark in 1941.

[. . .] The professional problems of Hollywood's actors are of a simpler character than those of Hollywood's producers, directors, and writers. For the actor is a talented mime or a beautiful person who is given a part and directed in the performance of that part. The decisions which actors make are relatively uncomplicated; their power to influence a story is relatively subordinate. Many stars in Hollywood do have 'story approval' clauses in their contracts, and can refuse to appear in roles which seem unsympathetic or unflattering. But in that event, another actor is hired for the part . . . The actor cannot shape the content of a film to the *degree* that a director or writer or producer can; the actor's power to affect the structure or the implications of a movie, or to exercise control over the point or the meaning of a film, is negligible. [. . .]

The popular impression of the actors' youthfulness is due to the fact that it is the younger stars who are best known to the public and most featured in films; the numerous middle-aged or elderly 'character' actors in Hollywood are generally ignored. The romantic roles around which most movies are built puts youthful actors at a premium in Hollywood, and gives them constant prominence in the public mind.

Hollywood's actresses, incidentally, are decidedly younger than Holly-wood's actors. The median average age for actresses is 34; for actors it is 46. [...]

[...] The top salaries are publicized in Hollywood and to the world: big sums, like big names, are always news. But the fallacy of the impressions created by the publicity is expressed by the actor who remarked, 'Sure, I get $500 a week. But I worked four weeks last year, six weeks the year before, and three weeks the year before that.'

The actors with personal box-office power won huge salaries from Holly-wood as far back as thirty years ago. A few striking cases will illustrate how much money the producers found it profitable to pay the stars, and at how early a point in movie history. In 1912, Mary Pickford was getting $40,000 for each picture in which she appeared. By 1914 she was earning $60,000 per picture. In 1917–18 she received $10,000 a week from Paramount, a percentage of the profits, and a bonus of $300,000 for signing the contract. In 1919 she was earning $500,000 a picture at First National. From 1919 to 1924, when she was a star, producer, and part-owner of the United Artists group, Mary Pickford was making as much as $1,200,000 from each movie in which she appeared. So great was the Pickford name, so enormous her drawing power, so devastating her competitive value, that when Adolph Zukor failed to hire her away from United Artists he then offered to pay her $1,000 a week for five years (a quarter of a million dollars) if she would retire from the screen for that period! It was worth that much to Paramount not to have to face the competition of Pickford films.

There were other dazzling personalities who commanded dazzling salar-ies. Charles Chaplin, 'the one universal man of modern times,' got $150 a week in 1913 and a year later was getting $1,250 a week. In 1915 Mutual Films paid him $10,000 a week plus a $150,000 bonus. When Chaplin joined the United Artists group as a member-owner, with a share in the profits of both his pictures and the United Artists corporation, his movies netted him well over two million dollars each; one film is reported to have earned four million dollars for Chaplin. [...]

[...] [I]n 1938 at least 80 Hollywood actors and actresses earned $75,000 and over. If we break this down we discover the following array:

TOP ACTOR EARNINGS: 1938

Annual Earnings	Actors
$ 75,000–$100,000	26
$100,000–$150,000	23
$150,000–$200,000	12
$200,000–$250,000	5
$250,000–$300,000	5
$300,000–$400,000	6
$400,000–$500,000	3
Total	80

[. . .] The following [fourteen] actors received [$250,000] or over in 1938:

Name	Earnings
Claudette Colbert	$426,944
Bing Crosby	410,000
Irene Dunne	405,222
Charles Boyer	375,277
Wallace Beery	355,000
Cary Grant	340,625
Shirley Temple	307,014
Joan Crawford	305,384
Norma Shearer	300,000
Warner Baxter	279,807
Clark Gable	272,000
Greta Garbo	270,000
Fred Astaire	266,837
Jack Benny	250,000

It should be pointed out that the discussion thus far rests upon *salaries* only. Some actors derive additional incomes from a variety of 'side-line' enterprises. Bing Crosby [. . .] draws heavy amounts from radio work, phonograph records, race track dividends, and different real-estate holdings. Such movie-radio stars as Bob Hope and Jack Benny earn almost as much—or more—from their work on the air as they get for appearing before the cameras. There are no authentic data for the total incomes of Hollywood's leading actors and actresses. We can, however, supply some random information.

W. C. Fields and Jeanette MacDonald are each reported to get around $5,000 for a radio appearance; Burns and Allen received $10,000 a week in radio one year and added $92,000 to that sum from movie work. Fred Allen's earnings from radio work ran $416,000 in one year; he appears in pictures infrequently, but picks up around $60,000 each time he does. The Messrs. Walter Winchell, Rudy Vallée, and Ben Bernie have garnered lucre in Hollywood to swell their radio royalties. Edgar Bergen has filled his coffers through radio and films, *via* Charlie McCarthy.

Some stars are blessed with incomes from a curious variety of commercial enterprises. Bob Burns made $85,000 in one year by permitting his name to be used on a musical contrivance called the 'bazooka.' The Disney animals and the Charlie McCarthy character have poured enormous sums into the laps of their creators, who lease the name and visage of their brain-children to manufacturers of dolls, dresses, sweat shirts, comic strips, drinking mugs, plates, flashlights, and other novelties. Shirley Temple is said to have earned fifteen times as much from her sponsorship of by-products as from her acting.

But let us descend from the Olympian heights, where the air is giddy, the inhabitants limited, and the statistics vaguely unreal. Let us consider the larger, more representative aspect of Hollywood's actors as a group.

[. . .] Nothing exposes the fallacy of Hollywood's *salaries* as an index of welfare so much as the contrast between weekly figures and the total amount which actors find they have earned at the end of the year. What were the actual annual earnings of the actors? A careful check of the evidence provided by 253 actors revealed that the annual earnings for 1939 ranged from 'less than $50' to $300,000. The median average was $4,700. This offers a startling contrast to the prodigious weekly figures which we have been examining; it means that half of Hollywood's class A actors earned $4,700 or less in 1939 and that half earned $4,700 or more. The violent exaggerations which are induced in the public mind by the $200,000 and $300,000 salaries of the most illustrious movie stars are deflated by a recognition of the meaning of the $4,700 a year median for Hollywood's actors—*excluding* the extras. There is a difference between the median annual earnings of male actors ($4,700) and females ($4,150).

12

Cinema Stars In South India

Sara Dickey

INDIA, HOME OF 'the world's largest film industry', has, since the 1930s, had its own massively popular film stars. India developed several separate film industries in different cities and languages. This extract refers not to Bombay (Mumbai) but to the Tamil-language film industry of Madras (Chennai); it focuses on the late 1980s, before India's big television growth. Film had a major political influence; here we are told how movie stars' fan club members became political activists in support of movie-stars-turned-politicians. Five individual film stars or film-makers each became Chief Minister of Tamil Nadu.

Although acting superstars were dominant (in terms of finance and public appeal), the Indian film industry generated other star categories such as music director, 'playback singer', and fight arranger. Film music also prevailed across Indian popular music, including radio. The star system had a big impact on film planning and finance. The main production phase was also strongly influenced by star actors' behaviour, not least their tendency to star in several feature films at the same time. In the post-production phase other stars (notably the playback singers and voice specialists) were wheeled in. Indian film acting has long been perhaps the most 'vertical' of all the world's media occupations, with top stars swallowing massive slices of the financial cake.

The arrival of sound in the early 1930s changed Indian films and the film industry dramatically. Previously, any movie could be shown throughout India with at most an addition of title cards in the regional language. Sound, however, made wide distribution much more difficult. It greatly increased the importance of 'regional' cinema (the label given to films in any language besides Hindi or English)—in fact, it effectively converted all cinema in indigenous languages into regional productions—and made the financial position of the Tamil production companies much more secure. (Competition from the US and Bombay had forced all Madras production to cease by 1932. The first talkies

Source: Sara Dickey, *Cinema and the Urban Poor in India* (Cambridge: Cambridge University Press, 1993), 51–5, 61–4, 120–1, 149, 152–3, 165–8, 170, 172.

reached Madras in 1931, the same year in which the first Indian sound feature, *Alam Ara* (Hindi), as well as the first Tamil sound shorts and feature, were produced in Bombay. By 1934 production of Tamil talkies had begun in Madras itself.

The switch to sound changed cinema in other ways as well. Sound allowed continuities with folk, classical, and modern drama traditions to be felt fully, and song and dance became a central part of all films. Suddenly singing actors, songwriters, musicians and dancers were in demand, prompting a mass exodus of personnel from the theater. Many of these stage artists had been involved with nationalist politics, and quickly injected their political concerns and social reformism into the new cinema. During the 1930s, a few Brahman women and others of 'respectable families' had begun to star in screen roles. This, plus film's growing association with politics, resulted in an increased aura of respectability that persuaded several of the most famous classical singers of the day—including K. B. Sundarambal and M. S. Subbulakshmi—to act. For a time, in fact, heroes' and heroines' singing ability played a greater role in their success than did acting.

The importance of the singer-actor declined when, in the first step toward creating what could be termed 'particulate' actors—the separate pieces of whose total performance are contributed by different individuals—filmmakers began employing 'playback singers' in the 1940s to dub over actors' singing parts. The purpose of the substitution was, according to Sarkar, 'to match an excellent voice with the most attractive possible image, which real life rarely provides.'[1] Unlike the western practice, in which, as Barnouw and Krishnaswamy put it, the playback singer's 'very existence is kept secret, with the assumption that audiences must be persuaded that the star does the singing,' Indian cinema 'scorns this deception'.[2] Where songs are one of the most important elements of the film, the most successful playback singers and music directors have become as popular as—and generally more long-lived than—the favorite actors and actresses.

Nonetheless, throughout India, heroes and heroines have become very significant factors in a movie's success. Cult-like followings of actresses and actors began in the 1930s, when famous singers entered the cinema. After Independence, screen stars began appearing frequently on platforms with politicians. As the overall popularity of individual stars grew, so did their importance to a film's success, and their salaries. Since the 1950s, which saw the rise of superstars like Shivaji Ganesan and MGR—and their increasing participation in politics—it has often been the star and not the director who has had greatest control in making a film. The stars' position has been further strengthened by growing networks of fan clubs, which first appeared in the mid-1950s. Fan club members engage in numerous activities in support of their idols, occasionally including political work. [. . .]

---

1   Kobita Sarkar, *Indian Cinema Today* (New Delhi: Sterling publishers, 1975), 104.

2   Erik Barnouw and S. Krishnaswamy, *Indian Film* 2nd edn. (New York: Oxford University Press, 1980), 277.

[. . .] [T]he postwar period witnessed a number of changes in Tamil cinema, primary among them the swing toward spectacular and [. . .] 'escapist' cinema. The initiator and foremost example of this new style was S. S. Vasan's dazzling *Chandralekha* (1948), an extravagant contrast to war-effort movies and the most expensive Indian film yet produced. One distinguished film editor and former censor stated that *Chandralekha* was the first film to combine all the elements now seen as essential to box office hits—comedy, fights, songs, and dances (R. K. Ramachandran, interview, September 1986). It was certainly the most successful movie to date. Vasan, who had recently established the important Gemini Studio in Madras, also produced his hit in Hindi for distribution in the north, where it was a similar success. This marked the postwar entry of Madras filmmakers into the northern market.

Another feature of postwar cinema in the South was an emphasis on Tamil linguistic pride, and the pro-Tamil, anti-Brahman, anti-North political sentiments that accompanied it. As before, movies became involved with politics because influential artistes were politically active. The first of these were leaders of the DMK (Dravida Munnetra Kazhagam) party, who in 1949 had broken off from the DK (Dravida Kazhagam) to establish an electoral party. C. N. Annadurai, the party's founder and chair, was a dramatist, occasional stage actor, and screenwriter. So also was Mu. Karunanidhi, another party leader. Such leaders found film an excellent vehicle for disseminating social commentary. In 1949, for example, Karunanidhi attacked social injustices and religious hypocrisy in his script for the film *Parasakthi*. An important new feature of these DMK and other films was 'dialogue'—extended critical speeches delivered in formal alliterative Tamil. The new social movies and their dramatic rhetoric proved very popular; indeed, a number of people can still recite favorite dialogues memorized during a DMK movie's first run.

The importance of screenwriters had greatly increased with the rise of Karunanidhi and Annadurai, but the actor too would soon gain in importance. Annadurai asked the young M.G. Ramachandran to star in one of his movies in the early 1950s. Ramachandran was a great success, and soon became a member of the DMK party. He and other movie stars were utilized to 'decorate' party functions and draw crowds. MGR began to use the DMK colors of red and black in his movies (after the switch to color in the late 1950s) and made frequent allusions to party policy and rhetoric, much of it anti-Congress. Injections of political spice became very popular in the 1950s and '60s, and it was said that no movie could succeed without some references to the DMK. MGR, the main star allied with the DMK, gained a large and devoted following and soon controlled many aspects of his movies, using them to promote an image of himself as the savior of the poor. Shivaji, who had starred in *Parasakthi*, had left the DMK for Congress by this time, and although he retained some interest in and association with politics, for the most part he was not as thoroughly political as MGR became. When I left Tamil Nadu in 1987, he and MGR were still the top two stars, as they had been for thirty-five years—despite the fact that MGR had not made a movie in a decade. [. . .]

Actors and actresses generally have more audience draw than the director, screenwriter or any other personnel. Tamil actors and actresses are idolized, and filmgoers fantasize about living the stars' glamorous lives. At the same time, however, performers—especially actresses—are seen as 'bad' or 'loose' people.

The esteem in which actors and actresses are held is reflected in viewers' typical reference to them as 'heroes' and 'heroines.' But, as one director pointed out, 'anywhere in the world it is hero worship, not heroine worship' (K. Balaje, interview, September 1986). In Tamil Nadu the lack of regard for actresses derives from the great number of actresses available, the relative shortness of their careers, and the 'aura of disgrace' that attaches to female performers in particular. Careers are short because almost all actresses quit as soon as they marry (just as most other young women who hold jobs do). The stigma derives from associations with prostitution early in the history of cinema, and even before that from the rather low reputations of all dramatic performers, who tended to be members of itinerant low castes.

Male actors have largely lost this reputation. Its continued association with actresses appears to stem from two or three possible sources. One is the common belief that women who act must be in close physical contact with men (as during romantic song sequences), and therefore 'go bad'. A few viewers believe that aspiring actresses have to 'do favors' for directors in order to gain movie roles—similar to popular belief in the US. The basis for the stigma attached to actresses, however, seems to be related primarily to the sentiment that no 'good woman' would display herself in public. [. . .]

The problem of maintaining popularity also encourages many artists to promote public images that will appeal to audiences. MGR was by far the best example of this, choosing his screen roles with great care to contribute to his image as member and defender of the people and making large and widely publicized charitable contributions to popular causes. Shivaji Ganesan also makes publicized donations to charities, and in recent years has preferred roles of upright family men. Younger actors have chosen different routes. Kamalhasan is said to have once used the press to advertise his virility; more recently he has advertised the work of his fan clubs ('social welfare organization') in establishing blood banks and eye banks. Most actors and actresses court their fan clubs, and see them as an important source of support. None of the top young stars is involved in politics as of this writing, but some with slipping careers have attached themselves to popular political issues—such as the problems of Sri Lankan Tamils—in order to bring their names back into the headlines. [. . .]

[. . .] Finance is difficult to come by, except for the most well-known directors, and can be withdrawn at any moment; actors and actresses work on several movies simultaneously wherever possible, making their schedule unreliable; film once completed may face difficulty with the censor; and even after passing and receiving a 'U' (unrestricted) certificate, they may never be released for lack of a distributor. Finally, after passing all these hurdles, most movies do not turn a profit.

Making a movie involves coordinating the work of a large number of people. The director bears most of the responsibility, although the producer, as the person pulling the financial strings, often has final say. In addition to technicians, the major personnel include the writer (who frequently is also the director), musical director, lyricist, choreographer, dance director, fight scene arranger, special effects director, dubbing director, dance team, stunt crew, playback singers, comedians, and actresses and actors. In India, many film artists attempt to make up for a short career by working in several movies at once. Actors and actresses are particularly notorious for this, and commit themselves to films months ahead of time—with the frequent result that a delay in shooting any one film delays the others they are involved in. This can be especially costly for directors who do not work for major studies and must rent their own equipment. [. . .]

After all the spoken scenes have been shot, voices are dubbed in the studio. Spoken parts used to be recorded on the acting sets with boom mikes, but this is no longer done. Stars' voices are often dubbed by other actors—completing the frequent phenomenon of the particulate actor, whose body, speaking, and singing voices are all contributed by different individuals. Dubbing is a time-consuming and expensive operation, and once again must be scheduled around the actors' and studio's availability, but it does have some advantages: it frees stars to spend their time more profitably (and to be replaced at lower cost to the director); it also allows filmmakers, as one director noted sardonically, to 'choose a beautiful star who can't speak rather than going to the work of finding an actress who can modulate properly.' Scenes are usually dubbed with actors individually rather than in groups, in fifteen-second loops of tape, and each loop requires several takes and usually a total of several minutes to dub. The director is present, and a take is not accepted until he or she approves it for dramatic qualities and the dubbing director approves it for lip synchronization. [. . .]

Fan Clubs and Politics

[. . .] Almost all fan club members are men, most in their late teens to late twenties. Women rarely join, and when they do they join women's-only clubs. By the time most women reach their late teens, they are being prepared for marriage, and it would be unseemly for them to participate in the public activities of a fan club. This remains true even after marriage, when the majority of women are at any rate too busy with household work to be involved in most outside organized activities. The vaguely licentious reputation of cinema also keeps women away, since they must be careful to keep their own reputations unsullied.

Young men, on the other hand, often have the time, the lack of family responsibilities, and the freedom of movement that permit participation in outside activities such as fan club work. Most fan club members come from lower to middle Hindu castes and the lower or lower middle class, and are not highly educated. The clubs also include Muslims and Christians in what appeared to be rough proportion to their numbers in the general population. Class and communal makeup vary according to the organization, however, and within it according to individual clubs. [. . .]

Each major actor has a distinctive image, and the choice to join a particular star's fan club implies a preference for that image since membership in one group bars a person from joining any other star's club. The images of the four stars mentioned most often here—MGR, Shivaji Ganesan, Rajnikanth, and Kamalhasan—merit a brief description.

M. G. Ramachandran began acting in films in the 1930s. Along with Shivaji Ganesan, he has been one of the most popular stars for the last forty years. MGR played swashbuckling heroes and victorious underdogs, and was closely identified with the poor. He was portrayed as the savior of the downtrodden and of the victimized heroine, and is the most renowned of all Tamil stars for his screen fights. MGR was said to be seventy years old when he died in December 1987 (although unofficially estimated to be five years older) and had ardent fans of all ages, both men and women.

Shivaji is about ten years younger than MGR. When young, he was associated with the DMK party and played a number of 'revolutionary' roles. He soon switched to the Congress party, however (and later to the Janata Dal), and is identified by fans today as a 'family man.' His acting is somewhat stylized and overdone by current standards, but less so than MGR's, and Shivaji is generally acknowledged to be the finer actor of the two. He too appeals to people of all ages, but this appeal tends to be stronger among the middle class than the poor. Nonetheless, he had many fans among the people I knew, especially women.

Rajnikanth is from the southern state of Karnataka, but has been starring in Tamil films since the mid-1970s. He has also worked as a producer and director. His characters are usually forceful men, and, like Raja in *Paṭikkaatavan,* sometimes experience the degradations suffered by the downtrodden. In his middle thirties in 1986, he is famous for his talents in dancing and fighting, and his appeal has been strongest among young men.

Kamalhasan's image is in many ways comparable to Rajnikanth's. Both men are about the same age. Like Rajnikanth, Kamal is celebrated among fans for his dancing and fighting abilities—although he is seen as a slightly more romantic hero than Rajni—and is also very popular among young men. He too is a director and producer. Kamalhasan is considered to be more of an 'artist' than most Tamil actors because he acts in nonstereotypical roles. In 1986, he and Rajnikanth were comparably popular (and commanded the same amount of money per movie), but by 1990 Rajnikanth was a more popular hero, though fans admitted his characters rarely varied; meanwhile Kamalhasan had lost some of his following but was widely praised as a highly talented, sensitive, and resourceful artist.

Fans of these heroes rarely describe their emotional attachment to the star in explicit terms, but their feelings can be inferred from actions and from statements about him. Fan club members were eager to talk about their star's personal character, and often went on at length about his goodness. Their descriptions focussed on the help he gave to the poor, goodnaturedness, humility, and strength. They might also include praise for his unique acting ability. All of these actors' public images emphasized each of these ingredients, but in varying proportions.

Rajnikanth's fans often pointed out that the actor was a bus conductor before he got his film break. The president of the Tholipatti Rajnikanth club reported that his club's main function was to promote Rajni by explaining to people, 'Rajni is a good actor. He is a great man. He suffered when he was young. He was a conductor and lived like an ordinary man, but now he has come up.' [. . .]

Of all the stars whom viewers applaud and fan clubs support, there is one who stands out in the depth of devotion he received and the skill with which he utilized his clubs. This is MGR. He was the first actor to take full advantage of cinema's features as a political tool—in particular, its potential for broadcasting a carefully crafted and widely appealing image in an area with no comparable mass media, and the accompanying network of fan clubs. Unlike the situation in many other industrialized nations, few people in India can watch the nightly news on television to see politicians and hear their speeches, nor can politicians rely on newspapers for contact with voters, since few people read the paper with any regularity. Even radio is limited as an information medium, since most people listen to radios only to hear movie songs. Film, on the other hand, is widespread and accessible to the majority of viewers. While several South Indian actors have made political use of their film success (including Shivaji Ganesan, Jayalalitha, and N. T. Rama Rao), MGR remains the most successful in translating a movie image into an effective political persona. In the process, he also transformed his network of fan clubs into a powerful political support system.

In forty years of film acting, MGR developed an image as a dashing romantic hero and the protector of the poor, an image that became accepted as a representation of his own personal nature. Born in about 1915 to a Malayali family in Sri Lanka, MGR is supposed to have left school at the age of six when his father died. His impoverished family then crafted his film and political image carefully. Called the 'Douglas Fairbanks of South India,' MGR had often played the swashbuckling hero in his early films. With his growing political involvement he added many roles that reflected the populist ideology of the DMK party, frequently playing the oppressed but victorious underdog. Like other Tamil movies, MGR's films were filled with flowery dialogue, love songs, and dramatic fights. I was told (always by men or by women who disavowed such feelings) that MGR's female fans were greatly swayed by his love scenes. His acrobatic fight sequences, however, were the most acclaimed of all. Handsome MGR fought the dark-skinned villains with swords, sticks, and fists—and always won. Good triumphed over evil as MGR rescued the heroine and brought justice to the poor. [. . .]

MGR's cinematically generated image survived many attacks by political rivals, and much evidence of his own corruption. Nonetheless, while the strong personal appeal of someone like MGR is difficult to combat, it is insufficient by itself to keep a leader in power. Hence the importance of his fan clubs. Their political significance derives first from their position as a crucial grass-roots network in the ADMK party, and second from the propaganda value of the social services they perform, which operationalize a star's philanthropic image.

MGR's clubs began organizing in the mid-1950s, the first of any fan organization. When MGR left the DMK he was accompanied by very few high-level DMK officials but took much of the party's mass following with him, including many thousands of fan club members. These groups soon evolved into a tightly organized, intricate network of political support. [. . .]

MGR has been the most successful of all actors in capitalizing on his film popularity. He was the only star whose image assured viewers that he had not only compassion but the potency to put it into action. Many followers saw him as someone who could actually change the circumstances that frustrate them and overcome the forces that make their lives insecure. His fans believed MGR to be an ally in real life just as he was in film. Perhaps the most effective action yet to grow out of cinema was the mass electoral support that pushed MGR and his party into power. Rather than resigning themselves to the present, an overwhelming number of viewers voted for a man who was identified as a hero of the oppressed, a man who had risen through a lower-class entertainment medium, and put him into power. For those who ask what effects the daydreams of cinema can have in real life, the crucial role of films in promoting MGR's ascent to power provides a striking answer.

13

Political Talkers on Radio

Richard Davis and Diana Owen

RUSH LIMBAUGH WAS the most notorious of the American AM radio hosts who in the 1990s attracted large audiences to angry conservative 'talk'. This extract suggests that the talk stars mainly reached an older (50+) male white working-class conservative audience. Ideological talk (or bigotry) was facilitated (after 1980) by deregulation—more radio stations, fewer owners, the migration of most music onto FM. This left AM radio looking for appealing cheap material and no longer needing to observe the rituals of political neutrality.

Often the more modest the outlet, the more dominant the star. Strongly rated dogmatic talk is a goldmine because (unlike live television) the production cost is minimal; the only significant cost is the host himself (seldom herself) and much of the gold ends up in his pockets. As in other types of stardom there is a tendency for the star to construct a persona which then cannot be altered. Like most other stars, these radio stars spill over, or cross over, into other media: they are involved in politics; they write books; and some also do television shows. Much of their notoriety (and material) comes from the big newspapers.

Who are the hosts who talk incessantly on tens of millions of radio sets all over the nation? It only seems like they appeared suddenly on the scene. In fact, many have been in broadcasting for years.

Still, they have proliferated rapidly in recent years. In 1990 there were only a few syndicated hosts, one of whom was a new entrant—the still relatively unknown Rush Limbaugh. Now, new nationally syndicated hosts have joined the growing crowd, and more hosts appear locally as stations turn larger blocks of their air time to a talk format.

Entrants since 1995 alone include Oliver North, former New York governor Mario Cuomo, and former U.S. surgeon general Jocelyn Elders. Some of those already in the business have seen their audiences grow exponentially during the 1990s.

The arrival of newcomers, particularly former politicians, has irked those who have made careers of the business. One longtime host starts his show announcing that he is not 'a right wing wacko or a convicted felon.'

Source: Richard Davis and Diana Owen, *New Media and American Politics* (New York: Oxford University Press, 1998), 56–61, 67–70, 72, 77–8, 81–2.

Another in the business since 1978 complains, 'Now it seems like everybody who can speak English has their own talk show.' The notable exception to the newcomers is long-standing host Larry King, whose late night talk program has been in syndication since the late 1970s. Even King has earned new notoriety as his radio program moved into television.

The rise of talk show hosts has been meteoric. A little more than ten years ago, Rush Limbaugh was a talker on a local program in Sacramento, Michael Reagan was a business executive, and Oliver North was still a little-known White House aide running covert operations.

One host, who worries about talk radio's influence, concluded that 'we're just commentators or columnists. That's all we are.' But who are these commentators or columnists who dominate the AM airwaves and whose presence is increasing on the FM dial?

There are basically two categories of talkers, the syndicates and the locals. The syndicates receive most of the national attention. They also carry great appeal for affiliates. Syndicated hosts already have name recognition, they have proven ability to attract audiences, and they almost always come free to the station. Only a few hosts, such as Rush Limbaugh and Howard Stern, charge for affiliates to carry their program, and even that development is relatively new. Most other shows negotiate barter arrangements that allow the affiliate to place approximately half the advertising time of the show while the network retains the rest. [. . .]

Who are these syndicated hosts? We now take a look at a sample of the most prominent of the syndicated talkers.

The king of the syndicates and talk radio generally is Rush Limbaugh. A native of Cape Girardeau, a small university town in southeastern Missouri, Limbaugh is the son of a local Republican leader and the grandson of a Republican state legislator. He dropped out of college at the age of twenty and bounced from one station to another until he was discovered by Ed McLaughlin, a former network executive. McLaughlin brought Limbaugh to New York in 1988 and gave him a nationally syndicated program.

Limbaugh's appeal stems from his entertaining, often bombastic, style. His flamboyance even makes liberals chuckle. He calls his style a 'unique blend of humor, irreverence, and the serious discussion of events with a conservative slant.'

A large part of the appeal of Limbaugh's show is his egotism. Limbaugh opens his show with the reminder that his listeners need only listen to him to get their information. In the introduction of one of his books he admits, with no hint of modesty, that 'I realized early on just how right I have been about so much.' He describes his books as 'loaded with insight, brimming with profundity.' And he predicts that this age will someday be referred to by historians as the 'Era of Limbaugh.'

However, Limbaugh's influence may already have peaked. His numbers (both in terms of affiliates and listeners) already have begun to fall off. One cause was his relentless attacks on President and Mrs. Clinton, which may have become too predictable and, thus, boring. Some argue Limbaugh's reaction to the 104th Congress hurt him. For a period, he became an unabashed supporter of Newt Gingrich, Bob Dole, and the Republican agenda, even when the public's support had eroded. His criticism of other candidates, such as Pat Buchanan and Ross Perot, also may have offended some of his audience.

Even with some drop in his audience, Limbaugh still is the most listened to host on talk radio. According to one survey, 37 percent of talk radio listeners tune in to Limbaugh, compared with 10 percent for the next most popular host, G. Gordon Liddy. Almost all political talk hosts compare themselves with Limbaugh. This is true not only for those who directly compete with him, both nationally and locally, but also for those who do not. Many other hosts respect him as a role model and listen to him regularly to scrutinize his style. It is interesting to note that Limbaugh's style is made-for-radio and does not translate well to television. His short-lived television program—a studio version of his radio show—did not succeed in attracting an audience.

Limbaugh's three-hour show is *the* topic of interpersonal conversation about politics for many Americans. Some restaurants have created 'Rush' rooms where 'ditto heads' (the self-attached label of devoted Limbaugh listeners) can gather to eat and listen. Callers to other talk shows often will make reference to some statement Rush Limbaugh has made. Moreover, all of his books have become national best-sellers.

Limbaugh's political influence has become legend. Some analysts credit his support for the GOP Contract With America with aiding the Republican take-over of Congress in 1994. Republican politicians crave access to his show, with the possible exception of 1996 presidential contender Robert Dole. Such influence even was noted by President Clinton when he criticized the fact that Limbaugh has 'three hours to say whatever he wants. And I won't have an opportunity to respond.'

One of the most remarkable rises in talk radio has been that of G. Gordon Liddy. Once the Watergate figure who refused to talk, Liddy now gabs into a microphone for three hours daily. His show is even more politically oriented and controversial than Limbaugh's. Although Liddy's statements about shooting federal agents and using cardboard figures of the Clintons for target practice has led some affiliates to drop his show, his popularity has risen dramatically since his first broadcast in 1992. [. . .]

[. . .] Liddy's sometimes nasty content has been termed 'beyond the pale of civil discourse.' Liddy was even singled out for criticism by President Clinton, who said that he had come to realize 'what a serious threat these ultra-right activist groups pose to America, and that G. Gordon Liddy is essentially their spokesperson.'

Yet none of this reaction to his broadcasts has changed his style. In fact, all of it has helped Liddy, who calls himself the 'G-man' and terms his show 'Radio Free D. C.' (his show is based in Washington), attract a niche audience eager to hear his fulminations about the crimes of the Clinton administration and the Bureau of Alcohol, Tobacco, and Firearms, in particular.

No nationally syndicated talk show host was better known prior to his talk show career than Oliver North. The featured witness of the Iran-contra hearings, North was a familiar face and voice to millions of television-viewing Americans during the summer of 1987. His appearance before the Iran-Contra committee dressed in his Marine uniform bedecked with medals made him a national hero among conservatives. North moved quickly from a possible prison term to the Republican nomination for the U.S. Senate from Virginia. North barely lost the race to a weak incumbent, Chuck Robb, another ex-Marine.

North launched his radio career soon after his defeat and has seen his show quickly gain popularity. At its inception, the show had only two affiliates—one in Washington, North's home base, and another in Houston. Three months later, he was appearing on 122 stations.

North generated less controversy than Liddy, but he also had acquired a devoted audience of conservatives. Yet, uncharacteristically, the former Marine colonel has included guests such as Mario Cuomo to take calls and debate with North on air. He was not, however, a skilled communicator nor quick on his feet, unlike many other hosts.

Michael Reagan, the adopted son of the former president, has been surprisingly successful as a talk show host, given his primary qualification as a relation to the star of the conservative movement. Reagan, now heard on over one hundred stations nationwide, publishes a newsletter that is popular among his listeners. Reagan is highly political, but also one of a few activist hosts who frequently urges listeners to take action on various bills before Congress. Listeners hear Reagan discuss specific bills, including the bill numbers, and then cajole them into becoming involved in the legislative process.

One of the few nonconservatives among the major syndicates, Tom Leykis is syndicated with Westwood One and has nearly two hundred affiliates. Leykis's fast-paced style is designed to draw younger listeners, a more favorable demographic for advertisers. 'We take shorter calls,' Leykis illustrates. 'We play loud bumper music. We have nasty promotion liners on the air that position the show as being dangerous or hard core or angry or whatever.'

Leykis's approach is less overtly political than Liddy, Reagan, or Limbaugh. He does not adopt the label of a liberal per se. Given the unpopularity of liberals in syndicated talk radio, it is not surprising that Leykis instead has proclaimed himself a 'populist.' [. . .]

Nationally syndicated hosts get the most attention from the press, but local hosts can become well-known personalities in their own markets. According to one talk radio survey, a majority of audience members listen to less well-known hosts, including local hosts. Success at the local level can then translate into national syndication. Most syndicated hosts started local and then moved into syndication with a different program. Some local hosts, such as Bernie Ward in San Francisco, maintain both local and syndicated shows.

Some local hosts refuse to make the move. There are distinct advantages to hosting a local show rather than a nationally syndicated one. The local host can cover both national and local issues, while the syndicated host is limited to national ones. Syndicated hosts say they also cover localities, but they must always relate such attention to a national issue.

The local angle is a powerful draw for listenership. The host can discuss issues proximate to the listener. 'You can talk about the fact that there are no traffic lights working,' explains one local host. 'On the syndicated show, you can't talk about that. You can only be very, very generic.'

It is imperative that local hosts exploit this advantage because, unlike syndicated hosts, they cost the station money. Local hosts must be paid, while syndicates, with few exceptions, come free, subsidized by advertising revenues.

Despite their costs, local stations, especially the larger ones, maintain a staff of local hosts in order to retain a local flavor for their programming. Local hosts can reflect the personality of the city. Former New York mayor Ed Koch is an example of a successful local host because of his close identification with the community. Koch would probably fail as a national host because his brash personality may be offensive to some and his accent grating to listeners in other parts of the country. But Koch thrives in New York. [. . .]

Ideological Bias and Host Personality

[. . .] Unlike traditional journalists, political talk show hosts are usually identified by their ideological bias. Hosts label themselves conservatives, liberals, or more frequently, 'moderates' or 'independents.' Some networks, such as ABC, Major Radio Network, and Westwood One, carry both liberal and conservative hosts. But others cater only to conservatives. The small Pacifica Network is an example both of a leftist radio network and of the lack of commercial success of left-wing radio.

Not only is ideological bias the sine qua non for publicity for many hosts, but for some it truly governs their approach to the show. Few hosts make an effort to be evenhanded in their discussions of issues. 'I don't see it as my role to be fair to both sides in my presentation,' states one host.

Responding to the criticism of unfairness, some hosts argue the callers will offer opposing perspectives. Hence, balance can be achieved. Balance, however, is not the main objective. Hosts are being paid to express opinions. With the exception of the few noncommercial radio outlets, ideological or partisan expression must be linked to profitability. The goal is appealing to the marketplace.

Additionally, it is not coincidental that the conservative views of hosts are reflected by many of the owners of networks and local affiliates. Local affiliates are the most resistant to the expression of opposing views, which, given the present conservative bias of talk radio, usually constitute liberal views. Some stations in largely conservative areas do not attempt balance, but program only conservative hosts.

The balancing of liberal and conservative hosts on a station might help promote fairness and attract more listeners. Still, several stations have successfully moved to all-conservative formats in line with commercial strategies. One talk analyst suggested that mixing liberals and conservatives is a bad strategy for the sales force 'almost as much as clearing Howard Stern on a religious station.' But from the perspective of public affairs debate, such a business strategy is likely to hurt liberals even more since an all-liberal station would be considered by the industry a potential commercial disaster.

Yet owners are not going to sacrifice the bottom line. The economics of radio broadcasting prevail over ideological considerations. Owners and executives may be able to weigh in on certain issues to direct the programming, but perpetuation of ownership is more important than fostering a particular ideology.

Station managers become highly responsive to what audiences will buy. In light of that fact, managers and hosts perceive ideological conservatism as a hot commodity. They point to one critical statistic to support that conclusion: the high ratings of conservative hosts such as Limbaugh, Reagan, and Liddy. [. . .]

As we have stressed, talk radio is primarily in the entertainment business. The host provides the main entertainment for every show and must maintain the audience day after day, week after week, for as long as possible. One talker described his job as 'a one man act, three hours a day, five days a week.' Understanding the nature of the personality traits that underlie a successful talk show host is a prerequisite to explaining talk radio's content. It helps illuminate how talk radio, even political talk radio, is at heart an entertainment medium.

One overriding characteristic of talk show hosts is the ability to sound passionate. According to Greg Dobbs, a Denver host, you must 'have passion for everything you bring up.' Although the average citizen possesses intense fervor about a few issues, the talk show host does not have that luxury when her or his goal is to sustain enthusiasm for issue discussion on a daily basis. Rush Limbaugh himself admits that there are 'some days I don't care if anybody knows what I think. But you gut it up and do it.'

Station managers encourage hosts to be provocative on the air, rather than to remain neutral or acknowledge the worth of varying opinions. 'I might actually think that an issue is complicated enough that there are two sides to it,' Victoria Jones confesses. 'But in the world of sound bites, . . . a lot of stations do not like you to go on the air and say "I'm of two minds about this issue and I'd like to discuss it with you." They just want fire and brimstone. You have to have an opinion or you don't do the issue.'

In conveying this passion, the hosts also must talk incessantly and try to make sense while they are doing it. According to one host, 'You have to come up with jokes, you have to be quick on your feet, you've got to think of quips, you've got to deal with the caller who thinks you're a dope.' All of this must be done at once.

To fit the personality, the host must be highly animated. 'Actually, off-stage, and I do regard this as a stage, I'm fairly quiet,' states one host. Sometimes hosts admit that their anger is not necessarily emotion, but serves commercial purposes. One talk show host once told callers that his anger is a form of play.

The host also must be willing to be superficial, that is, to address a wide range of issues while spending a limited amount of time on each one. Talk programs usually shift focus hour by hour (and sometimes even more frequently) in order to avoid losing listeners who are not interested in the topic. The array of brief conversations with callers reinforces the frantic shifting of thoughts from one conversation to another. As one host admitted, 'Maybe having a short attention span is part of me doing this job.' The result frequently is an artificial passion about issues the host does not really care about it, and a superficial knowledge of many issues addressed.

Hosts– Entertainers or Politicians?

Given the requisite traits for hosting a talk radio program, there should be little doubt about what talk radio hosts really are. Yet the questions persist: Are they journalists tracking down stories, political commentators whose responsibility it is to explain and interpret current issues and events, or primarily entertainers?

Even though they are primarily entertainers, sometimes talk show hosts do take their political role very seriously. Rush Limbaugh has called talk radio 'the portion of the media that the people trust the most.' Yet Limbaugh also calls himself primarily an entertainer. Other prominent hosts echo that self-description.

The problem for determining what talk radio hosts are is important particularly when talk radio is perceived as something other than what it is. If listeners perceive talk radio programs as public service-oriented, similar to public radio, then their response to the medium will be remarkably different than if they view it as primarily entertainment.

Such a misperception by the audience can be attributed, at least partly, to the rhetoric that has accompanied the rise in public attention to talk radio. Call-in programs, which prevail in talk radio and are also a common component of television talk, have been praised for their potential as venues for public discussion. [. . .]

Most talk radio programs follow a rough script that has become familiar to audiences. Talk radio programs routinely follow an established pattern: an opening monologue by the host, often followed by the introduction of a guest, who then interacts with the callers. Many hosts include guests for part of the program and then take calls alone for the rest of the program. Others rely more heavily on guests. Still others use guests infrequently. With or without guests, the host still serves as the star of the program. The host is more like Geraldo or Oprah than Dan Rather or Judy Woodruff.

One major difference between talk radio hosts and other media personalities is their direct association with advertising. While television network news departments' movement toward entertainment is commonly known, broadcast journalists still are more independent of ratings concerns than talk radio hosts.

Although their stories are placed beside bedroom furniture or farm implement ads, print journalists are separated from advertising in that they are not expected to write ads or place their name on advertisements. Even network news anchors or reporters, although they may introduce commercial messages, rarely actually deliver them.

Both national and local talk radio hosts do more than carry commercials on their programs. They often read them live (and sometimes ad lib through them), thus increasing the level of attention to the commercial. Like early television game show and variety program hosts, today's talk radio personalities are linked to specific products. [. . .]

[. . .] Newspapers, particularly, are critical sources for talk show preparation. One survey of talk radio producers in two major markets found they relied to a great extent on the morning newspaper for topics. Rush Limbaugh claims he reads nine newspapers a day. Other hosts say they read half a dozen or more newspapers daily, usually drawing on national newspapers such as *USA Today*, the *New York Times*, the *Washington Post*, and the *Wall Street Journal*. Some conservative hosts also rely on the *Washington Times* [. . .]

[. . .] While talk radio is promoted as a format for the expression of public opinion, this role is secondary. It is true that average citizens can call the toll-free numbers provided and converse with the hosts or articulate brief expressions of their opinions. That is not, however, their primary purpose on the program. Further, callers do not constitute a representative sample of public opinion.

Rather, the callers function as an integral aspect of the program's entertainment value. According to Rush Limbaugh, 'the primary purpose of callers on my show is to make me look good, not to allow a forum for the public to make speeches.' The caller's key function is to keep people listening. If listeners tune out because of boring callers, the show is over.

Since the callers' exchange with the host is a critical part of that appeal, the screener and the host attempt to control the type of caller who is granted time to talk. According to one host, it can be devastating 'to the survival of the station to put the wrong callers on.'

The dilemma for talk radio is the prevalence of older listeners in the audience and therefore among the callers. Talk radio does not appeal as much to those under thirty as it does to those over fifty. Moreover, the established superstitions in various metropolitan areas are likely to have built a devoted traditional audience, which is older. Talk radio programmers usually want a younger audience, preferably between the ages of twenty-five and forty-nine. In pursuit of a more youthful audience, talk radio structures the format to appeal to those who are younger. Callers, particularly, serve that role.

Hence, those callers who do not enhance the station's efforts to reach that goal are most likely to be discriminated against by the screener. They include callers who sound like they are over the age of fifty. A producer for a local host admitted that she screens out callers who sound like they are over fifty. 'In talk radio we want to put the best speakers on,' she confided.

Our content analysis of talk radio programs revealed that those who are estimated to be over fifty are less likely to talk on the air than those under fifty. Less than one fifth of the callers on air for the Limbaugh, Liddy, Leykis, and Colmes programs were estimated to be over the age of fifty.

14

Entrepreneurial Editors of National Newspapers

Jeremy Tunstall

BRITISH NATIONAL NEWSPAPER editors in the 1990s became more 'entrepreneurial', largely due to the extremely competitive conditions which followed the defeat of the London printing unions in 1986. This extract is based on interviews in 1994 with editors of 14 of the 20 daily and Sunday national newspapers. The 11 national dailies in 1995 together sold 13.67 million copies each weekday; nine national daily editors were interviewed.

These editors could perhaps be classified as a mixed case of baron/star. They were expected to be both editorially and commercially aggressive bosses of the editorial department. But they were also increasingly presenting themselves as star personalities on TV and radio, in other print media, and within their own publications. These editors also fitted the star profile in being both highly paid and highly insecure; editorships of two years or less were increasingly common. But 'failed' editors (like movie stars) tended to acquire other prominent media jobs—as high-profile columnist, as radio/TV personality, as book author, or as editor or senior executive at another newspaper or media group.

The term 'entrepreneurial editor' is used here to reflect the increased business involvement of the editor; the editor today is expected to lead, to innovate, to do new things, to take creative risks.

Decreased trade union power is one important change since the 1960s. Chief executives of newspaper companies have increasingly taken a more strategic interest in the business, leaving their highly paid and (they hope) highly skilled editors to take the editorial lead. Some chief executives and chief owners reside most or some of the time outside Britain and recognize the unwisdom of excessive interference in editorial detail. [...]

Editors also say that recent changes—in technology and competition—require quicker responses than previously. Comparing 1994 conditions with 1975, when he first edited the *Guardian*, Peter Preston mentioned three linked elements of speed-up. 'There has been a dramatic increase in the quantities of material coming in from news agencies and other

Source: Jeremy Tunstall, *Newspaper Power* (Oxford: Clarendon Press, 1996), ch. 7.

services'; the size of each day's paper is at least twice as big, while the number of journalists is the same or less; and thirdly there is heightened competition from press, radio, and TV. All of this, said Preston, means that the editorial day moves more quickly than in the past; 'if you lose an hour in the morning, you never get that hour back.' Chief executives are aware of this and do not want needlessly to waste the editor's time.

The managing director does not see the editor as a remote being; quite the contrary, the editor and the managing director typically work very closely together. The editor is seen as a highly paid creative manager, who will expect to be in complete charge of the editorial department. He expects to be judged primarily on circulation figures.

Most editors last either for about two years or for ten years or more. If the management are unhappy with the editor's and the newspaper's performance the editor is sacked and a new one hired, usually from outside. When a successful editor eventually is removed or promoted, the new editor is often chosen internally. Chief owners and chief executives recognize that much of the editorial control they can exercise is involved in their choice of a new editor. They thus look carefully. Rupert Murdoch tended to choose his editors from among British journalists he had already seen operating in New York. The people who appoint editors usually have some set of editorial goals and changes in mind—typically they want more readers in general and more young, female, and affluent readers in particular. The prospective new editor may well be asked about desirable editorial changes; as they arrive, new editors typically seek to make dramatic changes in people and pages.

Editors have also become public figures to a greater extent than was the case previously. In the 1960s one of the editor's duties was to get his talking head onto television, but by the 1990s there were more TV channels, and more radio stations inviting more editors onto the airwaves. Being a public figure has given the editor more internal company prestige. All of this has led company managements normally to support and to promote their editor as a star, rather than telling him or her what songs to sing.

Editors can be compared to prima donnas, or orchestra conductors, or film directors; in film terms these newspaper editors would perhaps best be seen as 'hyphenates', as people who do two or three creative jobs, like the producer-director-writer.

The trend has been for the newspaper editor to play a more active part in a wider range of activities than in the past. Today's activist entrepreneurial editors tend to engage in all nine of the following list of duties:

1. *Hire and fire* may well be the single most important prerogative; often the arrival of a new editor is quickly followed by half or more of the senior journalists being fired or moved. The editor then typically brings in several colleagues (from his previous jobs) into the top positions. This process may then be repeated once more or several times.

2. *Opinion.* The editor controls the formal policy of the newspaper, in particular the writing of the anonymous editorial 'leading articles'; most 1990s editors write some themselves and instruct leader writers each day.

The editor also controls the letters to the editor and chooses between sketches offered by the cartoonist. Even if ignored by most readers the anonymous editorials are not ignored by politicians and have their biggest impact on journalists in the paper; these editorials constitute a daily bulletin board as to what the editor thinks about current public issues. These opinions automatically flow into, and colour, reporting and feature-writing throughout the paper.

3. The *editorial budget* is controlled by the editor, via a managing editor. The budget is agreed each year and the finance department checks on each month's editorial expenditure. The editor holds sway over a budget of say £15 million; the editor in a fairly short period can make big changes in how this money is spent—less on foreign news, more on book serializations, and so on.

4. *Gathering of news and features.* The editor normally chairs a morning meeting at which the day's news menu is discussed. The editor also talks individually with senior news executives before or after this meeting.

5. *Processing of news and features.* The editor oversees the sub-editing and preparation of material for placement in the paper. Especially on tabloid papers, he is close to the 'back-bench' of processing executives, and—in discussion with them—he chooses the main front-page 'splash' story and decides which stories will be page leads on the main news pages.

6. *Presentation and design.* The general appearance and design is regarded as being salient in the newspaper's competitive effort. The editor typically has in train some planned redesign of some area or section of the paper. A major redesign is a matter of endless agony and effort; it needs the editor's approval.

7. *Systems.* The editor, these days, must make decisions (with production and information technology personnel) on the editorial computer system, the new page make-up system, the new computer graphics, the new electronic picture desk. Closely related to this are:

8. *The sections of the paper.* New sections often involve a different type of printing from the main paper. Merging old sections and creating new ones are major decisions which must be planned and discussed at length with advertising and other departments.

9. *Promotion and marketing.* This involves a range of activities. In recent years London newspapers have spent many millions of pounds on television advertising; the editor is closely involved in the creative message of such advertising campaigns. There is an increasing number of promotional games, co-promotions with television programmes, and so on, all of which involve the editor in issues of editorial compatibility, taste, and benefits.

In practice tabloid editors tend to be involved in all nine of these activities, while some broadsheet editors do not. However, an editor such as Max Hastings at the *Daily Telegraph*—who had little previous news executive experience—surrounded himself with a small team of senior colleagues, including one senior man (Don Berry) who was a design and layout expert.

The editorship which at first glance looks like a one-man band may on closer inspection consist of an editor, a deputy (who edits a daily paper perhaps on 100 days against the editor's 200 days a year), a managing editor (who runs most of the editorial finances), and two or three other assistant editors. There is usually at least one area (such as sport or finance) which the editor largely ignores. Nevertheless it is the editor typically who has chosen this editorial high command (and has decided to leave sport to the sports editor). [. . .]

Two [. . .] decade-long editorships of market-segment leaders helped to develop the new entrepreneurial editor pattern. These were Kelvin MacKenzie's editorship of the *Sun* (1981–94) and Andrew Neil's editorship of the *Sunday Times* (1983–94).

The *Sun*, which Kelvin MacKenzie edited, was a slim down-market daily tabloid and it looked very different from the fat once-a-week multi-sectioned upmarket *Sunday Times*. But the chief owner in both cases was mogul Murdoch and the manner in which he related to these two editors was very similar. These two editors were clearly regarded by Rupert Murdoch (and most other people) as successes and—after a trial period—they were granted steadily more powers.

In both cases there was an overwhelming emphasis on profitability. Both editors were successful at maintaining circulation and the *Sunday Times* was even more successful in expanding into ten advertising-laden sections. By the late 1980s the two papers together were probably making enough profits to provide between $200 and $250 million each year for investment in Fox television activities in the USA. These two commercially successful editors were given untrammelled power within their editorial departments.

Both Kelvin MacKenzie at the *Sun* and Andrew Neil at the *Sunday Times* were recruited personally by Rupert Murdoch before their 35th birthdays. Murdoch had already observed both young men when they were in New York; Andrew Neil was in New York for *The Economist* and Kelvin MacKenzie served a term as managing editor of the then Murdoch-owned *New York Post*. Both men, plucked from relative obscurity into these high-profile jobs, were utterly dependent on Rupert Murdoch's personal approval. Both seem to have modelled themselves on Murdoch's style of Aussie-New York personal directness and business pugnacity.

Murdoch was, of course, not an admirer of the traditional British establishment, and in Neil and MacKenzie he chose two middle-class but still very non-establishment journalists. Neil was a Scot who attended Glasgow University; MacKenzie, despite his Scottish name, was the son of two South London journalists and, as for many Fleet Street journalists, local London weekly papers and a local news agency were his journalism school. Both Neil and MacKenzie cultivated an aggressively street-wise 'common man' personal style. [. . .]

Both Neil and MacKenzie were hyperactive workaholics. Both editors were deeply involved in the news gathering as well as the presentation sides of their newspapers. Both were concerned to compete remorselessly against the market share of key rivals. Under Andrew Neil, the *Sunday Times* did win back the market share it had lost under Harry Evans. Under Kelvin MacKenzie the *Sun* fought back successfully against the *Daily Star*.

Both Neil and MacKenzie played very active parts in the migration of their newspapers eastward to the Wapping docklands in 1986. Both also found that the new technology (and weakened trade unions) after 1986 increased their powers. Both had now successfully completed a major test of macho management. Both found themselves buoyed up by the entre-preneurial excitement—and high newspaper profitability—of the late 1980s Lawson–Thatcher boom.

Both men were vigorous editorial promoters of Murdoch and News International interests. Both the *Sun* and the *Sunday Times* engaged in massive boosterism of Murdoch's Sky Television (and later BSkyB)—which led to accusations from competitors of abuse of monopoly power. Andrew Neil in 1989 was chief executive of Sky Television as well as *Sunday Times* editor. Both editors also gave huge editorial space to entertainment hoopla; the *Sun* was obsessed with showbiz, sex, and Hollywood—as was the *Sunday Times*. In 1992 Neil was willing and eager to fly to Los Angeles and—without reading the book first—to interview Madonna about her soon-to-be-released book, *Sex*.

Both Andrew Neil's and Kelvin MacKenzie's style of journalism was heavily criticized by fellow professionals in the competing publications. This criticism performed the function of completing a circle. Both Neil and MacKenzie, in their editorial columns as in their personal pronounce-ments, 'answered back' at their critics. Both had a well-developed line in personal abuse and vituperation. Kelvin MacKenzie, with his South Lon-don weakness for Cockney rhyming slang, made up insulting-jokey nick-names for his numerous enemies. Andrew Neil was not far behind in similarly childish abuse of competing editors, his numerous critics, and public enemies. [. . .]

The downmarket daily is the thinnest of the British national news-paper offerings. A daily paper of perhaps 48 tabloid pages has about 32 editorial and only about 25 non-sports editorial pages (equal to 12 or 13 full broadsheet pages). Although Colin Myler at the *Daily Mirror* admit-ted that he could not read all of this material each day, he could and did read all the bigger stories, such as page leads at the front of the paper. He also emphasized that with the once-a-week sections (which operate on earlier timetables) he also read the major stories and approved the main pictures.

The few biggest stories (which the editor monitors) are more dominant in downmarket tabloids. Bigger stories routinely are 'spread' across two pages, and the biggest stories often run across six or more pages. The choice of both feature and news stories is much less driven by outside agendas than with the broadsheets. The downmarket tabloid is not much affected by the agendas of politics, finance, and serious news generally. The editor is especially looking out for melodramatic human interest stories from a number of candidate stories being offered by features and news executives each day and each week.

Exclusive human interest and exposé stories often have legal and taste problems; the editor gets quick legal advice but he (or she) must decide whether to take the risk or send the story back for more research or rewrit-ing. Once it has been decided to go big on a particular story the editor can dictate or adjust the angle. The editor in effect often decides which character is the hero and which the villain, and also approves (or vetoes) the big headlines. Humour is often crucial to the headline and the story, and as always with humour there is the awkward question as to whether it really is funny; the editor's sense of humour is final.

Another key aspect of downmarket tabloids is that they revere youth and are suspicious of expertise. There are few editorial experts on serious subjects; the story subject expertise is in sport and entertainment where again youth is emphasized. Kelvin MacKenzie sacked many journalists who were aged over 40 and favoured '25 and 25'—25-year-old journalists who could be paid the junior reporter's salary of £25,000. With the emphasis thus on youth, inexperience, and entertainment, there were few outside forces or agendas to interrupt the flow of arbitrary editorial decisions. [. . .]

Major extensions of editor power occurred in the upmarket newspapers between the 1960s and 1990s. The clearest example of this was the *Daily Telegraph*, where the biggest changes occurred during 1986. In early March 1986 Max Hastings started work as editor. He was a surprising choice—he had established a unique reputation as a TV and newspaper war reporter (from Vietnam to the Falklands) and as author of solid works of military history, but he had never run anything bigger than the 'Londoner's Diary' in the *Evening Standard*. He recalled:

> We took over a near bankrupt company with an enormous number of people who were over age or no good. I sacked fifty journalists in the first two weeks . . . Nobody likes getting rid of people but we were driven by a kind of desperation. We simply had to do drastic things . . .
>
> On the way home in the car I used to go relentlessly through the staff list, night after night . . . frequently marking those who, one felt, were just not up to it. The proportion of staff who were not up to it used to terrify me . . . the ghastly collection of deadbeats who then involved huge sums of money and difficulty in unsticking . . . Jeremy [Deedes] gave me the score recently—in the first four years we got rid of three hundred journalists.
>
> God knows I've sacked enough people. But I went through the list again the other day and there's almost nobody we need to sack . . . We've also dramatically lowered the average age of our journalists.

Max Hastings in 1994—eight years into his editorship—was recounting to me his exercise of the editorial power of hire-and-fire. He had also hired a fresh team of senior editorial executives, nearly all of whom were still there eight years later. Hastings believed in delegating much editorial power to the heads of major editorial departments and to section editors; his attitude, he said, was that having put a lot of effort into trying to choose the right people, you then let them get on with it. If they failed they were fired, but 'I don't believe in much in between'.

Apart from this major exercise of hire-and-fire, Hastings took a special interest in the anonymous opinions. Most days the leader conference took about twenty-five minutes, with leader writers being assigned to topics and the general direction agreed. Hastings himself wrote one or two a week:

I write leaders on the big things—you know, whither the government, should the Prime Minister stay or go, and some Election ones. I sometimes write a leader to amuse myself, like one I did on unemployment last week. . . .

If it's something big or sensitive, it's quicker to do it myself. I can write a leader on anything in 40 minutes or under an hour. If you ask a leader writer to do it, he has to go through a lot of agonizing about what the *Daily Telegraph* ought to think about it, whereas I only have to think what I think about it. . . .

When I'm on holiday I reckon to speak to the paper every day, mainly because of leaders. I was on a fishing holiday when we fell out of the Exchange Rate Mechanism [1992], so I sat in the gillie's house watching the debate on television, and then I sat on a river bank, writing the leader myself.

Max Hastings had one other major area upon which he focused—the news coverage; it was agreed early in his editorship that the *Daily Telegraph* would continue to focus on news as its big strength. Having done a wide variety of reporting (and being a professional author) he tried to have 'a clear idea on the literary merits of all writers on the paper'. This notion of editorship amounted to a huge change from the previous regime. Here was a much more activist and entrepreneurial editorial approach than the *Daily Telegraph* had had previous to 1986. [. . .]

[. . .] [T]he *Guardian* editorship had also been moving in a more entrepreneurial direction. The *Guardian* editor for twenty years (1975–95) was Peter Preston, who had extensive writing as well as sub-editing and production experience on the paper. As editor he was extremely hands-on in terms of production, but he also continued to write anonymous leaders and occasional signed pieces throughout his editorship.

Preston played a major role in the *Guardian*'s introduction of a computer system after 1986, and in major redesigns. In particular he committed the paper to greatly increased pagination, funded by classified advertising. And in 1992–3 he was deeply involved in the *Guardian*'s acquisition of the *Observer*. Preston gradually became more directly involved in the overall newspaper business.

The *Guardian*, with its left-of-centre political views, its journalist-friendly traditions and its collegial style was obviously in danger of going stale and being run by a clique of ageing journalists. There was one such period in the late 1980s, but Preston was adroit both in promoting younger people and in reinventing himself. At the end of his editorship in 1994, Peter Preston was still working an eleven-hour day at the *Guardian* and chairing about thirty meetings a week within the editorial department and in the company. In 1975 he had 'never seen a balance sheet', but by 1984 (in close alliance with his chief executive) he had dragged a left-wing newspaper towards commercial success.

Preston's successor, Alan Rusbridger, was very much in the *Guardian* tradition; he had been features editor, presiding over what he told me in 1990 was a 'subbing empire'—processing all the sections as well as features. Like previous *Guardian* editors, Rusbridger was young (40) when appointed, and looked even younger than his age; he was also ideally equipped to continue the *Guardian*'s ancient tradition of editorial sovereignty and its new tradition of entrepreneurship. [. . .]

And finally, [. . .] *The Times*. William Rees-Mogg departed as editor when Murdoch/News acquired *The Times* in 1981; in the next eleven years there were five editors. For once Rupert Murdoch's famous luck deserted him, not least in that Charles Douglas-Home's broadly successful editorship was terminated by his death. [. . .]

However, eventually the choice of Peter Stothard as editor in 1992, together with massive price cuts in 1993 and 1994, led to huge (and hugely subsidized) circulation increases. [. . .]

Despite many surface differences, the pattern of editorship operated by Peter Stothard conformed to the entrepreneurial pattern in general and to the *Daily Telegraph*/Max Hastings model in particular. After Stothard's arrival in 1992 there was yet another cull of senior journalists at *The Times*; a number of new senior editorial executives were brought in, including several from the *Telegraph* stable. Like Hastings, Stothard took a particular interest in the anonymous leaders, in the political coverage, and the whole range of news. Peter Stothard also took a very big interest in features. Stothard seemed in his own skills and interests to combine the dual strategy of *The Times* in its price-cutting phase. Stothard was enthusiastic about news stories and features which would appeal to new young readers coming from the *Daily Telegraph*, but he was also seeking to preserve the strength of the editorial page and the facing 'Op Ed' page with its weighty columns. He regarded being serious and reaching the restless young as compatible editorial goals, telling me:

> You have to communicate difficult material reasonably quickly. The days when the typical reader of *The Times* was a bank chairman, who could sit all morning slowly turning the pages, is gone. That person now wants to access information quickly . . .
>
> Too much in *The Times* was self-serving, it was there for no reason other than to please the person it was about or the person who was writing it. We have squeezed that, and it's not much mourned . . .
>
> Young new readers like our music coverage . . . something they weren't expecting. Young people accustomed to taking information off screens particularly like the back page digest which directs them to the pages they want.

Peter Stothard had a number of maxims: only talk to politicians if you're sure you're getting more out of it than they are; and 'the editor must look for ways to make the biggest difference'. He also mentioned numerous initiatives—a new television section, a new team to edit the fat Saturday paper, and a new daily meeting for proactive ideas (before the normal formal news conference). Stothard had recently edited *The Times* from Bristol and from Liverpool.

Although *The Times* was carrying on some old traditions, including subsidy, the editorship had changed decisively in the entrepreneurial direction.

4

PART FOUR

Professionalizing Media Occupations

15

News Agency Foreign Correspondents

Oliver Boyd-Barrett and Terhi Rantanen

THIS CASE STUDY of Reuters traces the role of the news agency foreign correspondent over the last 150 years. Today's correspondents and Reuters bureaux send text, graphics, audio, video, and still pictures into newsrooms in every corner of the world. But back in 1850 Julius Reuter was tucking messages under the wings of carrier pigeons.

Both of these authors are leading authorities on the international news agencies. The activities of these agencies have been somewhat obscured by their tradition of anonymous reporting and by the technical complexity of their world-girdling operations. Because so few agencies have dominated the world news flow, they have also deliberately pursued a low profile.

Already in the 1870s these correspondents were learning to think globally and act locally. These correspondents played a key role in defining British 'neutral' news and then very gradually transposing it into global 'neutral' news. These agency personnel and their output also reflect (and reinforce) the steep hierarchies of world news. At the top end Reuters personnel handle fast world political and financial news (and even faster bulk financial transactions). At the bottom end, a local stringer in some rural outpost telephones a hundred-word small-earthquake story to the Reuters staff correspondent in the local capital city bureau.

In this chapter we further pursue the argument (see Boyd-Barrett 2000) that news agencies contribute significantly to the semiotic construction of images of nation and of relations between nations. National agencies' claim to national status rests on their capacity to gather and disseminate news across the geopolitical area that defines the 'nation'. They link capital cities to provincial media, taking the news of elite institutions headquartered in the capital to the country, bringing back information from the country for capital city media, business, and government.

International news agencies use national agencies and the national media served by national agencies as sources of news about nations, news they then disseminate to media of other nations. The role of national

Source: Not previously published. Oliver Boyd-Barrett is at the California State Polytechnic University in Pomona; Terhi Rantanen is at the London School of Economics.

agencies among the panoply of institutions that new nations develop in 'becoming a nation' is demonstrated by their near universality, and by the rapidity with which new nations in the post-colonial era established news agencies, or with which the ex-communist countries of central and eastern Europe established new legal frameworks for the operation of their own agencies. News agencies, from their beginning, have been agents of globalization (Boyd-Barrett and Rantanen 1998). They were the first electronic media to compress time and space, transmitting news globally with the speed of electricity. Global news transmission required close cooperation between international and national agencies. National agencies, whatever their relationship to national governments, had to meet certain international standards of news-gathering (set by the international agencies) to achieve influence, developing an international realm of news based on (unequal) news-exchange arrangements. Progressively through the second half of the nineteenth century, the three major agencies—the French Havas, the German Wolff, and the British Reuters—divided up the world's news market. They guaranteed a domestic market monopoly for any national agency allied with the Big Three (Rantanen 1998b), but the international agencies set the terms. They defined the news criteria governing the exchange. Reuters gradually grew more powerful than its counterparts. Only Reuters was predominantly international in scope: it was not in business to serve national British media with domestic British news (this was the job of the Press Association). Yet for much of its history until relatively recently (up to the Second World War, and then to a diminishing extent thereafter) Reuters was principally a British agency that served the interests of the Empire. It was British in the location of its headquarters and major news hub, its mission, and its senior staffing.

Agency journalists, at least of the agencies (not Reuters) which engage in reporting both domestic markets for domestic media and international news, work at the centre of a news node that connects news coming from abroad and news sent out overseas. They serve a double clientele: foreign and domestic. These demands set special requirements for the recruitment and training of news agency journalists, and especially their foreign correspondents. News agency correspondents must know how to gather and select: (1) domestic news that is interesting for their national media; (2) foreign news that serves their national clients' needs; and (3) national and international news that is interesting for other agencies and media worldwide. News agency foreign correspondents (including Reuters correspondents) are mainly responsible for the latter two tasks, and have sometimes been compared to diplomats, perceived as representatives of their country and its media.

News agencies recruit significant numbers of journalists and associated labour. In 1998, Reuters employed almost 17,000 staff in 182 editorial bureaux, in 218 cities of 96 countries, and delivered news services in 22 languages (*Reuters Annual Report*, 1998). Staff included 2,072 journalists working in print news, photography, and television news. Associated Press (United States) had a total of 3,421 employees (Boyd-Barrett 1998). In 1992, AP had 86 foreign bureaux staffed by 30 correspondents in the Middle East, 11 in sub-Saharan Africa, 10 on the Indian subcontinent, 35 in Asia, and more than 40 foreign correspondents in Western Europe, 7 in Scandinavia, 25 in Russia and Eastern Europe, and 40 reporters and editors writing in English and Spanish from South America. There were an equivalent number of local employees, half of whom were Americans (Hess, 1996: 91). Among national agencies the majority of journalists are nationals of the agency's home country. This is less the case for international agencies, although nationals from the agencies' home countries are over-represented in top positions. International agencies still like their news reported from the perspective of the needs and interests of clients in major markets, in particular the United States and Western Europe. But while national identity is significant in the analysis of the construction of images of the global and the local, it leaves open the question as to which categories of 'national' are favoured among the possible constituencies of region, ethnicity, social class, language, gender, and other differences that constitute the heterogeneity of any nation.

Reuters' First Correspondents

The founders of the first major agencies, the Frenchman Charles Havas, the German Bernhard Wolff and the (first German, later) Briton Julius Reuter had worked directly together for the Havas agency in Paris. They shared backgrounds in journalism and business. Julius Reuter, born a Jew and also German, struggled for acceptance of his agency as a vital source of news for major British newspapers and for government and commercial clients. As Israel Beer Josaphat he had worked in various banks. He later adopted a common German name, Reuter, and converted to Christianity (Read 1999: 8). While in Paris he met Sigismund Engländer, born into a Jewish family in Moravia (then Austria). Engländer had been a revolutionary journalist who fled from Vienna in 1848 under threat of arrest, and was later briefly imprisoned. He was to become Reuter's first chief editor. As Storey (1951: 16) puts it, Engländer had an 'extraordinary instinct for political news, and an entrance to most Radical and progressive societies on the Continent'. He set up Reuters' network of foreign correspondents.

Read's (1999) history of Reuters suggests that its senior journalists were typically well connected and middle class. Under Roderick Jones in the 1920s and 1930s, class connections almost became a prerequisite for the job. While news agency work never enjoyed the prestige that attached to the better-known correspondents of leading national newspapers, and was much less well paid, it was recognized as a valuable stepping stone to better jobs, for all except a small number of dedicated employees who climbed the company ranks. Leading Reuters journalists cultivated contacts at the highest levels of society and it helped if they were familiar with these by birth. They needed to acquit themselves favourably in such circles as credible and trustworthy individuals.

Edmund Buck, Reuter correspondent with the government of India from 1897, was the nephew of a senior civil servant in the government of India. He was on personal terms with every viceroy and vicereine and their staffs in the period between the 1890s and 1930s, and was awarded an Indian knighthood in 1929. David Rees, Reuters manager for Egypt from

1884 to 1914, 'spent much of his time humouring Egyptian politicians, whose goodwill was necessary to ensure payment of the indispensable Egyptian government subscription. He also successfully cultivated Lord Cromer, the powerful British government agent, and Sir Herbert Kitchener, the sirdar of the Egyptian army' (Read 1999: 88–9). Among the earliest and most successful Reuter journalists were several German Jews, although soon a majority of senior editorial staff were British-born, including Henry Collins, who had started working life as a preparatory school teacher, and who joined in 1862 (Collins 1925: 15). Linguistic skills typically figured prominently among recruits. George Douglas Williams, who joined in 1861, is described by Read as having fluent command of French, Italian, and Spanish, in addition to his native English. Walter Bradshaw, who joined in 1874, had good command of English, Spanish, and Portuguese. Frederic W. Dickinson, who joined in 1874, is described as 'multi-lingual'. Languages were clearly important, but other virtues were also in evidence, such as 'general culture and intelligence', 'enterprise and dedication, along with tact in handling people', 'well-informed, observant, sensible, yet humorous' (Read 1999: 33). Roderick Jones, who took command of the agency after the First World War, was the son of a hat salesman and the grandson, on his mother's side, of a cotton agent. He did not attend a fee-paying 'public school' or go to university, and was sent to live with his mother's married sister in South Africa, where he began work as an assistant reporter, working his way up to become chief sub-editor of the *Cape Times* and chief cable correspondent for Reuters. It was here that he came to the attention of Baron Herbert Reuter, who was 'impressed by Jones' success in raising the prestige of Reuters through personal contacts in the topmost social and political circles' (Read 1999: 125).

Read reviews the selection criteria employed by Roderick Jones (which combined those applied by the Civil Service and those necessary for a business enterprise): 'candidates should be hardworking, healthy, good at languages, good with people, prepared to travel and ready to commit themselves wholeheartedly to Reuters' (Read 1999: 162). A correspondent should know what sort of news his principals and his public want, i.e. should either be British or know the country. Jones (1921: 2) once said: 'The value of news depends very much upon its selection and its presentation. A man who lived all his life in Canada or France may be a first rate news man in his own country and yet easily fail as a correspondent for a newspaper or agency in the United Kingdom if he has never lived in the United Kingdom or acquired some knowledge of conditions and requirements here. He may telegraph from his country much news which is unexceptionable. But he certainly will also telegraph some news which an English trained journalist would know not to telegraph'. Some experience of newspaper work was regarded as useful. Jones liked to recruit young; he preferred public school (especially Old Etonians) with Oxford or Cambridge degrees and with private means and 'social polish'. There were few women. Women were expected to retire upon marriage, and even male employees had to ask permission to marry. Under-representation of women has continued: in 1990 there were only 66 women in middle and senior management, out of a total possible of 666. Under Jones, the emphasis on social and educational credentials increased. A prime example was Christopher Chancellor, general manager in the Far East from 1932, then joint general manager from 1939 to 1944 and knighted in 1951. From a Scottish landowning family, and the son of a colonial governor, Chancellor was educated at Eton and Cambridge. 'The respect for him among the Japanese was increased because they exaggerated his aristocratic connections. They were also sure that he was working for the British intelligence service as well as for Reuters' (Read 1999: 180). Another example of the importance of elite connections was Harold King, who as Paris correspondent sustained a close relationship with Charles de Gaulle, both before, and when, he was president of France.

Later Developments

From 1941, Reuters was owned principally by the associations of British national and provincial daily newspaper publishers, representing many wealthy and titled press barons. But more democratic patterns of recruitment were introduced after World War II and may be ascribed in part to the growing democratization of post-war society, and in part to the changing role of the news agency which, through its nurture of new technologies and rediscovery of the potential of finance news for specialist markets, became less dependent on traditional news sources, markets, and patronage. The impact was particularly noticeable for the middle and upper cadres of Reuters journalists, and in particular, its bureau chiefs, section chiefs, editors, sub-editors, and managers. These were the staff who either controlled the London headquarters or were responsible for organizing, recruiting, managing, selling, and supervising as well as star reporting and writing from different centres throughout the world. The growing importance of specialist news services delivered by means of advanced telecommunications and, from the 1960s, computerized communications placed an increasing premium on the importance of specialist knowledge and technical skills, and required increasingly demanding and complex management skills. The growth in importance of photography, and the addition of radio and television news services in the 1990s, has merely intensified these challenges. Since the Second World War, therefore, the importance of elite connections relative to other attributes and skills has become much less relevant.

Some senior Reuters journalists before and during the Second World War had 'problematic' social backgrounds but successfully overcame whatever social disadvantages they had. Those who were not middle class at birth, an increasing if still exceptional likelihood after the Second World War, had generally already achieved educational success at elite universities, particularly Oxford and Cambridge. Principal characteristics of the background and skills which typify Reuters correspondents in its first one hundred years include: experience of travel, fluency in two or more languages, commitment to impartiality in news and in attitude to clients, concern for accuracy, speed, emphasis on facts and precision, and refraining from party politics.

Heightened emphasis on graduate entry after the Second World War underlined the continued preference of Reuters for journalists of good social and educational standing. More systematic approaches to recruitment were introduced. The growing detachment of the news agency from the British State and Empire made it seem less necessary or desirable that Reuters journalists be part of the governing milieux, although they needed to be able to mix smoothly in it when the occasion required. Tony Cole's appointment by Chancellor as joint news manager in 1942 was a harbinger of change. Cole had left secondary school at the age of 15 to work as a junior reporter for *The Scotsman*. The first graduate editorial trainee, with the required minimum of one foreign language, arrived in 1947. By 1960, 43 university trainees had been accepted, of whom 23 subsequently left. Reuters' openness to graduate trainees was in advance of Fleet Street attitudes generally. Most journalists came to London via the provincial weekly and daily newspaper press, but Reuters was exempt from the trades union agreements which imposed this route on the national newspapers. It was therefore a particularly attractive entry point for cosmopolitan graduates who aspired to Fleet Street without suffering provincial banishment for several years. Gerald Long, later to become the general manager who helped Reuters exploit new technology for financial news markets in the 1970s, entered Reuters in 1948 as a graduate trainee. The son of a postman, he was a Cambridge University graduate in modern languages (German and French). Long's successor, Michael Nelson, who oversaw a succession of computer products, was the son of a carpenter. Nelson came to Reuters as a graduate trainee after graduation from Oxford University. His successor, in turn, was Glen Renfrew, son of an Australian coal-miner, and graduate of Sydney University. Renfrew's successor, Peter Job, was also a graduate trainee, recruited from Oxford University. Graduate entry was strong in economic news, where Alfred Geiringer, founder of the new generation of economic news services under the name of Comtelburo (which in 1960 had 186 staff in London, and 282 overseas), recruited and trained university graduates as financial journalists, salesmen, and managers. These represented a threatening new breed, nurturing quite different skill sets to the ones most commonly associated with the Reuters name. Traditional general news journalists continued to make their way to the top, and during the command of Gerald Long tensions between economic and general news journalists began to intensify, while management skills, particularly in financial news and technology, took increasing precedence in determining the highest fliers.

The significance of nationality declined. Boyd-Barrett's (1980) survey of news agency journalists showed there were many more locally recruited journalists than expatriates in overseas bureaux, but bureau chiefs were generally nationals of the agencies' home countries or were nationals of other western or Commonwealth countries. They were more likely to be university graduates than were newspaper journalists of their own agencies' home countries. Bureau leadership by expatriates was justified in terms of expatriates' presumed better sense of the news interests of media audiences back 'home' and their native command of the main language of distribution. They were considered less vulnerable than local employees to domestic political intimidation. Read (1999: 477) reports that during the

1980s, British predominance at Reuters was reduced, at least in terms of proportionate staff numbers. The 10,071 staff at the end of 1989 were drawn from 160 nationalities. However, ten nationalities achieved three-figure totals and the British (3,308) and the American (2,577) cadres reached four figures, accounting for over half the total.

Critiques The decade 1925–35 represented a nadir in the fortunes of Reuters. At its beginning, Roderick Jones was negotiating a share of ownership of Reuters with the Press Association, in a bid to resolve the agency's precarious finances. In 1932, Associated Press broke from the cartel, which Reuters had led for sixty years. This was a serious blow to Reuters' reputation and financial security and was a contributory factor behind Jones's intensification of links, formal and informal, with the British government in the prelude to the Second World War. Whereas in 1923 there had been 43 offices or bureaux, only 27 were operating in 1932. Reuters journalism came under fire, some critical voices suggesting that Jones' attention to the 'right background' had superseded attention to appropriate skills and attitude. One internal source (Catling) claimed that the 'average recruit appears to have no intention of becoming any sort of journalist', and that in covering the news these raw recruits were inclined to report passively on newspaper reaction to events rather than engage in original coverage (Read 1999: 216). A senior editor, Rickatson-Hatt, described editors in 1931 as 'conscientious cable transcribers' and urged that Reuters cease to be a 'mere purveyor of Foreign Office and Embassy statements' (Read 1999: 225). There was 'too much unwanted, under-edited wordage' according to Turner in a 1939 critique, with heavy reliance on local news agencies that had been junior partners in the worldwide news agency cartel. With only modest staff numbers, Reuters was too often late with the news. Understaffing was a continuing weakness into and beyond the Second World War relative to the leading competitors, Associated Press and United Press, and Reuters journalists continued to be poorly paid. In Germany in 1932, Reuters had one chief correspondent, and one full-time assistant. The number increased to four full-time correspondents by 1938. By then, Reuters fielded a world-wide total of 676 correspondents, of whom 282 were based in Europe. But only 19 in Europe were full-time staffers, only 23 in Asia, one in Africa and two in the United States. Four full-time correspondents covered Spain during the civil war, two on each side. One of these was Christopher Holme, competing with British and other correspondents earning twice as much. One Reuters correspondent in Spain was killed in 1937: Dick Sheepshanks, an Old Etonian and graduate. A third correspondent in Spain was Alex Clifford, public school boy and Oxford graduate (see Read, 1999: 237–43). Covering Prague in 1939, Reuters had only one stringer, against four fielded by a significant competitor, British United Press. Reuters had no foreign correspondent in Moscow from the late 1940s to 1953, other than a part-time American journalist, and it had no local stringers behind the Iron Curtain. While often beaten in spot news, Reuters prided itself on interviews with celebrated news sources, a tactic which enhanced its profile and drew precisely on those social connections and skills for which the agency was noted. But internal criticism of its journalistic style persisted into the war period. Tony Cole wrote that Reuters stories were too lengthy, did not respect news values, and were too often unsuitable for publication. Recruitment, he claimed, had been haphazard (Read 1999: 307).

Reuters' leading position as a worldwide agency provoked criticism among some clients, mainly of the agreements which national agencies had to sign with Reuters and Havas and by which they lost their right to transmit news abroad directly without the intermediary role of Reuters. This was a financial loss for agencies that were big and rich enough to expand their activities beyond their national borders. But it was also a matter of prestige, a question of national interest. National agencies considered it their right to decide what kinds of news to transmit from their home countries. As Kent Cooper (1942: 12), general manager of the Associated Press, once bitterly complained: 'So Reuters decided what news was to be sent from America. It told about the Indians on the war path in the West, lynchings in the South and bizarre crimes in the North'. The charge for decades was that nothing creditable to America ever was sent. American businessmen criticized the Associated Press for permitting Reuters to belittle America abroad. National agencies also targeted Reuters' staff, described by Rupert Murdoch's father in 1926 as 'a lot of broken down University men and snobs, arrogant and British, with no conception of Australian requirements'. There were increasing demands to replace Reuters' staff with Australians who would select the news for Australians (Rantanen 1998*b*: 42). One of the first agencies to challenge Reuters' position was the United States' United Press Associations (UP), founded in 1907. The UP was an independent agency that turned down Reuters' offer to act as its US counterpart in place of the AP in 1912. Roy H. Howard, UP president, and son of a railroad baggage man, wrote 'The reason for my deciding against the alliance was that I knew that it would put the UP as much at the mercy of those moribund and venal agencies, as the AP was' (Rantanen 1992: 13). Reuters' leading position was crushed in 1934 by the two United States agencies acting in concert with several national agencies (Rantanen 1994: 31–5).

The transformation of United States agencies into international agencies was a major loss for Reuters and resulted in considerable changes in its leadership and ownership structure. In 1949, Reuters entrusted considerable responsibility for coverage of significant areas of the world to partner agencies, notably PTI of India and AAP of Australia. The (brief) PTI partnership was particularly painful. The Indians did not want permanent Reuters correspondents being appointed within their zone of influence (which, strangely, included Pakistan). Chancellor pushed instead the case for non-Indian appointments in Karachi and Delhi by stressing the wish of the British Press and the BBC for Reuters to have London-trained correspondents in every capital. The Indian government considered that Reuters was still under the influence of the Foreign Office (Read 1999: 323).

If for much of its history many of its correspondents and a greater number of its senior staff were British-born, did this make Reuters a British agency? Up until some time after the Second World War, the answer was largely affirmative. The first Baron Reuter was concerned to assimilate into British society and to achieve good relations with the British government and its overseas offices. In various ways Reuters contributed to the war effort in World War I. There was a close relationship to the British government both before and for some time after World War II, although at times, this was as much due to Reuters' perennial search for financial security as to a specific government desire to influence Reuters.

The agency's most celebrated World War I correspondents were Lester Lawrence and Herbert Russell. Russell was later knighted for his reporting services during the war. Russell's son and two of Lawrence's brothers were killed in France. Read writes of Russell, 'he got on well with the military authorities. He did not regard it as part of his function to be critical' (Read 1999: 145). His good relationship with the authorities was bought at the price of both self-censorship and compliance with formal censorship. (He was not alone: 'many correspondents admitted after the war that they had misled their readers by exaggerating successes, minimizing failures, and never speaking of defeat'; cf. Read 1999: 146). Half way through his report of the first day of the battle of the Somme Russell wrote of 'good progress into the enemy territory beyond the front line. So far the day goes well for England and France' (Read 1999: 148). The British eventually suffered half a million killed and wounded, but Russell could never admit there was no Somme victory: 'Week after week Russell dwelt upon local successes, and insisted upon the good spirit of the troops' (ibid.). He never quite claimed the Germans had been defeated but suggested that this was a clear possibility, and that the battle had always been planned as a battle of attrition. A Reuters report by Christmas, 1916, even referred to the battle as a 'prodigious tonic'; the war had another two years to run. 'Reuters did not knowingly tell factual untruths. But it did maintain a steadily optimistic tone, whatever the facts' (Read 1999: 150). On the eve of the Second World War, Roderick Jones advised staff of their obligation to observe 'great prudence in handling any news, which may possibly involve the national interest, and to act in close collaboration and accord with Whitehall in this connection'. Failure to do so would mean the loss of Whitehall as a source. In partnership with Associated Press, Reuters formed the attitude by 1942 that the major agencies should insist on publishing only truthful news, but to accept that there were circumstances in which not all the truth could be told. Reports from the field left no doubt that the 'news agency of the British Empire was in total sympathy with the defiant mood of the British people' (Read 1999: 254). Some reporters, like Desmond Tighe, were assigned 'special tasks' on intelligence-gathering missions paid for by the Ministry of Information. The salaries of several Reuters correspondents in sensitive parts of the world were supplemented by payments from the Foreign Office.

The linkage between Reuters and the interests of Britain and the British Empire gradually fell apart following the Second World War. A 1949 editorial note urged correspondents and sub-editors to develop a 'world outlook', looking at the world as it would be viewed by each of the thousands of newspaper clients in different parts of the world. This struck a different tone from a note in 1906, which had instructed correspondents to ignore most mishaps affecting non-Europeans (Read 1999: 438). 'Britishness' as an absolute value was giving way to a more pragmatic regard for the interests of influential British media, and the relevance of 'London training'. More significant shifts became apparent during the 1956 Suez conflict, which linked Britain, France, and Israel against Egypt. Read writes (1999: 452) that its Suez reporting showed that 'Reuters no longer wanted to be a channel for writing the news from the "British point of view" even while claiming to be objective; and that instead it was developing a supranational attitude'. Indeed, the chief news editor explained to Cairo correspondents the 'world view' to which the agency was now committed. They were not to favour either side to the conflict, bearing in mind 'every news angle and every news market'. A circular from Christopher Chancellor noted that British opinion was divided; that Reuters 'does not represent the British Government' and that the agency had a duty to supply an unbiased service (Read 1999: 452). Chancellor stressed the new 'world view' in a 1958 radio interview: 'Reuters is not just a British news service; it is not an organ for presenting British news; it is not associated with the British Government' (ibid.). Yet this new world-view co-existed with collaboration with British government-subsidized bodies such as the Arab News Agency (on which Reuters depended for much of its news of the Middle East until 1969, and which disseminated Reuters news throughout that region), and generous official subscriptions, notably through the BBC External Service (these disappeared only in 1980) and the Foreign and Commonwealth Office (whose subscriptions were reduced to normal commercial levels in 1986) (Read 1999: 394–9).

Such subsidies were on their way out, therefore, by the time of the 1982 Falklands (Malvinas) War between Britain and Argentina. By now, computerized services for financial news clients had begun to impinge significantly on the bottom line, divining the possibility of complete independence of government patronage (stock flotation followed in 1984). Michael Reupke, German-born editor-in-chief, had resisted his boss's suggestion that a circular be issued similar to Chancellor's during Suez: he argued this would insult reporters' integrity. In Buenos Aires, Reuter staff with British passports were transferred to Montevideo in neighbouring Uruguay, while non-British staff were flown in as replacements. A Spanish-language file for Argentina was maintained, confined to official news from all quarters, 'often led by Argentine material but balanced from other sources'. Reupke informed the Argentine ambassador at the United Nations that Reuters was not a British agency, that it took no position, national or otherwise, in any situation or conflict and that the agency's respondents were drawn from forty-eight different nationalities. The Argentine authorities did not, however, permit a Reuter correspondent to go with their forces, although a parallel request to join the British task force was accepted. Reupke did not feel bound to take full account of the 'D notice' system in London under which British editors are requested to voluntarily suppress news for the sake of national security or national interest. Reuters was only prepared to hold back stories if the release might put lives in danger—lives, that is, on either side of the conflict (Read 1999: 462–4).

| The Bureau System | Reuters did not invent the bureau system of international news organization all by itself, but it had a pivotal influence in giving it shape and durability as a result of its central status within the cartel, together with its influence over the news values and practices of associate agencies. This system had a number of features: |

1. A star system of organization whereby a central office (principally, London) received dispatches from various countries of the world and took responsibility for the relay of those dispatches to particular regions of the world, countries, or even specific clients. This model is intrinsically hierarchical, and centrist. Jones was even known to refer to national agencies as Reuters' children (Cooper 1933). It is difficult to reconcile the ethnocentricity of such organization with pretensions to internationalism. By 1919 Reuters had four regional desks in London receiving and transmitting news: these were the European, American, Asiatic, and Dominions desks. Transmissions went to London newspapers, other London clients, the Press Association, and overseas. Some were sent by electric wire, others went by messenger.

There were sometimes several layers of hierarchy, whereby a junior bureau in a relatively marginal news location would take directions from a regional hub bureau and transmit its news to that bureau for editing before forward relay to the central bureau. There were many variations on this model over time, and the identity of central, hub, and junior bureaux did not remain constant. From the 1970s the system underwent significant transformation under the twin pressures of computerization and competition, which led agencies to allow designated bureaux and correspondents to file directly to particular client categories. Pressures of globalization introduced a more distributed system of control among the leading economic zones of the world, with Reuters allowing its bureaux in New York, London, and Hong Kong to hand over command of the global system according to market opening and daylight operating hours in each zone.

2. The global scope of the major agencies (albeit with strong specialization governed by the cartel agreements which, for example, dedicated nineteenth-century Latin America largely to Havas, Asia to Reuters, and central Europe and Russia to Wolff) meant that bureaux were in business not only to serve specific clients or countries, but all clients in all parts of the world, whether they were direct clients of their agency, or indirect clients (the clients of partner or client news agencies). Some clients were strongly preferred and recognized as pre-eminent, but the fact remained that news agency reporting was the first reporting in the world which had to construct a mode of journalism that was tolerably satisfying to clients of different persuasions, interests, time-zones, and languages. This did not mean that complete impartiality was achieved—we have seen that it was not—but it imposed pressure on news agency journalists towards brevity, precision, and inclusivity of reference within the privileged world of the dominant western powers and their global interests.

3. National and international news agencies were contributors to the

semiotic construction of the modern state: principal bureaux were typically located in capital cities; they monitored the main 'national' (capital city) newspapers and broadcasters, those they considered reliable (the more prestigious, up-market, and 'official'); they radiated connections with the principal sources of news in the political, military, financial, and, to a lesser extent, sports worlds. This entailed monitoring of the chief departments of state for domestic and foreign affairs, the armed services, local stock exchanges, and major banks and industries, most of which were based in or well represented in the capital cities. International agencies cultivated relations with national news agencies, especially if these subscribed to the internationals' service. The national agency, often sponsored or owned by the state, was itself a pre-eminent actor in semiotic construction of the state and, in so far as the international agency relied on it (while not infrequently regarding its junior partner with a patronizing contempt), the international agency bought into that construction, even advising its local partner how best to provide usable copy for international dissemination.

4. Bureaux represent a measure of permanence. The major agencies have bureaux in most countries of the world, and sometimes several in one country. They thus distinguish themselves from major newspapers and broadcasters, whose reporting presence is much less comprehensive and less permanent. Individual retail media generally have only one major market to serve in one time zone. News agencies, unlike some of their clients, cannot indulge in gratuitously unfriendly coverage of the country in which they are based, as it is their job to act as correspondent of last resort. Unlike most of their own client media they also have a business presence in the country of coverage; they are a commercial institution, with local property and clients, and obligations to local employment, tax, and business laws. In these conditions agencies may be more likely than other media to respect local elite perspectives on particularly sensitive issues. Boyd-Barrett (1978) listed such issues for several Asian countries in the 1970s: in Taiwan they included local political factionalism, instances of hostility in the relationship between Taiwanese who had originated from mainland China and indigenous Taiwanese, corruption in the administration, stories concerning the families of the political elite, stories critical of the government's anti-communist policy, and stories concerning the health of Chiang Kai-shek in his later years.

The presence of a bureau signifies the extent to which agency news is routinized. In Boyd-Barrett's survey, news agency work, for bureau chiefs, was largely a desk bound job (at least 60 per cent of the time was spent in the office), with most of the time being spent on news-gathering or -processing, and bureau administration. Writing stories, reading local news sources, and editing or filing copy were the most important aspects of news-gathering and news-processing. Local press media were the most important local sources. Bureaux typically sent out between 500 and 8,000 words a day, at least 75 per cent of which was spot news. Although considerable periods were spent in or close to the office, respondents none the less viewed their work as relatively unpredictable: most stories had had no advance preparation. Coverage was mainly metropolitan-focused. Other

things being equal, agency correspondents said they would give priority to
stories that were: metropolitan, had a dramatic/entertainment/human
interest orientation, international, addressed needs of an established
market, involved violence, and came from reputable sources. Hess (1996:
62–3) notes that more than others, wire service correspondents face
particularly daunting challenges to maintain speed and to keep up with
new technology in order to remain competitive. Hess quotes an AP correspondent talking of the pressure to compete against almost unedited
news from sources like CNN. Pressure of speed is perhaps greatest in the
financial news agencies, for which a few seconds can mean a loss of
millions of dollars for clients. This competitive pressure may yield to strategic alliances, as between Reuters and Dow-Jones newswires, published in
partnership with the Associated Press. As many as 26 Dow-Jones newswires
were available on Reuters services by the end of 1999. This alliance, in turn,
reflects the increasing pressure of competition on Reuters from Bloomberg
L. P. and Bridge Information Systems (both American). In television news,
the emphasis on speed increasingly ties reporters to the technology, and
ties wire service reporters to their offices monitoring television coverage.
The apparent 'reality' and wide diffusion of television news images inten-
sifies editorial pressure on wire service reporters to match the television
stories. This is one of the reasons why the two global agencies, Associated
Press and Reuters, now have their own wholly owned worldwide television
news services, distributing wholesale television news.

5. Up to the 1980s, bureaux were generally headed by white, western
journalists (American, British, French, 'White Commonwealth'), who were
moved around from bureau to bureau periodically. Over two thirds were
headed by Americans, Britons, or French nationals; a further 9 per cent
were headed by White Commonwealth or west European journalists
and only 24 per cent by locally recruited journalists or other nationals
(Boyd-Barrett, 1980: 49). Hess (1996: 78) notes in the case of United States
foreign correspondents that the more important a country was to United
States interests, the more likely it would be that American media would
use an American correspondent to cover that country. According to
Boyd-Barrett's (1980: 92) study, a western bureau chief might be supported
by one or two western journalists and additionally by many locally
recruited nationals (there were three and a half times as many locals as
foreigners, counting all employees). The local nationals were often the only
ones who commanded fluency in local languages, although in multilingual
countries the bureau would most likely command expertise in only a small
number of all the local languages. (Hess's study of international news
(1996: 81) notes that only 41 per cent of American foreign correspondents
claimed conversational proficiency in the language of the country they
were covering, excluding English-language countries). Journalists with
local-language fluency were reliable monitors of local print and broadcast
media, but they were much less likely to have authority to file stories, or to
write the final versions of stories. Stringers, the lowest in the hierarchy of
occupational prestige, were much more likely to be local (only 8 out of a
sample of 157 correspondents in Boyd-Barrett's study were non-locals
(1980: 92). The percentage of full-time journalists who were locals was 78

per cent. Non-journalist staff were the most likely to be locals. Locals were also much cheaper to hire.

A tendency therefore emerges up to 1980 for locals to outnumber non-locals, yet for non-locals to dominate top-ranking positions, to have the authority to transmit stories, etc. This was partly to ensure fluent writing in the hands of those who were most familiar with the expectations of media in the principal or home markets of the international agencies, in particular the United States market in the case of AP, the European for Reuters, and France for AFP. Non-local top-ranking journalists also reported that they had greater reporting freedom than locals, who might have more invested (property, family relations, etc.) in the country and hence were more vulnerable to intimidation. In its original form, the bureau conforms to a colonialist outpost model, which privileges expatriate command and communications between the expatriate community and the mother country, and where the whites are surrounded by compliant servants. At the same time there is a relative absence of big 'stars' in agency journalism; news agency reports may carry bylines, but it is the institutional source that counts more than the individual reporter. In as much as anyone has 'star' status in the news agency world it is the bureau chief or the visiting or roving correspondent who flies out from London or New York or Paris for coverage in a time of crisis or to undertake a high-profile series.

6. Bureau chiefs were either supported by bureau managers or, in smaller bureaux, themselves assumed management, sales, and technical leadership, which could then consume at least as much of their time as editorial work. Their responsibility sometimes stretched to include supervision of stringers or smaller bureaux in other countries of the region. Of all staff, slightly more than one half were journalists, the rest were ancillary. Only 20 per cent of the journalists were specialists, but specialists have increased in number since 1980 in line with the growth of economic reporting and of photographic and television services. There are strong competitive relations between the major agencies in terms of speed and accuracy. But this is offset by (1) forms of specialization: for example, greater attention to the needs of North American media by AP, or greater attention to the needs of its financial, economic, and other non-media clients in the case of Reuters, and (2) by strategic alliances, as between Reuters and Dow-Jones, previously noted, or between AFP and Bloomberg.

Global News Agencies as News Instructors

In the latter half of the nineteenth century Reuters was a primary contributor to the process of defining what 'news' was. In 1883, Reuters correspondents were advised that the service should include news of 'fires, explosions, inundations, railway accidents, destructive storms, earthquakes, shipwrecks attended with loss of life, accidents to British and American war vessels and to mail steamers, street riots of a grave character, disturbances arising from strikes, duels between, and suicides of, persons of note, social or political, and murders of a sensational or atrocious character'. This definition was at least in part Reuters' reaction to the 'Americanization' of news, and to attempts by some small competitor agencies, including Dalziel, Central News, and Extel, to satisfy American taste. The note then drew an early distinction between headline news and follow-up: 'It is requested that the bare fact be first telegraphed with the utmost promptitude, and as soon as possible afterwards a descriptive account, proportionate to gravity of the incident. Care should, of course, be taken to follow the matter up'. This suited the difference in style between the general service 'for the educated reader who preferred a sober style', and the joint Reuter/ PA 'special service' for the majority of readers who had only limited education and experience, and who liked colourful news and description. Since the bulk of paying clients were in Britain or represented expatriate communities overseas, the Reuters perspective on the world was nationally and ethnically loaded. Guidelines for correspondents in the Far East in 1906 suggested that only the murder of Europeans should normally be reported to London, unless the murder had a political dimension (Read 1999: 107). Boyd-Barrett (1980: 201–3) notes the significant role of news agencies, in particular Reuters and AFP (bearing in mind their relations with agencies of the previously colonizing powers of Britain and France), as mentors who, through consultancy and training missions, helped national news agency journalists assimilate western news values and reporting and writing skills that would help them produce the kind of copy that would be of most use to the global agencies. Boyd-Barrett also notes how national agencies, subscribing to global wire services that by definition have superior resources and thus tend to be the fastest and most reliable sources of news, are increasingly exposed to, and inclined to assimilate, the principles and practices on which global news is selected and presented. This is not necessarily a passive process and it is far from a new process. Palmer (1998: 180–3) has documented the influence of Reuters and Havas on Russian news-gathering practices in the period 1904–6. The Russian news agency at that time, Vestnik, was admitted into the cartel in 1904. Reuters and Havas sought to educate Vestnik in western news values. They repeatedly told Vestnik how to compress dispatches, and write them for their respective customers. They complained about Vestnik's speed, accuracy, news values, and presentation. Vestnik, an official agency, in turn expressed its concerns about 'colourful prose', 'sensation-mongering' reports, and rumours of political disturbances which were being reported by some western newspapers and rival, smaller western agencies and which were setting the pace of competition for Reuters and Havas.

For Reuters, news agency journalism had much to do with monitoring the deeds of high-ranking political and other sources, requiring of its correspondents a capacity for the demonstration of composure in dangerous situations and/or in foreign cultures, adaptable literary skills, education, and the kind of bearing that would have been more commonly expected of 'gentlemen' than of other social classes. If the major news agencies did indeed play a role as operations that were simultaneously engaged in the social construction of the 'nation' and of the 'global', then they did so with the full collaboration of cadres of journalistic workers who arguably had much to gain from their allegiance to the 'nation', and to the system of interlocking national military and economic alliances that constituted the 'global'. The semiotic construction of 'national' and 'global' was essentially a product about the activities of elites and their affairs, fashioned by a middle-class community whose interests were tied to those whose activities they covered. Up to the Second World War, Reuters was an institution that had worked hard to be recognized as a key British institution with world-wide influence, and which was permanently engaged in a struggle to sustain that image and reputation in the face of threats to its economic viability and its global credibility. The identification with British interest declined markedly in the era following World War II. One might say that the Second World War separates an era in which Reuters was a British institution that acted globally, from an era in which Reuters was a global institution centred in Britain and still sometimes associated with things 'British'. Throughout its history Reuters has been a significant definer of the nature of news, in particular news that is transmitted internationally, through its relations with clients and other news agencies. The nature of the news product, and the system of global relations within which it is contextualized, has helped to define the organization of news-gathering and dissemination, and in particular the pivotal role of the bureau system. Through its association with elites—as a participating member of the elite before the Second World War, and as a technical contributor to political and economic information infrastructures after the war, Reuters, like other international and national agencies, has contributed significantly to the semiotic construction of images of the 'nation', of 'international' relations, and of the globe.

References   BOYD-BARRETT, OLIVER (1978), *The World-wide News Agencies: Development, Organization, Competition, Markets and Product* (Phd. thesis, Open University).

—— (1980), *The International News Agencies* (London, Constable; Thousand Oaks, Calif.: Sage).

—— (1998), 'Global News Agencies', in Oliver Boyd-Barrett and Terhi Rantanen (eds.) *The Globalization of News*, (London: Sage), pp. 19–34.

—— (2000), 'Constructing the Global, Constructing the Local', in Abbas Malek and Anandam Kavori (eds.), *The Global Dynamics of News*, Contemporary Studies in International Political Communication (Stamford, Conn.: Ablex), 229–322.

—— and PALMER, MICHAEL (1981), *Le Trafic des nouvelles* (Paris: Alain Moreau).

—— and RANTANEN, TERHI (1998), 'The Globalization of News,' in Oliver Boyd-Barrett and Terhi Rantanen (eds.), *The Globalization of News*, (London: Sage), pp. 1–14.

COLLINS, HENRY (1925), *From Pigeon Post to Wireless* (London: Hodder and Stoughton).

COOPER, KENT (1933), unpub. letter to Frank B. Noyes, 23 Aug. 1933, the Kent Cooper Papers, Lilly Library, Indiana University, Bloomington, Ind.

—— (1942), *Barriers Down: The Story of the News Agency Epoch* (New York: Farrar & Rinehart).

HESS, STEPHEN (1996), *International News and Foreign Correspondents* (Washington, DC: Brookings Institution Press).

JONES, RODERICK (1921), 'International Telegraphic News', *The Reuter Service Bulletin*, no. 12 Reuters archive, London, box 431, 865310.

PALMER, MICHAEL (1998), 'What Makes News', in Oliver Boyd-Barrett and Terhi Rantanen (eds.), *The Globalization of News* (London: Sage), 177–90.

RANTANEN, TERHI (1992), *Mr. Howard Goes to South America: The United Press Associations and Foreign Expansion*, Roy H. Howard Monographs in Journalism and Mass Communication Research, No. 2 (Bloomington, Ind.: Indiana University School of Journalism).

—— (1994), *Howard Interviews Stalin: How the AP, UP and TASS Smashed the International News Cartel*, Roy W. Howard Monographs in Journalism and Mass Communication Research, No. 3 (Bloomington, Ind.: Indiana University School of Journalism).

—— (1998a), *After Five O'clock Friends: Kent Cooper and Roy W. Howard*, Roy W. Howard Monographs in Journalism and Mass Communication Research, no. 4 (Bloomington, Ind.: Indiana University School of Journalism).

—— (1998b) 'The Struggle for Control of Domestic News Markets (1)', in Oliver Boyd-Barrett and Terhi Rantanen (eds.), *The Globalization of News* (London: Sage), 35–48.

READ, DONALD (1999), *The Power of News: The History of Reuters*, 2nd edn. (Oxford: Oxford University Press).

STOREY, GRAHAM (1951), *Reuters' Century* (London: Max Parrish).

16

Correspondents and Individual News Sources

Jeremy Tunstall

THIS STUDY OF British specialist correspondents in the late 1960s covered the corespondents' use of organizational news sources such as government departments and commercial companies. But the present extract is about how correspondents used personal contacts and individual news sources. Most of these correspondents believed there was a small number of key individuals in their specialist field. The specialist fields were categorized according to the predominant goal in the particular field; this was determined on the basis of interviews with circulation and advertising executives, as well as by asking the correspondents about each others' fields:

Advertising goal	Fashion and motoring correspondent
Circulation goal	Crime and football
Mixed goal	Aviation, education, labour, political lobby
Non-revenue or prestige goal	Foreign correspondents (Bonn, Rome, New York, Washington, DC)

These correspondents worked for all of the then 21 London-based national news organizations—9 national daily and 7 national Sunday papers, 2 London evening papers, the BBC, ITN, and the Press Association.

For the national specialist the junior PRO has relatively little to offer. The prominent 'name', by contrast, knows many things the specialist would like to hear and he has the power to give 'exclusive' information. Many specialists describe their own relations with sources in terms of exchange and power; some Lobby correspondents see themselves as dependent on certain Cabinet Ministers while having little time to waste in talking to many Members of Parliament. Education correspondents admit to regarding their relations with the head of a major educational institution quite differently from their relations with an ordinary teacher met casually at a conference.

Source: Jeremy Tunstall, *Journalists at Work* (London: Constable; Beverly Hills, Calif.: Sage, 1971), 188–92, 194–201.

But among media Performers there is a very rapid turnover; many of the names in the headlines or faces on the TV screen will not be there in five years' time. The insecurity-at-the-top theme plays a part in specialists' perceptions of the balance of exchange and power. A Cabinet Minister may have been having publicity which he regards as wholly bad. Or another Minister, despite being in the Cabinet, may be getting very little publicity at all. In either case the Minister in question may be extremely anxious to get some 'neutral' publicity. [. . .]

Specialists were asked: 'Some specialists say that in their field there is a small number of key individuals and that over half the work consists of finding out what these people are up to. Is this so of your field?' 59 per cent said Yes with variations by goal as follows:

	%
Foreign	40
Political Lobby	84
Mixed fields	60
Audience fields	51
Advertising fields	73
All selected specialists	59 (N = 200)

The field with the highest proportion saying Yes was Fashion (designers especially). The next highest were the Lobby correspondents who identified the key people as being in opposition to each other, for instance not only the Prime Minister and other top Ministers, but leaders of factions in the government party and the official opposition. Other specialists identified their 'key individuals':

'Yes. Top management/politicians.' (Aviation)

'Yes. The leading figures of the teachers' Unions, local authorities, Ministry and top educationists.' (Education)

'Yes. Ministers, Union leaders, industrialists and "Civil Servants" in politics and both sides of industry. The important people are either innovators or so placed that their actions affect large groups.' (Labour)

'Yes. Middle and senior rank CID officers.' (Crime)

'Yes. Administrators and officials and players connected with the game's top dozen clubs.' (Football)

'Yes. In each political party, ministry or other organization there is some key man who either runs the show or knows all about it.' (Bonn)

'Yes. Basically the policy makers—Cabinet officials, government Department and private business heads, Chairmen of Congressional Committees.' (Washington)

'Yes. In the UN—the Leaders pro-tem of ideological or area groups of states.' (New York)

News criteria such as personalization and conflict tend to define 'important decisions' and 'key individuals' each in terms of the other. There are two main ways of 'finding out what these people are up to'. One is to talk to the assistants, intimates, allies (and perhaps opponents) of the key individuals in question. The other is to find out from the key individual direct, which is usually the most desirable. Access to a big name satisfies news values with a minimum expenditure of the specialist's scarce time. The big name can give a story more importance even if the connection is only a comment; a specialist with an item of fresh news phones a big name for his comment (enabling the story to appear: 'Minister denies charge . . . '). The top names have more information not only about their own but also about other organizations. Cabinet Ministers through Cabinet committees and Cabinet meetings know about important decisions in other Ministries. A 'name' who is unwilling to talk about his own organization will often talk about another organization of which he has knowledge. Such umbrella information may concern a subject strong in news value—for instance a clash between two large organizations or several big names. Big name individuals also are aware about *who* is taking a decision elsewhere and *when* the decision will be taken. Finally, regular access to personal conversations with top names in the news source area may become cumulative and help to open doors elsewhere.

But the meeting with one individual journalist is, for the name source, uneconomical in time—journalists are most keen for personal interviews when source individuals are most busy. Such personal interviews also may antagonize competing specialists. One resulting compromise is the short private interview after a press conference. Another is the small 'secret' briefing for a few correspondents. In Washington there is a tradition of 'backgrounders'—meetings between a senior political figure and a small number of correspondents, often over dinner. The source gets, on an off-the-record basis, publicity through *several* news organizations; the journalists get relatively lengthy and relaxed access to the 'name'. British correspondents in the US have long adopted this American custom. In the 1960's there were at least two such backgrounder groups to which some British Washington correspondents belonged. One was an all-British group, and the other a more exclusive European group. An example in the late summer of 1965 of an *ad hoc* small group meeting was a briefing given by President Lyndon Johnson shortly before he went to San Francisco to address the special anniversary meeting of the United Nations. The briefing, for a dozen correspondents of various European media, took place at the house of Max Freedman (a former *Guardian* correspondent and friend of L.B.J.) in Washington. One British journalist present reported President Johnson as making three main points:

(1) That a story by James Reston in the *New York Times* to the effect that the US would help the UN out of its debt situation had originated from the State Department. President Johnson would make no such statement at San Francisco.

(2) 'He gave us a pep talk about our importance in "explaining" US policy abroad. (Which I do not regard as my function.)'

(3) President Johnson said that at the end of 1965 he would concentrate

less on getting his legislation through Congress and would turn his attention more to foreign affairs.

In London the late hours and 10 pm voting habits of Parliament, plus the size of the city, made for a tradition of political *lunching*. A few specialists—who perhaps work for the same multi-media organization, or who co-operate in other ways—may take a prominent performer out to lunch.

Another compromise form of personal contact between a name source and individual specialist is the evening or week-end telephone call. One Lobby man said he knew four Cabinet Ministers sufficiently well to leave a message asking them to ring him back. The week-end is an especially popular time for phoning sources. Evening and weekends, of course, are the time when name sources are free of their advisers, staffs, or Civil Servants.

The 'tradition' of an anonymous and politically neutral Civil Service appears to leave the matter of explaining the policy of a government Department in the hands of the temporary political 'masters' and the public relations department. Silence on the part of the Civil Servants and close co-ordination between the politician-Ministers and PROs would thus ensure that the Ministry spoke with a single voice. This 'tradition' obtains, if to a lesser degree, in most large organizations; but, needless to say, the tradition is honoured a fair amount in the breach: Firstly, the name performers in political or directorial control may themselves be internally split. Examples include the common political practice of 'balancing' a right-wing and a left-wing Minister, or the directors of previously competing companies on a merged board. Secondly, a Foreign Ministry spokesman may be wooden and unhelpful at press conferences, but his personal contacts with Foreign correspondents may be quite different. London-based specialists say that a top PRO may be willing to say: 'This is the on-the-record line. But my own off-the-record assessment is this. [. . .]

'The more senior the more freely they talk.' The highest reaches of the Civil Service are the most 'political'—in the sense of having the most widespread contact with politicians and involvement in political decisions. The giving of information to journalists is one means of supporting, or of opposing, a political 'master'.

Other individual sources, although not media performers or public names themselves, are at the level of 'advising' or reporting directly to such names. An obvious example in politics are second rank members of the government; at least some amongst them—including some determined to become 'names' themselves—may be even more talkative than the more talkative Cabinet Ministers. Despite a particularly strict rule that policemen must not talk to Crime journalists, it is accepted in the upper reaches of the police force that this rule must be broken. Again in Football, the other audience specialism in which there is a firm rule against talking to journalists, this rule is inevitably broken. One Football journalist talked about how the *Daily Express* got the exclusive story late in 1967 that Dave Sexton would be the new Chelsea manager:

'The decision is made one day and perhaps half a dozen people know that day. By the next day a dozen people know, the next day two dozen—the information moves out in ripples. Probably the *Express* got the story from some local contact—a player or some other employee of the club, or maybe a freelance or local journalist. There are many backdoors in Football.'

'Backdoors' are perhaps especially numerous in national politics—where anything which has been discussed in the Cabinet may ripple out to at least some journalist within hours or days. Prime Ministers and other leading performers cannot, as a general rule, make major decisions without consultation. The increasing complexity of decisions tends to involve increasing access for journalists (although the access may not increase as fast as the complexity). [...]

In any field of journalism one or two specialist correspondents may develop superior access to sources, and become to some extent performers in their own right. [...]

There were one or two such élite correspondents within several of the specialist fields covered by the present study. Such correspondents were usually working for one of the 'quality' newspapers. Television journalists in general are less suitable for special revelations—and the less detailed coverage of TV often means that these journalists possess less detailed knowledge of the field generally. But in Foreign correspondence BBC men—and Reuters correspondents—perhaps because of their large international audience, appear more likely to have élite contacts.

Sometimes 'experience' is deliberately planned and cultivated in advance; for instance the youngest Football specialist may be assigned to cover the England Under 23 team—in the expectation that some of these players will later be in the full England team. Some Political Lobby correspondents in early 1968—over two years before the 1970 General Election—were already saying that they must pay more attention to likely members of the next Conservative Cabinet. Ambitious source individuals will also be cultivating publicity and 'experience' in dealing with journalists.

Prominent news source individuals will often have a record of rapid movement both hierarchically and geographically. A young Football journalist in Manchester may get to know a leading player, who ten years later shows up as manager of a team in the London area. Policemen similarly move from place to place on their promotion ladder. The Lobby correspondent of a provincial paper may get to know a local MP who later becomes a Minister; or a Lobby man may have contact with a young Civil Servant in a Minister's private office—who ten or fifteen years later may have become a much more senior Civil Servant. But Foreign correspondents are perhaps the most subject of all to the experience of finding old sources popping up in new places:

'Any correspondent who has served in several overseas posts is liable to find diplomat friends occupying senior posts in, say, the US State Department. By virtue of oldish acquaintance he'll use them as contacts, however senior they may have become.' (Washington)

Another aspect of 'experience' is ability to draw conclusions from what to a novice might seem rather flimsy clues. Senior Football specialists say they acquire an ability to narrow down the possibilities:

> 'If the Second Division league leaders are worried about their goalkeeper they will be prepared to buy a better replacement, in order to ensure their promotion to the First Division. If you know enough about the game you can list six possible goalkeepers they might be after. Then if you spot their manager watching a match involving one of these six goalkeepers, you're on to a big transfer story.'

This practice of 'putting yourself into the source's position' is common also in other fields. When the likely issue in a decision has been narrowed down, a small verbal slip at a press conference may suddenly acquire significance. Of course this practice of 'seeing it from his point of view', and using 'instinct and experience' can also be regarded as 'pure speculation'.

Two very senior Fleet Street News executives gave the following accounts of the personal approach to new sources:

> (1) A political journalist got to know the secretary of a Conservative shadow Minister. In bed with the secretary at a seaside hotel the night before the annual Conservative Party Conference, the journalist discovered that her boss was going to make an unusually important speech next morning. He immediately got out of bed, and phoned the theme of the speech to his Fleet Street office in time for that night's late editions.

> (2) The problem in covering the United Nations is to get hold of advance texts of resolutions which the third world nations are bringing forward. There are two ways of getting these texts. One is to have a white secretary who sleeps around with men in the African and Asian delegations. The second way is to station permanently at the bar in the delegates' lounge a journalist who looks like one of the potted palm trees and drinks like a fish.

Although many journalists have tales of this sort to tell—with the moral that the personal approach often pays off—such approaches are said to be more often of a food and drink, rather than a sexual, nature.

A few specialists said they tried to lunch with a source every day and a few said they tried to avoid all source lunching. Two fields where lunching is especially prevalent—Aviation and Motoring—are also fields in which there is much public relations activity. The two heaviest drinking fields appear to be Crime and Labour. There is a 'local' pub for each police station in central London—although it is never the pub nearest to the police station; Crime correspondents frequent these pubs as a means of breaking down the distance between themselves and policemen. For Labour correspondents, drinking is important in establishing personal relations with trade union leaders. Labour specialists say there is a noticeable difference in this respect between union and management negotiators; after a meeting, while the management men get into their chauffeur-driven cars and disappear, the trade union leaders are much more likely to take a pint of beer with the Labour correspondents.

The propensity of Labour correspondents to drink informally with union men, but not with management, arises partly from differences in status, salary, and way of life between the two potential source groups. But a good deal of drinking and lunching results from sources and journalists being in the same place at the same time—rather than from pre-arranged meetings; these places include the traditional Pall Mall gentlemen's clubs—but more important are pubs near to Ministries or other source organizations, restaurants in Soho and elsewhere, and other clubs of a specialized interest sort. Many specialists say it is largely a matter of 'hitting it off' and genuinely liking the man. Most are also agreed that there is a strong age-grading phenomenon—of ambitious young specialists having ambitious young sources, and older specialists older sources. Specialists talk about 'my generation' of policemen, MPs or footballers.

Both an individual source and a specialist may develop a common interest in building up the source's name—the source wanting to become a 'name', the journalist wanting to build up his asset ('I knew him before he became famous'). In some source-specialist situations this element of working together is more explicit. The source may write a signed article for the newspaper, which the specialist may help to commission or sub-edit; in television interviews there is an element of the reporter and the source putting on a dual performance and establishing a shared experience. Another situation where exchange becomes more explicit is when a journalist 'ghost' writes a book for the source—something especially common in Football journalism.

Although most of the information supplying comes from the source side, there are also several kinds of feedback of information from the journalist to the source individual:

(1) The simplest kind is the supply of 'stop-press' news from the journalist to a source. 'We tell them a lot of things which they would hear within an hour or two.'

(2) Sources are interested in gossip about their own field of activity. Since journalists are in the gossip and information gathering business full-time, they will usually have plenty of fresh gossip.

(3) Specialist journalists may act as unofficial 'go-betweens' or 'conciliators' on a word of mouth basis; an obvious example is the industrial dispute.

(4) Specialists may perform a somewhat similar role between groups or individuals within a single organization. Cabinet Ministers may consult specialists as to the wishes of their own backbenchers, or backbenchers may want to know about the intentions of their own Ministers.

Such provision of 'information' by specialists to news sources shades off into the supply of advice and 'suggestions'. Professional footballers ask Football correspondents for advice on career problems. Lobby correspondents 'suggest' to MPs that they put down a particular Parliamentary Question.

In exchange for information about a particular decision or conflict, a specialist can offer individual sources who opposed the course taken an opportunity to 'get back at' the perpetrators of the decision. There is the prominent politician who was over-ruled by the Cabinet, or was sacked— yet still has much interesting information in his possession; there is the highly placed man in the Aviation industry—such as a designer, test pilot, or export salesman—who thinks the blame for some failure should be placed elsewhere; there is the detective who was moved off a particular crime; or there is the prominent footballer who was dropped from the first team by the new manager. All information supplied by an individual source has some motive behind it—which the specialist must evaluate. One source may seem to be trying to get back into the first team; another source may seem to be heading for the third world war:

> 'On April 2, 1954, I sat in Mr John Foster Dulles's ante-room at the State Department, waiting to see him . . . After a long pause, he spoke, emphasizing every word: "I can tell you that American aircraft carriers are at this moment steaming into the Gulf of Tonkin, ready to strike. . . ."'
>
> 'He went on to explain that the US Government was convinced that it could not afford to let Indo-China go Communist. He favoured intervention, but President Eisenhower had made such action dependent on Britain's deciding to go in and Prime Minister Anthony Eden was stubbornly opposed to the idea.
>
> 'I knew, as Mr Dulles must have known, that the British Cabinet was to meet in two days' time, on Sunday, to make its decision for or against support. A lot depended on that Cabinet meeting, and I was certain as I sat down to write my weekly despatch to the *Sunday Times* (in which I could not quote from the interview) that in indicating such sensational developments Mr Dulles was hoping to use one more avenue to influence the decision in London.[1]

In the standard situation of a press conference, or with a mailed hand-out, there are certain agreed conditions—in particular a set time at which the material may be used. But this quasi-contractual element does not exist in dealings between an individual journalist and an individual source. Sometimes the source will say that his remarks are off-the-record or not for use, but where source and journalist know each other, this may be left understood rather than explicitly stated. Despite the special circumstances of some such meetings and the extreme 'frankness' with which the source may talk, usually no explicit bargaining over the exchange takes place. Henry Brandon says ' . . . I was certain . . . that in indicating such sensational developments Mr Dulles was hoping . . . '. Even when the story could influence a decision to make war, there is no explicit bargaining of an 'If I tell you this, you must undertake to say that' character. [. . .]

[. . .] Specialists say they are rarely approached on an explicit bargaining basis—and if so approached tend to become sharply hostile toward the bargaining source. Thus the exchange of publicity for information takes on certain elements of 'pure' exchange of the small group or friendship type. The very 'purity' of the exchange, however, leads to a certain interpersonal

---

1 Henry Brandon, *Sunday Times*, 13 Apr. 1969.

distance. The specialist does not ask the source's motives, and the source does not ask the specialist how he will word his story.

Specialists admit to treating major regular sources differently from minor irregular ones. Here is an account of a British Foreign correspondent handling a minor irregular United Nations military source in 1962 during the Katanga secession from the Congo:

> 'One enterprising *Daily Express* reporter had asked a high-ranking Swedish Officer about his medals; some of them, he learned, had been bestowed by the Germans in World War II, for successfully helping them to cross the country, once on their way in, once on their way out. Since the *Express* was both violently anti-UN and violently anti-German . . . this made a fine story.[2]

But even though a *major* news source individual would be unlikely to receive this kind of treatment from a specialist there are certain techniques which can be used for managing the critical dilemma:

(1) Criticize the organization rather than the man. One City editor said that because of his friendly personal relations with the current Chancellor of the Exchequer, he directed his regular criticisms mainly at the Treasury rather than its political boss.

(2) The 'moral division of labour' approach. Here the man is criticized, but the story is written by a general reporter.

(3) Division of labour within a team of specialists. Among Lobby correspondents some teams operate in such a way that in practice one man writes stories critical of Labour and another man writes stories critical of the Conservatives.

(4) Criticism does not always lead to source withdrawal. Some sources persevere and try to persuade the correspondent of the error of his ways.

(5) Specialists with a number of élite sources may find it easy to drop one source and establish relations with another. Criticism is said by some journalists to produce a new friend for each old friend it loses.

(6) Some specialists are less dependent on any individual source, because they choose to compete in originality of comment and criticism rather than in original newsgathering. This is especially possible for a very well-known specialist.

---

2 David Halberstam, *The Making of a Quagmire* (London: Bodley Head, 1965), 20.

17

The Changing Role of TV Network News Correspondents

Joe S. Foote

ESPECIALLY FROM 1963, when the American TV networks extended their early evening news to thirty minutes, some leading correspondents became stars. But after 1980—with more competition and lower news budgets—network stardom and network news coverage both became more restricted. Network news reporting in the 1990s reached fresh vertical extremes. At the peak were the superstar anchors and the top producers; then the stars of the prime-time weekly news magazine shows; then a few dozen top correspondents, mostly Washington-based; below these came the lesser reporters, who only got their faces onto the network news perhaps twice a month. At the bottom end of this vertical profession were many hundreds of local TV reporters who might appear regularly on that city's Big Local News, but who earned at most 2 or 3 per cent of the network news anchor's salary.

The twenty-year period from 1960 to 1980 represented the correspondents' 'glory days.' Budgets were flush, network news was growing in stature and popularity, there were only three competitors to serve a huge domestic market, correspondents had significant independence, and they dominated the newscast. During this period of skyrocketing morale and upward mobility, the role of the correspondent solidified. New York controlled the evening news broadcast, but correspondents had considerable independence. Top correspondents held specific beats or geographical territories. The domestic prestige beats were all in Washington with the White House, Congress, and the State Department heading the list; overseas—London, Moscow, and the hot spot du jour topped the pecking order.

Upwardly mobile correspondents rotated through a variety of assignments, ending up at a prestige beat like the White House. When CBS and NBC expanded their broadcasts to 30 minutes in 1963, correspondents

Source: Joe S. Foote, 'Introduction', in Joe S. Foote (ed.), *Live from the Trenches The Changing Role of the News Correspondent* (Carbondale and Edwardsville, Ill.: Southern Illinois University Press, 1998), 2–19. © 1998 by the Board of Trustees, Southern Illinois University, reprinted by permission of the publisher.

gained additional opportunities for exposure. During the next decade, high profile stories like the Vietnam War, the civil rights struggle, the space race, the cold war, and political assassinations provided a launching pad for a whole generation of correspondents. Talented young reporters rapidly climbed the television market ladder to the pinnacle of network news. Hundreds of others endured low pay and shaky job security in the hope that they one day would join the chosen network few.

Stories about obscure local reporters being 'discovered' by the networks while covering a major spot news story became legion. At the top of network folklore was CBS's Dan Rather—being catapulted to the network after reporting from the eye of a hurricane in Texas, then soaring to the White House as the CBS Dallas-based correspondent when the Kennedy assassination story unfolded. Just enough unknowns ascended to keep the network dream alive. Having so many in the hunt for a coveted network correspondent's job only enhanced the prestige of those who had already made it to the top.

During the sixties, the correspondent corps became the breeding ground for anchorpersons when the networks elevated substantive journalists with years of reporting experience rather than relying on news readers in the British tradition. For correspondents, the anchor slot became the pinnacle position. Anchors promoted through this system, however, often became embarrassed by the small amount of heavy lifting required in their new positions and clung to the correspondent title as a badge of honor.

Demand for correspondents' work soared when big news stories unfolded. Not only was there the evening news—the network flagship broadcast—but morning news programs, news specials, and radio as well. Rather than flood the market with an army of correspondents, the networks empowered a trusted few with more responsibility and gave them better resources to do their work. Correspondents headed four-person crews that included a producer, cameraperson, and sound technician. Sometimes a lighting technician, assistant producer, and a unit manager came aboard. Thus, the correspondent became a network prince of sorts with his/her own retinue of courtiers to provide support.

Correspondents basked in their greatest glory during the megastories when money was no object, and New York would move heaven and earth to get them to the scene. It wasn't unusual on a big story to have a network 'bag man' with a fist full of hundred dollar bills running interference for the network juggernaut. Pouring more and more money into the care and feeding of correspondents created a much-envied occupation and lifestyle. Chartering jets at will became the status symbol of the newly empowered correspondents, with a variety of secondary perks following closely behind.

Not only did network correspondents have the biggest budgets, but their stock as journalists was rising as well. Print reporters who used to turn up their noses at their lower status broadcast colleagues found themselves being gradually, but undeniably, pushed to the rear of the gallery. Public officials and high profile news sources eagerly sought the network correspondents first because they could deliver their views to an enormous nationwide audience. [. . .]

At first, the competition was limited to CBS and NBC, but underfunded

ABC caught up and eventually passed its elder brothers in the eighties. The correspondents were the infantrymen whom the field marshals in New York sent into daily battle. From the war room in New York, the producers moved pieces on the board in anticipation of the competition's next move. News executives scrutinized correspondent productivity closely. With fewer than 10 correspondents appearing daily on each of three newscasts before the largest television audience in the world, there was no place to hide.

The stakes were so high that competition for competition's sake frequently reigned. Correspondents were not always used productively to gather stories, but to 'stake out' locations where a news maker might make a pronouncement deemed an exclusive. The networks assigned a correspondent 24 hours a day to the president, just in case there was an assassination attempt. Rather than take pool footage of routine video, the networks insisted on being there themselves, often with a correspondent. Much of this individuality was purely cosmetic because, in the aggregate, the network broadcasts were becoming remarkably similar with at least two of the networks leading with the same story 90 percent of the time. At least two-thirds of the content during the seventies was nearly identical.

Television news took its cue from newspapers and followed a modified beat system to track and report news. Yet, unlike newspapers, the networks sought only 22 minutes of content from a half dozen correspondents each day and could not afford to station correspondents permanently in too many venues. Most of the networks' beats were in Washington—White House, State Department, Capitol Hill, Pentagon, Supreme Court—where the weekly yield of reports could justify the expenditure of keeping a correspondent there. More than half of the network news output came from Washington, where a majority of the correspondents were stationed. As serious news organization wanna-bes, the networks were obliged to have permanent correspondents at the prestige beats in Washington where correspondents would be hand-fed a daily diet of government news.

The network nerve center in New York housed the second largest stable of correspondents. Bureaus located in Chicago, Los Angeles, and wherever the networks owned affiliates were also prominent. Other geographic areas fared far less well. Studies showed a distorted coverage map with some major cities and states getting disproportionate coverage and some receiving no coverage at all. [. . .]

[1980:] The Great Divide

The first half century of network television news can be divided roughly into two eras: the loss-leader years 1950–1980 and the profit center years 1981–1999. During the formative years, network news was always a costly, but necessary item in the network budget. Networks built their franchises and credibility in Washington on the reputations of news organizations that hemorrhaged revenue. A mark of honor was to sacrifice the prime time schedule and its handsome revenue to cover a presidential speech, political convention, or breaking news story.

Yet this 'unscheduled news' caused expanding fault lines behind the scenes between the news division that promoted the broadcasts and the entertainment division that sacrificed prime-time revenue because of them. The correspondents and anchors loved grabbing prime time from the entertainment divisions because it meant huge audiences and more airtime than they could ever get on the evening news. The 'suits' in the executive suites cringed every time the news people came calling.

Ironically, it was during these money-losing days for network news that the correspondents enjoyed their greatest independence, highest morale, most lavish lifestyle, and widest budgetary latitude. Correspondents had as much money as they needed when news was a loss leader. It was when news finally became a profit center that management tightened the financial screws on the correspondents.

CBS's *60 Minutes* was the networks' first news cash cow and their first regular venture into prime time. Being positioned on the fringe of prime time after professional football on Sunday, the biggest viewing night of the week, large audiences automatically meant big money. The *60 Minutes* experience led to the production of other magazine-style programs in the evening that competed head-on with entertainment programming. Executives quickly realized that there was far more money to be made in prime time than with the evening news; yet, even the flagship broadcasts became profitable eventually.

When the prime time money machine began churning, the entire dynamic of the network news system changed. The insulation between news and entertainment eroded as the bottom line applied equally to news as entertainment. The evening news broadcasts remained partially sheltered, but the news divisions became big time profit centers with a prime time fixation. In some cases, news became more profitable than entertainment. Even news programs that finished last made money because their production costs were so low. The skyrocketing cost of talent and production for prime time entertainment shows pushed forward a rush of inexpensive news and reality-based programs.

The profitability of prime time news programming gave the beleaguered news divisions a reprieve from their downward spiral, but the field correspondents did not share in the riches. The magazine shows were producer-driven rather than correspondent-driven. Using the *60 Minutes* model, segment producers did all of the research and preliminary interviews, waiting until the end of the story to summon the correspondent. It could take as few as three correspondents to front for an entire hour of programming. Prime time magazines also had a habit of stealing story ideas from the evening news correspondents to use for longer magazine segments. Programs replaced news beats as the measuring stick of network news spending.

The emergence of prime time magazine correspondents planted a new tier of talent between the anchors and the journeyman correspondents. The prime time correspondents were better paid, had higher prestige, and reached far more viewers than their evening news counterparts. Field correspondents, thus, had to settle for third-tier status in this new hierarchy.

Despite a profitable move into prime time, the network news divisions faced serious challenges. New ownership of the networks, a declining audience share, new competition from cable, and the rising power of local news caused major change. The presumed cure for the network ills was downsizing. Management consultants swooped into the newsrooms in the mideighties with questions. Why was it so expensive to gather the news? Why did correspondents get on the air so little but cost so much? Why did it take so many staff and resources to support the correspondent? Would it not be cheaper to buy in coverage from a reliable, third-party source rather than always send a network's own correspondent to cover an event? Should not correspondents be reporting for more news programs to make their positions more cost effective?

During this period of management consultant influence, correspondents and bureaus started to disappear. CBS President Lawrence Tisch finished an international tour of the news division in the mid-eighties by decrying opulence and overstaffing in the overseas bureaus. Tisch and the management consultants never grasped the principle of redundancy necessary to staff a bureau's second day coverage with reinforcements. What they had would be good enough, they reasoned, considering the immense savings gained from lowering the news-gathering overhead. CBS and NBC whittled their forces to levels unbelievable for those who had dominated the globe just a decade before. By 1998, the networks had but a handful of foreign correspondents to cover the world. Global coverage was a Potemkin facade the networks constructed to hide the shell of a correspondent corps left behind.

A dramatic example of the networks' empty stable of correspondents occurred on August 31, 1997, in Paris, France, when Princess Diana died. Neither ABC, CBS, nor NBC had a correspondent stationed permanently in Paris. All three had permanent reporters there a decade earlier. CNN's Jim Bittermann, operating from Paris for more than 15 years and speaking fluent French, was the only broadcast reporter who seemed to know the lay of the land. [. . .]

With fewer correspondents in the field to gather news, parachute journalism became the norm for nearly all international correspondents and some domestic ones. Being based in London did not mean just cruising Whitehall and Westminster for stories, but being prepared to circulate in a 1,000 mile radius from home on a moment's notice. In this environment, knowing the local language or being intimate with the culture gave way to having street smarts and an incredible ability to assimilate and process information under highly stressful conditions. [. . .]

Producer-Driven Networks

Changes in the network news format gave producers an opportunity to tighten the command and control structure of the evening news broadcast. Network news would no longer be just a composite of the latest news of the day cobbled together with breakneck speed. It would be a selective portrait of the world carefully crafted by the executive producer and staff on a tighter budget. Producers had always scrutinized stories carefully, but deadlines and a culture of correspondent autonomy had held their power in check. As budgets tightened, the power of the managing producers increased.

Stringent budgets meant fewer stories commissioned. Gone were the days when correspondents did a spate of stories on spec and eventually got a few of them on the air. Correspondents began covering more of what producers wanted and fewer stories the correspondents initiated. The truly international story with no immediate and compelling American angle, never a popular item in New York, became a casualty of the news-gathering process. Only CNN had the airtime luxury to thrive in this area. Doing fewer stories meant less work for ABC, CBS, and NBC correspondents covering remote areas that rarely made the news, putting their jobs and bureaus in jeopardy.

The producers who commissioned a story often prescribed the content. Correspondents chafed at the numerous, often contradictory, rewrites demanded by producers. Every network correspondent has war stories about how the butchers in New York decimated a story. Correspondents lament that by the time 'stories by committee' are broadcast, their creative imprint has vanished. Executive producers have their own preferences for types of stories and presentation styles that frequently override correspondent initiative.

Network correspondents who have fled to CNN marvel at their new-found independence. Enterprise stories nearly always find airtime, and the editing process is much less severe. Most editing occurs at the bureau rather than Atlanta. To insure quality, bureau chiefs often have to impose a higher editing standard on themselves than headquarters producers require.

As budgetary pressures grew, more and more stories appeared on the evening news that were assembled by correspondents but not actually reported by them. Producers asked New York and Washington correspondents to do stories from the bureau that happened somewhere else. Without ever visiting the scene of the story, correspondents would try to report authoritatively on a story they never actually covered, relying on footage from a variety of locations. It really was, in Edward Epstein's words, 'News from Nowhere.'

Another variation on this theme was for the White House correspondent to give a presidential angle to an out-of-Washington story. For example, the death of a foreign leader could be reported from the White House or State Department rather than from the target country. While this tactic offered great economy to the networks, it took a huge step backward in the standards of field reporting. It also frequently distorted the reality of the story by giving the White House angle disproportionate influence. Under this network logic, almost any domestic or international story could be reported from Washington.

Taking a cue from their infotainment cousins, some long-form stories on the evening news began having an edge placed on them—an unambiguous perspective that drove home the overriding message in the story in a one-dimensional way. This heavy-handed scripting of the story greatly eroded the autonomy of the correspondent. [. . .]

Simmering below the surface of the executive producer/correspondent relationship is a resentment of the power producers wield and how they attained it. What particularly grates on the correspondents is that the executive producers of the evening news come from the producer corps, a group that the correspondents have always directed as subordinates. It is like drawing the generals from the enlisted ranks with the majors and captains caught in the middle. While rarely discussed openly, correspondent resentment of the topsy-turvy chain of command could be blamed for a variety of organizational ills in the network news system.

The New York producers, while powerful, still faced competition for control of the broadcast from the evening news anchors who fancied themselves as majordomos of the broadcast. Anchors have diluted producers' power by ensconcing themselves in the position of 'managing editor,' a phantom position awkwardly squeezed into the network hierarchy to appease the autonomous anchors. Rather than act as a counterbalance to the producers on behalf of the correspondents, the anchors have made the situation worse for their former colleagues. The correspondent-turned-anchors can be just as brutal and judgmental as the producers. With the managing editor title tacked onto their duties, anchors have banished several correspondents into oblivion, leaving little recourse for appeal.

Anchors can not only influence how often correspondents' stories are chosen for air but can also steal the stories out from under the correspondents. Anchors' natural instincts are to rush to the field to do high-profile stories, temporarily displacing a correspondent. Few things provoke correspondents like being 'big-footed' by an anchor. Correspondents get the double whammy not only because they are upstaged by a higher-status person but also because they lose the chance to cover the very best and most visible stories on their beats.

When anchors began making mega-salaries and became signature players, the pressure to put anchors on the air only increased, denying good stories to correspondents. As Penn Kimball wrote, 'Television news has a lot more to do with the presenter than the material being presented'.[1] Producers found that it was much cheaper and more efficient to have anchors read stories from the anchor desk with taped inserts than to rely on a correspondent report from the field.

The reliance on anchors over correspondents is more than cosmetic. It shifts the center of gravity from news gathering to news processing. When a correspondent reports a story, there is considerable news gathering in the field. A studio-based story using an anchor, however, presents the same story using hired-in footage from news wholesalers. An astute viewer of television news notices the anchor doing more and more stories from the studio amplified by video taken at the scene, but with no correspondent. Most of the time, anchor-based stories are a matter of necessity or cost because no network correspondent has been assigned to the story. Sometimes, however, anchors report from the studio when a correspondent is already on the scene ready and willing to report. This behavior clearly hits a raw nerve in any correspondent caught short by the intervening anchor.

---

1 Penn Kimball, *Downsizing the News* (Washington, DC: Woodrow Wilson Center Press: Baltimore, Johns Hopkins University Press, 1994), 4.

Getting on the Air

In a competitive, bottom-line environment where jobs and livelihoods are at stake, correspondents must be visible frequently on the high profile news programs. Not getting on the air is an ongoing worry of correspondents. Only the senior reporter at the White House can count on getting almost daily access to the evening news; everyone else has to wait their turn.

During the 15 years that I have kept statistics on correspondent visibility, the majority of correspondents get on the air less than once a week; only the top 10 will do more than two reports per week. The average number of reports per correspondent on the evening news in 1997 was 37 compared to 43 in 1993. Below the most visible 100 correspondents, reporters rarely get on the air more than every other week. As anchors do more and more of the work correspondents used to do, the number of correspondent reports per broadcast is steadily decreasing.

In 1984, there were 234 correspondents reporting regularly for the evening news at all three networks. Today, there are only 167—a decrease of nearly 30 percent. The number of correspondents reporting for the evening news has declined by nearly 20 percent in just five years as downsizing has taken its toll. The geographic spread of existing correspondents is also different as bureaus have been downgraded and closed. Bureaus like Chicago, which might have had three or four correspondents a decade ago, are now lucky to have one. [. . .]

Because the network assignment system creates automatic winners and losers, correspondents are sensitive to how assignment decisions are made. Minorities and women have long felt that the system discriminates against them. A disproportionate amount of the lower visibility general assignment positions have historically gone to women and minorities. During the eighties, women had virtually no upward mobility in the correspondent corps despite great gains being made nationally by women in other professions. It wasn't until 1991 that women showed a significant move upward into the top echelon of correspondents, including White House assignments. The best year for women was 1994 when they reported a quarter of all stories. That year, 3 of the 10 most visible correspondents were women. Three years later, women were reporting only 22 percent of the stories and had no correspondent in the top 10.

Minorities lagged behind women in their upward mobility at network news broadcasts, showing no appreciable progress until 1994 when they reported 13 percent of all stories on the evening news and had 17 of the top 100 correspondents. In 1997, 18 percent of correspondents were minorities and reported 15 percent of the stories. The ethnic breakdown of correspondents was 20 African-American, 5 Asian, and 3 Hispanic. In 15 years, there have been only 2 years where a minority reporter has finished among the top 10 most visible correspondents and that was because of extraordinary coverage of the O. J. Simpson trial and floods in the Midwest. Only a handful of African-American reporters have had a regular beat in network news, and because of high turnover, few have attained the seniority to claim a prestige beat. [. . .]

[. . .] Celebrity has recently become a by-product of the correspondent's lifestyle. In a culture that places a premium on media exposure, it is no surprise that men and women who are seen by millions daily have a public persona. Visibility opens doors to opportunity, including books, lectures, talk show appearances, and so forth. Nearly all correspondents now have agents who negotiate their contracts with the networks and sometimes help in their 'merchandising.' Many correspondents will not make a public appearance, even on a college campus, without a sizable speaking fee.

There has been controversy recently over correspondents taking speaking fees from or having a financial stake in companies they cover. Clearly, journalists are no longer completely detached observers but are high profile, wealthy individuals whose private lives become entangled in their professional lives. Correspondents worried little about these problems years ago, but six and seven figure contracts have catapulted broadcast journalists into different tax brackets and social environments. It is not unusual for correspondents to socialize freely with politicians and other sources and to send their children to the same private schools. Critics argue that this improved lifestyle not only places correspondents too close to sources but puts the correspondent out of touch with most ordinary Americans.

Corporate downsizing, centralized administrative control, and resource cutbacks have dulled the correspondent's luster. Most alarming, news gathering has taken a back seat to news processing at most networks, marginalizing the role of the field correspondent. A 24-hour news network can exist today with no news-gathering capability whatsoever. In one all-news channel, recent j-school graduates packaged news from third-party sources around the clock with no correspondents and no original news gathering. Even major networks are camouflaging their shell of a correspondent corps by the clever use of anchors and third-party vendors.

Yet, there are limited signs of renewal in some sectors. At CNN, BBC, and other global networks, news gathering is on the increase with new bureaus opening where there was none before. NBC's and CBS's burgeoning cable efforts are setting the stage for a renewed interest in news gathering. News wholesalers are methodically fanning the globe to keep primary news gathering alive, although it leaves only two or three crews interpreting events for an entire world in some remote areas. Cyberjournalism offers a nascent, but promising, supplement to print and broadcast reporting.

18

The Culture of Foreign Correspondence

Stephen Hess

DURING THE 1980s and 1990s, Stephen Hess was the leading chronicler of Washington journalism and journalists. This extract is from the fifth volume of his 'Newswork' series of such studies.

All foreign reporting is prestigious, but Hess points out that there is also a steep hierarchy within this field of journalism. He emphasizes in particular the prestige ranking which places the *New York Times* and its correspondents at the top. He also discusses the significance of the distinction between the salaried staff correspondent and the locally based freelance reporter or 'stringer'.

In foreign correspondence, as in college teaching or book publishing or automobile manufacturing, there is a distinctive culture, an amalgam of attitudes, practices, and ideas that informs the behavior of all involved—news organizations, staff reporters, and stringers. This amalgam presents itself in the hierarchy of prestige among reporters and the organizations they work for, the patterns of assignments and job changes, management and editorial practices, the personalities the business seems to encourage, and the particular problems the organizations and their personnel face. Unlike college teaching or book publishing, however, the organizations and personnel involved are very few (about 1,500 correspondents working for fewer than 50 organizations) and the culture therefore more concentrated.

That there is a hierarchy or pecking order among foreign correspondents can be discerned by examining what organizations or jobs journalists leave to take which jobs in which organizations. The moves reflect the existence of an implicit ladder with freelancers on the bottom rung and the *New York Times* at the top, with parallel paths for television journalists and those who write for certain newsmagazines.

Although an occasional freelancer may prefer the latitude of being his or her own boss, most see permanent employment, with its health insurance and other fringe benefits, as a step up. 'Freelance correspondents, even the

Source: Stephen Hess, *International News and Foreign Correspondents* (Washington, DC: The Brookings Institution, 1996), ch.4.

most professional and relied upon, are treated terribly by news organizations, both financially and editorially,' according to Nomi Morris, a freelancer in Berlin. Fees are modest, often $50 for a radio spot, $75 for a newspaper photo, and $100 for a 700-word article. And the work is less than steady. 'When they need you they're great and when they don't they're horrid,' says Sarah Gauch, a freelancer in Cairo.

The permutations of moving from freelance status to a full-time staff position are various. Alma Guillermoprieto was a freelancer in Managua and San Salvador from 1978 to 1982, when she was hired by the *Washington Post* and assigned to Washington as a metro reporter. Julia Preston was a freelancer in Mexico City from 1976 to 1977 and El Salvador from 1981 to 1983, when she was hired by the *Boston Globe* to be its correspondent there. Peter Ford, a freelancer in Managua and Buenos Aires from 1984 to 1990, was hired by the *Christian Science Monitor* and sent to Jerusalem. The talented and lucky, after churning out considerable quantities of piecework for a particular organization, are hired because of a special need, such as fluency in Arabic or the ability to get good stories in dangerous places, and will be kept where they are. Or a freelancer may be admired for general reporting skills and given a domestic assignment (tempted, perhaps, by a hint of future foreign correspondence). Of all those in our survey who first went overseas as freelancers, 47 percent eventually gained jobs in the mainstream media, although not necessarily as foreign correspondents.

Working for the wire services, especially the Associated Press and Reuters, constitutes a major step up from freelancing, although working for United Press International is a special case. Recalling the 1950s, when he worked for UPI in Paris, London, and Geneva, Jonathan Randal commented, 'I left because of money. Yves Montand starred in a movie called *The Wages of Fear*. UPI was known as 'The Fear of Wages' in my day.' It was the only news organization that journalists regularly quit to become freelancers. Yet foreign correspondents speak fondly of it for giving them an opportunity, if not a living wage.

Being a correspondent for the wire services represents a trade-off. Reporters must work in relative anonymity, but they enjoy the possibility of having an entire career as a foreign correspondent, a prospect that has grown dimmer at other kinds of news operations. The careers of top AP reporters, for instance, can be made up of one interesting assignment after another. Mort Rosenblum moved from the New York foreign desk to Kinshasa, Zaire (1967–69), Lagos, Nigeria (1969–70), Singapore (1970–73), Buenos Aires (1973–76), and Paris. Harry Dunphy left the New York foreign desk for Beirut (1970–74), Cairo (1974–77), Moscow (1977–79), and Paris. William C. Mann moved from the New York foreign desk to Manila (1971), New Delhi (1971–74), New York (1974–76), Manila (1976–80), Copenhagen (1980–85), and Cairo.

Working for the wire services can also create the chance for considerable mobility among news organizations. From the wire services, foreign correspondents may transfer to such major regional newspapers as the *Boston Globe* and the *Chicago Tribune* or to Cox, Knight-Ridder, or other chains. The lure, in part, is the opportunity to write more interpretive pieces. Ethan Bronner, who reported from Israel for Reuters and later returned

there for the *Boston Globe*, said he admired the clean, precise prose of
Reuters writing, but believed more analysis was needed to adequately pene-
trate 'the layer upon layer of the Middle East story.'

The top of the hierarchy is the organization with the most 'serious'
approach to news. Seriousness to foreign correspondents is defined by the
amount of print space or broadcast time that is made available to them, an
organization's willingness to commit resources, and its willingness to cover
topics that are considered more important than interesting. Julia Preston,
the freelancer who went to the *Boston Globe*, moved up to the *Washington
Post*, covering the United Nations in New York, and then left for the Mexico
City bureau of the *New York Times*. Alma Guillermoprieto, the freelancer
who went to the *Washington Post*, later joined the *New Yorker*. The *Baltimore Sun* and *Miami Herald* lose correspondents to the *Los Angeles Times*,
the *Los Angeles Times* to the *Washington Post*, the *Washington Post* to the
New York Times. Freelancer David Rocks remarked to a table of journalists
in Prague in 1992, 'There are two types of foreign correspondents—us and
the *New York Times*.' Except that there are different levels of 'us,' and some
organizations, such as the *Wall Street Journal*, whose reporters produce
both hard-edged business news for inside the paper and lengthy cultural-
political features for page one, are outside the schema.

Does this suggest a '*New York Times* type' or other types? Our survey
included forty-four persons who were working for the *New York Times*,
thirty-six for the *Washington Post*, and twenty-one for the *Los Angeles
Times*. Those who have reached these levels are past or present foreign
correspondents, although they have not necessarily worked abroad for
their present employer. Catherine S. Manegold, for example, had been a
foreign correspondent for the *Philadelphia Inquirer*, then for *Newsweek*,
and is now in the Washington bureau of the *New York Times*. I will loosely
characterize an elite reporter as one who comes from a managerial or
professional family and has attended a highly selective university, usually
majoring in the humanities or liberal arts. (Journalism majors in the survey were 20 percent less likely to have fathers whose occupations fit in the
managerial or professional category.) On these criteria there are distinct
differences among the three top dailies, differences most pronounced in the
prestige of the universities their reporters attended, which suggest that
there is a relationship between journalists' backgrounds and their place on
the ladder (Table 1).

Journalists do leave the *New York Times* and other top-of-the-line organizations. In the steeply pyramidal world of the newsroom—where there can
be only one executive editor, one managing editor, one foreign news
editor—some seek comparable positions at other organizations. Clifford
May, for instance, who reported from Africa for the *New York Times*,
became a columnist and editor at the *Rocky Mountain News* in Denver.
Others want to pursue journalism beyond the confines of a daily. Pulitzer
Prize winners David Halberstam and David Shipler left the *Times* to write
books and long magazine articles.

But not all foreign correspondents are constantly seeking higher rungs
on the ladder. There can be considerable longevity, especially at the newsmagazines. Robin Knight joined *U.S. News & World Report* in 1968; Barry

TABLE 1. *Characteristics of Journalists at Three Major Newspapers, 1992*

Percent unless otherwise specified

Characteristic	New York Times	Washington Post	Los Angeles Times
Managerial or professional father	74	69	62
Attended highly selective college	82	69	57
Humanities or liberal arts major	89	89	55
Journalism major	7	8	32
Graduate degree	82	95	77
Humanities or liberal arts	74	56	31
Journalism	17	33	54
Number	44	36	21

SOURCE: Author's survey of journalists who are or have been foreign correspondents.

Hillenbrand and Ron Moreau have been overseas for *Time* and *Newsweek*, respectively, since 1972. There are even examples in television news. Bob Simon (CBS) and Keith Miller (NBC) have been abroad for the same employer for decades. Correspondents' patterns of movement among the networks are less discernible; personality and money play bigger roles in broadcast journalism than in the print media.

Because reporters move easily from one type of print journalism to another, there is not much variation in the profiles of newspaper, wire service, and newsmagazine writers. Jonathan Randal can move from UPI to *Time* to the *Washington Post* without changing a vital statistic. But there are notable differences between print and television journalists. (Only 2 percent of the correspondents surveyed worked exclusively for radio.)

Television correspondents abroad are less likely than their colleagues in the print media to come from managerial or professional backgrounds, less likely to have graduate degrees, and less likely to be women. They are also older and have been overseas longer. Forty-one is the mean age for newspaper and wire service reporters, forty-eight for those in television journalism. The TV correspondents average twelve years abroad compared to eight for newspapers and nine for the wire services.

But it is less who they are than what they do that separates the TV and print foreign correspondents (Table 2). The television correspondent is the consummate parachutist, an expert in crisis journalism, on call to jump into a country he or she is not familiar with, often during an armed conflict. When I visited Bob Simon in his Tel Aviv office in 1992, he had just finished writing a book about his capture by the Iraqis during the 1991 Gulf War. He seemed restless. I said, 'It's only been four months since the last crisis [Moscow, December].' He shrugged, 'Hey, we're talking news.' His book's dust jacket reads, 'Bob Simon, CBS News chief Middle Eastern correspondent, has covered wars in Vietnam, Lebanon, Israel, and Central America, as well as virtually every major news story of the last twenty-five years.'

TABLE 2. *Work Characteristics of Foreign Correspondents in Four Types of News Organizations, 1992*

Percent

Work characteristic	News-papers	Wire services	News-magazines	Television
Covers more than one country	79	60	66	93
Spends time away from home base	32	22	25	40
Involved in key stories about armed conflicts[a]	25	28	19	36
Able to conduct interviews in language of base country	42	54	46	21

SOURCE: Author's survey.

[a] Respondents were asked to list the three key events they covered at each post.

The culture of foreign correspondence categorizes journalists about equally as specialists—Asia hands, Africanists, and so forth—and generalists. For the generalists the lure of assignments in different corners of the world is perhaps the main attraction of their work. Robert Zelnick of ABC remembers that when he was a child, the other kids drew pictures on the blackboard, but he always drew maps. Mort Rosenblum of the Associated Press has been posted on four continents. Ray Moseley's career for UPI and the *Chicago Tribune* started in Rome in 1962 and has encompassed ten postings on three continents, including Nairobi, Cairo, and Moscow. A reporter who has had a particularly stressful assignment is likely next to be sent to a more joyful place: Harry Dunphy went from Moscow to Paris. Organizations that rotate their correspondents every three or four years work as if they were creating a crossword puzzle. Alvin Shuster kept a list of his reporters' wishes in the top drawer when he was foreign editor of the *Los Angeles Times*; a correspondent who wished for Warsaw rather than London was more likely to have a wish come true.

Still, a profile of foreign correspondents by region—which reporters are located in the Americas, Europe, Asia, Africa, the Middle East—does not show an equal distribution by demographic characteristic. Partly this is because, in 1992 at least, African-American journalists were more likely to be assigned to Africa—for example, Keith B. Richburg of the *Washington Post* was in Nairobi and Kenneth Noble of the *New York Times* was in Abidjan, Ivory Coast. Asian-American journalists were more likely to be in Asia: Teresa Watanabe, *Los Angeles Times*, was in Tokyo, and Lena H. Sun, *Washington Post*, in Beijing. Women have been more likely to gravitate to Central and South America. [. . .]

The correspondents who are specialists have three characteristics that make them statistically different from their more nomadic peers: they are more likely to be married to a person from the region, they have greater proficiency in the language of their posting, and they are more likely to have had a connection with the region in their youth.

One of the unique characteristics of foreign correspondents is the amount of time they have spent abroad with parents or in university programs or serving in the military or Peace Corps. This time is not greater for geographic specialists than it is for the generalists, but it has more often been spent on the continent to which they are ultimately posted. This is especially true of those who report from the Middle East and Africa. Those who become European specialists, however, are no more likely to have spent early years there than other foreign correspondents.

In the culture of foreign correspondence, news organizations have various schemes for arranging their workforces. [. . .]
 The system chosen in each case has as much to do with organizational maintenance, with how large enterprises try to keep their employees functioning as productively as possible, as with perceptions of how best to gather information abroad. The management of the *Los Angeles Times* may believe it could not retain high-caliber foreign correspondents if they were expected to spend most of their careers in Los Angeles, which is not a governmental or financial capital. The management at the *Philadelphia Inquirer* seems to prefer a rigid three-years-and-home policy, knowing it will lose talented reporters as a result but concluding that keeping some of its best and brightest is a good trade-off. Some policies may see foreign correspondence as a means of providing additional skills. 'I think being overseas gives you a little perspective on your own country,' said the *Wall Street Journal*'s Tony Horwitz, who returned from years in the Middle East to win a Pulitzer Prize for reporting on working conditions in minimum-wage America. Some smaller papers offer reporters an overseas tour mostly as a reward for good work. [. . .]

Susan Linnée, the AP bureau chief in Madrid, has said, 'There really isn't much difference between a good cop reporter and a big-time foreign correspondent.' She is right to the extent that many qualities desirable in foreign correspondence—tenacity, integrity, intellectual honesty, precise and graceful writing—are also important to good domestic reporting. And, of course, seasoned reporters of whatever background can eventually learn to deal with censorship, disinformation, corrupt officials, thuggery, anti-Americanism, dysentery, and other overseas hazards. For example, 'Never wash your car,' says John Pomfret, who is in Bosnia for the *Washington Post*; 'If someone plants a bomb under it, you'll see fingerprints.' Other useful advice: 'Finding a good local driver is your key decision, since he'll know how to keep himself out of danger' (Martin Fletcher, NBC), and 'In a military convoy, never ride in the lead or the trailing vehicle, as they are the first targets in an ambush' (Oakland Ross, *Toronto Globe and Mail*). Nevertheless, foreign correspondents do need some special qualities and do face some special problems. [. . .]
 Foreign correspondents carry with them a good deal of baggage other than their résumés and backgrounds that ultimately influences where they want to go and what they want to explore. There is a culturally transmitted romantic tradition to which the antique word 'swashbuckling' is sometimes attached: Eric Sevareid 'running just one step ahead of the Nazis as

France fell to the Wehrmacht, bailing out somewhere over the Burma Road into a jungle peopled with headhunters,' as Russell Baker recalled. (Consumers may share these trench-coated expectations.) 'There is too an appealing camaraderie in war,' remembers Stanley Karnow.

> Show up in Tel Aviv or Srinagar during a crisis and you encounter colleagues who reach back to Kabul or Kinshasa. American, British, French, Russian—you belong to an exclusive international fraternity. The mood is familiar, perhaps a bit boisterous, as you catch up over drinks and dinner, or trade rumors and sources. Above all, war is rejuvenating, and journalism is the only métier in which you can remain an eternal adolescent—if you survive.

New York Times correspondent John F. Burns said in Sarajevo: 'It seems so indecent to say we are having the most tremendous amount of fun in the midst of all this misery. It's not fun, but it's an experience I would not want to miss.'

From my first interviews with foreign correspondents in Paris in 1983, they talked of dealing with danger, often of being scared, sometimes of exhilaration. 'You get hooked on your own adrenalin,' said E. J. Dionne in Rome in 1985, thinking about Beirut. Peter Arnett wrote in his memoirs, 'What I had learned to love [was] the thrill of covering wars, for which there was no substitute.' I met few who loved war. I did meet a lot of fatalists. When the Committee to Protect Journalists sought to codify safety information for reporters on their way to the former Yugoslavia in 1993, its executive director, Anne Nelson, noted, 'We were surprised to learn how little dialogue existed on a formal basis about safety measures, both among journalists and between journalists and their news organizations.' 'There's a kind of hubris among reporters,' Geraldine Brooks said. 'They think they're bulletproof.' When they learn they are not, they think they are lucky or unlucky. 'The 9 mm bullet bored a hole through the humerus bone in my left shoulder—without breaking it—smashed a rib in my back, then ricocheted harmlessly toward my breastbone—without breaking it—rather than toward my heart or lungs. Everything the bullet did to my body, nature is going to undo.' So wrote the *Washington Post*'s Paul Taylor from South Africa.

This is a variation of the personality type I had found in journalists when I first studied Washington reporters. Then I wrote, 'The attraction of reporters to excitement biases news gathering in favor of certain institutions and certain types of newsmakers.' There are similar attractions abroad. National Public Radio's Noah Adams, assigned to cover the fall of communism in Romania, quoted a fellow reporter as saying, 'When the shooting stops it's time to go, otherwise you'll have to stay around and do the economic stories.'

The importance of foreign correspondents expands proportionately with the decrease in their numbers. Although the major newspapers tended to protect their foreign bureaus during the retrenchment of the past decade, the three broadcast networks cut their ranks in half, the number of *Time*'s foreign correspondents decreased by a third, and United Press International became a shadow of itself. The total shrank to fewer than

1,500 reporting full time for the U.S. media, and many of them worked for business and other specialized publications. In the culture of foreign correspondence, Tom Mathews of *Newsweek* told me, 'News passes through a narrow needle.'

19

Foreign Correspondents: A Team, B Team

Mark Pedelty

THIS EXTRACT IS from Mark Pedelty's book *War Stories*; more precisely his research in El Salvador in 1990–2, just after the main civil war of the 1980s. With the near cessation of killings, most of the staff correspondents of major United States media had been withdrawn. Pedelty is critical of the remaining 'A Team' of 13 staff correspondents working for major US media; this 'A Team', he says, are too involved with their own careers, their home news desks, and elite news sources in El Salvador. Pedelty clearly prefers the much larger 'B Team' of another 67 journalists, who are closer to El Salvador's suffering people.

Pedelty's A/B Teams classification is very simple and too US-centric. Half of the 67 'B Team' journalists are local El Salvador nationals, but his B team also includes correspondents of major European and Latin American media. However, this account of between-war-and-peace reporting is important, not least because a substantial slice of all foreign correspondence falls into this loose category.

Stringers harbor a great deal of animosity towards staff correspondents, whom they call the *A Team*. Their complaints are as follows: 1) staff correspondents are both physically and culturally removed from Salvadoran society, 2) *A Team* correspondents exploit stringers' knowledge and labor without offering adequate compensation and 3) staff correspondents rely much too heavily upon elite, propagandistic sources—especially U.S. State Department officials—and are, in turn, treated preferentially by them. While such complaints often take the form of gossip—'dirt' concerning *A Team* reporters—they cannot be completely dismissed as products of professional jealousy. These tensions indicate the importance of the hierarchical stringer/staff system, an issue almost completely ignored by academic researchers despite the fact that it plays a fundamental role in structuring the activities of foreign correspondents and influences the news they write. The *A Team/B Team* structure is not only a question of professional status, but a political, economic, cultural, and ideological divide as

Source: Mark Pedelty, *War Stories: The Culture of Foreign Correspondents* (New York and London: Routledge, 1995), 69–78, 80–1.

well. Although the ratio of staff to stringers shifted over time, the dichotomous structure continued to be a fundamental part of SPECA[1] life until the very end of the war.

As is true of U.S. foreign correspondence in general, the *A Team/B Team* conflict was heavily influenced by the U.S. State Department. For SPECA reporters, the State Department is represented in the form of 'The Embassy.' Journalists speak of the U.S. mission, 'The Embassy,' as if there were no others in El Salvador. It is by far the single most important source of news for the U.S. press, and has a significant influence on the reporting of other nations' journalists as well.

SPECA journalists speak of The Embassy continually, many of them critical and resentful of its inevitable influence. Troy, an *A Team* journalist, said the following:

> Oh yeah, it is important in every way you can imagine. I can't think of another country, with the possible exception of Haiti, where the U.S. Embassy is anywhere near as important to a reporter . . . I did a long interview with the Ambassador here, who compared himself with Henry Cabot Lodge in Vietnam as being this kind of guy who practically ran everything. I asked him what it was like to run everything. You would think that most diplomats would demur or say something to the contrary. [Ambassador] Walker, quite to the contrary, affirmed it, explaining how he was a guy who could pull a lot of strings here.

As the mouthpiece for U.S. policy, The Embassy is involved in almost every issue SPECA journalists cover.

Most editors demand that news stories include the perspectives, or at least the quoted statements, of official U.S. government sources. As a result of these pressures, intimate access to The Embassy is crucial to most SPECA journalists. Those who are able to get exclusive, quotable interviews with decision-making embassy staff have an advantage over their colleagues who must rely on the oblique, though ubiquitous, press hand-outs and infrequent embassy press conferences.

Cognizant of its worth to the SPECA community, The Embassy only provides interviews to certain reporters, namely those who can be trusted to use the information in a safe and sanctioned manner. Bob, a stringer who spent over seven years in El Salvador, explains:

> You get a certain access when you are a staff reporter for a major U.S. paper that you don't get as a freelancer or someone who works for less prestigious papers . . . Have you heard of the *A Team* and the *B Team*? It's very true. The Embassy will only invite certain people. The big boys will go to the little, intimate briefings. [U.S. Ambassador] Walker only does briefings with people that aren't going to disagree with him that much. They'll get more disagreements if [Ronald] or I are there. It's a question of them doing a triage with the most important papers they are trying to affect and those reporters with whom they get along best. It

---

1 [Salvadoran Foreign Press Association.—ed.].

tends to work out that they get along better with those people because their minds are in the same place.

I interviewed two USIS press representatives, both of whom affirmed Bob's contention. [. . .]

I interviewed another State Department official, an amicable bureaucrat who said he earned a 'grad level education in dealing with the press' while working in Panama during the 1989 U.S. invasion. He expressed a favorable view of staff correspondents:

> They figure to be around a lot longer. They are less likely to burn you. They see people we can't and provide us with information. It is an exchange, a nice working relationship.

In other words, there is a coincidence of interests between The Embassy and the *A Team*. Given access to the valuable quotes of embassy decision-makers, *A Team* correspondents return the favor by allowing the State Department inordinate power to shape the news discourse.

This professional 'exchange' often develops into personal friendship. Pati, a Canadian reporter, explains that 'it is impossible to isolate yourself and not identify with the people who you quote on a regular basis.' Indeed, most USIS officials count several staff correspondents among their best friends, a natural outcome of their mutual 'working relationship.'

USIS officials have a very different attitude towards stringers. 'They are generally not as good,' said one. 'They are less prepared. They are trying to sell a story, which is more dangerous.' The main 'danger' he and his agency fear is that stringers will deal with State Department information in a critical, or at least idiosyncratic fashion. As information managers, they must carefully weigh the potential risks and benefits of providing access to journalists. For them the staffer/stringer dichotomy provides a convenient and fairly accurate guide for determining who can and cannot be trusted to represent State knowledge in sanctioned form. As will become clear in the following descriptions of each team, The Embassy's filtering process imbued the already contentious staffer/stringer structure with even greater cultural meaning.

A Team Most SPECA staff journalists received their degrees from prestigious universities in the eastern United States or Britain, including Harvard, Cornell, Oxford, and Cambridge. Most of the *A Team*'s editors and sources were educated at similar institutions. [El Salvador's] President Christiani, for example, attended Harvard. Conversely, most stringers earned their degrees at public universities.

The staff members identify themselves quite closely with their institutions. When asked to describe her past, Nell explained that she had attended 'private schools in New England' before enrolling at a 'good Ivy League university' and then, in fulfillment of her career plans, received a position at a 'very prominent, large newspaper.' Through her association with these 'good' and 'prominent' institutions, Nell has gained a greater sense of self worth, professional prestige, and inclusion in an elite clique. *A Team* journalists like Nell are cognizant, and sometimes even boastful of their institutional role in informing and influencing policy makers. Nell conceived of her work as an attempt to 'bring these problems to life for an affluent, educated and possibly policy-making audience'.

The *A Team* maintain constant contact with their editors and associate themselves closely with them (though a certain level of tension always exists between author and editor). Katherine, a staff correspondent, explains her relationship with her editors:

> Having been an editor, I think you are more inclined to write the story the way you think they are going to use it than trying to confront them, maybe . . . You get along better with them if you do that. It is self-defeating to fight them.

A Team journalists see editors as fellow professionals and ultimately part of the same team. Bob explained:

> Many journalists, if they tend to want to get ahead, basically will play along with the prejudices of their editors. Bit by bit they will learn to become like their editors. And, eventually, they will become their editors. The system rebuilds, re-cements, and re-propagates itself.

While stringers prefer to project an air of independence, the staff correspondents' professional identities are largely constructed in relation to their news institutions. Correspondents employed by the *New York Times*, for example, rarely refer to themselves as generic 'journalists' or 'foreign correspondents.' Instead, a '*New York Times* correspondent' will almost always refer to herself as just that. This tendency is part of what other journalists call 'the *New York Times* disease.'

The '*New York Times* disease' also manifests itself in a sort of institutional solipsism. The *New York Times*' reporters enjoy quoting the behind-the-scenes maxim: 'If the *Times* isn't there, it isn't news.' This statement has a double meaning. On the surface it promotes the idea that the *New York Times* will cover all newsworthy events. Therefore, if something is not covered it is because the issue or event itself lacks intrinsic news value. That is not how the *New York Times* reporters use the phrase, however. For them, 'If the *Times* isn't there, it isn't news,' is a boastful and self-conscious realization that they, as an institution, play an instrumental role in defining the national, and sometimes international, news agenda. In a world of infinite issues and events, the *New York Times*' very presence often defines what is or isn't news. One reporter for the *New York Times* put it bluntly: 'The *Times* has the attitude that if we weren't there, it didn't happen.'

Rosenblum cites the example of the *New York Times*' R. W. Apple Jr., whose coverage of the war in Chad in the late 1960s caused the rest of the mainstream U.S. press to 'catch up' on events there as well. The European and African press had been writing about the Chadian conflict for several years, but the United States did not consider it a newsworthy story until Apple wrote of the war while touring Africa. In typical *Times* style, Apple boasted, 'I discovered a war.'

The *New York Times'* correspondents exhibited similar self-referential and agenda-setting tendencies in their coverage of the Salvadoran War. A parachuter for the *New York Times* interviewed FMLN[2] Commander Jauquin Villalobos near the end of the war, portraying Villalobos' rather typical statements as a 'striking departure' from the 'Marxist rhetoric' of the past. Reporters more familiar with El Salvador were outraged. They knew Villalobos had been making such statements for several years (and that the FMLN was never simply a 'Marxist' institution). Three days later another *New York Times* reporter contextualized Villalobos' statements in the 'striking departure' frame as well. I asked why and he replied:

> There is a very clear reason. It had been on the front page of the *New York Times* two or three days earlier . . . [Jauquin Villalobos] could have been saying it for five years, but until it is in the *New York Times*, nobody believes it. The *Times* makes a story . . . Christiani even said that the only thing new [about Villalobos' statement] is that it appeared in the *New York Times*. He said that at a press conference. Which is true. The *Times'* editors are funny. They take the attitude, 'Well, we don't necessarily have to be first. The important thing is that when we have it, then it is important.'

In other words, the ideological shift may have not been a recent, nor even major change, but once printed in the *New York Times* it became reality. Because the first *Times* correspondent had written in the 'striking departure' frame, the second felt an obligation to do likewise. It had become *Times*-sanctioned truth.

The '*New York Times* disease,' a virulent hubris more common than its label implies, manifests itself in additional ways. According to the stringers, staff correspondents 'feel like they are purely objective, sort of above it all.' They are 'above it all,' literally. Most of them live in the Escalon, a wealthy residential and shopping district which lies along the raised shelf leading up to Volcan San Salvador. The place is closer to Miami than the slums of San Salvador.

Their geographic isolation is matched by even greater social distance. The *A Team* members rarely mix with middle and lower class Salvadorans. 'Those people who make it through the hoops and become staff,' explained a stringer, 'tend to be people who also get along better with other conservative people in the Salvadoran establishment.' As usual, Paul put it more bluntly:

> They are married into the class system . . . They live in scrumptious mansions just like the [U.S.] AID people, among the oligarchy. They have no contact with other classes, except their maids.

This may be overstated. Not all staff journalists live in 'scrumptious mansions.' Furthermore, the *A Team*'s frenetic parachuting schedule is rarely as pleasant as the stringers contend. 'I'm sick of living in hotels,' complained Katherine. 'It is hard on your health. I'm gaining weight.'

Nevertheless, stringers perceive of *A Team* life as culturally distant and

---

2 [Farabundo Martí National Liberation Front. —ed.].

materially ideal. In their indignation, SPECA stringers not only demonstrate a strong disdain for *A Team* behavior, however, they also implicitly make a claim towards greater involvement with, and understanding of, the Salvadoran masses.

B Team   Staff and stringers are usually drawn to El Salvador for different reasons. Bob explains:

> Freelancers (stringers) tend to be in a country they like. They are interested in it and what is going on, whereas a staff correspondent may be put here when he wants to go to Paris. El Salvador is a stepping-stone for where he wants to go later in life.

Indeed, the two highest profile *A Team* correspondents were constantly complaining about their assignment.

Conversely, stringers choose their posts themselves (although there must be a market for their work). Thus, they 'tend to be in a country they like.' Several SPECA stringers were first drawn to El Salvador for non-journalistic reasons, such as human rights work, development, or tourism. Marla's first exposure to Central America came in college, where she met several Nicaraguans. A trip to Central America sparked an interest for Marla which 'continued through to today.' 'You have to go where your personal *ganas* [desire] is,' said Marla; 'I think that ultimately it makes more sense to cover the story that you find most engaging, as opposed to a career decision.' Others left positions at small market domestic newspapers in order to work internationally.

The stringers' interest in and dedication to Central America is so pervasive that many have lingered well beyond news editors' interest in the story. Cary is one of these. According to a housemate, every month for the last several years Cary has threatened to leave El Salvador for a more marketable story. Nevertheless, he remains with his community of Salvadoran friends and SPECA colleagues. [. . .]

[. . .] While *A Team* journalists mainly hang out with local and foreign elites, the stringers tend to socialize with a slightly more diverse group including church workers, human rights activists, members of international solidarity groups, and a few local intellectuals. These groups, like the stringers themselves, tend to have liberal to left political views.

While most of the stringers come to the country with liberal views, others gravitate toward those perspectives after dealing with the Salvadoran army and government. Tracy, a fixer, claimed that Cal, a wire service reporter, was more conservative than she because he had 'only been in the country for a year.' According to this popularly held view, the more time reporters spend in El Salvador the more liberal their political perspectives generally become. Michael, an *A Team* magazine correspondent, explained:

> Because stringers get to know a place so well they tend to become a little bit more liberal. A correspondent flies in and he's much more detached. I tend to have a much more—not conservative—but detached attitude.

> He [the stringer] sees all the abuse and so isn't so detached . . . The
> service stringer's sell is familiarity. Complete familiarity can lead to
> pretty strong emotions towards the story. The [staff] correspondent flits
> in and out.

In sum, a combination of factors—motivation, experience, and social
environment—conspires to provide stringers with a more liberal outlook
than their higher-status colleagues.

Although the stringers' personal politics tend to be more liberal, however, their news reports do not generally contain liberal biases. Stringers
must conform to the political and editorial wills of their clients. Bureaucratic exigencies and restrictive journalistic conventions generally prevail
over individual politics. For this reason, they feel much more freedom
when writing occasional pieces for alternative press organizations such as
the *Village Voice, The Nation, The Progressive* and other institutions whose
editorial politics mesh much more closely with their own. Unfortunately,
these institutions cannot afford to pay very well and constitute a very small
part of the overall news market.

Sometimes the difference between the two teams is not just *how*, but
even *what* they see. An FMLN soldier flagged down a press vehicle during
one pack outing. He exhorted the journalists—one staff correspondent and
several stringers—to take an injured child to the hospital. The stringers
were later surprised when the staffer wrote: '[A] mother carried her nine-
year-old daughter in her arms, pleading with passing cars for a ride to a
medical clinic.' He was evidently unwilling to present an image editors
might construe as favorable to the FMLN. He had to construct a more
suitable reality.

Reporters who wish to rise in the press hierarchy must learn that sort of
editorial discipline. The stringers are, for the most part, young reporters
who will either leave the profession, gain one of the relatively few, under-
paid positions in the alternative press, or become staffers themselves.
Unfortunately, it is difficult for a stringer to become staff. 'Having been a
stringer actually hurts you,' explained Adriana, 'because you haven't been
under the editor's constant eye.'

For reporters, 'the editor's constant eye' forms an inescapable center.
Editors exercise control over their charges' postings, their writings, public
exposure, and career-chances. For these and other reasons, editors can
depend on staffers to perform their duties with relative compliance.
Stringers, however, develop their craft slightly outside the boundaries of
any single institution's gaze or disciplinary regime. This makes them 'dangerous' and 'subjective,' two words often applied to stringers by the U.S.
and Canadian editors I interviewed.

Nevertheless, it is occasionally possible for stringers to shed their stigmatized status and become staff correspondents. However, most stringers
must greatly modify their writings, if not their attitudes, before making this
upward leap. Capitalist enterprises, corporate media included, must make a
profit to survive. [. . .]

As a result of these pressures, stringers must usually move right to move
up. Therefore, most stringers-turned-staff have been accused by other

stringers of having modified their reporting in order to advance, of 'selling out.' Four ex-stringers were most often cited as examples, including two stringers-turned-staff for the *New York Times*, one *Washington Post* correspondent and a *Miami Herald* correspondent. 'They began blaming the FMLN for everything,' complained one of the stringers left behind, perhaps an unfair characterization, although their reporting certainly became more conservative after they made the transition from stringer to staff.

Stringers who submit reports to alternative press are particularly stigmatized by corporate media, even though it comprises a small part of their overall news output. Ronald, an intense and intelligent young stringer who writes regularly for alternative media, was rejected for a staff job at a U.S. daily for this very reason. The offending editor told Ronald he greatly respected his work, but that it was too 'left-wing.' 'It is apparent that if performers are concerned with maintaining a line,' argues Goffman, 'they will select as teammates those who can be trusted to perform properly'. The *A Team* and their bosses find Ronald's performance anything but proper.

The *A Team* correspondents vehemently disagree with the *B Team*'s contention that ideological criteria are used in the staff hiring process. Troy explained:

Papers don't choose to send people here based on ideological disposition. I was never asked about politics. I was not involved in Latin American politics. I didn't speak Spanish. I considered myself innocent. Nobody could accuse me of anything.

This is probably true. The gatekeepers have little need to ask people like Troy about their politics. Politically moderate and compliant, Troy fits the needs of his news institution quite well. The hiring system acts as an ideological thermostat, allowing consenting and compliant reporters like Troy to enter while keeping dissenters like Ronald standing outside the company gates. In short, media corporations regulate their workforce, as must any successful corporation or governmental bureaucracy. [. . .]

Despite their mutual antagonism, *A* and *B Team* journalists are heavily interdependent. A great deal of international news is produced via their collaborative efforts. Most staff journalists rely heavily upon stringers for knowledge of ongoing events and to make contacts among sectors not readily accessible to their parachuting practice. 'I am a correspondent,' explained Michael, 'but I rely on the stringer that lives here. He lives and breathes it.'

The stringers provide their labor and knowledge to staffers in exchange for money, institutional resources (an office and secretary), and an opportunity to reach wider audiences. Paul, a veteran photographer, equated these relationships to international oil dependencies. Like oil-bearing, Third World nations, stringers need cash. Like First World industrial powers, staff correspondents need the reporting 'resources' stringers possess: contacts, knowledge, and reporting skills.

Cary aids a parachuting staffer. Whenever his staff patron flies in, Cary provides him with an update, arranges necessary contacts among nongovernmental sectors (i.e., the FMLN or popular organizations) and provides logistical aid. Like most stringers, Cary feels inadequately compensated for his hard work and expertise.

Cary occasionally publishes his own articles in his staff patron's newspaper. He feels exploited in this role as well. As evidence, Cary displayed his check stubs. Most of the payments ranged between $25 and $80 per story. Cary held up one $60 stub, total recompense for an article that took several days of work. Such meager compensation is the norm. Stringers receive an average of $150.00 for each 900 word report. This is practically nothing when compared to a staff correspondent's salary, which is usually well over $50,000 a year. Distance and dispassion certainly have their rewards.

20

The Hollywood TV Producer

Muriel G. Cantor

MURIEL CANTOR'S CLASSIC account of *The Hollywood TV Producer* is based on interviews with 80 producers. Of these, 59 were producing 'live action filmed dramas' currently showing in network prime time during 1967–8. Only one producer was a woman. These men were in charge of most of the high-rated non-comedy series of that year. The median producer was aged 42 and was making an annual batch of 26 one-hour series episodes. Cantor identifies the 'old-line producers', the 'writer-producers', and the (mostly younger) 'film makers'. However, all of these individuals are basically writer-producers, because the producer controls the series via the scripts.

Once again there is a steep hierarchy. The TV series producer is a highly paid, senior person, in a high-pressure and hard-slogging job. Above him are the top executives of the Hollywood production company and the relevant network executives. Far below him in vertical Hollywood are thousands of under-employed people, aspiring to get work on even one episode of a popular TV series.

The interviews clearly showed that certain producers shared a common view of the audience and a pattern of relating to the networks and their fellow craft workers. An analysis of the material reveals three types of producers. These types are heuristic models, not descriptions of actual producers, although in each group there are typical cases. The first group, the film makers, are usually the younger producers who have little experience in other media. Most of these men considered series film making a training experience that would enable them to make more artistic and personal films in the future. Fame more than money seemed to be the goal, but the two are obviously related. Their training was more likely than the other two groups to be in the formal schools of communication and in film making rather than in writing, the theater, or pretelevision radio and the movies. The next group, the writers-producers, had been free-lance writers before they went into production. Unlike the film makers, their aspirations

Source: Muriel G. Cantor, *The Hollywood TV Producer* (New York: Basic Books, 1971), 74–85, 92–7, 100, 106–10, 131–5, 137–8.

or ambitions are connected with television rather than with theater films. They would like to make more 'meaningful' television films, that is, films with social messages. Therefore, they were more concerned with story content and less interested in technical aspects of film making. The third type, the old-line producers, had worked in several media, but primarily had been in movie production or radio before coming to television. Their main goal seemed to be maintaining financial success in any entertainment field. They are able to move easily from one medium to another, depending on the financial gains and the popularity of the medium with the public. [. . .]

[. . .] The interviews show that most producers, regardless of type or age, had been writers early in their careers. If someone were to ask what would be the best route to becoming a producer, the simplest answer would be that somehow the aspirant producer should try to write a script. The realities of the steps leading to the occupation are more complex than simply trying to write a script and selling it. However, in answer to the question 'How did you get started in the industry?' almost all mentioned script writing at some time in their careers. The role of producer is complicated and as such demands individuals who possess a variety of skills and knowledge that are learned by first filling other roles (usually assistant producer or assistant to the producer). Therefore, while it is not a formalized apprenticeship and often not a direct route, a training period is necessary before one can 'produce.' [. . .]

The Film Maker for the most part had grown up professionally with television films; their work experiences and even their education was connected with communications, often film making. Most of those closely fitting the model had college training in a relevant field, such as theater arts, television communications, journalism, or English with emphasis on writing. Those who had no such training were either business majors or had major work in a preprofessional program. The group had several distinctive characteristics: all had completed two or more years of college; most worked for a large, bureaucratically organized studio that rotated producers from show to show; all had had no experience in live television and began their careers either as a copywriter in advertising or as a contract writer for a studio making movies and television films. [. . .]

[. . .] The respondents in this group, almost without exception, started by writing free-lance scripts or short stories. They spent much of their time in the beginning either working in the mailrooms or for the publicity departments in some clerical capacity before being noticed by someone and moved up the hierarchy. Their spare time was spent writing more scripts, and this writing effort was shown to directors or others in the studio in the hope that their scripts would be produced. Occasionally, this did happen, but it was more likely that, because of their presence on the scene and their ability to write, they were moved up the production ladder within the organization.

How mailboys, messengers, and the like are recruited is not known. It may be necessary to know someone (only several admitted to this), or it may be that recruitment for such highly prized jobs is based on recommendations from the local schools. Most of the film makers were educated in the Los Angeles area. Both the University of California, Los Angeles, and the University of Southern California have excellent departments in film making and electronic communications, and men from the industry teach students and sometimes recruit and sponsor favorites.

Most of the *Writers-Producers* had their work experience in television and related communications, but they differed from the film makers in several ways. Because many had started their working careers shortly after World War II, several had had experience in 'live' television and radio before television films were being produced in Hollywood. Many of them started as script writers under contract in the studios, which at that time were concentrating on feature-film production. In addition, their career patterns varied: they were more apt to have had both failures and, of course, more successes than the film makers. They did not show the same occupational stability in either the kinds of jobs held or the length of time under contract to a particular studio or to a production. In fact, these men seemed closer to the prototype of the producer that is generally accepted around the studios and in the press. They were not only less stable in jobholding but were often unemployed; thus they often described their work experience as 'feast or famine.' Upon questioning, their 'feast-or-famine' declaration seemed to stretch the facts considerably; when the men in this group were without producing contracts, they were able to do free-lance writing or possibly directing and consequently were rarely without income. This was true in the past, but as film-making opportunities 'dry' up, the writer-producer may be the least likely to survive the 'new Hollywood.' Thus, their lives (and incomes) were not as orderly as the film makers under long-term contracts. However, one compensation for such job instability was much higher income when working as producers.

Members of this group were less apt to be trained in academic programs in the Los Angeles area, although several were. However, they did have training related to their work, but this training was more likely to be in advertising, journalism, or the theater. The schools attended ranged from Ivy League institutions to commuter colleges of large metropolises. It should be stressed that their education usually was not in film, radio, or television. When they did work in communications, they were usually writers in either Hollywood or New York in the early days of television. [. . .]

This group of producers were satisfied with television work, although they had the most problems in producing freely and therefore the most role conflict. The reason given most often for continuing to produce series was the financial rewards. Those who were just salaried (all but three, who as independent producers still worked on the line) made extremely high salaries, over $50,000 a year. Besides the financial rewards, they apparently liked the fast-moving pace of television and took pride in their ability to make the decisions that their jobs required of them. [. . .]

While the overall work experience of the *Old-line Producers* differed markedly from the others, most also had been writers at the beginning of or during their careers. Their writing experience had often been in several media and was not part of their immediately previous occupation. Many of them had been in production for a number of years and, although they had once been writers, it was not an occupation with which they usually identified. Several had started as journalists, a few had been playwrights and worked as screen writers, and a number had written for 'live' television in New York. For this group the two main paths into television were from network radio and Hollywood film production; those who had started with radio were more likely to have worked in 'live' television, while those who had been with the movies usually went into television when it moved to Hollywood. However, several of the former movie people had experience in 'live' television in New York as well in the early 1950's, because they had been unable to find work in Hollywood when movie production was low.

Fewer of this group had some college education; of those who had attended college, most had majored in fields of studies that were unrelated to their occupations or career. Two of these producers were trained in the law, one in engineering, and the others were former teachers or had general business or liberal-arts backgrounds. Of those who were trained in related fields, just one had training in the communication field (radio); the rest were English, advertising or journalism majors.

Many of this group had colorful careers or job histories. One producer, for example, had been a radio comedy writer for many of the notable comedians in the 1930's. He went from local radio performing to network writing, then to 'live' television in New York and to films in Hollywood. At the present time he is the producer of a successful show. He said he was responsible for the first filmed series in the early 1950's. [. . .]

Others, of course, did not have as colorful or as successful former careers, but there was no question of current success because all of them had one or more series on the air for more than one season. In addition, this group included the majority of originators of ideas for new series. They were responsible for over twenty series ideas that were made into pilots and sold for series production. An accurate number of pilots made that did not becomes series (that is, were shelved) could not be obtained. However, each producer who sold one or more series did recall making at least one pilot that did not sell. These men frequently worked on the line with the series that they created. Sometimes, however, the production company of the network removed them from producing their own series, but all at the time of interviewing had been on the line some of the time during the season.

In this group four granted interviews although they had either returned to a former occupational role (in two cases, writer and story editor) or were no longer with the show. It is of interest that the group also seemed to have more recollections of periods when work was impossible to get. Several recalled the lean days in Hollywood in the early 1950's when movie production was at a low ebb and television was not yet in full swing. At that time several moved to New York to 'try their luck' with 'live' television. Several also mentioned how difficult it was to find other assignments as producers when a series they had in production was not renewed. During such times they would usually turn to free-lance writing, but several preferred to wait so they would be available for production and story development when a production company wanted their services. One producer was unemployed for a year after producing three series that had remained on the air for a number of years. (The last series with which he had been associated was a critical success but a failure in the ratings, the type of failure, according to him, that makes it difficult to find new assignments.)

The respondents were asked to state their present income and also their highest and lowest incomes for the past five years. This group reported the greatest variation ranging from no income for one year to over $100,000 for one year. [. . .]

Role Partners: Writers, Directors and Actors

[. . .] [M]ost of the producers started their careers as free-lance script writers, contract writers, or story editors. Forty-eight of the fifty-nine first interviewed still considered themselves writers or 'hyphenates' (writers-producers), and, as such, were members of the Writers Guild of America West. The most important 'other' to the producer probably is the free-lance writer, not only because producers basically identify with writers as an occupational group, but also because the two occupational roles are by necessity mutually dependent.

The producer of a series on the air for a full season needs at least twenty-six scripts from writers unless he or his story editor are themselves able to write a script or two. More than twenty-six scripts are actually needed even if the series is on the air for just twenty-six episodes; several extra scripts are required for emergency contingencies. There have been cases where the network or advertiser who has final script approval would not permit filming of a particular script. [. . .]

Because so many scripts are needed, most producers were continually concerned with stories, story ideas, and script development for almost the entire season. A few producers were able to line up scripts early and finished that part of the work sooner. One producer did his own writing. However, usually producers were concerned with some stage of script development until the end of the season.

The first problem for a producer of a new series or even a continuing series is to find those writers able to do the exact kind of scripts necessary for that particular series. The scripts have to adhere to the story theme of the series. Obtaining story consistency is a major concern of most on-the-line producers and is considered their primary responsibility. Several producers or production offices give writers descriptive brochures or statements of the series' basic concept and philosophy before they start writing. If the series has been on the air for a few years, the producers may use writers who have already written scripts for the series. [. . .]

The work arrangements between the producers and the writers follow certain formalized (rational) rules, which are in the contract adopted by the Writers Guild and Motion Picture and Television Producers Association. Although most producers are members of the Writers Guild, while playing the role of producer they represent the Motion Picture and Television Producers Association and therefore must follow their rules. The contract was adopted after a writers' strike in 1960. Presently, the collective-bargaining and negotiation procedures protect the Guild members and established writers. These procedures make it difficult for those trying to get started as writers; thus, finding new writers is not easy under the present legal structure and Guild rules. It is rare indeed at this time for a writer to do a script on speculation and expect to sell it, though this was rather common during the early days of television. The practice is discouraged today, and, if an entire script is submitted for reading without a contract, the writer is asked to sign a waiver in case the same idea is already in production or in a story-presentation stage. It is much more common to have writers near at hand begin to write scripts under the guidance of someone in the studios. This accounts for the 'discovery' of writers in mailrooms and publicity departments explained earlier. [. . .]

Whether the producer tells the writer that he wants a story about a certain topic or the writer suggests the idea, the producer's office is the place where most stories originate. The story conference seems to be institutionalized in the industry. The producer, the writer, the story editor (if there is one), and an assistant producer meet to discuss the story outline or presentation. After the first draft of the script, therefore, it is rarely the effort of one man; it is usually the work of a 'committee.' The term 'committee' as used in the industry is an euphemism to mean an effort by a group of people, rather than the creative effort of one man. By the time the script is mimeographed and ready for distribution to the network censorship office, the director, and others with a stake in the production, it might no longer resemble the script the writer originally submitted. Rewrites are commonly done by the producer or the story editor (or both) to represent the desires of the producer, of the production company to whom the producer is directly responsible, or of the network. [. . .]

[. . .] Some producers stated that they never rewrote. Others thought that, along with selecting writers, it was most important that they not only rewrite when necessary, but that they change every script to fit the series. In fact, several insisted that they rewrote at least 50 percent of all the scripts but took credit just 2 to 4 percent of the time. As one producer noted:

> There are very few scripts that come into a television office that are shootable the way they stand. There are only a handful of writers in this town that deliver scripts which are shootable in the first draft. This is an extremely difficult business, and you have to shoot a show in six days, and on budget. You have forty-eight minutes of film, certainly half a feature and you know how long it takes to shoot the average feature film, and we do it in six days. Obviously, something has to give. You have to be able to tailor scripts to what you can afford, produce, and also you have problems with stars. This show has been going on for——years, and the characters of the people are set. New writers coming cannot always catch the flavor and *somebody has to catch that flavor* or the show does not go on and that's my function. Many times when we are shooting on the very next day, I have been up 'til three o'clock in the morning to finish the pages we are going to shoot the following morning. [. . .]

[. . .] A director is hired to direct and does so usually with minimal interference. If the producer-director wants to direct an episode (and several did throughout the season), he is the only director and responsible for the entire directing job. There is nothing comparable to rewriting because there is no chance to redirect the film. There could be artistic and personal quarrels over direction, of course, and these possibly did occur, although no such cases were reported. However, directing a television episode is not considered as 'artistic' as feature-film directing, and the freedom of the director is limited by the brief time spent in production and the general structure that has developed. A director is usually brought in a week or so before filming begins. Along with the producer, he helps select actors for supporting roles. He has the final scripts to 'prepare' for shooting. Sets, costumes, and music must be selected. Subsidiary personnel, who do these jobs week after week, assist the director. The director with the producer has a 'say' in such matters, but the producer is the final arbiter. According to some of the subsidiary people around the studios, the producer's tastes are considered first when making certain selections.

In motion-picture film production the director has the right to the first 'cut,' in accordance with an agreement between the Directors Guild and the Motion Picture and Television Producers Association. The right to edit his film is important to the director because he can choose scenes to keep or cut, a prerogative highly prized because the sequencing and editing of a film constitute much of the creativity of film making. The same contract, of course, holds for television film making, but because of time limits and economic considerations, few directors take advantage of this prerogative. [. . .]

Even though most of the editing was done by the producers or by film editors selected by the producers, there seems to be no institutionalized conflict between directors and producers as between free-lance writers and producers. This possibly can be explained economically because by contract the director does not share credit with anyone else, whether or not he cuts his own film. In all cases he gets residuals for reruns of the film.

The free-lance writer and the free-lance director reflect the producer's ideas and through them he controls the material presented. Another important element in film making, of course, is the actor, because without appealing actors, a series cannot be a success. The permanent cast has usually been chosen before the working producer enters the scene, and often the choice is made on the popularity of the actor with the general public. Therefore, the producer has less control over the main or starring actors than he has over the others who play an important part in film making.

Many important stars have clauses in their contracts giving them consultation rights over scripts. This does not mean full creative control, but they could refuse to do an episode they consider out of character for them, or in the case of comedy stars, a scene that they do not consider funny. Some stars have the right to refuse to do scenes that make them uncomfortable or that might not show them off 'properly.' This was not true in the early days of television when many of the performers were relatively unknown and therefore less powerful. Now, because many are well-known personalities, they have much more influence over what goes into the script. [. . .]

The relationship between the actor and producer seems quite different from that between the producer and writer or producer and director. Regardless of the difficulties they have with each other, the producers consider writers and directors as colleagues. Most producers, for instance, named other writers as the close friends they would choose to spend their leisure time with, and they considered directors to be craftsmen and, as such, much admired them. But the actor was considered either a 'child' to be humored or a valuable 'property' who might halt the series if not treated with kid gloves. This relationship was prevalent in Hollywood in pretelevision days, and as certain Hollywood 'superstars' turn to television and build their following, it is recurring. It should be noted, however, that television stars differ from movie stars because there does seem to be evidence that the series makes the star famous rather than the star making the series famous. [. . .]

[. . .] According to the producers interviewed, many very talented performers would rather not work on television series because the range of the part is not rewarding enough. The challenge to the producer is to use their talent without sacrificing simplicity and losing an audience, which, many believe, does not want to see arty films or stories with a message. In other words, many producers felt that some of their permanent cast had a great deal of ability that went untapped because the series concept does not allow the plot to be too complex or the acting roles too demanding.

The Producer and the Network

[. . .] When conflicts occur between the producers and the networks, they are often subtle and devious. If a producer is willing to take a strong stand, which will result in either doing the show his way or else, it usually results in his removal from the job. Since producers value their jobs for a variety of reasons (economic considerations are just part of the story), few were willing to confront the networks too directly. Whether producers have direct or indirect conflicts, those who perceive the networks as interfering with the selection process and those who are more willing to fight this interference have outstanding things in common.

Why some producers are pressured and others not seems to depend on several factors. The type of show being produced is certainly one factor. [. . .] [T]he more successful the show, the less likely the network is to interfere; the less political or controversial the show, the less likely the network is to interfere. The type of producer is also important; some producers experience no interference because they carry out the network's suggestions and directives without complaint. Others seem to try to thwart the network directives at every opportunity and therefore are under constant pressure. [. . .]

The film makers have few expressed conflicts with the network. Because they see their function more as coordinators than as creators, they are less likely to view the network as a constraining influence than are those in the other two groups. They are also less likely to take a stand on story content than the others. It is more important to them to learn all aspects of production, especially direction and editing, so they can go on to make theater films in a more artistic way. They believe in holding their talent in abeyance until the time is right for them to leave series television and become movie-makers. To learn their craft well is the key distinguishing ambition of this group. Because of their craft orientation and comparative youth, they experience little conflict in pleasing network officials by subordinating their own artistic values about film making.

Because they do not think that their function is to be a taste leader or that television's function is to proselytize for political and social change, they see no inconsistency in 'giving the public what it wants.' Rather, they see television's function as entertainment, not delivering messages. Most claimed to be politically liberal and usually voted for Democratic party candidates, but their personal political views caused few if any conflicts because they had no desire to use the medium as a means of political expression. [. . .]

The *writers-producers* have the most conflicts with the networks because they are most committed to the ideals of their craft: basically, the writer should have control of what he writes. The writers-producers see themselves more as the chief writers of their series than as film makers. Most became producers to begin with because when they were free-lance writers, the producers they worked for changed or rewrote their scripts, and they prefer to be in a position to control their material. Being involved with both the series concept and the individual scripts and being the most politically committed, they are more likely to incur both network interference and pressure.

Most of their difficulties with the networks are more covert than overt because they know that they must please the network officials to remain in production. For them the story is the most important element in film making. They are also more likely to believe that television should be used to express political views and to change society. Several thought a major qualification for producing is knowing how to fight the network and related numerous incidents describing how social or political messages were put into particular stories over network opposition or deviously. [. . .]

The *old-line producers* believe television's function is to sell products by reaching large audiences; they think their role is to provide simple entertainment to large audiences. This group was the most successful of the producers interviewed, with success measured by highest incomes and responsibility for more original series ideas (the writers-producers were next). Because they were successful and were oriented toward the same goals as the network, one would think that they would have few conflicts with the networks. But such was not the case. Since they were responsible for many successful series, they often believe that they are more aware of what would appeal to the viewing audience than the network officials. [. . .]

[T]he network liaison men are more likely to interfere in story selection for a new series and try to give expert advice to the producer. As the series becomes successful, there is less interference. When an old-line producer becomes involved with a new series, he often battles with the network not so much over political and social ideas but over casting decisions and story ideas, having little to do with social messages. [. . .]

Like all the others interviewed, this type of producer would oppose the networks just up to a certain point because they also depend on network approval to continue producing the series. However, because the nature of the conflict is usually apolitical and they have more successes to their credit, the old-line producers are more likely to convince the networks to do things their way than are, for example, the writers-producers. The conflict between the old-line producers and the networks seems to be overt; it is more a contest between equals than between a superior and a subordinate. The political orientation of this group varies from conservative to liberal (most again are Democrats), but this does not influence their roles as television producers because they separate their personal politics from their job performance.

21

BBC Trade Unions

Tom Burns

TOM BURNS'S 1977 book was based on extensive interviewing conducted inside the BBC in 1963 and 1973. This extract looks back to the late 1950s, when—spurred by the new commercial competition to the BBC—trade unions became much more salient. By the late 1950s the BBC had accepted four trade unions and a fifth union (ACTT) had organized much of the new commercial ITV. In the BBC (Burns suggests) the trade unions became almost a second management system operating in parallel to the official system.

The trade unions in the 1950s and 1960s became an integral part of the British public broadcasting project; the unions also supported some 'craft' as well as 'professional' orientations, especially in terms of job security and quality production. But the BBC (like ITV) was a highly complex, compartmentalized, and hierarchical organization. The loyalty of most BBC employees, Burns's work suggests, was either to the BBC itself or at the level of a small and specialized sub-occupational fragment.

The Independent Television Companies, in their hurry to put into use their 'licence to print money', as Lord Thomson so embarrassingly called it a few years later, had to outbid the BBC for trained producers and technicians, and were in no mood to haggle over union recognition. The Association of Cinematograph Television and Allied Technicians (ACTT), still denied recognition by the BBC, stepped in quickly and assumed the role in commercial television which the Staff Association had in the BBC. And it negotiated agreements which went beyond anything the Staff Association had dreamed of. 'This Week', the oldest Current Affairs programme in Independent Television, to take one example, accepted an agreement with ACTT which was based on the union's experience and success in negotiating contracts for its members engaged for 'short' documentary films. [. . .]

The 'shorts' agreement was the only precedent for the kind of work which was envisaged; the new television companies were venturing into new territory which might conceivably prove risky, so that it was hardly possible to guarantee the security of employment characteristic of work for BBC television. The 'shorts' agreement incorporated such elements as the

Source: Tom Burns, *The BBC: Public Institution and Private World* (London: Macmillan Press, 1977), 63–71.

'four, four and four' composition of teams—four cameramen, four sound technicians, and four 'production' staff, including the producer. This kind of agreement had been fought for and won over a period of many years from British film managements which were, as they still are, suicidally opportunistic and irresponsible. Nobody knew which model—BBC or film industry—the independent television industry would follow. As it happened, the situation in television followed the BBC model, with the industry providing a structure within which people could follow a career, hold down jobs for as long as they wished (provided their competence stayed with them), and have pensionable employment. Also, over the next ten years, the industry provided more work and offered more jobs than there were people qualified to be able to fill them; even up to 1975, the ACTT kept entry open to most categories of qualified staff. Later programmes were manned according to less extravagant agreements, but 'This Week' still operated under the old 'shorts' agreement, even including provision for first-class travel for the whole team.

> One of the most contentious areas of all this is the 'buying in' of material. One of the reasons why there is very little independent production in this country is that the union (ACTT) acts in total concert with the management over the question of 'outside material'. In the ACTT-ITCA agreement there is a clause about 'unique material'. The interpretation of that clause is extremely rigorous . . . If somebody had managed to film, say, Fidel Castro in the early sixties, that would be 'unique material', but basically there is complete hostility to the importation of 'outside' material; there's a very close watch kept on where material comes from, who shoots it. It very rarely happens, but for that reason there is the absolute sanction of 'blacking' the material; and managements tread very carefully in that sort of area.

The changes which the coming of Independent Television [in 1955] wrought on the BBC's situation were more immediately apparent in the pattern of industrial relations than on programme policy. In one regard, the Corporation stood firm; it refused recognition to the ACTT—even though many BBC producers and technicians joined the union so as to gain access to a labour market which provided, for the first time, employment options. The BBC Staff Association changed its name to the Association of Broadcasting Staff, the better to recruit members of the Independent Television Authority and the Independent Television companies—many of whom, of course, were departed members of BBC staff. After 1954 there was a three-year struggle between the ABS and the ACTT for recruits in independent television; the ABS lost out to the rival union so far as the companies were concerned, but gained a foothold in the Independent Television Authority itself and in the end became the sole union recognised by the Authority for its 1000 staff. A further move to broaden out from its 'house union' status by affiliating to the T.U.C. was voted down by the T.U.C.; but in 1963, when it tried again, it was successful.

On the other hand, 'outside' unions quickly got a foothold inside the BBC. The first, the National Union of Journalists, gained recognition early in 1955, though, following the recommendation of the Beveridge

Committee, it had to join forces with the Staff Association in negotiations concerning particular categories of staff. A few months later, the Electrical Trades Union, which had had a sizeable membership among engineering craftsmen in the BBC, also gained recognition, largely because it was showing signs of becoming the dominant engineering union in independent television [. . .] Lastly, the National Association of Theatrical, Television and Kine Employees (NATTKE), which had begun as an industrial union for all non-performers in the entertainment industry, was recognised by the BBC in 1958, again after it had established itself in Independent Television as the representative of the wide range of craftsmen, semi-skilled operatives and clerical workers employed in television.

In the space of five years, the BBC had become 'unionised'. It had happened largely because of the advent of independent television, and again it was a change which reduced the unique institutional quality of the BBC as well as its monopoly of broadcasting services—a unique institutional quality which consisted largely in the way in which the staff as a whole were incorporated in the BBC. In the days when Reith could speak of 'what the BBC does' as coming not from what one individual thinks but more and more 'from a consensus of opinion and experience', and when an administrative official could declare that 'the BBC is one Corporation, and can only be thought of by the listener as one individual', differences of opinion, disputes and negotiation between management and staff had been a matter of dealing with individual dissatisfactions and grievances.

In the 'control and consensus' regime established under Reith, which lasted until the creation of commercial television, loyalty could indeed be expected, and everything did follow from that. The establishment of the Staff Association after the war did recognise the possibility of divergences of interest between the 'Corporation' (i.e. management) and staff, but, as the Staff Association's memorandum to the Beveridge Committee had made clear, it was at one with the Corporation in the purposes and values to which it subscribed, and served to 'make representations' to senior management about such discontents and grievances as existed among its individual members. Trade unions, however, are founded on the assumption of ultimately conflicting interests between management and staff, and exist for the clearly stated purpose of defending or improving their members' pay and conditions of work. And the open conflict between the ABS and ACTT for recognition as the sole representative of staff interests in all broadcasting organisations could only be waged in terms of each demonstrating its ability to achieve that stated purpose more quickly and more effectively than its rival. In fact, with the ABS retaining 'recognition' in the BBC and ITA, and ACTT gaining 'recognition' in the commercial television companies, large numbers of BBC staff found it useful to join both unions; indeed, since the commercial companies were virtually fully unionised from the beginning, BBC programme staff and technicians might well become members of ACTT as an insurance policy against the time they might want to move, while staying out of the ABS. Either circumstance constituted a further incentive to the ABS to prove itself as militant as its rival.

The immediate consequence of the recognition by the BBC of the NUJ,

ETU and NATTKE, alongside the ABS, as unions with which management would be prepared to negotiate on matters affecting the pay and working conditions of the members each union represented was what was called, by one union official, the 'industrialisation' of people in the lower grades of the Managerial, Production and Editorial (MP) grading structure and a definitive shift of technicians and manual workers into regarding 'working for the BBC' as something completely undifferentiated from working for any other employer, something, in fact, which was covered appropriately by the institutional framework of collective bargaining which prevailed throughout industry. Some of the older hands in the Personnel Division were all too conscious of this:

> Can I go back to one other thing you mentioned?—this 'dedication' among engineers. This is still present [in 1973], but possibly not to the degree it was. I think there is still a very healthy pride in BBC engineering; they're very much inclined to believe, though they might not be quite so ready to say so in these days, that the system is the best in the world, second to none in techniques and everything else. *But*, ten years ago we still had a lot of the pioneering sense; even some of the really early boys were still with us. I think broadcasting has become to some people—some of the younger chaps—just another job in the technical field. I wouldn't want to overstress this, but, in a way, it's bound up with the increased unionisation of the BBC. The union position has changed markedly over the past ten years. We've got a great deal more union problems than we used to have. Strangely, when you were here before [1963] it was only the ETU that gave any real trouble. The ABS—which used to be just a staff association—were relatively non-militant; still fairly cosy, rather house-union. They've developed quite a lot since then; their shock troops have tended to be the technical operators in television. And there are a lot more hard-minded union members among the engineering fraternity than there used to be.
>
> *Why is this?*
>
> I honestly believe—yes, I think it's a national trend. We live in an age when doctors are active in trade unions, when airline pilots go on strike, teachers march past here in great columns shouting and handing out leaflets—it's the 'in' thing. We had a very light time with the unions for a very long time, really, and we're just catching up with what it's like in the big world outside.

For him, and for many others in senior management, 'unionisation' had lessened the 'sense of dedication' which had characterised BBC engineering. But for technicians and craftsmen as old as he in the game, it was 'managerialism'—what they called, of course, 'red tape', or 'using the proper channels'—which had punctured enthusiasm. [. . .] People [. . .] who knew and usually respected the producers and editors they worked for—and with—saw the 'management' at higher levels, or, rather, the system of management through which directors and production assistants had to work in order to meet emergencies or resolve dilemmas, as a bureaucratic maze, or as a kind of smog, which lowered morale and reduced people's effectiveness. And the union organisation comes to be seen as a way of short circuiting 'procedure'—of penetrating the smog.

If there's a problem on the floor, the proper channels, the paperwork, seeing all the different people before you can get a yea or nay—it all takes time. People get very frustrated. Before I relinquished the post of union representative I could get on the phone straight away to the Head of Studios and say 'This isn't on, this is against the rule book', and the thing would be done there and then. But for the normal man on the floor to try to get to him . . . ! It's a feat if you can even get inside his door . . . The only way of stating a problem is through your Establishment Officer, who will look at you, you know, understandingly, and then say, 'I'll have a word'. Which is no satisfaction, you know. Before you came in we were talking—the things which amaze me about this vast Corporation! After all, if you're interested in your job and you ask for a tool which you feel is—relevant, it's only because you're interested in your job that you realise the tool is relevant. So you put the suggestion forward—but by the time it's come to fruition, it might be years.

What do you mean, exactly, by a tool relevant to the job?

Well, say, if I wanted a pair of stepladders—I mean, this is bringing it down to basics, and eventually I thought it ridiculous. We really do need stepladders. You tell your immediate superior, and then you wait, and wait, and wait. So in the end you can only go to your shop steward to represent you and make a louder voice. Because, after all, he is the Union, not just one man.

In this way, the industrial relations machinery in the Corporation has become lumbered with business which is properly the concern of management. Often enough, the consequence is that anxieties in senior management about the trade unions are heightened. [. . .] In the minds of at least some senior managers, the problems of industrial relations which had come with unionisation—and which, moreover, were regarded as entirely the consequence of increased union militancy which, they were persuaded, was a nation-wide trend—were, albeit tedious, exasperating, and, in the long run, expensive, less of a threat to the Corporation than the presence of what was always called 'a small minority' of politically left-wing people, many of them very talented, among production and editorial staff and among the upper levels of technical staff. These senior managers were particularly upset by the 'underground' press established within the Corporation—very much a spin-off from the underground press and the student movement of the late sixties—which mixed information 'confidential' to senior management with scathing, and often scatological, criticisms of individual managers, and with challenges to the constitutional legitimacy of the bureaucratic structure of the Corporation.

22

Television Producers

Jeremy Tunstall

THIS EXTRACT IS from *Television Producers* (1993), which involved interviews with 254 producers and senior executives in 1990–2. The study encompassed a wide range of genres—comedy, documentary, drama/fiction, game and people shows, news and current affairs, youth programming, and sport. Television is indeed a producer-driven medium. But the producer's work varies greatly between these different genres; a sitcom producer has fairly little in common with a natural history producer or a producer of live sports. Moreover producers are already well placed on a career ladder which stretches from the very bottom to the very top of British broadcasting.

In practice most producers seem to think 'horizontally' in terms only of their own genre, and vertically mainly in terms of their own career. They show little interest in attempting to construct a horizontal and demarcated self-governing profession for all producers.

Each specific genre has its particular requirements and working cycles, which tend to cut its producers off from producers and others working in different fields with different timetables. Most British producers spend between 4 and 6 months each year locked into the intensive effort involved in meeting deadlines for a series of programmes; during this intensive phase they may well work 7 days a week for many weeks in succession. The other half of the year includes vacation time and perhaps 5 months of less intensive work. During these other months the producer may be supervising writing, casting supporting roles, engaging in research, looking at locations, seeing possible interviewees, talking to actors' agents, and so on. Producers spend much of the time out of their offices—in the studio, at the location, viewing the raw rushes and, later, the rough edited film or tape.

Even at the quieter times of the year most producers do not arrive home until after the London rush-hour. They often take home with them scripts and programme outlines to read, as well as cassettes of programmes submitted by available writers, directors or performers. Much of their domestic TV viewing is of programming in their own genre. Thus producers tend to be locked into a genre-specific world even when at home.

Source: Jeremy Tunstall, *Television Producers* (London: Routledge, 1993), 2–3, 13–16, 24–6, 104–5, 202–7.

Each of the genres is located within a department or departments; and even independent production companies specialize, so that here also producers are locked into the private world of a single genre. Each genre has its own specific goal or goals; it has a characteristic style of production— location film, or live studio, or the 'outside broadcasts' of sport. Each genre has its own internal system of status and prestige, its own values and its own world-view.

Departments and genres also function as career-ladders. There is continuing movement between organizations: many producers have started in the BBC, moved to ITV, then back to the BBC, only finally to go freelance or to set up as independent producers; but such job-moves all take place within one small world which shares one broad career-ladder. It is common for a producer's career to have involved several job-moves, each move following one particular senior colleague. Producers also in turn tend to be surrounded by production team-members with whom they have worked on several previous programmes and projects.

Thus the producer's own work-career advances within the private world of a particular genre whose peculiar work-mix of timetables, goals, production schedules and world-view largely shuts its members off from the members of other private genre-worlds. [. . .]

In contrast to their private world of genre, work and career, producers are aware of being in some respects dependent on the public forum of the British national newspapers.

Producers know that newspaper coverage of television is read by the general public, by other print journalists and by politicians. The producer's colleagues comment on press coverage in corridor conversations; the producer also knows that the barons at the top of the system see a daily digest of press comment from all newspapers and specialist publications. The barons themselves anxiously scan the press because they know that press comment helps to establish the public image of their channel.

The producer eventually receives several kinds of feedback on his or her series. Audience ratings only become available a week or so later; even letters take a day or two to arrive; the opinion of the controllers upstairs also takes time to filter down; the press coverage, however, is not only public but also immediate. [. . .]

Producers are aware that many audience members only 'discover' the series by, say, the fourth or fifth episode, when the short run is nearly finished. For this reason, and because the press is believed to relish novelty, publicists and producers tend to focus on the first programme in a new series run. This leads the producer to place his or her potentially most popular or sensational programme at the start (while hiding 'weaker' episodes towards the end).

Many producers, having focused their promotional efforts on the first programme, decide that their publicity work is now completed. Other producers continue to battle away at the promotional effort, sending out fresh publicity material (and fresh motorcycled tapes) for each programme in the series. The height of such publicity efforts is found in some of the factual TV areas; some programme teams include a high proportion of personnel from journalism who spread the word to their newspaper friends.

In the 1980s factual TV producers in general (and perhaps independent producers of Channel Four programmes in particular) increasingly offered newspapers background articles linked to a TV programme scheduled for that evening. The newspaper gets a solidly researched article, perhaps based on several weeks of preparatory investigation by a researcher and a producer. It might be said that investigative journalism in the British press is alive and well and based on TV programme research.

This multi-faceted dependence on the press serves to underline for the producer the fleeting nature of television: press cuttings are part of the industry's available record, whereas most British TV programmes in practice fail to register in the industry's collective memory. This dependence upon newspapers, which are regarded as covering television in such an amateurish and unsystematic manner, also reminds the producer that the industry's overall system for awarding prestige and recognizing 'quality' is itself highly uncertain or—as some producers say—'whimsical'.

Very few people in British television today would deny that producers are now less secure than they used to be. It is also widely agreed that producers now carry additional responsibilities.

In the past the producer was simply required to make a batch of programmes in an integrated factory, within which a large range of back-up services were available on tap. Today many producers are out in the independent-production world, running small businesses in which nothing is provided on tap. Even the producers within the large organizations have additional tasks: today many series are made primarily in-house, but also contract out, say, 3 or 4 of a run of 13 programmes to outside producers. The in-house producer thus has to learn the skill of commissioning programmes out to other producers; this activity also brings with it extra tasks in the form of a flood of supplicants looking for finance for their programme projects.

In some of the more expensive areas, such as drama and documentary, producers are also increasingly expected to arrange co-production finance. A US or Australian channel may be willing to pay one-third of the cost but this involves additional diplomatic-entrepreneurial tasks for the producer.

More generally, the tightening-up of budgets and programme finance has meant that producers spend more time talking about, and working on, budgets and money.

Increasingly also producers are required to make choices over what technical facilities they use. The 1970s practices—always making the programme in the integrated factory's downstairs studio, or always using a company film-crew for outdoor filming—no longer automatically prevail. The BBC in 1992–3 introduced its 'Producer Choice' initiative which encouraged producers to 'choose' between using in-house studios and facilities or using outside specialists. Again, sizeable sums of money are involved; again, there are new work-tasks, and new expertise is required. [. . .]

Anyone who works in an organization, and within an occupation or profession, must accept many constraints. The lawyer in court and the surgeon
in the operating theatre are both constrained in obvious ways. The British
television producer is also located within an industry, an organization and
an occupation, and must accept many constraints. In particular, [. . .] TV
producers are subject to strategic decisions about commissioning and
scheduling programme series. Much power is located at the level of the
channel baron who sanctions finance and places programming in the
schedule.

Once the go-ahead for the new series or the new season has been
obtained, the producer has a substantial level of autonomy. Much of the
guidance that comes down from above is indeed guidance; much of it says,
in effect, obvious things about not breaking the law and not over-spending
the budget. Another (perhaps unspoken) piece of guidance is to maintain
last season's audience level, or at least to do roughly as well in relation to
the relevant competition. A final piece of guidance requires the producer to
stick broadly to the approach agreed when the series run was commissioned; often this involves a target audience, a specific time of day on the
particular channel and an agreed sub-genre style.

Unless the series producer is a total novice, he or she is typically left in
day-to-day and programme-to-programme control. The broad subject-
matter of the projected programmes needs to be known higher up—not
least to avoid clashes with the output of other producers and other programmes; but typically the series producer does not show scripts to a
superior and is trusted to be the person in charge, whose day of reckoning
comes only at the end of the series run.

The factual-series producer has a budget to spend—varying from hundreds of thousands to millions of pounds—and is typically left very free to
decide how this sum will be spread between the programmes in the series.
Many series combine some expensive programmes (and distant filming)
with some cheaper studio-based (stay-at-home) programming. It is the
series producer who decides the actual combination and the topics to be
covered.

The producer also chooses the production team. Especially in the first
season there may not be a free hand, because some personnel are inherited
from the previous season or assigned by a departmental superior, but after
two or three series runs, the producer can re-shape the team or acquire an
entirely new team—new directors, writers, reporters and presenters.

This team-building autonomy also allows the producer to decide precisely what kind of producer to be. In factual television the series producer
often has a team of several directors, each of whom is responsible for
supervising the filming and editing of two or three programmes. In some
cases the series producer personally also directs one or two programmes.

The director role varies greatly between genres. There is a sharp difference between the studio director, who oversees several cameras simultaneously operating on a studio floor and the outside location director,
who, working with one camera [. . .], provides the main artistic input to a
documentary film.

The producer in factual television is often a 'hyphenate'—most usually a producer-director; but the producer may (or may not) also be actively ('hands on') involved in writing scripts, in editing film and tape, as programme publicist, and so on.

In British factual television an important decision for the producer is whether or not to have one 'presenter'—a single face which will become identified with the programme—and whether to use a famous or an unknown face; other alternatives are to have no presenter (common in British documentary) or to operate as producer-presenter (like Melvyn Bragg in *The South Bank Show*) or to adopt some other radical hyphenate solution such as the researcher-presenter. These decisions rest with the producer and often lead to extended agonizing and indecision.

Factual television involves a myriad of small details. The team's producers or producer-directors in charge of specific programmes will have the fullest knowledge of those details. Only the series producer, however, will have broad insights into the whole series. The series producer, for example, may regard some programmes as potentially stronger as well as more risky than others. The series producer often must ponder a proposed foreign-filming story which is potentially the best programme in the series, but which is also the most costly and may seem to have only a 50 per cent chance of reaching the screen. Because of the risks of losing money here, the series producer may have decided to make several much cheaper and safer programmes in the series.

Producers who have been in charge of programmes over several years typically list the major changes that have occurred in them. These changes can include a nearly complete change in personnel, a different set, different opening titles and so on. The producer may also have changed the programme series in more fundamental ways: these changes can include reshaping the programme in its general goals; the programme may have become much more orientated towards entertaining a younger audience—perhaps with the use of appropriate music, graphics and presenters. Or the programme may have been steered in a more educational direction—with a greatly increased emphasis on associated printed material. 'The book of the series', the related consumer magazine, or 'Write in for the Fact-sheet' can have major impacts on the production team's work-effort and on the character of the series.

Autonomy, in TV production as elsewhere, also depends in part on the potential availability of alternative career-moves. One consequence of the pursuit of a distinctive production style may be the enhancement of the producer's reputation within television; but the career implications of this—like so much else—may differ from field to field.

In documentary the producer-director can make a reputation as a film-maker, which may or may not lead on to employment outside television. In news and current affairs there are big hierarchies up which to advance and career-paths which lead into TV general management as well as outside employment in journalism, public affairs and public relations. However, the successful sports producer is not typically aware of many colleagues who have moved on to much higher things.

Fiction and Entertainment Producers

[. . .] British TV regulators, legislators and channel controllers have long had a kind of Gresham's Law of Entertainment as one of their main anxieties – a fear that bad entertainment will drive out good. 'Good' has tended to be equated with British-made, a formulation to which the trade unions for many years gave their muscular support. If British is best, however, British is certainly also more expensive. Thus better moral value, higher cost, better artistic value and better industrial value have coalesced together; cheapness has tended to be equated with lesser virtue.

Consequently, a fog of moral values hangs over the fiction and entertainment areas. Across the various genres, the quiz/game show has a lowly position because it is seen as a US formula and cheap in most respects. 'People' shows, such as chat shows and people/surprise shows, are also seen as cheap imported formulae. On the other hand, both drama/fiction and comedy are seen as occupying higher positions on several moral dimensions. British TV dramas are seen as truly British, as artistically superior, as dealing in non-factual forms with real issues and real concerns; British drama and comedy series are both expensive and prestigious.

This moral hierarchy, which operates between genres, also operates within each genre. There is a more-deserving (and more-expensive) and less-deserving (and cheap) dimension within each field. Within drama/fiction the multi-episode soap ranks bottom and single plays or TV films rank top in both prestige and cost. Similar rankings are recognized between better and worse comedy; between more demanding or difficult or simple and cheaper game shows. There is also a hierarchy between the top chat show and the lower depth of chat shows.

These fiction and entertainment genres of programming have gone further than has British factual programming towards the publisher model. Television fiction programming has long been more freelance than most British television; and much drama is contracted out to either a freelance producer or an independent production company. The picture is more varied in the other genres.

Each of these genres has its own variants of the standard TV division of labour. The producer's own job-definition and tasks vary between genres. In studio-based game shows, for example, the studio director controls the multiple in-studio cameras and camera-operators. But in comedy there is quite a long tradition of the producer-director. In drama the separation between the producer and director roles is sharpest; since drama involves a lot of money, people and logistics, the task of directing the actors and filming the scenes keeps a director extremely busy; in a single drama the director may dominate. Most drama is, however, in series and here a single series producer usually employs several directors.

British television tends to honour the sole writer, or the comedy-writing partnership, and allows the writer's creative instinct to play a very big part in the comedy enterprise. Writers are clearly also crucial in drama; but the number of writers varies greatly with the number of episodes, although soaps are the only British entertainment area fully to have accepted the large team of writers.

Research, more than writing, is of central importance to both game shows and people shows. This 'research' differs from that found in, say, current affairs. These entertainment researchers are looking for contestants and participants and for questions. Larger shows employ sizeable teams of such researchers.

The more expensive forms of drama, comedy and studio entertainment are expensive mainly because of the large technical crews, the design and related specialists and the acting and other talent. In some cases there is a dominant star and the producer and the star may effectively control the show between them.

More common, however, is the show that is led by its script. This is true of most drama and comedy. In this case the script-editor part of the producer's role is crucial. [. . .]

Insecurity, Autonomy, Profession?	During the recent years of turbulence, British TV producers have undergone a paradoxical combination of changes: they have become less secure but more autonomous.

Few British TV producers would deny that producers overall have become less secure in recent years. This study has focused on producers whose names were in the *Radio Times* attached to productions just being transmitted. Many other producers were becoming ex-producers; indeed, a number of the producers we interviewed in 1990 were already ex-producers by 1992.

How, then, can they have become more autonomous at the same time? The paradox derives from a significant shift in the nature of the producer's job. Those producers who are (still) working are being asked to do more things than was the case before 1986. First, producers have been forced to take budgeting more seriously. Second, producers (especially in fields such as documentary and drama) are increasingly expected to take part in raising finance. Third, with the increasing contracting-out of programming by the BBC and ITV, many working producers are not only producing programmes but commissioning them out to other producers.

Fourth, producers are required to make more decisions about resources and encouraged to use outside freelance camera-crews, studios or graphics specialists, instead of the BBC's or the ITV company's own in-house facilities. The BBC in 1992 launched its new effort of this kind called 'Producer Choice'; the BBC made clear that choices would rest with series producers and not with heads of output departments.

All this adds up to more work, more responsibility, more control and more autonomy – for those producers who are still producing. [. . .]

[. . .] Television producers collectively have some similarities to the many occupations which have been professionalizing in recent decades; but TV producers have not tried very hard to do the classic things normally done by occupations which have a strong urge to professionalize.

Television producers have not tried to control entry; on the contrary, entry has become more open. Television producers have not set up a 'qualifying association' which vets qualifications, establishes standards and the like. Television producers lack 'clients' of the kind that doctors, lawyers, architects or teachers claim to serve. Although TV producers are serving the general public, their 'hands-on' work refers not to clients or patients but to cameras, scripts, editing, performers – the business of TV production, not TV consumption.

There is another simple reason why British TV producers are not likely to go much further in a professional direction. In British television the producers – more than any other occupational category – are, or become, the general managers. Apprentice producers can start as 'researcher' and eventually become chief executive. This occupation of producer is not only a lengthy career-ladder, but also fits closely with the organizational hierarchy from bottom to top.

The TV-producer role covers a very wide horizontal range in terms of genres and types of output. In recent years the producer role has become further fragmented by the introduction of two new industrial systems, each of which introduced new definitions of producer to the British scene. The publisher model introduced the 'commissioning editor' and the 'independent producer'; the satellite or cable channels give weight to the acquisition and packaging of large flows of pre-existing production.

Some associations and organizations of a 'professional' kind do exist. There is the Royal Television Society which holds conferences and awards prizes. There are bodies which lobby on behalf of independent producers. Trade unions, although now weaker, still exist.

There is, however, no single body which seeks to preserve, defend and advance the interests of TV producers in Britain. The producers are too involved in their organizations – many devote their 'professional' loyalty to the BBC which they see as preserving the kind of television they believe in; indeed, many ITV and independent producers also express deep loyalty to the BBC and what it stands for.

Producers' deep involvement in their private genre-worlds is also in part both cause and effect of this lack of professional feeling or organization. [. . .]

[. . .] This study indicates that TV production is a well-established occupational category but the term 'elite' certainly does not fit many producers' social backgrounds. The producers interviewed in this study are not a representative sample of all TV producers. Of those interviewed about one-quarter were educated at either Oxford or Cambridge; about another quarter were at one of another small group of institutions (including two London University colleges – the London School of Economics and University College – as well as Bristol, York, East Anglia and Manchester Universities). The majority of these producers did not attend fee-paying schools; more went to grammar schools or comprehensives. In terms of their social and educational origins these producers' backgrounds are broadly middle-class and meritocratic. Despite having lived in London most of their adult lives, many of these producers speak with some trace of a British regional accent. In this respect, and in others, the producers are probably very similar to their presenters whose faces appear on the screen.

These are jobs, however, which many young people would like to do. A number of producers complained about the huge numbers of applicants that a single newspaper advertisement for a 'TV researcher' would attract. This occupation, of course, has no specific entry-qualification. [. . .]

In British television, the producer (of various kinds) has taken over some functions previously performed by management and also by trade unions; increasingly, the producer is becoming the effective employer.

'We have removed an entire tier of management' said one senior executive of an ITV company. Some of the functions previously performed by both specialist and general management are now heaped on to the producer.

The same is true of the trade unions, which until about 1986 in practice managed much of what went on in the craft areas. For example, the unions operated penally high overtime rates of pay which greatly affected the entire practice of location filming. The construction of sets, the operation of studios, the outside broadcasting of sporting events – all of these areas of work were partly managed by unions and partly managed by management. When trade-union power radically declined after 1986, these management tasks were not given back to management, which itself was slimming down radically.

The producer of a series run often has one, two or three million pounds to spend; and there are several possible strategic paths which could be followed. Do you do all the location filming first? Do you work alternate weekends? Do you start in the studio when the days are shorter in March? In the past all such decisions were heavily influenced by union rules. Now it is the producer who sits down, maybe for quite a long time, worrying away at the cheapest and most efficient use of the available time, resources and people. The producer makes a management plan, carries it out and is held responsible for it.

Increasingly, the producer is not just a general manager; the producer is also coming to be the effective employer. This latter has happened most obviously in independent production; but it is happening also within the BBC and ITV. With the short series runs so common in British television, employment is very often for a few months; it is the producer who effectively employs the production team, and increasingly also the technical crew, for those weeks or months. The producer who from 'inside' the BBC or an ITV company takes on a production team – via the personnel department – is increasingly likely to be either a freelance producer employed for that short series run, or a producer on a contract of perhaps one year.

British television is no less – probably more – producer-driven today than before 1986. The production systems have changed and the publisher system has become central; but the production culture has remained the same, in focusing on the producer as the person who holds the reins. The overall system has increasingly fragmented into smaller programme-making units. Everyone seems to agree that to the question of who should be in charge, in most cases the answer has to be the producer. If the producers are not driving the system, no other suitable occupational category – under British conditions – is available to do the job.

23
The Television Labour Market in Britain

Richard Paterson

THIS ARTICLE REPORTS on a panel study which had several rounds of questionnaire and diary data collected from an initial sample of 436 British television production workers during 1994–8. The study was based at the British Film Institute in London and the Judd Institute of Management Studies at Cambridge University. Here we see data covering the entire behind-the-camera TV workforce; it excludes all actors and performers and almost all of the people whose faces appear on the screen. By eliminating actors, it excludes the most 'vertical' of the media-related occupations. Within this TV production workforce there is a significant bulge in the middle; about half the workforce earn not much more than, or not much less than, the overall average. But there is also a big range from top to bottom. A thousand securely employed men at the top earn at least ten times as much as a thousand insecurely employed women at the bottom.

Moreover, while some TV workers successfully ascend the steep career ladders, many clearly do not; there is a lot of slipping down the ladder (working, or earning, less this year than last year) and of falling—or jumping—off the ladder. The polarization between successful and failed careers also appears to be increasing.

The television labour market in Britain has been significantly transformed since 1980 with an increase in freelance employment as a consequence of new labour laws and reductions in union power and membership, the rapid pace of technological change, and the emergence of a large, but poorly capitalized, independent production sector. Where before the 1980s, there was controlled entry and a high level of staff jobs in broadcasting organizations, the onset of independent production and the end of a 'closed shop' in television led to a profusion of new entrants willing to work within the freelance employment mode, which in Britain had previously been typical of the film industry. These changes have, in turn, led to an environment of increased uncertainty for those working in television.

There is a wide range of jobs in the television production and

Source: Not previously published. Richard Paterson is at the British Film Institute in London.

post-production chain across a range of firm types. Alongside the major broadcasters (BBC and the major ITV companies), the independent production sector in Britain includes over 1,000 companies, most of which are located in London and the South-East. Three are large and well capitalized (GMG Endemol, Chrysalis, and Pearson), approximately 50 are medium sized (including leading companies like Mentorn Barraclough Carey/TVC and Wall to Wall), and some 600 receive a commission in any given year. Many independents specialize in documentary and factual programming and there is intense competition for commissions in this area, and a need for a constant flow of new ideas. The drama and entertainment genres tend to be more talent-led and there is a project-based approach to employment similar to that which has operated in the film industry for the past fifty years. Factual production tended in the past to offer more continuity in employment than is the case today. In addition, the post-production sector includes a range of facilities houses which offer services to production companies. This sector has witnessed fast technological change and talented editors have been able to trade their skills effectively.

This essay reports on research undertaken by the British Film Institute between 1994 and 1998: the Television Industry Tracking Study, a longitudinal study of the careers of 450 creative workers in television.[1]

Employment and Income

Employment in the British television production industry was, until the early 1980s, available only in a limited number of production companies (usually within a vertically integrated broadcaster-producer structure), and was predominantly staffed by full-time employees. Careers were marked by a gradual progression, and training was offered by most employers, and in particular by the BBC. Since the mid-1980s there has been a marked rise in freelance employment. Of the 28,000 people estimated now to be working within the British television industry some 60 per cent are working in freelance employment. In 1994 25 per cent of freelances were producers/directors and assistants, 18 per cent were involved with production support, and 11 per cent worked in post-production. Just over 20 per cent work with camera, lights, or sound and approximately 8 per cent were researchers/writers.[2] Over two-fifths of freelances have worked in more than one sector of the industry. The workforce is affected by regional factors, with the London effect on work availability both creating more opportunities, and therefore acting as a magnet for new entrants, but also forcing greater competition for work than elsewhere. There is a preference on the part of the majority of workers (56 per cent) for continuity of employment and staff status whether in the independent sector or in a broadcasting organization.[3]

1 This research benefited from a major grant from the Economic and Social Research Council (Contract R000237131) as well as initial funding by the Hoso Bunka Foundation and Skillset. Data were collected in 9 waves at 6-monthly intervals. Contributions to this paper have been made by Janet Willis, Elaine Sheppard, Megan Skinner, and Shirley Dex.

2 M. Woolf and S. Holly, *Employment Patterns and Training Needs*, (London: Skillset, 1994).

3 See *British Film Institute Television Industry Tracking Study: Third Report*, May 1999 (London: BFI), 29.

The hierarchy of labour in television has been accentuated in recent years because of the changed conditions of production. In this regard, television as an industry offers an example of how changes in modes of employment can have very contradictory effects. Greater management control has been established with the discretion to hire and fire increased by the normative contractual environment, but all firms require the trust and commitment of their employees to sustain creativity and provide a competitive advantage in the search for commissions and this factor is undermined by the uncertainties inherent in a freelance labour market.[4]

The increasing power of those in commissioning roles across the television channels has recast relationships in television and put a new emphasis on institutional 'knowledge' skills (which DeFillippi and Arthur call 'knowing-of' skills[5]). Creative work in television varies between genres but there is an accentuated emphasis on the central role of the producer. The producer is effectively the packager, the person who secures the funding for a project, and as broadcasters seek to lower costs and spread risk this has become an ever more important role.[6] It is a position which was formerly attained only after a relatively long 'apprenticeship' moving from researcher to assistant producer or director over a period of a decade or more but which can now be attained within a very short time. Management and cost control have become watchwords for modern TV, with those working in staff technical posts put increasingly under pressure in recent years. There have been important developments which have affected the television industry in recent years: the advent of digital technology having a fundamental effect on the costs and relations of production, and organizational changes in the industry, including the decline of trades unions.[7]

Television is marked by a culture of long hours. Thirty-six per cent of the Tracking Study sample stated they had worked 50 hours or more in the previous week, and 8 per cent were working over 70 hours—well beyond the 48-hour limit indicated by the EU working time directive. For some, the long working hours experienced were felt to be attributable to decreasing budgets and increasing pressures of time and it was thought that the project focus of the industry encouraged a culture of long working days. Different age groups were affected differently by this regime: those over 51 years of age were working the longest hours (almost 60 per cent working over 50 hours in a week), compared to just over 50 per cent of those aged 41–50 and 30 per cent of those aged 31–40.

There were slight regional differences, with 14 per cent of those living in London and the South-East working over 70 hours compared to 7 per cent

4 cf. Duncan Gallie, Michael White, Yuan Cheng, and Mark Tomlinson, *Restructuring the Employment Relationship* (Oxford: Oxford University Press, 1998).

5 R. DeFillippi and M. Arthur, 'Boundaryless Contexts and Careers: A Competency Based Perspective', in M. B. Arthur and D. Rousseau (eds.), *The Boundaryless Career* (Oxford: Oxford University Press, 1996).

6 cf. Jeremy Tunstall, *Television Producers* (London: Routledge, 1993).

7 On technology see Chris Thompson, *Non-Linear Editing* (London: BFI, 1994); on trade unions and organisations see, *inter alia*, A. McKinlay and B. Quinn, 'Management, Technology and Work in Commercial Broadcasting, c. 1979–98', *New Technology, Work and Employment*, 14: 1 (1999), 2–17; G. Ursell, 'Labour Flexibility in the UK Commercial Television Sector', *Media, Culture & Society*, 20, (1998), 129–53; and R. Paterson, 'The Economic Organisation of Production', in R. Paterson (ed.), *Organising for Change*, (London, BFI, 1990).

of those living elsewhere. However, approximately 50 per cent of both samples reported working over 50 hours a week. Those in managerial/executive producer jobs were the most likely to be working over 50 hours of all the job groups in the study. Company owners and those with staff jobs were more likely to work over 50 hours than freelancers. However, freelancers, due to the nature of their work, are not consistently employed throughout five working days in any given week, thereby reducing the average hours worked for that group. Freelancers who had worked a full week were found to have worked longer hours than staff who had worked a full week, with 53 per cent of freelancers having worked over 50 hours compared to 48 per cent of broadcaster staff and 44 per cent of independent staff.

Television has the image of a glamorous industry and is associated with high rewards. Uncertainty and risk are usually recognized as being matched by good pay. In fact, the income profile of TV workers fluctuates. In the Tracking Study the numbers earning under £20,000 generally decreased over time, from 31 per cent in 1994 to 24 per cent in 1998 (no doubt in part because of wage inflation), while at the other extreme those earning over £50,000 increased from 10 per cent to over 21 per cent. However, it is possible that those who remained in television throughout the study's duration were those who were better rewarded for the job they did, or were more resilient to work-related stresses, or in some cases remained hopeful of breakthrough and eventual success in television while seeking work in related sectors.

Such aggregate figures conceal important trends. The income of new and young entrants to the industry is often still very low and, for some positions, even unpaid. Often there is a reliance on parental financial support in the initial stages of their employment, which clearly gives an unfair advantage to a relatively small group. One small independent producer commented that 'The gap between rich and poor in TV is widening all the time—so many young people work for nothing. This advantages the middle-class children of London and the South-East, against the rest of the country'. It is also notable that there is a marked disparity emerging between age groups in terms of background and secondary education, with a rise in the proportion of entrants who have benefited from private education.

For those who were in the 31–40 age group at the start of the survey, incomes dispersed and polarized over the four years. This age cohort has been most obviously affected by the changes in employment practice and the general conditions of the labour market. They are squeezed between a large number of entrants to the industry willing to undercut them in salary terms and a lack of more senior posts to progress to. The young industry syndrome identified in the US entertainment industry, which gives greater opportunities to the younger parts of the workforce (who are seen as more attuned to the needs and wants of the crucial under-35 demographic), may be increasingly applicable in Britain. In the US TV fiction production sector this is only discountable where an individual has had a recent commercial success.[8]

---

8 William T. Bielby and Denise D. Bielby, 'Organizational Mediation of Project-based Labor Markets: Talent Agencies and the Careers of Screenwriters', *American Sociological Review*, 64 (1999, 64–85).

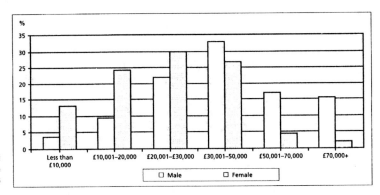

Fig. 1.
Percentage of males and
females within each
income bracket, May 1998

Generally, women tend to earn significantly less than men. Throughout the course of the Tracking Study women's salaries remained significantly lower than men's. For example, between May 1994 and May 1998, the percentage of men earning over £50,000 had risen from 16 to 32 per cent, but only 3 per cent of women were earning this much in 1994, rising to 6 per cent in May 1998. At the other end of the scale, the percentage of men earning less than £20,000 almost halved over the last four years, from 25 to 13 per cent. Yet the percentage of women earning less than £20,000 fell by only two per cent during this time, from 39 to 37 per cent (see Fig. 1).

Freelancers and those on short-term contracts consistently appeared in the lower income brackets compared to staff, although their incomes increased relative to staff during the course of the study. However, almost 85 per cent of respondents earning less than £10,000 were freelancers. As might be expected, there were significant differences in income for different types of jobs, so that by May 1998, over half (57 per cent) of the managers/executive producers were earning over £50,000, whereas only 16 per cent of producers and directors earned this much.

Changes in income level are very responsive to labour market conditions in a sector with a predominantly casualized and flexible workforce.[9] In 1997, 38 per cent of the respondents indicated that they had been able to push up the rate for the jobs they had done in the previous year. But another 42 per cent indicated that they had been offered or had been obliged to work for lower than their usual rate. Factors determining a willingness to accept a lower rate included interesting work and the possibility of making useful contacts, but were more often a response to the necessity of earning some income.

Short-term Contracts and Conditions of Uncertainty

Short-term contracts of a few weeks or months have become a defining element of employment for many of those working in the television industry. For some, this has provided a chance to enjoy the flexibility and freedom offered; for others, it has made it difficult to plan their career in a strategic way, or receive the security and stability associated with permanent employment as a member of staff in a company. One

9 cf. Gallie et al., *Restructuring the Employment Relationship*.

freelance producer/director described freelance work as 'a euphemism for uncertainty and unemployment'.

The search for secure work has meant that almost a third (32 per cent) of those who had worked on short-term contracts had taken less skilled jobs and almost a quarter (24 per cent) agreed that they had had to put aside ambition for the sake of security. One young researcher wrote: 'Applied for every long [i.e. one year] contract that I see in the BBC. Worried now that they think I'll go for anything but I do need the stability.' Characteristic of short-term work is the lack of benefits such as pensions, sick leave, holiday pay, maternity provision, and often the financial stability required by mortgage lenders.

Another young researcher noted that: 'In fact no security exists—how can it on a one-month contract? I have no pension plan or health scheme and am paid at the same rate as I did [sic] . . . over a year ago although I've developed and pitched ideas and worked as an assistant producer. I now feel little loyalty to the company and . . . I seek to leave as soon as possible. There should be very strict parameters for employing an ever-increasing short-term contract workforce.'

Some expressed the view that fewer and fewer employers are willing to take risks with ideas or to innovate. In a market where uncertainty is prevalent, it is possible that the most secure career path may mean taking the least risky option or the least innovative direction.

However, short-term contract work can provide an opportunity to gain a range of experiences at work, and 73 per cent agreed that it had given them a taste of another genre. In addition, 40 per cent of respondents agreed that short-term contracts had given them more time with their family, an advantage seen as especially beneficial by mothers.

For some of those who were unable to see a way of breaking into more secure or lucrative TV work, the situation had led them to consider whether or not to continue pursuing a career in the TV industry. One young assistant producer wrote: 'Strongly considering leaving TV produc-tion, but for one thing—what else can I do? The cons outweigh the pros hugely, but it's very difficult to leave when you've worked so hard for it.'

One difficulty in assessing why people leave the industry is that, in the main, we have the views of the 'survivors' in an industry which has a very high attrition rate for entrants. The most common responses of those leaving were that they were 'unhappy with their job' or that they had been made redundant (13 per cent each). A further 11 per cent wished to 'change their lifestyle' and 11 per cent had decided to take up another career.

Whilst a substantial proportion (some 40 per cent) of those working in television still retain staff status and life-long careers, workers in all parts of the industry are now having to adapt to uncertain work conditions. In their response to an uncertain working environment individuals have adopted a series of 'coping' strategies. There have been changes in the way work is secured or recruitment is carried out in television. There is less use of traditional procedures like formal applications or responding to advert-isements and greater use of personal contacts or pitching projects. For example, between 40 and 57 per cent of the sample at all times indicated the use of 'personal contacts' as the 'most important method' of finding work. Less than 5 per cent of all respondents indicated 'response to adverts' as their most important method for finding work.[10]

Freelancers reported being more likely to use personal contacts as a method of finding work than those with staff jobs. In May 1998, 63 per cent of freelancers indicated personal contacts as their main method of finding work, compared to 33 per cent of independent staff and 36 per cent of broadcast staff. Broadcast staff were those most likely to use job adverts and formal applications. A much larger percentage of freelancers were job-seeking at any time compared to staff. Freelance TV work involves either high turnover of jobs or periods of unemployment. Working freelance or on short-term contracts by necessity requires an almost constant eye on the job market, especially through the avenues of networking and personal contacts.[11]

With constant competition for work on new productions, reputation and the informal network of contacts are critical for continued employment. As Burt has suggested, 'the information benefits of a network define who knows about [. . .] opportunities, when they know, and who gets to participate in them,'[12] so that weak ties across a large network which also has a diversity of members working 'under a presumption of trust' is optimal.

Two-thirds of employers in the Tracking Study indicated using personal and work contacts, and 44 per cent reported using personal recommendations, as their main method of recruiting staff. All other methods mentioned (newspaper ads, trade press, in-house or internal ads, agencies, and speculative sending of CVs) each accounted for less than 15 per cent of the responses. Recruiters in the independent sector were more likely to use informal methods for seeking staff—69 per cent, compared to 32 per cent of those in the ITV companies, and 33 per cent of recruiters at the BBC.

Multi-skilling and Gender Issues

One major consequence of the increasing uncertainty associated with an industry so reliant on a casualized workforce and under budgetary pressure, but with a whole range of new technology to deploy, has been the rise of multi-skilling. There is a growing trend of merging posts and expecting staff to learn additional skills to take on the extra work involved. This can result in increased frustration and dissatisfaction with the individual's role in TV production, especially when the extra work is not accompanied by improved recognition or salary. One young researcher described why she

10 cf. Candace Jones, 'Careers in Project Networks: The Case of the Film Industry', in Arthur and Rousseau, *The Boundaryless Career*, 71: 'In industries with extensive subcontracting and permeable firm boundaries, tightly knit relations exist in the inner core, which are connected to loosely woven interactions on the peripheries. The peripheries of the industry's structure are open; those individuals with the necessary skills and desire [. . .] may enter'.

11 Cf. Wayne E. Baker and Robert R. Faulkner, 'Role as Resource in the Hollywood Film Industry', *American Journal of Sociology* 97: 2 (1991), 279–309.

12 Ronald Burt, *Structural Holes: The Social Structure of Competition* (Cambridge, Mass.: Harvard University Press, 1992), 13.

had left what had previously been a satisfying job: 'I had been unhappy in my job—I felt that I was doing a lot of work as a researcher which really should be classed as assistant producer work. Yet my boss was unwilling to give me acting pay or change my job title.' Some respondents felt that creating a 'jack of all trades' culture within the industry was eroding the skill base and would eventually erode quality.

The lack of continuity of employment has also led some workers to diversify their sources of income and work. Many indicated that they were using the skills gained through television work to find work in other, non-television fields. The need to supplement income by doing work in parallel with television, for example in radio or the growing multimedia field, was deemed essential for maintaining a career in the media. One freelance writer/producer/director, when discussing his diversified interests, wrote: 'Flexibility is the key to my survival, I feel.'

Flexibility in the labour market has also engendered exploitation. There is now a common expectation that freelance work, particularly in the development phase, may be unremunerated. Where in the past research and development were part of the work of staff members in large organizations, now it often takes place outside the organization, leading to freelancers sometimes working without any payment. This trend is exacerbated by the need to establish a reputation for high-quality work and for reliability with potential employers. In May 1998, 63 per cent of the freelancers stated that they had worked unpaid at some point in the last year. Producers and directors were found to be those most likely to have worked unpaid. The majority of freelancers undertaking unpaid work were researching and developing ideas (83 per cent), whether it was commissioned or speculative development work. Aside from research and development, 38 per cent of freelancers also reported having undertaken a fixed-fee project which had run overtime, and had therefore been paid for less time than they actually worked. Thus at both the beginning and end of a production project a freelance producer or director may be unpaid.

Women in the sample were much more likely to be single than men (29 per cent of women over 40 compared with 4 per cent of men) and 53 per cent of women over 40 did not have children compared with only 15 per cent of men. Women who take maternity leave or take a career break to have children proved extremely unlikely to continue in employment in such a high-stress industry. As part of the Tracking Study 13 of these women were interviewed in 1995, all of whom were over 30 when their first child was born.[13] They found that having children can disadvantage women in terms of career progression in ways that do not affect men. Two years after the interviews, only two respondents were in full-time continuous work. Whilst some had managed to sustain their job grades, only one had made career progress. Most women in the sample were not in jobs of comparable status to their pre-childbirth work. One producer in the independent sector commented: 'I think I certainly delayed having the first

---

[13] Reported in Janet Willis and Shirley Dex, *Mothers Returning to TV Production Work: Equal Opportunities in a Flexible Labour Market*, Research Papers in Management Studies (Cambridge: Judge Institute of Management Studies, 1999).

one until I was reasonably well established as a producer because I had seen lots of friends have babies when they were assistant producers and they just could never seem to crack being a producer or director afterwards'.

In addition to the gender differential found in earnings, a number of other notable differences were found. In May 1998, similar proportions of women and men in the study were working as producers or directors, but more women than men were working in the often lower-paid production support roles with men more likely to be filling managerial/executive producer roles and post-production or technical jobs. The percentage of women working as producers or directors during the course of the Tracking Study remained marginally higher than men, peaking at 9 per cent more than men in May 1997. This would indicate that women are able to compete strongly with men in the producer/director role, but are more likely to remain in this position after their male counterparts have moved on to more managerial roles. The percentage of those working in managerial and executive roles over four years increased from 6 per cent to 13 per cent for women, but from 20 to 26 per cent for men. At the important post-production/technical or 'craft' levels, which historically have been well paid and secure in Britain's television industry, men continue to outnumber women significantly.

A greater proportion of women in the study were found to be working freelance compared to men. When the study began, 51 per cent of women and 44 per cent of men were working freelance. In May 1998, 39 per cent of men were working freelance, compared to 48 per cent of women.

The implications for equal opportunities are not clear. Men as well as women find that new conditions and competition in the workplace generate uncertainty. Moreover, crude gender stereotypes are gone in the cost-cutting, low-budget environment where who will do the job at the price is far more important than whether it is a man or a woman. Opportunities for men and women are now more equal, so long as women remain childless, but this equality has been brought about by the worsening of men's conditions of work as much as it has been by improvements in women's.

Creative work in television remains a challenging and often enjoyable (if sometimes stressful) set of tasks. Its attractiveness has been dimmed by the life of uncertainty which those working in its structures have to bear. As one young researcher noted, one important factor affecting her move into television was that she 'wanted to be part of a larger "creative" process', but later notes that there is 'always a sense of insecurity caused by the constant shifts in the work place—and the constant need to be looking for "the next job"', and that there is 'a sense that I'm compromising everything else in order to be successful in TV'. The changing nature of the career anchor is further attested by a successful female producer in her forties: 'The loss of jobs for life means that everyone, no matter how successful, is insecure. This is good as well as bad—no one can be complacent but the insecurity can wreck some people's confidence'. Finally, a long-time staff member at the BBC in a secure staff position commented, 'often people within the BBC feel so undervalued that it comes as a surprise that they're rated in the outside world'.

Many of the aspects valued most highly for creative work were also those experienced positively by respondents in their current or recent job. Over 80 per cent of respondents had experienced 'working in a team', 65 per cent a positive 'exchange of ideas', 70 per cent 'working with talented individuals', and 67 per cent a positive level of 'trust between colleagues' in their current or most recent job.

However, only 28 per cent of respondents had experienced 'effective management', even though this had been rated highly as a factor in encouraging creativity of work, while less than 30 per cent of the sample had received 'good pay' or 'sufficient time'. Although 85 per cent of respondents gave leadership a high score as an important factor in encouraging creativity, less than 40 per cent of respondents indicated that they had experienced 'effective leadership' in their current or most recent job.

Almost all respondents who had staff positions were more likely to experience aspects of the creative work environment more positively in the workplace than those working freelance and on short-term contracts. Over half of staff had experienced 'adaptability to change' in their current workplace, whereas less than a third of freelancers reported the same. Thirty-nine per cent of staff had experienced 'staff stability' compared with only 21 per cent of freelancers. Large differences for contract type were also experienced for 'responsiveness to ideas', 'exchange of ideas' and 'working as a team'.

When looking at the type of organization worked for, several differences are revealed between those working for the BBC or the ITV companies and those in the independent sector. Almost 60 per cent of those working for the independent sector were positive about working in their company compared with 18 per cent of those in ITV and 7 per cent in the BBC. Furthermore, twice as many workers in the independent sector reported having positively experienced 'effective management' compared to those from the BBC and ITV companies, and half of those working for independent companies had experienced 'effective leadership' in their job compared to only a third of those at the BBC. This suggests that working for a small company gives individuals better access to effective management and leadership, perhaps because the creative team works more closely together than do those in larger companies, where more structured management hierarchies apply.

The changes in the television industry in the past two decades—both through direct intervention as a result of new legislation and through technological and other contingent changes—have led to a radical alteration in the working lives of those employed there. These changes have opened up the industry to new ways of working and offered the opportunity to many more to seek success in it. However, the long-term effects on output remain uncertain. There has been a reduction in direct training in the industry by the large organizations and for some a perception of a drop in standards.[14] Work in television remains for now a highly attractive proposition to ambitious individuals despite the high attrition rate for new entrants. As media convergence gathers pace, television production work (a

---

14 See *British Film Industry Tracking Study: Third Report*, 41.

very specialized form of knowledge work) may become just one option for the aspiring worker wishing to perform a job with social purpose and glamorous associations. The wider issue of appropriate work environments to encourage creativity, and appropriate employment modes to retain talented staff in a highly competitive arena, will remain key factors in all media industries. Workers planning their careers will need to negotiate the major labour market transitions, which seem certain to continue, and will also need to retain and market their knowledge and skills to ensure sustained employment.

24

New Technologies and Changing Work Practices in Irish Broadcasting

Ellen Hazelkorn

FROM THE 1980s onwards most national broadcasting systems around the world experienced radical change. New technologies, new liberalizing policies, more competition between more channels, and more importing were accompanied by radical changes in production and work practices; these included the elimination of many technical jobs, as well as much de-skilling, multi-skilling, and re-skilling. There was a weakening of public broadcasting, of trade unions, and of male dominance; there was a growth in 'independent' production, in freelancing, and in non-staff employment, and a switch towards the feminization of some work areas.

Even in the UK (where the change was slower than in the USA, Italy, France, and Germany) it is now quite difficult to explain precisely what the main changes were. In the UK the relatively simple BBC versus ITV situation underwent complex changes; many companies changed ownership, trade unions merged, and even the regulatory agencies changed their names, areas of competence, and regulatory approach.

Ellen Hazelkorn's chapter focuses on the somewhat clearer picture in Ireland, where the public broadcaster (RTE) retained a central role. Ireland, like other smaller-population countries in northern Europe, tried to introduce its radical changes a little more slowly and wisely than had some of its larger neighbours. Nevertheless Ireland itself faced special difficulties, not least in terms of limited TV production capacity. Ireland also, like other low-population nations, had to confront not only the Hollywood challenge, but also a nearby big brother; in Ireland's case this was the UK, with its big broadcasting base in northern Ireland.

This chapter gives an exceptionally sharp picture of these profound late-twentieth-century broadcasting changes. Hazelkorn makes clear that the entire occupational structure—with its previous patterns of skill, craft, and professionalization—was radically and permanently changed.

Source: Not previously published. Ellen Hazelkorn is at the Dublin Institute of Technology in Dublin.

Competition and Technological Change

Established in 1960, RTE (Radio Telefís Eireann) enjoyed the status of being the sole broadcaster in Ireland despite effectively operating within a broadcasting environment dominated by the UK's BBC and independent networks. Beginning in the 1980s, however, fundamental changes in the global broadcasting market place, including the emergence of new media technologies, the multiplicity of (public and commercial, terrestrial and satellite) broadcasting channels, the fragmentation of the audience, and the mogulization of media ownership, combined to undermine broadcasting-in-one-country. Given Ireland's peripheral economic status, policy moved quickly to recognize and realize the opportunities: the media/cultural industry could be economically advantageous. Accordingly, the view that government would be better off regulating rather than owning various key utilities, including media and telecommunications, is now ideologically uncontentious. Emphasis has been on liberalization, privatization, and diversification of the broadcasting, cable, and telecommunications market place, active promotion of Internet and e-commerce technologies, and significant investment in technological infrastructure.

The conjuncture and implications of these developments (economic, political, and technological) has not been lost on the public broadcaster, RTE, which had arguably enjoyed a monopoly position. In recent decades, there has been a rapid growth in the number and formats of media providers. Teilifís na Gaeilge (TnaG—now TG4), the Irish-language station, began broadcasting in October 1996, followed by TV3, Ireland's first commercial station, in September 1998. The popularity of local, community, special interest, and commercial radio stations has further challenged the once-prevailing wisdom that a country with a population as small as Ireland's (3. 6 million) could only handle a limited number of media. Thus, despite RTE's winning the right to be a major provider of digital television in Ireland, its declining audience figures and peak-market share, rising costs of programme purchase and production, deteriorating financial position, requirements to partially fund the Irish-language TnaG, challenges to its 'right' to the television licence fund and the transmission network, and the 'forced' sale of its share of the largest cable company (Cablelink) suggest that RTE's circumstances will be significantly different in the new millennium.

A 1985 government-commissioned study assessed the challenges to broadcasting 'in the era of competition', and recommended a reformation of RTE's corporate organization and strategy to prepare it for a changed domestic and global media environment: transformation from producer to publisher, externalization of programme-making through active commissioning and purchasing of independent productions, aka the Channel 4 model, and changes in heretofore restrictive work practices and conditions of employment. The study was strongly critical of RTE for failing to take advantage of new technologies, where such technologies would help reduce staffing levels and costs. Indeed, in comparison with other broadcasters, RTE had shown itself to be a reluctant user of new technology. As a result, a new management strategy was adopted. *Competing in the New Environment—Our Strategy for Survival* was a detailed account of RTE's response to the changed media environment:

We must produce and transmit more and better programmes at lower cost and with fewer staff. This is the essence of the challenge, which we face and must overcome. If we fail to do so now we risk getting into a spiral of decline, which will become impossible to halt and which would undoubtedly have disastrous consequences for RTE and RTE staff [. . .]

Multiskilling must become the norm, and while preserving how [sic] essential production and operational core skills and maintaining programme quality and output standards, staff in general will need to cover a range of duties for which they are competent or for which they can, with limited effort, be trained and scheduled to work as a team. [. . .] reasonable flexibility within a team concept has to be the norm. (RTE 1988: 2, 6)

Remarkably similar in tone to the UK *Broadcasting in the '90s: Competition, Choice and Quality—The Government's Plans for Broadcasting*, RTE's strategy emphasized flexibility, efficiency, and lower costs. It accepted the need for technological innovation and deployment of new media technologies, although it promised there would be no compulsory redundancies; job reductions would be achieved by 'natural wastage' and early retirement. Hence, restructuring the organization, introducing new technologies, and changing work practices were seen as key mechanisms to help reduce costs, create greater efficiencies, and enhance broadcasting and programming output. In response, the trade unions argued over issues of deskilling and reskilling and compensation; there were two industrial disputes in 1991 and 1992.

At the end of the century, the challenges posed by 'the pace of change affecting both the technology and the public policy of broadcasting' (RTE 1998*a*: 3) required that RTE embrace a strategy of continuous change. To meet these challenges, the Executive Board instigated a 'thorough review of the organisation [. . .] not merely anticipating the imminent arrival of keener domestic and international competition [. . . but] to project itself into the future' (ibid. 25). Following an intensive six-month review, the RTE Authority and senior management issued a blueprint for the future, *Review of RTE's Structures and Operations*; at the same time, the trade union group within RTE, with management support, published their own review, *Towards a Shared Vision*. The Review identified 'modern technologies, structures and accompanying work practices [. . . and operating] in a commercially enterprising manner in order to maximise its revenue' as fundamental to any strategy for survival. In so doing, the report acknowledged significant changes in work practices that had already occurred and anticipated further changes to ensure that RTE's 'methods of operation [. . .] conform to best practice' (RTE 1998*b*: 11).

Technology and the Broadcasting Labour Force

From inception, technology and technological change have been central to radio and television. The introduction of FM radio broadcasts, the invention of the transistor radio, and the move to colour television increased the consumption of media products in the 1970s. More recently, computerization and digitalization have swelled the possibility of media platforms, often enabling new audiences to be captured by simply reformulating existing media products onto new technologies. New technologies have also led to significant changes in media production techniques and practices, most notably smaller crews and simplified post-production. These developments have generated economies while substantially raising production standards. Digital technologies have also altered or eliminated many traditional skills required in the media production process by rendering them obsolete or less efficient. They have shifted the balance between large media institutions and small independent production facilities in favour of the latter.

RTE has not been a market leader in the early adoption of new technology, partly due to the financial constraints under which it has operated. Unlike other broadcasters who had embraced new technology with lower operating and cost structures, RTE sought initially to rapidly downsize and casualize. Nevertheless, its decision to implement changes in working modes and practices is demanded by the new broadcasting environment and the problems it poses, particularly for broadcasting in and by a small, peripheral society. Recognizing that these developments will have major implications for those working in RTE, the Review specifically asks employees to directly address the issues of change:

> The RTE that thrives in this new environment will be a different organisation. [. . .] Renewing RTE means creating new relationships, new structures and new ways of doing our work [. . .] Each of us asks—what does this mean for me? Will RTE be harder, leaner, more focused on the bottom line? Will it still do public service broadcasting? Will there be a job for me? Will I want to work in such an organisation? (RTE 1998*b*: 1)

The Review team concludes that through this process, RTE is 'capable of achieving a minimum reduction of 270 posts and a minimum total savings of £15m.' Given the strategy of transferring programming to the independent sector, there could be a further reduction of 100 jobs and savings of £2m. Much of the 'savings' will come from greater efficiencies gained through wider use of new technologies (ibid. 9).

A study of changes in work practices arising from the impact of new technology was conducted in RTE in the late 1980s. Fig. 1 provides an updated look at the changes within particular divisions.

Labour Restructuring

Labour flexibility is a key advantage of new media technologies: slimmed-down production teams and the contracting-in of cheaper programming and/or skills from independent production and facilities houses. Single-operator crews are fast becoming the industry norm. With the introduction of self-editing, there is greater convergence between the technical and the production sides of broadcasting, eliminating traditional boundaries; for example, technicians are retrained as journalists and journalists re-skilled to edit their own interviews. During 1997, RTE, following trends elsewhere, introduced the position of multi-skilled 'technical operator'. Another

- ■ **Engineering**
- ◇ Changes in transmitter technology and specifically modular circuits through microelectronics.
- ◇ Transmitters now controlled directly from studios.
- ◇ Decline in the demand for engineers partially offset by demand to service the growth of IT systems – a situation not repeatable in other areas.

- ■ **Radio**
- ◇ Digital technology has led to self-editing, a technique suitable for people with little or no sound operating background.

- ■ **Digital switching**
- ◇ Move from analogue to digital equipment means integrated circuits and touch-screen VDUs are controllable from anywhere in the studio.
- ◇ Capability to 'go directly to the transmitter network', thereby making it possible for a single presenter to control programme output on radio, without a sound operator needing to be present.
- ◇ Transformation of that part of television studio operations which mixes sound and vision for final live broadcast, cues and announces programmes, and sends out the broadcast signal.
- ◇ Significant scope for efficiencies arising from further introduction of new technology and its integration with Master Control.

- ■ **Graphic design**
- ◇ Revolutionized practice of producing artwork on paper and then filming it with a camera.
- ◇ Integration of skills with other technical aspects of production, transmitting work from computer to videotape directly without involving a video tape operator.
- ◇ Increased quality of work and speed of delivery has increased demand, with the result that staff numbers have increased in this section.

- ■ **Lighting**
- ◇ New saturated lighting rigs, which are quickly rigged and derigged, means that operations can substantially be carried out at the flick of a switch.

- ■ **ENG/EFP equipment**
- ◇ User-friendliness, light-weight, and superior technical capability of video over film processing has virtually led to the replacement of the latter by the former.
- ◇ Extend use of one-person crews to other areas, 'e.g. current affairs'.
- ◇ News crews should 'begin to use laptop field editors, as they become available'.

- ■ **Telecine VTR**
- ◇ Equipment is more reliable than cinecameras; increased number of VTRs and cameras.
- ◇ Commitment to 'in-house' repairs has led to increased numbers.
- ◇ Imminent replacement of videotape formats by compact disc and networked file-server technology.

Fig. 1
Summary of Impact of
Technological Change on
Selected Departments in
RTE, 1988–1999
Sources: Hazelkorn
(1996); RTE (1998b).

change has been the decline in full-time employment, with a move towards casualization of employment through a shift towards short-term contracts lasting either for several months or the duration of a series.

Unlike its counterparts in the UK and the US, the prevailing political and public climate in Ireland has proven itself intolerant of large-scale redundancies, especially in state institutions. Thus, RTE has used a combination of early retirement, redeployment, retraining, and alterations in staffing structures to effect the necessary cost efficiencies required. In this way, the full extent of the impact of new technology is masked by RTE's social responsibility. Thus far, the pace of change has been able to absorb the level of redeployment and retraining, albeit the unions have expressed concern that the speed of change might begin to outpace the organizational ability of the corporation to absorb displaced labour.

The industrial disputes of 1991 and 1992 began when RTE sought to introduce two-person camera crews without trade union approval for the level of compensation to be awarded to members displaced by technology. The unions claimed that they did not seek to overturn the decision to use new technology but rather sought compensation for those members affected by its introduction. In this regard, the dispute illustrates the inability of the unions to influence the 'product strategy' of RTE as regards the quality and nature of programmes produced. Previous efforts to influence the nature and extent of technological change had also been thwarted. Explanations for this failure rest to some extent on union unwillingness to become involved in retraining, preferring instead to negotiate increased wages. Worrying from the union's viewpoint must be the fact that RTE views the introduction and use of technology as an essential means to achieve greater efficiencies and competitiveness, and accordingly intends to work with those who are 'prepared to change and take on new work'.

Another aspect of labour restructuring has been changes in employment categories. In the early 1980s, the government introduced an embargo on full-time employment in the public sector as an on-going policy of reducing current expenditure. To meet the recommendations of the 1985 consultancy study, RTE has sought to make new appointments and promotions by contract only. This trend towards casualization of the labour force is best illustrated by Table 1: in 1988, 2,146 people were employed, 99 of whom were in non-permanent employment; in contrast, by 1998, 761 people held non-permanent employment. By 1999, almost half of RTE's employees were non-permanent!

TABLE 1. RTE Labour Force, 1988–1999

Year	Total employed	Permanent	Non-permanent	% Non-permanent
1988	2,146	1,867	99	4.6
1994	1,973	1,643	330	16.7
1998	2,100	1,399	761	36.2
1999	2,093	1,147	946	45.2

Source: RTE Annual Reports.

A closer examination illustrates that the pattern of casualization of employment is not universal. There is a marked contrast between employment patterns in the technical and production divisions, albeit all areas showed a fall in the numbers employed. Technical areas, such as radio and television facilities, show a steady contraction in permanent and pensionable employment, with no comparable increase in non-permanent employment. For example, total engineering staff fell from 379 in 1988 to 199 in 1994, of which non-permanent contract staff constituted 26.1 per cent in 1988 but only 3 per cent in 1994. Thus, no new employment has been generated in this area. In contrast, permanent and pensionable staff in production areas, most notably in television programming, radio, and news, are being replaced or displaced by non-permanent contract staff; the latter has increased from 10 per cent to 19.9 per cent, from 3.8 per cent to 15.8 per cent, and from 2 per cent to 28.2 per cent, respectively (see Table 2).

TABLE 2. Employment categories in selected divisions in RTE, 1988 and 1994

		Total staff	Permanent and pensionable	Continuous employment	Employment contract	Temporary contract	Non-permanent contract (%)
Radio facilities	1994	58	57	1	0	0	0
	1988	91	89	1	1	0	1.1
Engineering	1994	199	190	2	6	0	3
	1988	379	359	11	99	0	26.1
TV programmes	1994	351	239	42	60	10	19.9
	1988	399	302	57	40	10	10
Radio 1	1994	177	127	22	27	1	15.8
	1988	212	177	27	8	1	3.8
News	1994	142	102	0	39	1	28.2
	1988	137	118	16	3	1	2.2
Total	1994	1973	1508	135	292	38	16.7
	1988	2146	1867	180	99		4.6

Note. Non-permanent contract category includes those employed on both employment or temporary contracts.

Source. RTE.

The relationship between technology and labour restructuring within RTE is complex and often contradictory. While competitive and political factors have stressed technological innovation, other factors have slowed its implementation and effects. Both deskilling and reskilling are occurring, sometimes in tandem. Their impact has been felt unevenly by the labour force; for example, while all areas have experienced a decline in employment, new employment is less likely in technical areas most affected directly by new technology, for obvious reasons. This suggests that if and when the embargo on permanent and pensionable employment is lifted, new recruitment is likely in non-technological areas. This represents a shift in the balance of skill/power relations between technology ('blue collar') and production ('white collar') jobs. This rebalancing carries significant implications for the rate of 'productivity' as new media technology opens up the possibility for a shift from 'variable' (wages) to 'fixed' (plant) capital by reducing the production process and the cost of production. Effectively, technological developments have enabled many more people to make programmes more easily. People with little or no technical skill can with little or no additional training undertake traditionally quite skilful operations, a factor illustrated by the experience of self-editing. Additionally, the latter workers carry none of the benefits of premium payments (e.g. for unsociable or overtime hours) associated with the formally well-organized technical staff.

Another factor is gender. Women constitute only 31.8 per cent of full-time but 60 per cent of part-time staff. The technical areas of media production (lighting, camera, sound, etc.) have traditionally been male bastions but these areas are most vulnerable to incursions of new technology. In contrast, women are likely to be employed on contract as production support staff (e.g. administrative activities, researchers, production assistants, secretaries, receptionists, programme directors, etc.). Employment patterns within RTE, like its international counterparts, continue to show a strongly segregated skill and grading structure: men dominate the technical areas while women are over-represented in administrative activities. While RTE is an 'equal opportunity employer', distinctions in recruitment and promotion continue to be highlighted. Although skill sounds like something that can be measured objectively, skills have increasingly become a 'masculine prerogative'. Indeed, the demarcation between 'women's jobs' and 'men's jobs' is as strongly marked as ever throughout the industry (see Table 3). One explanation for the significant recruitment of women into some production grades, categorized as 'pink collar' or 'velvet ghetto', is the declining status of the specific medium (e.g. radio vis-à-vis television, broadcasting vis-à-vis film).

For understandable reasons, journalists and producer/directors have more readily embraced multi-skilling than their technical counterparts; the former see it as a means of enhancing their control while the latter see it as losing control over the finished product. The evidence further suggests that women are more likely to be the beneficiaries or victims (depending on one's analysis) of casualized employment in the sector. Given the media's predilection to image, gender factors such as 'technological know-how' and 'personality/looks' may play a key role in explaining new forms of sex

TABLE 3. Distribution of Male and Female Employees in Independent Film and Television Production Companies and Facilities Houses, Ireland, 1995

Group	Permanent					Contract		
	Male		Female			Male	Female	
	Number	%	Number	%	Total	(Number)	(Number)	Total
Production management	82	77	24	23	106	9	5	14
Production support	18	16	97	84	115	7	9	16
Operational	122	83	25	17	147	26	4	30
Total	222	60	146	40	368	42	18	60

Source: Statcom/FAS (1994).

segregation, e.g. behind vs. in front of the camera, directing vs. producing. Technology may be capable of bridging the gap between conception and execution in the 'artistic' production process but the rewards are not necessarily evenly distributed.

Implications for Broadcasting (in Ireland)

The internal changes in RTE are taking place against a backdrop of, and in response to, a revolution in broadcasting. The establishment in 1982 of Channel Four in the UK proffered a new model of broadcasting, formally separating production from broadcasting, thereby transforming the 'integrated factory production into the publisher model' and creating 'a new industrial model'. This process was seen as both a means of reducing public-broadcaster costs and stimulating the development of an independent production sector, from which both the BBC and ITV were to commission 25 per cent of programming. In Ireland, the shift to the independent sector was initially quite modest; TnaG would operate as a publisher-broadcaster, with most of its programmes commissioned from independent producers or bought in and dubbed (mainly from languages other than English, and particularly from lesser-used languages). The Broadcasting Authority (Amendment) Act 1993 marked a more determined effort to 'jump-start' an independent film and broadcasting sector. RTE was required to make available IR£5.0 million in 1994, rising in each financial year to 20 per cent of television programme expenditure or IR£12.5 million (whichever is greater) by 1999 for programmes commissioned from the independent sector. The Independent Production Unit (IPU) was established to liaise with and commission such programming from the independent sector. This was essentially a strategy of managed privatization, based on fiscal and legislative restrictions on the state sector and incentives to the private sector with the intention of jump-starting an independent media production sector and marketing the country as an English-language beachhead producing content for the rapidly expanding global media/cultural industries.

While that sector has received significant public policy attention in recent years, it remains small: 84 per cent of production and facilities houses have ten or fewer employees and 69 per cent five or fewer. Many were start-ups by former RTE employees who opted for early retirement during the initial mid-1980s destaffing. While operating on a financial precipice, they survive through a combination of flexible work practices and multi-skilling, a low-cost base with low overheads, and contracting-in both labour skills and equipment as required. It is their ability to undercut significantly the cost of programme production by the state broadcaster, because of the latter's rigid structure of secure employment contracts and conditions of employment, that signals the most revolutionary challenge to broadcasting and to its labour force.

Essentially, the independent sector is a freelance sector—more aptly referred to as a 'system of sub-contracted labour'—although the precarious nature of much of its employment precludes an accurate picture.

Between 1991 and 1994, permanent employment increased by 18 per cent but freelance employment grew by 58 per cent. Of the 3,500 people employed in the entire audio-visual industry in Ireland during those years, including those employed by RTE, almost half or 1,500 were freelance. While the trade unions still control access to employment in the sector through a closed-shop policy, they are in no position to present any serious challenge. More flexible work practices, the often intimate employment relations, where recruitment and promotion is often on a basis of personal contact and the 'old boy network', and the precarious and spasmodic nature of media production work militates against this. This is well illustrated by the 1992 strike in RTE; although ostensibly over the size of camera crews, some union organizers did proclaim it as a strike in defence of trade unions against a 'management offensive'. Despite the unions' 'success' in persuading the majority of their members to stay outside the gate, new technology had simplified broadcasting to the extent that a few managers could sustain the national radio and television station. New media technologies, which have resulted in the reduction in the size of camera crews, have made it more difficult for unions to 'produce technical arguments to support their negotiating position' (Sparks 1982: 26). The open acknowledgement of defeat by union strategists illustrates the depth of decline from its legendary bargaining strength of the 1970s. While the Irish situation is a long way off from the UK, where the independent sector is fast becoming the largest production base in the country, the fact that TV3 operates as a 'publisher', with an annual budget of £6 million (£10–12 million initial capital costs) and a staff of 100, suggests clear parallels.

Many of the changes described above correspond to normal economic developments, whereby technology is introduced in order to reduce labour costs and secure competitive advantage and audience/market share. RTE is just one of many broadcasters implementing change:

1. a continuing decline in full-time employment;
2. a move towards casualization of employment through a shift towards short-term contracts, lasting either for several months or a series' duration;
3. erosion of the demarcation between the technical and production areas, both within broadcasting and between broadcasting and film, and a rebalancing of the power relationships between the two;
4. slimmed-down production teams;
5. contracting-in of programming and/or skills from independent production and facilities houses;
6. routinization (or redefinition) of many previously skilled tasks.

There is little dispute over the significance of these changes. Economic, ideological/political, and technological developments, arguably in that order, have combined to change the environment in which broadcasting has and will operate. Several concluding comments can be made. First, all broadcasters face the struggle for economic survival; competition for audience/market share is, because of technology, truly global. Public broadcasters, especially small ones, operate in an increasingly more aggressive climate in which even public support can no longer be taken for granted; broadcasting-in-one-country is no longer tenable. This certainly has implications for 'national culture' but also for sheer survival. Second, new technologies have had a major transformative impact on the nature of work, work practices, and the product. It has changed for ever the way programmes are made and distributed. Strict demarcations between skills, which traditionally required an 'apprenticeship', no longer exist. Employees must be multi-skilled and flexible. The structure of the firm has also changed. Third, access to technology is now widely available at decreasing cost. Web publishing will place broadcasting into more and more hands, theoretically diminishing the power of the majors to control the equipment. This has opened the door to the emergence of an independent sector, cheapening the cost of the product they produce. In turn, the independents, which often operate a 'kitchen table' operation, continually force down the cost of production within traditional broadcasting corporations. Fourth, while ideological dislike for state broadcasting systems may have been an initial rationale for some policy initiatives, there are now sound economic reasons to support the shift from producer to publisher. It is not just in Ireland that the sponsorship of an independent commercial production sector has become both 'the nuclei of cultural industries' and the undertaker of the large public broadcasters. Recent experiences of change in the Irish media industry are representative of change experienced elsewhere. Technology, overdetermined by ideological and economic imperatives, has engineered a revolution in the social and economic relations of production, involving deconcentration, decentralization, and 'democratization' of the audiovisual industry.

References

DELOITTE and TOUCHE (1998), *A Strategy for Digital Television and Broadband Communications Services* (Dublin: Deloitte and Touche).

FRENCH, N., HAZELKORN, E., and TRUETZSCHLER, W. (1990–) (eds.), *Irish Communications Review* (Dublin: Dublin Institute of Technology; also available on-line at www.icr.dit.ie).

HAZELKORN, ELLEN (1995), 'Ireland: From Nation Building to Economic Priorities', in M. de Moragas Spá, C. Garitaonandía, and B. Lopez (eds.), *Decentralisation in the Global Era: Television in the Regions, Nationalities and Small Countries of the European Union* (London: John Libbey).

—— (1996), 'Technology and Labour Restructuring in Public Broadcasting: The Case of Ireland's RTE', *Irish Communications Review*, 6.

—— (1997), 'Digital Technologies, Work Practices and Cultural Production in Ireland', *Economic and Social Review*.

—— (1999), 'Competitive Challenges for Irish Television in the Digital Age,' in M. de Moragas Spá, C. Garitaonandía, and B. Lopez (eds.), *Television on Your Doorstep: Decentralization Experiences in the European Union* (Luton: University of Luton Press).

RTE (1988), *Competing in the New Environment: Our Strategy for Survival* (Dublin: RTE).

RTE (1998*a*), *Annual Report* (Dublin: RTE).

—— (1988*b*), *Review of RTE's Structure and Operations* (Dublin: RTE).

SPARKS, COLIN (1992), 'The Impact of Technological and Political Change on the Labour Force in British Television', *Screen.*

Statcom/FAS (1994), *The Independent Film & Television Production Sector in Ireland: Training Issues to 2000* (Dublin: Statcom/FAS).

SKC (Stokes Kennedy Crowley) (1985), *Review of Radio Telefís Eireann: Report to the Minister for Communications* (Dublin: Government Publications).

5

National and Regional Overviews of Media Occupations

25

Media Occupations in Sub-Saharan Africa

Graham Mytton

THE MEDIA IN Africa are generally less developed than elsewhere. There are fewer press titles enjoying lower circulation per capita. There are also fewer radio and television stations, and fewer sets per head of population. The underdeveloped nature of the media reflects both Africa's poverty and its colonization by the European powers. Low levels of literacy, underdeveloped infrastructure, especially for distribution, low levels of advertising spend, and the high cost of mostly imported newsprint and ink have restricted the growth of the press. Radio has the ability to overcome some of these barriers but poverty has slowed the development of broadcasting, both at the transmitting and receiving ends. Many African countries still do not have universal radio or TV services capable of being received in all parts by all people. While in some countries radio now reaches almost everyone, there are others where it does not.[1]

Africa's corps of professionals in media occupations is small. Professional standards are, in many countries, not very high. Media professionals tend to enjoy rather low status. In many cases they are poorly paid government officials, especially in broadcasting, which has long been regarded as part of the apparatus of the state. Some journalists in the independent sector, which has grown in many countries in recent years, have been harassed, detained, and imprisoned by governments.

There is today, however, a growing sense of professionalism. Media professionals are increasingly challenging interference by the state and in many countries we are beginning to see the development of professional organizations capable of mounting successful legal and moral challenges to state control and interference. This, coupled with the decline in state control of media, gives some grounds for optimism.

Source: **Not previously published. Graham Mytton's book *Mass Communication in Africa* was published in 1983; he was subsequently Head of Audience Research at BBC World Service Radio.**

1 In Tanzania, for example, radio has a weekly reach of over 90% of the population. Even in rural areas, almost 9 in 10 Tanzanians hear radio programmes at least once a week. In contrast, there are rural areas of Mozambique and Sudan where only a minority hear any radio.

The dominance of the state in the media predates independence, achieved by most sub-Saharan African countries in the 1960s. The European colonial powers controlled all broadcast media. The press was mostly formally independent but in very many cases was dominated and owned by colonial settlers, or by European religious or commercial organizations.

There were some indigenous newspapers and magazines. Most of these were in the British territories of West Africa, and in Liberia and South Africa. Faringer estimated that by 1900, sixty-three African newspapers had been published in Britain's West African territories—Gambia, Sierra Leone, Gold Coast, and Nigeria.[2] This was evidence both of their uncertain financial basis—few titles lasted more than a few years—and also of what another writer and distinguished editor and teacher Frank Barton described as a 'bush fire out of control'. He was referring to the way in which Africans with aspirations saw the press as a way to campaign for emancipation.[3]

Herbert Macaulay established a daily newspaper in Nigeria in 1925. The *Lagos Daily News*, affiliated to a political party, set a pattern that continues to this day. Many if not most daily papers in Africa's most populous state are politically affiliated. Macaulay was a radical and some feared the influence of his paper. A group of conservative business people started a competing newspaper, *The Daily Times*. This was to become a very successful and widely read paper in modern Nigeria. It soon set professional standards, both in journalism and in print and layout, that have had considerable influence in Nigeria and beyond. There soon developed vigorous competition for readership and sales between these and other new titles.

The West African tradition of the press as a campaigning medium survives quite strongly today. One famous Nigerian nationalist campaigner and politician, Nnamdi Azikiwe, started the *African Morning Post* in 1934 and later the *West African Pilot*, a paper that was to become a major force in the nationalist campaigns of the 1950s and in the party rivalries that were to follow the achievement of independence.

In other parts of Britain's empire and in the French and Portuguese territories, no significant African press was to emerge for many years. In East and Central Africa, settlers had been involved in newspaper production for several years, but there was little African involvement and no important titles appeared until well into the twentieth century. In both Kenya and Tanganyika, nationalist leaders like Jomo Kenyatta and Julius Nyerere were involved in some early African papers. But, Erica Fiah in Tanganyika is probably the only East African who can be compared to Azikiwe or Macaulay in West Africa. In a more modest way, Fiah used his own paper to promote African emancipation and political power during the 1930s.[4]

A tradition built up in British West Africa of the press as a campaigning, anti-authority instrument for political and social change. Elsewhere, even

---

2 Gunilla L. Faringer, *Press Freedom in Africa* (New York: Praeger, 1991), 6.

3 Frank Barton, *The Press of Africa: Persecution and Perseverance* (London: Macmillan, 1979), 15.

4 Rosalynde Ainslie, *The Press in Africa* (London: Victor Gollancz, 1966), and John Iliffe, 'The Age of Improvement and Differentiation (1907–1945)' in I. N. Kimambo and A. J. Temu (eds), *A History of Tanzania*, (Nairobi: EAPH, 1969).

without such indigenous challenges, the British colonial authorities acted in response to these actual or perceived threats with their own sponsored or financed press. There were the government official gazettes.[5] And as a counter to feared subversion and opposition to colonial policies the British authorities also supported through direct or indirect subsidy a range of nominally independent press titles, especially during the period immediately before independence.

Competition was entirely absent in the broadcast media. Here the government—colonial before independence and African governments thereafter—had complete control. Radio, and later television also as it emerged during the 1960s and 1970s, were run as departments of the government. While governments, both colonial and independent African, had been and continued to be *involved* in the printed press, they were in total *control* of broadcasting. No independent voices were permitted. The radio was as much an instrument of the state as the national armed forces or the police. Broadcasters were civil servants, if not always in name, certainly in their relationships to the rest of the state apparatus.

The Immediate Post-Independence Period

When independence was achieved, the media quickly became instruments of power in the new states. They were believed to have an important role in the very creation and shaping of the new states. They were expected to portray in a favourable light the personalities, images, and symbols of the new state and its rulers. Media professionals were expected to be obedient if not enthusiastic and committed advocates in this portrayal. This was not all a matter of building up the political position of the new rulers. There was also a good degree of optimism about the modern mass media and what they could achieve for the general good. Given the absence of infrastructure and the low level of literacy in many states, radio was especially seen as having great potential to bridge developmental gaps and to help to mobilize people. Radio, it was argued, could bring education and information to people who would otherwise not have it. It could inform farmers, publicize educational and health campaigns, act as an effective communicator of essential information, and generally contribute to the well-being of the whole of each state.

There is little doubt that radio did play a role of this kind. The remarkable historical coincidence of the invention in 1948 of the transistor and its commercial development in the 1950s and 1960s, and the coming to independence of some forty nation states during the same period, has been ignored in literature on communications. The transistor made radio portable and cheap and liberated it from reliance on main electricity supply, which most African homes did not have. Radio rapidly became the most widespread medium in Africa and this had important consequences for Africa's culture and political life.[6]

---

5 African scholar Professor Ali Mazrui has put forward the theory that the reason why the Swahili word for a newspaper is *gazeti* is that these government gazettes were so prominent.

6 I explore these issues in *Mass Communication in Africa* (London: Edward Arnold, 1983).

The new governments were nervous of this new and now more widespread medium. They sought to maintain maximum control over media, including the printed press. The then President of Zambia said this at a conference of the International Press Institute in Nairobi in 1968:

> The press is capable of making or destroying governments given appropriate conditions; it can cause war or create conditions for peace. It can promote development or create difficulties in the way of development.

This influence, he said, could also have international consequences:

> It is largely true that a country is also what the press makes it. Once they stick a label on it, what was a lie can slowly be converted into truth in the eyes of other members of the international community.[7]

In Zambia and in many other countries, the new governments feared the ability of the press to provide or promote conflicting or alternative 'truths' and took the view that this placed enormous power into the hands of the proprietors. This was the main reason why during the period 1960–90 we saw a steady increase in political power exercised over the printed press, either by direct take-overs or by censorship and suppression. In Zambia itself, the then ruling party, UNIP, took control of the *Times*, but even before this happened the president had acquired the power to hire and fire its editor, a power he used on several occasions.

Journalists who had become used to being outspoken and forthright about those in power during the colonial period soon found that they had less freedom in the new post-independence era. African newspapers that had campaigned for majority rule often became sycophantic and uncritical. In many cases this was not an imposed position. There was a will to assist new administrations with what was seen as a national and patriotic venture—the establishment of legitimacy and good government in the new political order. However, in time strains inevitably appeared. Then a variety of measures were taken. At one extreme governments brought in new laws to curb what they saw as seditious journalism. Thus Tanzania passed a law in 1968 enabling the state to close, or refuse to permit publication of, any newspaper if it was seen as posing a threat. But lesser measures were more common and probably of greater significance. Everywhere in Africa, the state is a major advertiser, either in its own right or through its various para-statal bodies and institutions. Before the widespread privatization that became such a feature of the structural adjustment programmes of the 1990s, many African states owned many of the major industries, from brewing to banking, insurance, mining, and agricultural marketing. All of these place advertising in the media. It was a relatively simple matter to ensure that business went to favoured press outlets rather than to those that were in any way hostile or critical. Other means of bringing pressure to bear could range from withholding importation licences for newsprint or essential equipment, to the actual detention or harassment of journalists. Moreover, the government, as a major employer and purveyor of patron-

7 Address to IPI Assembly, Nairobi, 4 June 1968.

age, could create many other difficulties for journalists or press proprietors seeking to establish credible independence.

These measures certainly helped to create in many countries a rather dull press for most of the period from 1970 to 1990. But it would be a mistake to interpret this as a dead period of African journalism. There were always ways in which journalists and other media professionals could work within existing restrictions and create interesting and lively copy. Both in radio and the press there are many examples where the creative genius of professional writers, photographers, and artists broke through and communicated alternative ways of seeing events. Through cartoons, poetry, picture stories, and personal columns, newspapers were able to enliven their output and often touch obliquely on sensitive issues. Radio stations similarly were able to carry singers and poets whose actual words, if reported in a less stylized way, would have incurred wrath or worse. For example, in Tanzania, satirical poetry would sometimes be carried in the ruling party's daily papers. In Zambia the main government daily carried a weekly column by an anonymous columnist who made fun of government announcements, lampooned party leaders, and created general hilarity about subjects normally treated with great solemnity.[8]

Even so, most media content demonstrated the slavish role of the media as little more than a mouthpiece of the government. A high proportion of news bulletins on radio and lead stories in the newspapers featured the head of state visiting some project or speaking at an event. Coverage in the media would mostly report what he said and who was present. Sometimes remarkably uninteresting speeches would be carried in full on the radio and printed at length in the papers. The head of state may have been visiting several projects in different places and saying more or less the same things. The coverage would usually repeat the same details. Other stories would be of a similar kind; ministers and other state officials making speeches or announcements, visiting state institutions, opening schools or hospitals, and so on. Each would be reported, with the focus being always on what the official or leader said and little on any other aspect of the story.

If you asked an African radio or TV director what his or her major problems or shortages were, transport would come high on the list. But whatever the shortage or difficulty, transport and other resources were usually quickly available when it came to covering the activities of the head of state. I saw a memorable example of this at the OAU conference in Kampala in 1975. President Ahidjo of Cameroon attended the conference for one day. He arrived in his plane with an entourage of officials and media people from Cameroon. The first to emerge from his plane at Entebbe Airport were staff of the national broadcaster with their TV cameras and tape recorders and photographers from the daily press. They positioned themselves at the foot of the aircraft steps to film Ahidjo descending. They then followed him to the conference, where he made a speech. They filmed his entrance and departure. Later they were seen returning with him to the airport, where they repeated their earlier activity

---

8 Some of the weekly columns were also published in a book, *The Kapelwa Musonda File* (Lusaka: Neczam, 1973).

in reverse and departed with him back to Cameroon. Presumably much of the coverage of the conference in the Cameroonian media concentrated on Ahidjo's short visit.

I am conscious of the fact that I am writing this account from the perspective of a journalist and broadcaster who has been trained in a different tradition. Within the Western tradition of critical enquiry it seems absurd to use the media in this way and one can very quickly dismiss these uses of the media as mere examples of African dictatorships at work. This may miss a vital point of difference in ways of seeing and doing things. What I saw in Uganda in 1975 was an extreme example that derived from Ahidjo's own way of being that country's leader. But the same tendency could be seen in more liberal states. In Tanzania, President Julius Nyerere was known to dislike the fact that even his very minor activities were reported as headline news in the press and on the radio. I once asked a senior radio manager in Tanzania's state radio why they continued to give the president such prominence at all times. His answer was illuminating: 'That is how Mwalimu talks. He is a very modest man. But he is the president and the father of the nation.' The news was seen as a formal requirement. Just as in a ceremony there is an order of precedence, so also in news.

Louise Bourgault has provided a fascinating, if controversial, view of the differences in European and African communication traditions. The discourse tradition which separates subjective and objective categories is, she says, largely absent from Africa. Africa's communications norms do not expect nor put a high value on critical, objective and distanced positions, typical of a literate tradition. Africa's communications traditions are largely oral and the dominant discourse is speech. Media content often reminds one of the praise songs typical of many African cultures. The journalist in this cultural context does not distance himself or herself from the audience: 'In effect, the reporter, subject and audience all form part of the same team, i.e. they are part of a larger whole. Objectivity as it is understood in the Western sense becomes impossible'.[9]

We can see different discourse traditions operating alongside each other. The tradition in some countries of journalism as anti-authority which developed in the campaigns for social and political emancipation and freedom created a relationship between rulers and the press that did not sit easily with the established forms of discourse, nor with the expectations and views of the new rulers. Former chairman and managing director of the *Daily Times* in Nigeria, Babatunde Jose, who had been a distinguished journalist and reporter himself, had this to say about his craft and the changes that independence had brought:

> In the name of press freedom and nationalism we deliberately wrote seditious and criminally libellous articles against colonial governments. Today, at least ten years after independence, many African journalists still believe that a good press is one that is in a constant state of war with the government, that a progressive journalist is one who writes anti-

9 Louise Bourgault, *Mass Media in Sub-Saharan Africa* (Bloomington, Ind.: Indiana University Press, 1995), 182.

government articles and a leading journalist is one who is in and out of prison for sedition.[10]

Strategies that had been used to end colonialism should not, he said, be used against the new African governments. He gave the example of a reporter who wanted to expose corruption in high places but was unlikely to have the training or experience required to do the kind of professional job of investigation that was required to back up such a story.

A few years later, Jose's gloomy view of some of his press colleagues seemed to be vindicated when unsubstantiated allegations about political opponents became a normal part of the daily press during an intense period of political rivalry during the 1979–83 era of multi-party politics. Virtually all the daily papers of that period were either the mouthpieces of one of the five political parties or the property of a state government or the federal government, which were each in the control of one or other of those five parties. Similarly, the state broadcasting networks, either at the federal or state (i.e. regional) level, also became the mouthpieces of the respective state governments. This trend even led to the creation of rival federal and state TV and radio stations that were in essence party mouthpieces.

Soon after the establishment of the short-lived democracy of 1979 to 1983, Nigerian newspapers which were affiliated to one or other of the five parties began to report largely unsubstantiated allegations of corruption or even of subversion against their political rivals. For example, the *National Concord*, launched by the millionaire businessman Chief Abiola to support the NPN, alleged that the leader of the UPN, Chief Awolowo, had hatched a plot to subvert the constitution and was about to use a foreign radio station to promote this. Other NPN supporting papers took up the story. But I found that many Nigerians seemed to regard such stories as part and parcel of the political battle and not to be taken too seriously. They did, however, undoubtedly contribute to widespread unease about the behaviour of politicians and a weariness with party politics that contributed to a lack of support for the continuance of constitutional government.[11]

Political Reforms and Deregulation post-1990

Today the political atmosphere in which the media operate is changing. So also are the laws that govern media ownership, especially radio and television. Few states retain the high level of control they once had over the press and broadcasting. The state remains a dominant force, especially in broadcasting, but there is an increasing amount of choice. Alternative media are emerging. There are four broad trends. One is the emergence of commercial media companies with pan-African ambitions, especially in television. The second is the growth of politically sponsored media, mainly

---

10 Alhaji Babatunde Jose, 'Press Freedom in Africa,' unpubl. address to the Royal African Society in London, 10 Apr. 1975.

11 See Luke Uka Uche, *Mass Media, People and Politics in Nigeria* (New Delhi: Concept, 1989). There was little opposition from any of the newspapers when the military ended civilian rule. This was probably because of the extent of corruption that had been reported.

in the form of newspapers, as one-party states have given way to multi-party competition. The third is the emergence, especially in francophone West Africa and in South Africa, of community-based media, using FM radio in particular. And the fourth is the emergence of commercial radio stations, principally confined to the main cities.

The South African digital satellite TV service, Multichoice, which reaches the whole continent, has developed local partnerships with many African commercial media companies to provide services on subscription. A multi-channel bouquet of networks, mainly originating from outside Africa, is offered. Multichoice has been the stimulant to commercial TV ventures in several countries, often in partnership. In the francophone countries similar arrangements have been seen in partnership with Paris-based companies. Several other companies are competing for deals. Some of these involve the packaging of programming with advertising, offering the advertisers a package of countries or markets, and the TV stations a mix of well-made and attractive TV programmes ready for broadcast at low or no cost. We are beginning to see the development of new media companies with interests across different media, print and broadcast.[12]

The second trend, the emergence of new politically affiliated media, is a by-product of more pluralistic political systems. As what became known as 'multi-partyism' emerged in the 1990s, a bewildering number of newspaper titles emerged in many countries. Many disappeared as suddenly. These papers have been of very mixed quality and have often reflected the faults that Jose described in the remarks noted earlier. A prominent Zambian journalist commented to me that media professionals generally saw them as 'gatecrashers' who were not committed to professional standards but merely to the promotion of a particular political cause or faction.[13]

The third and fourth trends are to be seen in radio. A remarkable feature of African radio is that almost everywhere it has been national rather than local in focus. Ghana had a Ghana Broadcasting Corporation for the whole country, a state-managed and -run broadcasting station. But until the advent of private radio in the 1990s Ghana had no local radio. The same is true for most African states. The arrival of local and community radio is a very recent phenomenon and one that is still not very widespread. Until very recently, the standard reference book on world radio listed national radio stations for all of Africa's 53 nations. Less than ten had any kind of local radio and until 1989, all of these were state-run.[14] When writing a book on Africa's media in 1983 I was able to find only three radio stations on the entire continent that did not belong to the state. By June 2000 there

12 For example, in East Africa, for several years, the Aga Khan has owned the *Daily Nation*, a successful daily newspaper, as well as several smaller daily, weekly, and monthly titles in both English and Swahili. When the state monopoly of broadcasting was ended in Kenya one of the first to bid successfully for a broadcasting licence was the *Nation* group.

13 Several sources have documented these developments. See, for example, W. Joseph Campbell, *The Emergent Independent Press in Benin and Côte d'Ivoire* (Westport, Conn.: Praeger, 1998), and 'Newspapers Mushroom in Ghana', *New African*, Mar. 1992.

14 *World Radio-TV Handbook*, annual, (1946–).

were more than 500 private radio stations.[15] Some of these are fully commercial radio stations, living off advertising revenue and mainly focusing on audiences in the cities, attractive to the advertisers of consumer goods.

But many of these 500-plus new radio stations are not commercial, but community-based. Community radio has emerged especially strongly in francophone West Africa and in South Africa. NGOs or other charitable bodies, including some Christian churches, have supported some of these stations. The stations tend to rely heavily on volunteer effort. Unlike the new commercial stations, many of the new community stations are based in rural areas.[16]

Many new skills are being looked for in Africa's contemporary media. Whereas state-run broadcasting formerly relied on a civil service mentality and culture, the state monopolies have been compelled to be more competitive. Marketing has become an important factor in success or failure but this is not something that emerges with ease within a bureaucratized culture. Advertising sales personnel are becoming key figures. Advertising revenue is increasing and we are likely to see this sector of broadcasting growing in the years ahead.

In the area of journalism and production the situation of the African media professional is also changing. Some of this can be attributed to outside pressures, especially from Western governments promoting good governance, accountability, and democratization. Professional journalist associations, independent of the state, have emerged in many countries.[17] Such have often vigorously taken on the role of supporting journalistic independence and the maintenance of professional standards.

International bodies have also played a major role, in monitoring the media, the treatment of journalists, laws governing the media, the availability of training, and related matters. Prominent among such bodies have been Reporters sans frontières, the Panos Institute, and Article 19.

Reporters sans frontières concentrates on the treatment and professional status of journalists. Article 19, the International Centre against Censorship, was founded in 1986 to campaign for the promotion and protection of freedom of expression. It argues that the right to impart and receive information regardless of frontiers is now firmly enshrined in international law, as well as in the constitutions of a large number of countries. It publishes reports on many countries, including several in Africa, in which censorship and the associated human rights abuses are exposed and challenged. Its aim is said to be to ensure not only that standards in this area

---

15 Mytton, *Mass Communication in Africa*. There is no single source for radio stations today. The *World Radio-TV Handbook* does not list all private stations. The best source for news about broadcast media is the weekly publication of BBC Monitoring, *World Media*.

16 They are especially strong in Cameroon, Mali, and Burkina Faso. See Francis Nyamnjoh, 'Media Ownership and Control in Cameroon: Constraints on Media Freedom', *Media Development*, 4 (1998), 25–33.

17 It is interesting to note that in many countries, while there may have been a professional journalists' association to which most journalists belonged, new associations have now emerged with the word 'independent' in their title. Whereas the single national association would have as members many who were employed in the state apparatus, these new associations would take only those working in independent media.

continue to rise, but that actual practice keeps up with those standards. The Panos Institute concentrates more on the development and educational aspects of the media in the poorer countries and specializes in information for development. Like the other two, it argues that diversity, or 'pluralism', in civil society is essential to good government. Access to, and freedom of, information is essential for informed and vigorous debate and allows people to play a constructive and often challenging role in public discourse and decision-making. All three bodies support training efforts and help to maintain networks of support for African media professionals.

Schools of journalism have emerged in several countries. Some, like those in Zambia and Kenya, have taken in and trained media professionals from several African countries. European governments through their departments of international assistance have also played a role in these developments. A growing amount of aid and technical assistance has been given by, among others, the UK, Germany, Sweden, and the Netherlands. The BBC African Service, broadcasting to Africa in English, Portuguese, French, Arabic, Swahili, Hausa, and Somali, has employed many African journalists. Several have returned to Africa and occupy senior positions. Many professional African journalists view the daily English programmes, *Focus on Africa* and *Network Africa*, as setting a standard for African reporting. The two programmes rely not only on many journalists from the continent, among them Elizabeth Ohene, former editor of one of Ghana's leading daily newspapers, but on a network of local reporters in every African country. Many African leaders and politicians in the anglophone countries regard it as required daily listening. When former President Kenneth Kaunda invited me to dinner at his private residence in Lusaka in 1972, the meal was interrupted in the middle when the time came for the President to listen to *Focus*.

The influence of the BBC, and to a lesser extent Radio France International and other foreign radio stations, continues to be strong but is likely to decline as greater media autonomy and professionalism gain ground. Elsewhere in the world, when autocratic or undemocratic regimes have passed away, audiences for foreign radio always go into steep decline as the local media improve.[18]

While the professional autonomy and status of the press journalist has improved in recent years, the status of radio broadcasters seems to remain rather low. I was engaged in research for the national broadcasting station in Zambia in 1972. I discovered that poor translation and presentation considerably weakened the impact of some broadcasting in Zambian languages. A lot of output was translated from English. This was done by young men and women straight out of secondary school, who had received no special training and whose knowledge and experience was very limited. They had a position in the civil service equivalent to very junior clerical grades. Most Zambian listeners' knowledge of national and international events, as well as a lot of what limited information they received on matters of health, education, and agriculture, depended on the poor and often inaccurate translation of under-educated and untrained staff. Attempts to persuade officials that this was a problem which needed to be urgently

---

18 For data on this trend see Graham Mytton (ed.), *Global Audiences* (London: John Libbey, 1993).

addressed were a failure. Translation was not seen then as a professional skill of high importance. This situation has not yet changed very much.

Deregulation may change this as stations begin to compete. They may soon be competing not only for audiences but also for creative professionals, something that has hardly happened hitherto, and this will strengthen the professional status of broadcasters. In the past, creative people have tended either not to seek employment in the first place or else not to remain in government-run media for very long. This is either because the prospect did not appeal or because they soon found that they were out of place and not wanted. Being part of the state apparatus led in many cases to a civil service way of doing things. It meant that decisions tended to be made at the top and passed down. People making programmes tended to play safe and not to make creative decisions and choices, and to stick to established programme formulae.

In the early 1970s when I worked in Zambian broadcasting, broadcasting journalists who showed investigative initiative, reporting controversial issues and trying to do professional and interesting current affairs broadcasts, soon found that their efforts were disapproved of. I know of several occasions when staff were reprimanded for not following the government line on some matter of controversy. Their attempts to reflect and report different opinions and attitudes were often suppressed. Some dispirited broadcasters left radio and television altogether. Elsewhere in Africa also, talented and creative professionals sought and found jobs in public relations or advertising, or left the media altogether. Broadcasting staff have tended not to be innovators. This is now very likely to change as the result of competition.

Of course the media thrive on more than mere news. Most of the time the media, radio especially, are used for entertainment. While a cautious approach has generally been seen in news and news-related programmes, this has not always been the case in other creative areas. African radio stations have been important patrons of music and, in some countries, of poetry and oral literature. In the 1970s many radio stations made regular programme-collection safaris into remote parts of the country to record songs, drama, poetry, and other indigenous material for later broadcast. However, in recent years these activities have been curbed by financial restrictions. Similarly, the studios of many national radio stations were once a focus for much new music. This happens less now, largely because many state-run radio stations have stopped most payments to artists. African radio used to play a major role in popular music. It still does play a role, but mainly through the playing of commercial records. Many African musicians find that they do better financially by marketing their own cassettes through street sellers.[19] Copyright laws are not widely enforced. Few African artists are members of rights societies. These same financial pressures have also held back the growth of (and sometimes even reduced the amount of) original indigenous drama and other spoken-word programmes on both radio and television.

---

19 Most African commercial recordings on sale in the shops and markets formerly appeared on discs—usually vinyl 45 rpm or 33 rpm records. While in the developed world, vinyl records have largely been replaced by the compact disc, in much of Africa they have now been supplanted by the audio cassette.

26

Servants of the State or the Market?: Media and Journalists in China

Chin-Chuan Lee

IN 1938 CHU ANPING interrupted his study with Professor Harold Laski at the London School of Economics and returned to China, then at war with Japan. He was an editorial writer for the *Central Daily News*, the chief organ of the ruling Nationalist Party. Before long, he turned against the Nationalists and became a Communist sympathizer. In 1947, writing for an influential intellectual magazine he edited, this Fabian Confucianist none the less remained suspicious of the Communists' dictatorial tendencies:

> To be honest, under the Nationalists our fight for freedom is really over the question of 'how much freedom'. If the Communists come to power, the question is going to be 'Will we have freedom at all?'[1]

Chu was prophetic. After the Communist Revolution, he was consigned to several minor positions before being installed as editor-in-chief of the *Guangming Daily* in 1957. This was at the peak of the 'Hundred Flowers' movement. Many intellectuals were moved to tears when the supreme leader, Chairman Mao Zedong, implored them to speak out and criticize the Party. Chu took advantage of this invitation and his own prominence to castigate the Communist Party for forgetting that only the people, not the Party, were the 'true masters of the country'. As the going got rough, however, Mao abruptly decided to retaliate without mercy and purged 550,000 intellectuals as 'anti-Party, anti-Socialist rightists'. Chu held his editorship only seventy days, and died mysteriously. His story was emblematic of the fate of thousands of idealistic intellectuals and journalists in Mao's China, all victimized by Communist intolerance of dissent.

The foremost and enduring problem of Chinese journalism has been its

Source: Not previously published. Chin-Chuan Lee is Professor of Journalism and Mass Communication at the University of Minnesota and editor of three books on Chinese media and political communication.

1 The story of Chu Anping is based on Dai (1990: 131–279); the quotation is from p. 186. Throughout this chapter, Chinese family names precede their given names.

lack of press freedom since the inception of strict party-state control. Very few political regimes in history have been more conscious than the People's Republic of China (PRC) of the vital importance of ideological indoctrination and thought management among its people. Even fewer could match the extent to which it has exploited mass media to achieve such goals. The PRC characterizes what Su (1994) calls 'cultural despotism', imposing an all-pervasive network of ideological control across various systems and levels. But this twisted history can be roughly divided into the Maoist era from 1949 to 1977 and the post-1978 Dengist era (including his successors), manifesting notable differences in operation and outlook. The earlier quote from Chu is significant, in the context of this chapter, as a mirror of change: after two decades of economic reform China seems to have moved, in relative terms, from the Maoist absence of media freedom to the question of 'how much freedom'. This change is momentous, but by no means linear or smooth (Lee 1990), as the Tiananmen crackdown testifies. In the 1990s the momentum of market forces and increasing commercialization has set the media relatively free in non-political reporting but political control remains stringent (Zhao 1998; Lee 1994, 2000*b*).

| Politics Takes Command | The key to understanding the media in Mao's China (1949–77) is his dictum that 'politics takes command'. Mao inherited but embellished Leninism by intensifying every device of propaganda and agitation invented by the Bolsheviks. He claimed that thought determined action: if the masses are imbued with the 'correct' thought, they will act 'correctly'. The media must therefore be responsible for creating social impact and must be closely related to the grand ideology and political 'lines' rather than political or economic reality (Liu 1975; Lee 1980: 210–19). During this period, the media were subjected to control which oscillated between Mao's left-wing policy of totalistic state penetration (1949–52,1958–9,1963–77) and spells of the bureaucratic-pragmatist policy of societal identification (1953–57, 1960–62). These policy shifts reflected intense power struggles, with Mao defeating his political rivals. |

Mao's penetrative policy exalted the power of human will to the extreme in pursuit of permanent revolution—often at odds with the legal-rational authority, bureaucratic apparatuses, or the economic infrastructure. Mao wanted to pursue his ideological visions through voluntarism and mass spontaneity. In sociological terms, he was extremely pro-agency and anti-structure. He initiated a succession of large-scale and nationwide mass campaigns, criticisms, and self-criticisms, not only to eradicate the legacy of the old social order but also to swiftly transform the 'revolutionary spirit' of the people (Su 1994). The media assumed the responsibility of injecting political authority and bringing forth a new political consciousness in the people from without. For example, in 1957, Mao berated the *People's Daily* editors, led by Deng Tuo, as 'a bunch of dead men' who had not done enough, in Mao's eyes, to propagate his 'Hundred Flowers' policy.[2]

---

2 For a recollection of this encounter by one of the participants, see Wang (1987: 369–417).

Mao's symbolically romantic mass campaigns, such as the Anti-rightist Movement (1957), the Great Leap Forward (1958), and the Cultural Revolution (1966–76), however, all relied predominantly on the use of coercive power or terror to foster the appearance of mobilized 'mass spontaneity'. Chu Anping died in the Anti-Rightist mass liquidation that displaced the 'Hundred Flowers' policy. The leading Party journalist-propagandist, Deng Tuo, joined numerous others in committing suicide in 1967 while his deputies became janitors.[3] The ensuing Cultural Revolution, according to post-Mao officials, implicated 100 million people.

Mao's rivals, in contrast, adopted a policy of identification which was closer in spirit to the Bolsheviks in encouraging long-term cultivation of national culture and consciousness through persuasion. This faction, led by Liu Shaoqi and Deng Xiaoping, briefly returned to the forefront of power after Mao's reckless Great Leap Forward policy had caused a mass famine, resulting in 30 million deaths from 1959 to 1961. Having borne the brunt of Mao's wrath for not supporting his 'Hundred Flowers' movement only a few years back, the *People's Daily* now fell under Liu's sharp lash for manufacturing falsehood during the Great Leap Forward campaign.[4] Liu said that having a lying paper was worse than having no paper. Declaring class struggle in the PRC to be over, he was determined to harness the media for socialist economic construction and political integration among the whole population (*quan min*) rather than only the proletarian classes (Lee 1980: 210–19). Liu favoured the development of propaganda organizations and professional ideologists. This policy was terminated when Mao persecuted him to death and sent Deng to do manual labour in the countryside.

The Cultural Revolution started when Mao mobilized the young 'Red Guards' (high school and college students) to rampage around the country destroying the existing Party-state apparatuses, including media propaganda organizations. But as the Red Guards later appeared to be out of control, he summoned the Liberation Army to suppress them. Mao's thoroughgoing populism despised bureaucratic regularization, role differentiation, and professional expertise. In the name of 'mass-line journalism' he purged tens of thousands of 'reactionary bourgeois liberal' journalists and sent many others down to do hard labour in factories or communes three months a year—to receive re-education from the revolutionary masses. Taking their places were amateur ideological enthusiasts, known as barefoot correspondents, whose lack of intellectual knowledge was lauded as a virtue. Loudspeakers kept blasting out the temporarily 'correct' thought and policy nationwide. The cult of Mao's personality was almost unprecedented in world history. For years the media praised a student who submitted a blank examination paper as a Maoist model who rebelled against authority. Ideological conformity was so absurd that every

---

3 For a study of Deng Tuo, see Cheek (1997). Deng's deputy, Hu Jiwei, was demoted to janitor of the *People's Daily* building. Hu came back to be editor-in-chief of the paper in 1979 (replacing a Maoist who did not even have any knowledge of Mexico), only to be sacked 5 years later and almost ousted from the Party in the wake of the Tiananmen crackdown in 1989. In 1998, friends reportedly congratulated a retiring editor-in-chief of the *People's Daily* for hanging on to his job until retirement, because almost all of his predecessors had been purged.

4 Interview with Hu Jiwei, Minneapolis, summer 1993. He was present at both meetings with Mao and Liu.

newspaper in China, large or small, copied the *People's Daily* verbatim, ranging from the editorials down to such minute details as the typeface and positioning of articles.

Revolutionary rhetoric turned out to be a tool for rationalizing the established factional power interests, even between Mao and his erstwhile closest allies (Pye 1979). Mao himself wrote newspaper editorials to launch political campaigns. Political agitation was so intense that Pool (1973) argued that China offered 'something like a laboratory test of the limits of what propaganda can do'. As power struggles led to unpredictable policy reversals and personnel purges, the media constantly contradicted their own rhetoric. Mao's handpicked successor, Lin Biao, became an official traitor overnight, and Premier Zhou Enlai was Mao's confidante allegedly turned schemer. Not until then did many journalists, writers, and intellectuals who had been previously purged begin to develop *private* doubts about the correctness of Mao's visions. They had been blaming themselves for not being able to root out completely the deeply ingrained 'legacies of the Old China' from their minds (Liu 1989; Hsiao 1990). These unbridgeable gulfs between words and reality, and between a 'symbolic China' and an 'actual China', fooled many Western students of China and its media (Harding 1982). The telling of big lies created the most severe crises in public confidence and media credibility in the history of the PRC (Nathan 1985), which has not fully recovered.

Economic Reform

The Cultural Revolution ended with Mao's death in 1976. What was arguably the most significant work of journalism was undertaken from 1978 to 1979, when post-Mao leaders used the media to expose the excesses of the Cultural Revolution and to blunt the ideological opposition of the remnant of Maoists, thus consolidating the power of Deng Xiaoping, now rehabilitated for the third time (Goldman 1994). Those few years saw the adoption of many bold measures to correct the blunders of the Cultural Revolution and to rehabilitate the wrongly persecuted cadres. A refreshing political wind swept through Beijing, so that, in 1978, members of the Red Guards generation wrote wall posters denouncing Communist dictatorship. Once Deng was in firm control, however, he jailed leaders of the wall-poster democracy movement and forbade any challenge to Communist leadership. To salvage the Party from the brink of losing its legitimacy, Deng also juxtaposed ideological compliance with vast economic modernization programmes.

Abhorring Mao's ideological clamour, Deng single-mindedly pursued economic reform under the dictum that 'Practice is the sole criterion of truth.' (As a pragmatist, Deng said, 'Whether it is a white cat or a black cat, as long as it catches mice, it is a good cat.') Deng showed little patience for Maoist polemic and even less tolerance of ideological challenges to his power. The media quickly retreated inside the bounds of convention to rationalize economic reform under Communist initiatives. But the path to economic reform was ferociously contested between proponents of greater market incentives and orthodox advocates of a Soviet-style centrally planned economy. The media were caught up in rounds of factional warfare, which Deng managed to arbitrate, as both sides tried to enlist them for political gains. The leaders even went beyond manipulating domestic media by exploiting international news and translations of foreign reports on China to solidify their domestic policy position and disparage their rivals (Hood 1994). The media were reviled by Party ideologues during the short-lived Anti-spiritual Pollution Campaign (1983), the Anti-bourgeois Liberalization Campaign (1987), and the Tiananmen crackdown (1989). On each of these occasions some of the best journalists-writers were ousted on account of their investigative exposés or theoretical arguments (see, for example, Liu 1989; Wang 1987).

Two of those considered to be Deng's most enlightened reform protégés, Hu Yaobang and Zhao Ziyang, who ruled China throughout the decade and whom Deng eventually sacrificed, held restrictive views toward the media (Lee 1990: 8–9). Hu granted literary writers greater latitude to choose subjects and develop themes with 'completely comradely suggestions and advice' from the Party, but insisted that journalists must devote 80 per cent of their coverage to proclaiming the Party's achievements. Zhao was hesitant and ambiguous in his position. He discouraged greater media autonomy by espousing the neo-authoritarian view that iron-fisted rule was a prerequisite to economic growth (Ruan 1990). But he also implicitly or explicitly endorsed—even manipulated—the ferment of media reforms, in part to put pressure on his critics (Goldman 1994; Zhao 1998). Scholars and journalists proposed various media reforms to prevent the mistakes of the Cultural Revolution—those of blindly following the Party's whims to the detriment of the people—from being repeated. Media laws were drafted. The media were openly urged to enhance policy transparency and to monitor government abuses. Many of these voices were heard in closed-door deliberations by an advisory group to Zhao (Wu 1997). From 1986 on, the *World Economic Herald* in Shanghai, despite its alleged 'elitist' orientation (Zhao 1998: 162), was the leading advocate of political reforms in alliance with—or at least with the tacit support of—Zhao's reformist faction. By metaphorically 'hitting line balls' (*cha bian qiu*)—aiming for the very edge of the ping-pong table where a ball is almost out of bounds but remains a fair hit—the paper ventured to the edge of the permissible. The contradiction between political control and economic change came to a head in the abortive democracy movement of 1989, in which the paper was closed and Zhao lost his power amidst a brutal crackdown. Media reform suffered a comprehensive political setback.

In the 1980s, notwithstanding the eruption of turmoil, the media shifted their focus from class struggle to economic modernization. The market mechanism was beginning to intervene in media management but its full force would not be felt until the 1990s. Deng quelled dissent and opposition by using the state apparatuses rather than mass mobilization from below. The retreat of the state from mass campaigns and certain social domains meant that the media did not intrude into the private sphere to the same extent as in the Cultural Revolution. The cult of personality was diminished, while professional media organizations and journalists were resurrected. A proliferation of media outlets emerged to serve specialized interests and constituencies as a consequence of economic reform. The de-emphasizing of revolutionary ideology also made it possible for various cultural genres, livelier media entertainments, and other less ideologically loaded materials to flourish as long as they did not pose a threat to state power (Lee 1990).

Raging Commercialization[5]

Deng Xiaoping's legitimacy was severely damaged by the Tiananmen crackdown in 1989. To lift China out of international isolation and domestic stagnation, Deng re-ignited the flame of economic reform in late 1992 under the name of 'socialist market economy with Chinese characteristics'. This time he used his supreme authority to nip in the bud another ideological debate about whether the market economy was capitalistic or socialist, but he had no desire to define what 'socialist market economy' or 'Chinese characteristics' meant. For Deng, making money is not a sin as long as you don't defy the party-state. Since then, all the media have jumped into 'the ocean of raging commercialization'.

Economic reform necessitated the decentralization of political and financial power to local units. Even back in the 1980s, the central government found itself increasingly at a loss to subsidize a mushrooming number of media outlets that were concurrently being beset by rising costs caused by market competition. After 1992 the state decided to cut off media subsidies and expected media to be financially self-sufficient. Non-Party organs, especially the evening press, no longer had to carry dry ideological Party propaganda and television was allowed to provide more lively entertainment. Rapid and vast economic development has produced a phenomenal growth in advertising, of which the media are the prime benefactors because of their monopolistic status. The wheel of fortune has turned against the previously dominant central and regional Party organs, which have been losing ground in market competition to mass-appeal newspapers in the major coastal cities of Guangzhou, Shanghai, and Beijing. Size of salary is no longer dependent on the journalist's professional rank, but on the media outlet's ability to garner advertising revenues (Chen and Lee 1998). For example, the *Xinmin Evening Daily* in Shanghai is politically marginal but financially rich, and its regular reporter makes as much money as the top editor of the chief Party organ, the *People's Daily*. While the Party press remains the major ideological instrument, television has risen to be the most potent shaper of popular images. Of the 4,000 primitive and low-budget cable operators in China, fewer than 1,200 are officially approved. Offering popular programmes with the so-called 'Coca-Cola flavouring' in contrast to Central Television's (CCTV's) 'distilled water', they are a driving force behind the tabloidization of Chinese television (Gordon 1999).

Economic wealth does not guarantee media independence (Chan 1993). Unlike the politically defiant and active media in the late 1980s (Polumbaum 1990), the media of today have learned to improvise a variety of

---

5 This section is partly adapted from Lee (2000a).

seemingly paradoxical editorial or marketing strategies, all geared toward catering to the market without violating official bounds (Pan 2000). These strategies span the gamut of non-routine news genres, formats, and techniques (such as sensational crime stories, investigative exposé, and prestigious-sounding opinion polls), all developed with the full backing of available organizational resources and personal or business connections. All media outlets have tried to 'make the most out of policy' by probing the edges of the shifting official boundaries. Many newspaper editors have confessed—to me and to others—that their front page endorses the planned economy, their second to eighth pages support the mixed economy, and their ninth to sixteenth pages advocate the market economy. He (2000) therefore describes these schizophrenic market-oriented media as 'a capitalistic body' that wears 'a socialist face'. The content is still conventionally framed but its genre of discourse is being expanded. The *Beijing Youth Daily*, for example, has used investigative reporting and debates on controversial issues—for example, a ping-pong player who became a member of the Japanese team by marriage and beat her old Chinese team-mates—as popular marketing devices. Many of these seemingly disarming reports have provided fertile ground for readers to rethink certain core values (such as 'good citizenship' or 'nationalism') from a broader perspective (Rosen 2000). A number of positive examples of reform, such as phone-in radio shows in Guangzhou and Shanghai as well as the highly successful news commentary programmes on CCTV, are most instructive (Zhao 1998). He (2000) ventures to argue that China's Party press is being transformed from a strict mouthpiece of the government into what he calls 'Party Publicity Inc.' to promote Party images and legitimacy rather than to brainwash people. However, China's media reform is not guided by a coherent framework but grows out of ad hoc and practical needs, prompting Pan (2000) to caution that news improvisation is bound to be shortsighted, opportunistic, and vulnerable to the shifting winds of Party opinion.

In order not to lose its grip on the media in the tidal wave of media commercialization, the state must both cede to *and* capitalize on market dynamics. The national channel CCTV is so lucrative (with an advertising revenue of US$600 million in 1998) as to need no state subsidies, but the state is eager to retain its role as patron and insists that CCTV accept a meagre allowance anyway. When I visited Beijing in the summer of 1998, several leaders from a top Party organ boasted of its ambitious plans for becoming a press conglomerate and asked me for my thoughts. Mindful of Communist badgering of Western media conglomerates, I told them I thought that conglomeration was a new scheme for state management of the emerging ramifications of media economics and politics in China. As a matter of fact, these press conglomerates are being organized around a group of 'core' and affluent Party organs (such as the *Guangzhou Daily*), which serve as big sponges to absorb unprofitable, chaotic, or disobedient 'small papers' and magazines (Chen and Lee 1998). The state absolves itself of financial obligations while the core media profit from takeovers and mergers. My hosts did not bother to justify the ideological inconsistency, other than noting in agreement that China's media conglomerates would remain under the control of the Party rather than 'rotten capitalists'.

Nothing can corrupt Communist ideology more insidiously and effectively than money. Media ethnographers (Pan 2000; He 2000) have told many startling tales which suggest that media corruption is almost a way of life in China. Zhao (1998) documents five forms of corruption: journalists go on sponsored junkets; they solicit advertising contracts to the extent of blurring editorial functions; many of them moonlight for public relations firms and enterprises; they individually and collectively take bribes for news ('paid journalism'), not only from business clients but also increasingly from government units; and they even fabricate news in exchange for advertising. Almost all media units actively seek advertising sponsors for their projects, and many editors contract out their programmes or space for extra money. A disheartened old journalism professor tells me that even his former students would not report the results of his opinion polls unless they receive 'red envelopes'. I know a county Party chief in Guangdong who runs the local cable TV system and owns a collection of Mercedes cars, a country club, and an apartment in Hong Kong—while his wife and children live in Canada. Such unseemly conduct cannot exist without collaboration between an authoritarian power and an unchecked market. The various government crackdowns have not been effective.

Professional Role and Ideology	Despite anti-Confucian rhetoric, PRC journalists are Confucians in Leninist disguises. The Confucian tradition bestows moral legitimacy on intellectuals who serve the rulers and speak for the people, whereas its Leninist incarnation recasts the Party as the vanguard of the proletariat (Lee 1990: 7–8). Most 'ideological priests' in the PRC media follow what Cheek (1992) calls 'the mandarin vocation': patriotic toward the state, receptive to patronage toward superiors, peers, and subordinates, and paternalistic and elitist in self-expression.

Journalists—like Chu Anping (Dai 1990), Deng Tuo (Cheek 1997), and many others (Liu 1989; Wang 1987; Hsiao 1990)—are both integrated into the system as part of the cultural elite and treated as part of an ideological instrument. They inherit a tradition of intellectual advocacy on behalf of reform and enlightenment—typical in the 'transitional' society (Passin 1963)—but now are expected to play a revolutionary role. The first to be glorified or vilified, most PRC journalists do not seek to separate their work from statist arrangements; they demand instrumental reforms *within* the system rather than a fundamental change *of* the system. The Western bourgeois-liberal concept of 'neutral journalism'—let alone the development of an oppositional culture to the state—is officially rejected.

The Chinese media comprise an interwoven network of functionally differentiated ownership and target audiences, all under Party-state control. While the PRC has allowed joint ventures with foreign interests and has sought to divest itself of state enterprises, it has closed the media to private or foreign ownership. All journalists are literally state employees. Official statistics record a total of 86,646 full-time journalists employed by more than 3,600 news media—a figure not including the most junior staffers and contract workers. On the basis of two mutually corroborating national surveys conducted in the 1990s (Chen, Zhu, and Wei 1998; Yu 1998), a general portrait of Chinese journalists can be painted:

- They are evenly divided between newspapers (49 per cent) and broadcasting (radio 22 per cent, television 28 per cent). Two-thirds are male. The median age is the mid-thirties. Four-fifths have some college education, a third in journalism. But little on-the-job training is provided.
- Journalists are unevenly distributed, with a majority of them (60 per cent for newspapers and 52 per cent for broadcasting) congregating in the most developed urban and coastal areas, where only 20 per cent of the population reside. In developed areas, newspaper journalists make more money than television journalists, who in turn make more money than radio journalists.
- Seven in ten journalists are members of the Communist Party (50 per cent) or the Young Communist League (20 per cent). This is particularly true of those in senior ranks.
- Most journalists regularly read the *People's Daily*, the *Reference News*, the *Economic Daily*, the *Southern Weekend*, and other evening papers published in Shanghai and Beijing, all of which serve as their frame of reference.[6] They also watch CCTV news the most frequently. Two or 3 per cent (perhaps under-reported) admit listening to the Voice of America, the BBC, or CNN.
- Fifty to 80 per cent cite professional experiences, public reaction, the *People's Daily*, and the opinions of immediate superiors or other leaders as major factors influencing their news judgement. It is hard to know how they would resolve possible conflicts between different sources of pressure. Less important factors are news sources, peer news organizations, colleagues, and personal friends.
- Sixty or 70 per cent of journalists agree that they enjoy 'a great deal of job autonomy'. They feel that their supervisors listen to their opinions and suggestions patiently, and give them important assignments (Chen, Zhu, and Wu 1998). They value cordial relationships with their colleagues and respect the ability of their supervisors. However, the rank-and-file staff reported less autonomy than their supervisors did.

The strikingly high degree of perceived job autonomy (Chen, Zhu, and Wu 1998: 24) is a far cry from other studies (Polumbaum 1990; Yu and Liu 1993) conducted in the era of political activism a decade earlier, when discontent with lack of professional autonomy ran high.[7] Previously, journalists expressed widespread aversion to the Party-state's meddling

---

6 Popular among intellectuals, *Reference News* prints translations of foreign media reports, especially those on China. *Southern Weekend* offers the most daring coverage in China; were it not for the protection of the Party chief in Guangdong, the paper would have been punished by the central Department of Propaganda.

7 The gap can be attributed to today's improved work conditions, broadened media genres, and relaxation of detailed control. It may reflect the prevailing climate in the 1990s of channelling creative energies from politics into commercial pursuits. Since most journalists are privileged Party members, their widespread acceptance of—or acquiescence to—the status quo could be caused by self-censorship, or the sort of ideological conditioning that makes submission to authority seem natural.

in journalism, particularly in the day-to-day conduct of newswork. They aspired to greater independence within the bounds of the Constitution, the laws, and the facts.[8] Since the mid-1980s cries for more media autonomy have gained only precarious ground, but the media as information provider (*vis-à-vis* the class struggle) has been duly legitimized by the logic of the market.

A scrutiny of both of the recent national surveys discloses the emergence of a mixed and ambiguous normative conception about the role of journalism in the 1990s. First, most journalists continue to view news as propaganda. The media should act as Party mouthpieces to help people understand government policies, but they should refrain from using old tactics of 'indoctrination'. Second, journalists are no longer pure 'Party folks'. They recognize that the media should provide news and information to 'reflect the objective world'. But what is 'the objective world'? Since they repudiate the Western norms of separating facts from values and presenting balanced views on controversial issues, they solemnly undertake to uncover the truth before they start work on a story. But 'the truth' from what or whose vantage points? Their answers are vague. Third, they remain highly paternalistic toward 'the people', failing to endorse the media as a 'public forum' or a provider of popular entertainment. They perceive their own role as going far beyond informing the people; they see themselves as 'guiding public opinion' and 'bringing the influence of public opinion to bear on the government'. These goals—as stated in surveys and other writings—remain highly abstract, leaving unarticulated the *modus operandi* for realizing them or for resolving possible role conflicts (for example, the Party versus the people). Finally, most journalists surveyed resolutely disapprove acts of corruption and the practice of 'paid journalism' (Yu 1998), contrary to what seems to be ample evidence of widespread corruption (Zhao 1998: 73–81).

Conclusion The most distinctive mark of Deng's economic reform, in my opinion, has been the transformation of Mao's *totalitarian* regime into an *authoritarian* regime. On the surface, China retains many or all of the formal characteristics of a totalitarian regime (Friedrich 1969): a totalist ideology; a single party committed to this ideology; a fully developed secret police; and monopolistic control of mass communications, operational weapons, and organizations. In essence, much has changed. Deng's ideology is intent on preserving entrenched Communist power and thus can be ruthless toward dissidents, but it does not seek to intrude on *all* domains of social life. It is also more pragmatic, less absolutist, and less exclusionary—devoid of Maoist fervour for mass campaigns or for perpetual attempts at reshaping socialist consciousness. Market power,

---

8 According to a national survey conducted in 1988 (Yu and Liu 1993: 131–47), 79% agreed that there were too many restrictions and taboos with respect to media coverage and criticism; 90% called for increased media autonomy; 80% rejected the claim that socialist newspapers could not be privately run; and 75% rejected the claim that 'freedom of the press' is a bourgeois slogan fundamentally opposed to the Party principle of the dictatorship of the proletariat.

despite its corrosive influences, has to some extent created a countervailing force to state power, while the state has had to negotiate with, incorporate, accommodate, and at the same time take advantage of market forces. These modifications seem to have moved China closer to an authoritarian regime (Linz 1975: 189) akin to the Bonapartist model of Marx (Linz 1974: 250).

At the beginning of this chapter, I quoted a remark by Chu Anping to illustrate the fact that after two decades of economic reform, China's media have moved from having no freedom to having some freedom in non-political areas, although their freedom in political areas remains highly restricted. Similarly, Hu Shi, the most renowned liberal intellectual in modern China, against whose 'poisonous' thought Mao launched a nationwide campaign in 1955, once remarked that under Nationalist rule people had no right to speak out, but under Communist rule people had neither the right to speak out nor the right not to speak out. They could not withdraw into silence because the Communists did not take passive acceptance as sufficient proof of loyalty: mass campaigns required the people to fully display their 'colours'. By this crude and relative yardstick, Chinese journalists may now have earned the right to remain silent and even to speak out on *some* issues in public, and especially in private, with little fear of persecution, such as they faced during the Cultural Revolution. The media have tried to bypass sensitive political issues or to turn them into a form of commodity. I would characterize these various develop-ments as signs of 'demobilized liberalization'. They are obviously far from democratic or celebratory, and may indeed seem trivial and mundane to those who do not have to live under state terror or to those who are attracted to a variety of more radical-romantic imaginings. But I believe that the gains are real, substantial, and hard won in the context of the PRC's media history.

The incorporation of market forces into the Party media system has been characterized as a process of 'peaceful evolution' (Huang 1994) or as 'strengthening' the power of the Party (Yu 1994) by 'repackaging the official ideology and selling it at a profit' (Zhao 1998: 147). Both views may be right in some ways, but they are surely exaggerated in others. A prudent view must be more dialectical, in that the media have tried to benefit from the market *without* affronting state power, but the official ideology of today is also qualitatively *different* from that of yesterday. The market has produced a powerful liberating and subversive potential to relax the rigidity of the official ideology, especially in the long run, while it has also created corrupting influences on newswork, especially under authoritarian and crippling market conditions. What we are seeing is a painful working-out of contradictions and ambiguities inherent in these state–market interactions in which the media both operate and participate. How can civil society and the 'public sphere' emerge and be widened enough to ensure greater press freedom and equality in China? What will the emerging global network of communication technology do to China's state-controlled commercialized journalism? We shall continue to ponder these questions.

References   CHAN, JOSEPH MAN (1993), 'Commercialization without Independence: Trends and Tensions in Media Development in China', in Joseph Y. S. Cheng and Maurice Brosseau (eds.), *China Review, 1993* (Hong Kong: Chinese University Press).

CHEEK, TIMOTHY (1992), 'From Priests to Professionals: Intellectuals and the State under the CCP', in Jeffry N. Wasserstrom and Elizabeth J. Perry (eds.), *Popular Protest and Political Culture in Modern China* (Boulder, Colo.: Westview Press).

—— (1997), *Propaganda and Culture in Mao's China: Deng Tuo and the Intelligentsia* (Oxford: Clarendon Press).

CHEN, CHONGSHAN, ZHU, JIAN-HUA, and WU, WEI (1998), 'The Chinese Journalist', in David Weaver (ed.), *The Global Journalist* (Caskill, NJ: Hampton Press).

CHEN, HUAILIN, and LEE, CHIN-CHUAN (1998), 'Press Finance and Economic Reform in China', in Joseph Y. S. Cheng (ed.), *China Review, 1997* (Hong Kong: Chinese University Press).

DAI, QING (1990), *Wo de ruyu* (My Imprisonment) (Hong Kong: Ming Pao Press).

FRIEDRICH, CARL J. (1969), 'The Evolving Theory and Practice of Totalitarian Regimes', in Carl J. Friedrich, Michael Curtis, and Benjamin R. Barber, *Totalitarianism in Perspective: Three Perspectives* (New York: Praeger).

GOLDMAN, MERLE (1994), 'The Role of the Press in Post-Mao Political Struggles', in Chin-Chuan Lee (ed.), *China's Media, Media's China* (Boulder, Colo.: Westview Press).

GORDON, KIM (1999), 'Special Report: China Speaks Out', *Prospect*, Mar., 48–52.

HARDING, HARRY (1982), 'From China, with Disdain: New Trends in the Study of China', *Asian Survey*, 22: 934–58.

HE, ZHOU (2000), 'Chinese Communist Party Press in a Tug of War: A Political Economy Analysis of the *Shenzhen Special Zone Daily*', in Chin-Chuan Lee (ed.), *Money, Power and Media: Communication Patterns and Bureaucratic Control in Cultural China* (Evanston, Ill.: Northwestern University Press).

HOOD, MARLOWE (1994), 'The Use and Abuse of Mass Media by Chinese Leaders during the 1980s', in Chin-Chuan Lee (ed.), *China's Media, Media's China* (Boulder, Colo.: Westview Press).

HSIAO, CHIEN (1990), *Traveller without a Map*, tr. Jeffrey C. Kinkley (London: Hutchinson).

HUANG, YU (1994), 'Peaceful Evolution: The Case of Television Reform in Post-Mao China', *Media, Culture, and Society*, 16: 2, 217–41.

LEE, CHIN-CHUAN (1980), *Media Imperialism Reconsidered* (Beverly Hills, Calif.: Sage).

—— (1990), 'The Media: Of China, About China', in Chin-Chuan Lee (ed.), *Voices of China: The Interplay of Politics and Journalism* (New York: Guilford Press).

—— (1994) (ed.), *China's Media, Media's China* (Boulder, Colo.: Westview Press).

—— (2000a), 'Chinese Communication: Prisms, Trajectories, and Modes of Understanding', in Chin-Chuan Lee (ed.), *Money, Power and Media: Communication Patterns and Bureaucratic Control in Cultural China* (Evanston, Ill.: Northwestern University Press).

—— (2000b) (ed.), *Money, Power and Media: Communication Patterns and Bureaucratic Control in Cultural China* (Evanston, Ill: Northwestern University Press).

LINZ, JUAN J. (1974), 'The Future of an Authoritarian Situation or the Institutionalization of an Authoritarian Regime: The Case of Brazil', in Alfred Stepan (ed.), *Authoritarian Brazil* (New Haven, Conn.: Yale University Press).

—— (1975), 'Totalitarian and Authoritarian Regimes,' in Fred I. Greenstein and Nelson W. Polsby (eds.), *Macro Political Theory: Handbook of Political Science*, vol. 3 (Reading, Mass.: Addison-Wesley).

LIU, ALAN P. L. (1975), *Communications and National Development in Communist China* (Berkeley, Calif.: University of California Press).

Liu, Binyan (1989), *Liu Binyan zizhuan* (Autobiography) (Taipei: China Times Press).

Nathan, Andrew J. (1985), *Chinese Democracy* (New York: Knopf).

Pan, Zhongdang (2000), 'Improvising for Reform Activities: The Changing Reality of Journalistic Practice in China', in Chin-Chuan Lee (ed.), *Money, Power and Media: Communication Patterns and Bureaucratic Control in Cultural China* (Evanston, Ill.: Northwestern University Press).

Passin, Herbert (1963), 'Writer and Journalist in the Transitional Society', in Lucian W. Pye (ed.), *Communication and Political Development* (Princeton, NJ: Princeton University Press).

Polumbaum, Judy (1990), 'The Tribulations of China's Journalists after a Decade of Reform', in Chin-Chuan Lee (ed.), *Voices of China: The Interplay of Politics and Journalism* (New York: Guilford Press).

Pool, Ithiel de Sola (1973), 'Communication in Totalitarian Societies', in Ithiel de Sola Pool and Wilbur Schramm (eds.), *Handbook of Communication* (Chicago: Rand McNally).

Pye, Lucian W. (1979), 'Communication and Political Culture in China', in Godwin Chu and Francis Hsu (eds.), *Moving a Mountain* (Honolulu: University Press of Hawaii).

Rosen, Stanley (2000), 'Seeking Appropriate Behavior under a Socialist Market Economy: An Analysis of Debates and Controversies in *Beijing Youth Daily*', in Chin-Chuan Lee (ed.), *Money, Power and Media: Communication Patterns and Bureaucratic Control in Cultural China* (Evanston, Ill.: Northwestern University Press).

Ruan, Ming (1990), 'Press Freedom and Neoauthoritarianism: A Reflection on China's Democracy Movement', in Chin-Chuan Lee (ed.), *Voices of China: The Interplay of Politics and Journalism* (New York: Guilford Press).

Su, Shaozhi (1994), 'Chinese Communist Ideology and Media Control', in Chin-Chuan Lee (ed.), *China's Media, Media's China* (Boulder, Colo.: Westview Press).

Wang, Ruoshui (1987), *Zhihui de tongku* (The Pains of Wisdom) (Taipei: Renjian Press).

Wu, Guoguang (1997), *Zhao Ziyang yu zhengzhi gaige* (Zhao Ziyang and Political Reform) (Hong Kong: Pacific Century Institute).

Yu, Guoming (1998), 'Chinese Journalists' Occupational Ideology and Ethics', *Xinwen Jizhe* (Journalists), 10 Mar., 57–64.

—— and Xiayang, Liu (1993), *Zhongguo minyi jianjiu* (Public Opinion Research in China) (Beijing: People's University Press).

Yu, Xu (1994), 'Professionalization without Guarantees: Changes in the Chinese Press in the Post-1989 Years', *Gazette*, 53: 1–2, 23–41.

Zhao, Yuezhi (1998), *Media, Market and Democracy in China* (Urbana, Ill.: University of Illinois Press).

27

Australian Media Occupations

Rodney Tiffen .

For above all Australia is Australian. It is indeed an astonishing thing how strong a character Australia has—so strong that the ever-continuing waves of British migrants have no impact on it but are ruthlessly bent to its pattern. It is a character immediately recognisable in her soldiers as in her poets, in her politicians as in her cricketers—rough rather than tough, kindly but not tolerant, a generous, sardonic, sceptical but surprisingly gullible character, quick to take offence and by no means unwilling to give it, always ready for a fight but just as ready to help a fellow-creature in distress.[1]

IRONICALLY JOHN DOUGLAS PRINGLE was able to pen this 1950s testament to Australian independence because he had been brought to the country to edit its oldest newspaper, the *Sydney Morning Herald*, whose then proprietors, the Fairfax family, still, half a century after federation, had a tradition of appointing English editors. It is also ironic that the articulation of national characteristics is an enterprise dominated by immigrants and expatriates. While in the wake of World War II, Australia began one of the largest immigration programmes in history (and today is second only to Israel in the proportion of overseas-born in its population), at the same time many artists and journalists left the country in search of financial success or professional fulfilment. They were rarely shy about describing what they had left behind. Germaine Greer, for example, thought Australia was 'a huge rest home, where no unwelcome news is ever wafted on to the pages of the worst newspapers in the world.'

While expatriates and immigrants have been disproportionately influential in shaping Australia's international image, one suspects their constructions of the country are often designed to serve as the backdrop to highlight their personal journeys. In contrast, the national imagery

Source: Not previously published. Rodney Tiffen teaches Government at the University of Sydney.

1 John Douglas Pringle, *Australian Accent* (London: Chatto and Windus, 1959), 20.

produced for domestic consumption exhibits more unqualified celebration, and more often serves a political rather than personal agenda. Sometimes this has a direct policy purpose. For example, in recent times television industry representatives, fighting a rearguard action against the introduction of new services, have taken to claiming that Australia has the best TV in the world. It seems almost unpatriotic to point to the lack of evidence in such invocations.

Perhaps all attempts to define national cultures are doomed; perhaps the effort must be intrinsically confounded by over-generalization and subjective judgement. National portraits typically underestimate change as well as variation, and their explanatory schemas commonly invoke unobservable traditions more than socio-economic institutions. Rather than probing convict origins, a larrikin streak, a cultural cringe, or any other allegedly defining national characteristic, if we wish to understand the flavour of Australian media content and of the people producing it, it is more fruitful to begin with the key aspects of Australian media structures.

The most basic feature of the Australian media market is its smallness. This was even more pronounced in the past. While Australia's current population of 19 million is almost one third that of the United Kingdom, in 1950 the proportion was one sixth (8 million to 51 million), while when Australia achieved independence in 1901 the population was just 4 million.

Australia's newspaper market comprised a series of six city-states rather than a single national structure. Each had one central city, which in nearly all of them constituted considerably more than half the population. The capital city newspapers dwarfed the provincial titles, few of which had any substantial news-gathering capacity outside their local area, and most of which enjoyed a local monopoly. Many were (and are) quite small operations, family companies where the relations between employer and employee ranged from the paternalistic to the tyrannical. Being the only newspaper in a relatively tightly knit community had consequences for the flavour of the news, which often seemed to outside eyes stiflingly parochial and conformist. However, many journalists who later went on to enjoy success in the metropolitan media praised the discipline that working in such an environment necessitated. Inaccuracies or irresponsibility were immediately apparent to the audience, and feedback was direct and personal. It should be added that despite such fond memories, few of these journalists seemed inclined to return to their provincial roots.

The metropolitan newspapers were more substantial operations, but not large in either circulation or staffing by comparison with the most prestigious international papers. Over time, their position changed in two major ways. On the one hand what had begun as locally owned enterprises gradually became parts of nationally owned chains. In addition, within each major city the number of competitors was reduced. Thus while there were 21 metropolitan newspapers and 17 independent newspapers in 1901, by 1972 this had been reduced to 17 titles with three different owners.[2]

---

2 Henry Mayer, 'Press Oligopoly', in Henry Mayer and Helen Nelson (eds.), *Australian Politics: A Third Reader* (Melbourne: Cheshire, 1972). Mayer's figures differ slightly from my own, because I include Canberra, and because almost immediately after he wrote his article, the number of owners was reduced from 4 to 3, when Frank Packer sold out of newspapers, selling the *Daily Telegraph* to Rupert Murdoch. The number of papers produced for the 6 state capitals had declined from 21 to 14.

By the 1960s only Sydney and Melbourne had directly competing metropolitan newspapers.

This was not a formula for dynamism. Especially in the smaller capitals, the papers' styles tended to be centrist, eschewing both the ambitions of the quality press and the marketing gimmicks of the British tabloids. Politically, they tended to be close to the business establishments and to the state Liberal parties. There had never been an influential or vibrant mainstream pro-Labor press in Australia, but in the decades following World War II, during the long period of rule by the Liberal–Country Party coalition, the major press was almost unexceptionally supportive of it. In that generation Australian society changed much more than its press. Its increasing education, multi-culturalism, and internationalization, and its greater subcultural diversity, were only dimly and belatedly reflected in its newspapers. Their oligopoly cushioned them from the need to be more responsive to their changing audiences. This cosy conservatism extended also to management practices. The employment situation for journalists was very much a buyer's market, and power inside the newsrooms rested unambiguously with top management.

Entry to journalism was heavily influenced by nepotism. Recruitment was overwhelmingly at a very young age, with a disdain not only for formal qualifications but for vocational training, often justified by the belief that journalists were born not made. Since colonial days journalism had often been, in Walter Lippmann's phrase, a refuge for the 'vaguely talented', or in the words of Bert Cook, the founder of the Australian Journalists Association (AJA), for 'that frayed type of somewhat cultured mankind who had fallen to the temptations of the wayside'.[3] The other major recruitment pool was from the talented upwardly mobile, often individualistic but eager for opportunity and so wishing to please their employer.

It was not fertile ground for a strong trade union. Indeed at a meeting in 1910 leading to the formation of the AJA, one reporter passionately told of how due to their collective bargaining strength, the slaughtermen on his round got much higher pay than journalists, and moved a motion that journalists deserved to be paid as much as slaughtermen.[4] Although the AJA was one of Australia's earliest white-collar unions, its bargaining strength has always been limited.

From the mid-1960s on the situation for newspaper journalists began to change under a variety of influences. One was the coming of two national newspapers—the *Australian* and the *Australian Financial Review*. Although they only took a small share of the circulation in each city, they created a more competitive market for quality journalism. This combined with the disunity inside the coalition and its sharply declining political fortunes to encourage an improvement in federal political reporting.[5] A change in journalistic formats—namely the switch from anonymous reports to the increasing use of bylines—was a further factor bringing a shift in the

---

3 Clem Lloyd, *Profession: Journalist* (Sydney: Hale and Iremonger, 1985), 20, 25.

4 Ibid. 62.

5 C. J. Lloyd, *Parliament and the Press: The Federal Parliamentary Press Gallery 1901–88* (Melbourne: Melbourne University Press, 1988); Rodney Tiffen, *News and Power* (Sydney: Allen and Unwin, 1989).

internal power balance between journalists and management. Most importantly, the monopoly position of the newspaper proprietors could not stop
newspapers themselves losing their monopoly role. Change in the press was
necessitated most fundamentally because their role as the initial and
primary conveyor of the latest news was supplanted by television and radio.

As with other democratic countries, Australia's broadcasting was shaped
much more directly by government policy than its press history had been.
Australia's constitution has often been described as a Washminster political
system, combining the Westminster system's emphasis on the parliamentary accountability of executive government and an impartial public
service with the American federal system, and a strongly bi-cameral
national parliament. Similarly, Australia adopted a hybrid broadcasting
system, midway between the American and British systems. Television was
introduced in the 1950s initially with two, later three, commercial channels
in the biggest cities. In addition, there was a public service channel, the
ABC, modelled on the BBC. In 1980, the multi-cultural channel, SBS
(Special Broadcasting Service), was added. All the major population
centres, and all but the most remote parts of the country, now have this
five-channel structure.

A British observer would find the mix of commercial and public service
in Australia's television structure deceptively familiar. However, three far-
reaching differences are likely to confound our visitor's assumptions. The
first is that the ABC has never gained the centrality or self-assurance of the
BBC. Whereas the BBC has for most of its history commanded more than
40 per cent of the TV audience, the average ratings share for the ABC is
around 12 per cent. The second is that the outlook and behaviour of
Australian commercial TV more closely resembles a radically scaled-down
version of the US networks than the more regulated, public service ethos of
the ITC. The third is that Australia's media oligopoly has given the major
proprietors far more leverage in policy formation, and the system is much
more weighted to their interests.

Government broadcasting policy has always been surrounded by high-
sounding rhetoric, but the need to ensure financial viability while filling
the programming needs of a voracious medium has always been the basic
driver of TV practice. The smallness and geographic dispersion of the
national market were initially central in shaping Australian television.
When television began in the 1950s, it was impossible to transmit instant-
aneously between the major cities. The technological limits, the structure
of the advertising market, and an official ideology of localism meant that
the early days of Australian television, like the press, were marked by relatively dispersed ownership, by a series of relatively small commercial enterprises with variations in competence and professionalism. However, the
economic realities of national networking soon became paramount in TV
decision-making. Any substantial production needed to sell to a national
market with a key 43 per cent provided by the Sydney–Melbourne axis.

Even more importantly, it was far, far cheaper to import programmes
from the United States than to produce them locally. If television programming were left to market forces, Australian content would be very
limited. Australian TV was swamped by imports not because of lack of

demand for the local product—the programmes on television with the highest ratings have always included a large proportion of domestically produced programmes. Rather it was the comparative cost of supply, added to the attraction of purchasing a programme already proven in the American market rather than investing in a new local product of unknown appeal. However, overwhelming political sentiment, plus an array of active pressure groups, have created one of television's longest-running and most entertaining sagas—how to ensure Australian content.[6]

The imposition of quotas, and the ways the industry has coped to meet these with a minimum of expense, has been an interesting example of the interplay of policy and practice. Regulators had to find ways in particular to ensure that local content included drama rather than just being filled by cheap alternatives like game shows. One consequence of the local drama content was the flowering of soap operas, especially on the least successful of the three commercial channels, the Ten network. Soap opera is a genre ideally suited to the commercial institutional logic of television. It encourages habitual viewing, with each episode being part of an ongoing story, an extended neighbourhood to which regular viewers become more attached with familiarity. It does not depend on one or two stars, but a stable of (at least initially) cheap and if necessary replaceable actors and writers. Typically the sets are minimal as the camera focuses upon individuals and their interactions. Cheapness and consistency of supply met the commercial imperatives, while the production industry and unions liked the revenue and employment generated. Ultimately one such programme, *Neighbours*, originally sneered at by TV critics, became one of Australia's most successful TV exports,[7] proving even more popular in Britain than it had been in Australia.

Government policy was always mindful of setting requirements which did not challenge industry profitability. It has been even more respectful of the proprietors' interests when it has come to media ownership policy. In fact governments have consistently acted to reinforce oligopolistic tendencies rather than trying to stimulate diversity. Two decisions, both reeking of political patronage, were most important in influencing the control of Australia's media. The first came when the Menzies government allocated the original television licences to consortia dominated by newspaper proprietors. The combination of historical advantage and institutional logic produced in Australia one of the most oligopolistic media in the world. By the early 1980s, four major companies dominated not only the metropolitan daily and weekly press and the major TV markets, but also magazines, newsprint, and ownership of the national news agency, and were significant players in the provincial and suburban press, commercial radio, book publishing, and record companies.[8] The financial muscle and

---

6   Albert Moran, 'Three Stages of Australian Television', in John Tulloch and Graeme Turner (eds.), *Australian Television: Programs, Pleasures and Politics* (Sydney: Allen and Unwin, 1989).

7   Stuart Cunningham and Elizabeth Jacka, 'Australian Television in World Markets', in John Sinclair, Elizabeth Jacka, and Stuart Cunningham (eds.), *New Patterns in Global Television. Peripheral Vision* (Oxford: Oxford University Press, 1996), 207.

8   Henry Mayer, 'Media', in Henry Mayer and Helen Nelson (eds.), *Australian Politics: A Fifth Reader* (Melbourne: Cheshire, 1980).

marketing advantages of the four giants, as well as their political connections, meant that the odds were greatly loaded against new entrants.

The four companies each had their distinctive managerial and personnel styles. Unusually, three of the four were dominated by a single family. The exception was the Herald and Weekly Times, which never gained a foothold in Sydney, but was the largest player in all the other state capitals. It had been built up through the mergers of the 1930s and '40s, principally by the efforts of Sir Keith Murdoch, who, famously for the initial prospects of his son, Rupert, owned little stock. The Herald and Weekly Times had a reputation as the blandest of the media corporations. Its critics saw it as the epitome of monopoly comfort, of grey mediocrity, with an emphasis on unadventurous conformity not only in its investment policies and its media products, but in its internal practices. Seniority, patience, and diligence were the way to the top. Almost invariably senior editorial positions were filled by people with long experience on the production rather than the reporting side of journalism. Initiative was discouraged, but the company's reputation was as a paternalistic, rather than ruthless, employer, still reflecting the spirit Sir Keith had proclaimed in the 1920s of offering 'our young men' 'sound careers'.[9]

In contrast, right from its origins, the Packer company had a rough edge in both its internal and external dealings. Tales of bullying and stinginess abounded.[10] As its empire grew, some of that ethos changed. Some of the company's loyal lieutenants were lavishly rewarded. Moreover, the company proved a market leader in providing the 'perks' that became synonymous with the upper levels of commercial TV. However, the cardinal sin was always assertion of independence. Among journalists, it was reputed that the Packers could sack you many times, but you only resigned once.

The fastest-growing of the four major corporations, Rupert Murdoch's News Corporation, had a similar, although slightly more civilized, reputation. Murdoch's management style, like his investment strategies, has been high-risk and unconventional, one designed to maximize his own control, with a premium on effectiveness over procedural niceties. Both rapid promotion and job insecurity have characterized his companies. As Maxwell Newton, one of his former editors, put it, 'He's a tremendous sacker. But of course he's also a tremendous hirer. He's always sacking them and hiring them.'[11] He has given people opportunity, but he has also handled them ruthlessly and manipulatively, often adopting divide-and-rule strategies, using one person to undermine another, breaking promises when convenient, and of course always subordinating the individual's interests to the corporation's.

The Fairfax organization, which owned most of Australia's highest-quality newspapers, had a very different ethos, one which was much more respectful of the prerogatives of middle management, and which, most

9 Lloyd, *Profession: Journalist*, 143.

10 Paul Barry, *The Rise and Rise of Kerry Packer* (Sydney: Bantam Books, 1993); Bridget Griffin-Foley, *The House of Packer: The Making of a Media Empire* (Sydney: Allen and Unwin, 1999).

11 Michael Leapman, *Barefaced Cheek: The Apotheosis of Rupert Murdoch* (London: Hodder and Stoughton, 1983), back cover. See also George Munster, *A Paper Prince* (Melbourne: Viking, 1985).

importantly, typically allowed a greater sense of editorial integrity. This did not always result in more harmonious internal relations, however, partly because the tendency of the upper echelons to management by memo tended to escalate conflicts.[12] Moreover, they often tended to view internal conflicts as matters of principle, so adopting a more rigid approach, where the more buccaneering, domineering, but ultimately pragmatic style of Murdoch and Packer would look for accommodation. Nevertheless, outside the ABC, the Fairfax organization was the most nurturing of journalistic talent.

Government policy was also the catalyst in ending this stable oligopoly, but the result was a structure even less likely to serve the public interest. The second fateful decision in the development of Australian media came in 1986–7. After prolonged conflict and indecision within the Labor Government, TV networks were allowed to spread their ownership to own stations in markets comprising up to 60 per cent of the national market. But at the same time the government imposed limits on cross-media ownership, not allowing a proprietor to own a TV station and newspaper in the same city. This policy helped Packer—who did not own any newspapers— and Murdoch, who by acquiring American citizenship had forfeited his right to an Australian TV licence, and would soon have had to sell his existing stations. Although existing arrangements were grandfathered, the new policy inhibited future growth by both the Fairfax and Herald and Weekly Times companies because of their patterns of cross-media holdings.

In the convulsions which followed, the great majority of newspapers and TV channels changed owners, some more than once. Murdoch took over the Herald and Weekly Times. All three TV networks finished up with new owners. Packer took a short holiday from TV ownership thanks to an absurdly generous bid by Alan Bond. The activity brought to a head tensions in the Fairfax family, which then imploded in an ill-fated attempt at total control by one family member.[13] The result, after a few years, was a series of bankruptcies, which left Packer in an even more dominant position in TV than he had been, and Murdoch controlling newspapers which accounted for around two thirds of daily circulation. The seven existing afternoon newspapers all closed. The high levels of debt led to rounds of cost-cutting, which impacted directly on the programming performance of the networks. The journalists' union estimated that over 1,200 jobs were lost in less than three years, by far the biggest loss in history. Official figures showed that employment in commercial TV dropped from 7,745 in 1988 to 6,316 three years later.[14] Qualitatively, these changes seemed to be

---

12 The memos did, however, make possible two of the best corporate histories ever written in Australia. See Gavin Souter, *Company of Heralds: A Century and a Half of Australian Publishing* (Melbourne: Melbourne University Press, 1981); Gavin Souter, *Heralds and Angels: The House of Fairfax 1841–1990* (Melbourne: Melbourne University Press, 1991).

13 V. J. Carroll, *The Man Who Couldn't Wait: Warwick Fairfax's Folly and the Bankers Who Backed Him* (Melbourne: William Heinemann Australia, 1990).

14 Rodney Tiffen, 'Media Policy', in Judith Brett, James Gillespie, and Murray Goot (eds.), *Developments in Australian Politics* (Melbourne: Macmillan, 1994), 329–36. See also Paul Chadwick, *Media Mates: Carving Up Australia's Media* (Melbourne: Sun Books, Macmillan, 1989), and David Bowman, *The Captive Press* (Melbourne: Penguin, 1988).

accompanied by TV executives going increasingly down-market in their programming, notably in their news content.

Australia's media thus entered the 1990s in a battered state, but the decade has continued to be a dynamic era of expansion and innovation, stimulated by technological change, globalization, and the seemingly ever-expanding variety of media markets. This dynamism, wedded to changing patterns of employment in the economy generally, has changed many of the assumptions that marked career routes, management practices, and industrial relations in media organizations.

Probably nowhere in the world does journalism meet the requirements for being called a profession. Certainly in Australia it has lacked most of the essential attributes. No professional body controls entry, or has the power to enforce observance of professional standards. Journalists are employees having no direct relationship with their clients, who interact with them only as consumers of the larger product to which they contribute.

One of the prerequisites which it has lacked is public prestige. Only 8 per cent of Australians rate newspaper journalists high or very high for ethics and honesty, towards the bottom of occupational groups, along with advertising people, estate agents, and politicians, but all above the lowest group, car salesmen (2 per cent). TV journalists rate slightly higher at 13 per cent. In contrast the top groups are nurses (88 per cent), pharmacists (80), school teachers (71), and doctors (69).[15] These results have been broadly consistent with a slight downward trend for a generation.

In stark contrast to journalism's low public standing, it is one of the most sought-after careers among young people. The demand to enter journalism is so strong that in the mid-1990s, the ABC received 800 applications annually for an intake of six cadets. Typically newspapers were receiving perhaps 500 applications for the half dozen new cadet positions they annually offered.[16]

To continue with the apparent contradictions, the occupation which is so difficult to break into has a very high voluntary departure rate. This is despite the fact that from quite early in their careers, journalists may gain a public profile through their bylines in print or their on-air reports in broadcasting. But this upward mobility often plateaus. The high exit rate from journalism is partly because of increased opportunities elsewhere. Cognate occupations, most especially public relations, have grown much faster than mainstream journalism itself, and frequently they offer more pay, more security, and better working conditions. 'Push' factors in the nature of journalistic work itself are also pertinent. Many tire of the daily pressure involved in meeting deadlines. What produced an adrenalin surge early in their careers may later just become tiresome and stressful.

Traditionally Australian journalism was not good at creating rewarding career development for those who did not become editors. (Moreover, the requirements to succeed in a managerial role do not necessarily correlate strongly with those that produce a successful reporter.) Australian media

---

15 See the Roy Morgan Research Centre website (http://www.roymorgan.com.au/polls).

16 David Conley, *The Daily Miracle: An Introduction to Journalism* (Melbourne: Oxford University Press, 1997), 2.

organizations do not seem to have been characterized by enlightened personnel practices. Negative feedback has traditionally far exceeded positive feedback in most newsrooms. There has been a reluctance to invest in staff development, partly because there has been a feeling that the organization will not get a return on their investment because the journalists will then leave for greener pastures.

In recent decades, and at an ever accelerating pace, far more individualistic and various career patterns have emerged. The capacity of the media to manufacture 'stars' in journalism as well as in entertainment gives those individuals much more leverage with potential employers, and often an increasing sense of their own worth as commodities. The increasing number of niches and individual outlets has broadened the talents that are rewarded. The ranks of journalism have become more socially diverse. (The 1970s was the crucial decade for women to break into the occupation in large numbers, and since then successive glass ceilings have been broken.)

At the same time, job security has become even more tenuous, and instability the norm in many organizations. The bargaining position of all of the unions has become weaker as national award structures give way to enterprise bargaining amid high rates of unemployment. The union movement from the 1980s has followed a policy of amalgamation. As part of this the Australian Journalists Association became part of the Media, Entertainment and Arts Alliance. Its industrial capacity has been eroded by the trends of the last two decades, but it has broadened its concerns, and become a more effective advocate on issues of professional ethics.

Nevertheless any consistent sense of professionalism is at least as precarious as at any time in the past, especially as informational programming has become increasingly diversified but frequently with fewer controls on standards. The rise of infotainment programming, of supplements attractive to advertisers in newspapers, of more 'tabloid' current affairs programming on commercial television, and of talk-back radio have all contributed to a richer mix of information, but with fewer checks on editorial standards. The old division in quality newspapers between 'church' (editors) and 'state' (publishers) has been obliterated, as editors have also become publishers, now attending more directly to revenue as well as to editorial concerns. In 1999, a spectacular scandal broke out over 'cash for comment' as radio's two highest-paid and most famous talk-back presenters, John Laws and Alan Jones, were revealed as having taken huge payments to promote certain goods and viewpoints in their on-air comments.

The trends in Australian media are acutely contradictory. The power of the major moguls is as great as ever, while the bipartisan desire of governments to please them continues unabated. There are also trends making for greater pluralism in access to the media, more varied routes to career success, and more competition between different media, as the impact of new technologies becomes increasingly important. The material rewards for the successful are greater than ever, but how that success correlates with a professional excellence beyond immediate market forces is becoming more problematic. It is likely that these contradictory trends extend beyond Australia, as part of the reason for them is how our media developments are increasingly influenced by global forces. In another generation, when we talk about national traditions in media occupations, whatever the differences in origins, the destinations may turn out to be increasingly similar.

28

Journalists and Media Professionals in France

Michael Palmer

'**T**HE PEN IS mightier than the sword.' This cliché comes from the play *Richelieu* (1839), by the Victorian writer Edward George Bulwer-Lytton, focusing on the French seventeenth-century statesman. The preceding line (less often quoted) is 'Beneath the rule of men entirely great'. The two lines sum up two recurrent ways of perceiving the role of journalists and writers on public affairs in France: Firstly, *an adversarial (or else subservient) relationship* to those who wield power (political, religious, economic, and other); and secondly, *the importance of writing skills*—some today would broaden this to 'production skills'—either in a given polemical exchange or the coverage of a particular story. For centuries, it appears, skills and power relationships have fashioned a journalist's self-perception and the way media professionals—beginning with journalists, but now including other 'intellectual publicists' and 'media' workers whose products address a public or market—perceive themselves collectively.

The terms 'journalists' and 'journalisms' were in use in French in the early 1700s: but it was not until the late nineteenth century that the notion of journalism as a profession, with distinctive characteristics, gained currency. This was the period when the press became an industry, with some dailies having circulations exceeding a million copies, and when other terms of the vocabulary of 'modern media' likewise gained currency: in 1898, the sociologist Gabriel Tarde wrote of 'the sense of the topical' ('la sensation de l'actualité').

Recent research by media historians in France highlights how, from the 1880s, the emergence of a professional identity—a sense of 'self' (collective self-interests and the need for collective self-help)—slowly gathered momentum. 1881 was the year of the law on the freedom of the press—freedom from state control. Although amended, and sometimes suspended, during France's chequered political history during the following century, this law continued to underpin freedom of expression in France. Broadcasting likewise had a varied history from the 1920s to the 1970s: the July 1982 law, proclaiming the freedom of audiovisual media from state

Source: Not previously published. Michael Palmer is Professor of Communications Theory, University of Paris III, Sorbonne Nouvelle.

control, echoes in some respects the freedom of the press and publishing celebrated in the first article of the July 1881 law. For centuries, therefore, issues of state control, and other influences on freedom of expression and on journalists in particular, have been centre stage in many writings on the press and, subsequently, on the media (a term which gained currency in France from the 1960s).

Many legacies have resulted: the Revolution of 1830—leading to the overthrow of the king, Charles X—was sometimes dubbed 'the journalists' revolution': this exemplifies 'pen versus sword' rhetoric. For much of the Third Republic (1870–1940) there were many instances when journalists' self-awareness continued to feed off the 'power of the press': the self-importance of 'her majesty the press' grew with the chronic parliamentary instability and crises of the Republic. Yet during this period, the years 1881–1914, and especially 1918–40, witnessed phases in journalists' awareness of their common professional concerns and identity: the 1880s to 1914 saw the development of mutual benevolent funds and associations or guilds and a rhetoric of journalists as 'a big family'. By some estimates, there were about a thousand journalists in Paris in 1885; individualism and careerism often appeared triumphant and the hoary adage, 'Journalism can be a springboard to anywhere, provided you escape its clutches', remained emblematic. Yet historians have revealed the other side of the coin: awareness of the precarious working conditions and income of most rank-and-file journalists, of their subservience to employers who might dismiss them at a whim, of the vagaries of power relations within any given newspaper title, slowly resulted in moves to better organize 'the profession'.

Already in the 1890s, there was a growing number of comparisons with the 'professional situation' of journalists in Britain, the US, and elsewhere. During the First World War, the French government often provided better facilities to British and American war correspondents than to French journalists, who were operating under censorship constraints. These and other factors led in the 1920s to the growth of a trade union—le Syndicat National des Journalistes (founded 1918)—and to pressure that culminated in the 1935 law recognizing the existence of journalism as a profession: a journalist was defined as a person who derives the major part of his income from employment in a French magazine, daily newspaper, or news agency. From 1936 a professional identity card was issued by a body on which sat—in equal numbers—representatives of news media employers and journalists. In early 1939, there were 3,459 card-carrying members: 3.5 per cent were women; 56.5 per cent were based in Paris.

The number of card-carrying journalists—the recognized professional measuring-rod—doubled between 1955 (6,836) and 1975 (13,635) and doubled again by 1990 (26,614). In 1998, there were some 30,000. Parisian-born journalists have consistently represented about 50 per cent of all card-carrying journalists. The profession has become more feminine—about 30 per cent (in 1990, 33.2 per cent of the total, and 48.7 per cent of those under 31 years of age). But the diversity of socio-economic origins, of working conditions, and of stability of employment, remains considerable. The traditional perception of journalists as 'petit bourgeois' persists: in 1983, only 6 per cent were of working-class origin. The growing number of stringers ('pigistes') illustrates the precarious working conditions of many journalists: the proportion of this group among card-carrying journalists had risen to 14.7 per cent in 1990; 40.5 per cent of them were women; 44.1 per cent of photographers were stringers. There is thus a world of difference between stringers, on the one hand, and elite journalists on the other, some of whom allegedly constitute a 'mediaklatura'. The latter, much attacked in recent years by fellow-journalists and by leading intellectuals (including sociologist Pierre Bourdieu), indeed belong to—or perceive themselves as—the privileged interlocutors of an elite of some 5,000 people who, it is claimed by many these days, provide the backbone of the class that governs France (just as in the 1930s, anti-Establishment figures held that 200 families controlled much of the wealth of France).

'Pigistes' develop multi-skilling, as do many young recruits to journalism: these include those who successfully enter the limited number of elite journalism schools, whose graduates, however, form only a minority of professional journalists. It is sometimes observed that journalists from the print media make the leap into audiovisual media, and have the necessary writing and production skills: it does not necessarily operate the other way. It is also claimed that many of the 'mediaklatura' are more in the vein of op-ed page commentators and columnists than hard-nosed newsmen, with a proven track record of investigative reporting. All these ingredients are part of the debate concerning journalism and journalists. Let us explore some of them.

French and US academics studying the sociology, professional practice, career patterns, and relationships with sources of various journalists over the past twenty years agree, by and large, on the following: there is a certain *connivence* or complicity between journalists and their sources, including political and government sources, irrespective of the editorial stance of the media the journalist works for. The more measured academic studies of 'converging media and government elites' have been amplified since the mid-1990s by vigorous, polemical exposés, conducted by prominent intellectuals headed by Bourdieu, denouncing both this complicity and the 'mediaklatura', i.e. the limited number of commentators who hold forth across a range of broadcast and print media. Intellectuals who criticize media pundits are a distinctive feature of French public life—as is the desire of many leading journalists to be considered as intellectuals, more perhaps than those who want to be thought of as seasoned hard-nosed investigative reporters. Let us consider some of the recent events in this debate.

Near the pinnacle of the profession, the chief editor of *Le Monde*, Edwy Plenel, is a seasoned newsman, with many exposés of nefarious political malpractice to his credit—his telephone was tapped while investigating murky undercover activities sponsored by the Elysée during the Mitterrand presidency; he, and colleague Bertrand le Gendre, led the *Le Monde* team that uncovered the participation of French intelligence in the blowing up of the Greenpeace ship *Rainbow Warrior* (July 1985). Plenel—aged 15 in 1967, at the dawn of his political consciousness (Plenel 1999: 13–14)— argues that the phrase 'investigative journalism' is tautologous: every journalist investigates. But Plenel also engages in dialogue with the intellectuals whose often controversial stands on topical issues nurture the agenda of public debate; Plenel's books on journalism, on public affairs, and on dialogue with intellectuals who intervene in public issues are grounded in his reading of Charles Péguy (1873–1914), the poet, nationalist, socialist, and Catholic writer; this situates Plenel in the 'man of letters' tradition of French journalism. In mid-May 1999, *Le Monde* published an open letter to the president of the republic by Régis Debray, in which this leading intellectual sought to publicize the Serb viewpoint on what was happening in Kosovo; within weeks Plenel had penned a reply to Debray, modifying in the process a manuscript he was writing centred on the 'national republicans', a 'new feature of the French politico-intellectual landscape'. Meanwhile, a few weeks before the publication of Plenel's book, entitled *L'Épreuve*, another *Le Monde* journalist of the same generation as Plenel, Daniel Schneidermann, published a riposte to the critique of journalism made by Bourdieu. Schneidermann writes a weekly column on television and public affairs in *Le Monde*, and presents a TV programme, *Arrêt sur images*, analysing television news coverage.

Thus, within weeks of each other, two leading *Le Monde* journalists took issue with prominent intellectuals who periodically criticize the media. As skilled journalists, they persuaded some of the latter to appear in the columns or programmes of their respective media: Debray's controversial article on Kosovo appeared in *Le Monde*, and Schneidermann succeeded in getting Bourdieu to appear on his TV programme (in 1996). Where Schneidermann writes as the humble journalist proud of the fact that the emininent sociologist debates with other journalists on his programme, Plenel admonishes Régis Debray, in a tone 'more in sorrow than in anger', based on thirty years of following Debray's writings and statements. In so doing, the two *Le Monde* journalists—both still under 50 years of age—stand in a long line of journalists-publicists debating, not as equals, but not as inferiors, with leading intellectuals whose views they dispute. Other *Le Monde* journalists have documented this tradition (Ferenczi 1993). 'Quite simply', argues the American scholar Clyde Thogmartin, 'French journalism *is* opinion journalism' (1998: 5, emphasis his). And, in a way, the battle of ideas—commentating from the sidelines, or even joining in the jousting oneself—attracts many journalists more than does laborious and long research into technical or abstruse subjects that their editorial news managers might not consider worth the time and energy involved: for every *Le Monde* that invests heavily in digging into the background behind the *Rainbow Warrior* scandal, there are many newspapers where editors believe they do not have the budget to fund investigative research requiring time and energy and whose results may not be publishable.

Just as some claim that the *cadres* or leading figures of French mainstream political parties have failed to generate much new blood over the past twenty to thirty years, there is also criticism that a limited number of pundits and commentators hold forth, year after year, in the major mainstream media pulpits; the generation that came to the fore in the 1960s—before and after the events of 1968—still holds many elite 'mediaklatura' posts. There have been real-life incidents that seem more typical of caricature: two leading and professionally respected women journalists, Christine Ockrent and Anne Sinclair, have hosted television current affairs programmes where each interviewed the other's husband or companion, who were both government ministers (Bernard Kouchner and Dominique Strauss-Kahn, respectively). The director of the French Press Institute, Rémy Rieffel, quoted Christine Ockrent thus: France is a small country, with a very centralized government. Therefore the journalistic community operates side by side with the hermetically sealed world of politics, trade unions, artists. [. . .] These people know each other too well, because it is the same 5,000 people who are going to do things, comment on them, react to them' (Rieffel 1984; Thogmartin 1998).

Belgian by origin, Ockrent, whose career has included posts as a television anchorwoman, publisher of the weekly news magazine *L'Express*, and untold commentator-columnist activities on radio and television, started her career in France after holding an internship at CBS in the US, while beginning a doctorate in political science. American news-presentation skills and a French multi-media presence are assets that made her something of a role model.[1] The two main anchormen fronting the prime-time evening newscast on the rival private and public service channels in 1999— TF1 (Patrick Poivre d'Arvor) and France 2 (Claude Sérillon)—both worked in the early 1970s for the same public service channel, Antenne 2. Critiques of *connivence* accordingly draw attention to the longevity of professional relationships between colleagues who may work together at one time only to be in competition later. But the point is rather that it is only during the past twenty-five to thirty years that professional skills and performance (and networking) have become the determining criteria across a wide range of public service and private sector media.

Observers of regional and local media sometimes remark that a similar complicity exists there also, or rather, that regional press barons may employ chief editors who occasionally criticize the local powers that be— but it is not in such mainstream media that exposé investigative journalism in, say, a Chicago or New York muckraking tradition is to be found. 'Don't bite the hand that feeds you': this maxim is frequently heard, in exchanges about journalists and their sources, and about media owners, top editorial management, and major advertisers. (There are celebrated instances where newspapers and magazines—including *Le Monde* and *Le Nouvel Observateur*—have lost advertising budgets following hard-hitting articles.) Prominent public and private sector companies and utilities own substantial—sometimes majority—shareholdings in major mainstream media: perhaps the most symbolically charged instance of this in recent years was the privatization in 1986 of TF1, and its subsequent sale in 1987 to a consortium headed by the major construction utility, Bouygues; more

---

1 That is, a role model as a professional of her generation (she was born in 1944). She writes that during the events of 1968 she preferred to cover the story rather than to mount the barricades; having already proved herself as an anchorwoman, she found hard to stomach the attitude of the construction magnate Francis Bouygues, when Bouygues acquired the TV channel TF1 in 1987 and told her: 'I'd like to see you present the news at the weekend: it's good to have a woman presenting the news over the weekend' (Ockrent 1997: 215).

recently, and similarly, France's leading subscription TV channel, Canal Plus, set up by the state in 1984, became part of the media and public utilities company owned by la Compagnie Genérale des Eaux, itself rebaptized Vivendi (1997–9). These trans-media conglomerate corporations are commonplace in 'developed' capitalist societies, although in France, privatization, transnationalization, and the emergence of modern-style corporate media conglomerates occurred relatively late. Developments in the 1980s accelerated the trend. Robert Hersant, the 'Citizen Kane' figure who crystallized the opprobrium journalists felt towards media capitalism and concentrations of ownership from the 1950s to the 1980s, died in the mid-1990s; in 1999 eight industry and media moguls had, in a sense, taken his place. None of them—unlike Hersant—had ever been a practising journalist; six of them—Jean-Marie Messier (Vivendi, Havas); François Pinault (Pinault-Printemps-Redoute), Bernard Arnault (LVMH), Jean-Luc Lagardère (Aérospatiale-Matra-Hachette); Serge Dassault (Dassault Aviation); and Jérôme Seydoux (Pathé)—controlled a host of media assets and advertising budgets. Thus, in France, some journalists are beginning to echo the apocryphal remarks attributed to employees of the Murdoch press (outside France): 'Every journalist once worked, now works, or will in the future work for a Murdoch media interest'—i.e. for a media asset directly or indirectly controlled or influenced by one of the eight. French journalists and media workers often think of media conglomerates as tentacular creatures: Hachette (publishing, print media distribution, etc.) was long called 'the octopus'.

In the context of contemporary media capitalism, many journalists experience the atmosphere of uncertainty and instability characteristic of many other employees in cultural, advertising, and entertainment industries. Networking and the cultivation of contacts are both professional skills and survival skills, as is the continual updating of technological expertise. The French news agency, Agence France Presse, was still considered in the late 1980s as the major news media company, employing 700 professional journalists: graduates of journalism schools or of political science and international relations planning a career in journalism, possibly as a foreign correspondent, knew that AFP was a choice career target. But many French journalists believed that AFP was weighted towards serving the needs of the French print media and of Francophone media worldwide. In the 1990s, AFP developed its English-language services: its chief news editor in 1999 was a Scot. And it developed a joint venture with the American-based Bloomberg news agency, so as to acquire television experience: AFP built a TV studio to provide a feed of French general and business news to Bloomberg. The AFP staff journalists who were seen as good recruits for the TV feed were relatively young (many were in their thirties) and had a TV presence. Even older staffers, working primarily for print media and 'conventional' wire services, expressed enjoyment at doing a ninety-second or three-minute piece for the TV feed. Multi-skilling and diversification out of the traditional print media base proceeds apace. Even *Le Monde*—the journal of reference and the leading quality daily—is developing radio and TV programmes and interests: their journalists are more 'up front' than their pre-1968 predecessors. For many

25- to 40-year-olds, mobility remains the name of the game: the chief editor of a leading trade magazine in the early 1980s, *Médias*, went on to become a major producer of independent films. None the less, everyone claims that a grounding in the print media remains an indispensable prerequisite. Many journalists make a more-than-decent living out of the profession; but a substantial minority live precariously and vicariously.

Many of the most stringent critics of the practices and performance of journalists come from the press itself. This has long been the case. One of the most astute recent historians of French journalism, Christian Delporte, points out that the self-criticism which the profession frequently embarks upon publicly is somewhat self-serving: 'There are black sheep, but these are exceptions to the rule,' runs the argument. Since the attempts at radical reform of the French press immediately following the Liberation (1944), media industries and professions have mainly followed political and economic trends common to (middle-class) French society as a whole. In the mainstream media, consumerism and marketing techniques impinge on news-editorial content and presentation. This is true of the leading national and regional dailies and of general interest and thematic news magazines that generally occupy centre stage. But studies show that technical, professional journals and specialist, thematic titles aimed at a mass audience (TV magazines, for example) employ over 35 per cent of card-carrying journalists—the same proportion as that of journalists employed in national and regional dailies, in non-daily regional newspapers, and in general interest magazines (1990 data). Radio, television, and news agencies each employ about 6 to 8 per cent.

The multimedia, multi-skilling career patterns of a growing number of young and early middle-age journalists emphasize technical and verbal skills in an advertising-funded and consumer-targeted media rather than the ideological struggles which marked much of French journalism until the 1950s. Delporte puts it thus: 'the French journalist is a paradox: on the one hand he is marked by a missionary ideal, nurtured by a glorious past, which makes him think of himself as destined to fulfil an exceptional role; on the other, he simply wants to be considered a citizen just like any other' (Delporte 1999: 426). There is ample evidence that the latter concern is ever more important as the ranks of the profession—peopled by younger, better-educated recruits and a higher female intake, and requiring ever more human management, as well as technical skills—increase. The American observer Clyde Thogmartin, puts a positive gloss on this: 'in the last twenty years, French journalists have tried to develop a professional and ethical culture in which news serves as an end in itself, not simply as a pretext for commentary defending a particular political ideology' (Thogmartin 1998: 265).

Both Delporte and Thogmartin are correct. But a further point lies in the sheer range of media outlets of all kinds where (card-carrying and other) journalists work. The greater the range, the greater the premium on presentational and news-editorial skills. There have been anguished debates in the commission that issues these cards as to whether journalists in the 'institutional press' (municipal bulletins, for example) are entitled to have the card, and thus the privilege and standing that it confers. There are recurring concerns that TV, radio, and now Internet styles, with chatty, oral skills in evidence, will militate against the more formal written skills, and the greater range of news-editorial genres practised in the print media.

But the point is rather that journalists use the technical resources available—Internet, satellite phones, laser printers, etc.—as tools to enable them to produce copy for an ever greater array of media and with an ever growing list of urgent deadlines, and often on more and more of a piece-work basis. Published accounts of day-by-day, week-by-week logbooks or diaries of journalists—be they stringers or former staff correspondents of *Le Monde*—testify to the various work pressures and to the competitive, insecure climate in which many journalists operate (Accardo 1998; Lacan 1994). Stringers sometimes produce piecework in ways reminiscent of eighteenth- and nineteenth-century uses of the term. There are more and more 'self-media': local or thematic media produced by small teams where distinctions between journalists and technical staff, and even between journalists and marketing/advertising staff, are less watertight than the traditional distinctions—'separate news from comment and both from advertising'—would have one believe. The phrase 'information service'—the provision of practical information in a user-friendly mode—or else debates about journalists who use their professional reputation and celebrity status to make money on the side by hosting various commercially sponsored, or industry-promoting, conferences ('faire des ménages'), exemplify this blurring of distinctions (Roucaute 1991).

The reputation of journalists working for *Le Monde* was long associated with the ascetic, austere personality of its founder-director Hubert Beuve-Méry, who nurtured and managed the daily for a quarter-century (1944–69). Thirty years later, many leading newspapers and magazines stress how they maintain a 'professional culture', rooted in the 'personality' and traditional practice of each title, rather than in collective debates or soul-searching conducted by the profession as a whole. There are, of course, instances when leading news-editorial figures put on a collective front: this occurs when the government, the parliament, or media bosses or employers are perceived as threatening the working conditions, freedom of expression, or salaries and other perks and privileges of journalists; in the 1990s, attempts to eliminate various tax rebates, or to limit reporting freedoms, were resisted collectively.

But 'in-house' debates and exchanges between staff colleagues matter more in fashioning today's or this week's issue. Journalists write and produce with their colleagues in mind: some have a somewhat jaundiced view of the effect of their labours—uncovering misdeeds, for example—on their readers. Company mission statements, news-editorial style guides and conferences, in-house assessment procedures of audience reaction or of client feedback, help determine the collective tone and help make necessary incremental adjustments. *Le Monde* and public service television channels France 2 and France 3, respectively employ media ombudspersons (Robert Solé, Didier Epelbaum, and Geneviève Guicheney, respectively), who act as mediators between the public and the news-editorial staff when the former write in to complain about the performance of the latter. Some argue that the danger of 'dérapages', of professional misconduct, increases as a newspaper, magazine, or television channel uses more and more material that comes from outside contributors or 'independent' production houses: in France, as in Britain, many sections or segments of a newspaper (other than the main section) are sub-contracted out, with feature material from outside contributors.

In television, private channels commission most of their material from outside: many of the major 'household names' associated with a given channel's public image, in fact, own and operate their own production company, which sells its programme series to the channel. There have been many instances—'causes célèbres'—of excessively generous payments from channel executives to the production companies of their 'star names'. Scandals have resulted, but the state or various regulatory bodies (le Conseil supérieur de l'audiovisuel, or parliamentary watchdog committees) rarely intervene other than with 'a light regulatory touch', to use a British euphemism. Such scandals have contributed, however, to the fall of some of the top figures in French broadcasting in the 1990s—for instance, Jean-Pierre Elkabbach, the chief executive of a public service channel; the young independent producer and talk-show host, Jean-Claude Delarue, whose contract allegedly contained the over-generous terms that contributed to Elkabbach's fall from grace, continued to produce and present his programme *Ça se discute.*

Traditional news and entertainment media develop web-sites, electronic media, and data storage and retrieval experience. Journalists become ever more skilled in using these resources and monitoring the output of other news and data organizations. Worldwide, on-line facilities proliferate. Digitalization is spreading fast. In Agence France Presse, journalists are preparing for the News Industry Text Format, whereby news organizations world-wide will access data and information classified for usage by all media equipped with the necessary web protocols or hypertext mark-up language. AFP journalists in its multi-media division are continually having to update their knowledge: they rewrite or modify texts produced initially for 'traditional wire service' clients. This may require repackaging the news item in a 'bullet-style' mode. Sentences become ever shorter, tauter, news-nugget-like. Or rather, some of the pieces of information that traditionally figure in the lead sentence or opening paragraph—for example, the source of the information—may be shunted further down.

These developments are by no means unique to France: research engines to help prevent information overload are used by journalists everywhere. But they contribute to a lessening of what have been some of the distinctive features of French journalism for at least two centuries: literary skills, high-profile politics, ideological commitment, and a polemical tradition. The state is less of an 'intimidating presence' than it used to be. In developing professional norms and practices and multi-media skills, journalists are moving closer to the culture and practices—the verbal and visual practices—of other media and entertainment industries in an advertising- and sponsorship-dominated, consumerist and user-friendly environment.

References ACCARDO, A. (1998), *Journalistes précaires* (Bordeaux: Le Mascaret).

BOURDIEU, P. (1996), *Sur la télévision* (Paris: Liber éditions).

CHARON, J. M. (1993), *Cartes de presse: Enquête sur les journalistes* (Paris: Stock).

DELPORTE, C. (1995), *Histoire du journalisme et des journalistes en France* (Paris: P.U.F.).

—— (1999), *Les Journalistes en France* (Paris: Seuil).

FERENCZI, T. (1993), *L'Invention du journalisme en France* (Paris: Plon).

HALIMI, S. (1997), *Les Nouveaux chiens de garde* (Paris: Liber éditions).

I.F.P. (1991), *Les Journalistes français en 1990: Radiographie d'une profession* (Paris: La Documentation française-SJTI-CCIJP).

LACAN, J. F., PALMER, M., and RUELLAN, D. (1994), *Les Journalistes* (Paris: Syros).

OCKRENT, C. (1997), *La Mémoire du coeur* (Paris: Fayard).

PLENEL, E. (1999), *L'Épreuve* (Paris: Stock).

RAMONET, I. (1998), *La Tyrannie de la communication* (Paris: Galilée).

RIEFFEL, R. (1984) *L'Élite des journalistes* (Paris: P.U.F.).

ROUCAUTE, Y. (1991), *Splendeurs et misères des journalistes* (Paris: Calmann-Lévy).

RUELLAN, D. (1993), *Le Professionalisme du flou: Identité et savoir-faire des journalistes français* (Grenoble: P.U.G.).

SCHNEIDERMANN C. (1999), *Du journalisme après Bourdieu* (Paris: Fayard).

THOGMARTIN, C. (1998), *The National Daily Press of France* (Birmingham, Ala.: Summa Publications).

29

Media Professionals in the Former Soviet Union

Brian McNair

THE CURRENT SITUATION of the media professional in the Russian part of the former Soviet Union is the contradictory outcome of an uneasy co-habitation of old and new. There is an almost manic enthusiasm for reform amongst some, countered by stubborn resistance to change on the part of others. Some eagerly embrace the importation of Western concepts of objectivity and pluralism into their professional lives, as well as foreign assistance and investment in Russian media ventures, while others react to such developments with denunciations of 'cultural imperialism'. Ten years into the reform process the question of how these tensions will be resolved is still difficult to answer, dependent as that answer is on economic and political trends beyond the control of the media (and beyond the capacity of any analyst to predict with reasonable certainty). Although, as I will argue, Russia at the turn of the millennium can be described as a *media-ocracy*—a country governed by a media-industrial complex, in which the barriers between those who own the media, and those who run the country, are more than usually blurred and fluid—the individual media worker, and his or her employer, exert only marginal influence against the tidal wave of the processes now under way. Their professional futures, and the future of their professions, are only partly in their own hands. That said, they have achieved much in difficult conditions, and can reasonably claim to be, from a professional perspective, better off now than they were before the roller coaster of reform started off in the late 1980s.

The Russian Media, 1991–1999: Two Steps Forward, One Step Back

The 1990s, it need hardly be said, were a period of rapid and far-reaching change for the Russian media and those who work in them. The failure of the coup attempt of August 1991 ended the Soviet tradition of authoritarian media control at a stroke. A transition from Marxist-Leninist media principles to liberal democratic ones began, while a privatized media economy came into existence for the first time, subjecting print and broadcast organizations to the harsh logic of the market place. These processes were

Source: Not previously published. Brian McNair is at the University of Stirling in Scotland.

generally welcomed, at least by those in the media who had campaigned for liberal reform since the 1980s, but their consequences for individual organizations and media workers were unsettling, and frequently traumatic.

■ The Russian Media and the Law

In the sphere of media law, for example, the post-Soviet state acted to abolish political censorship and to guarantee a measure of freedom of information, transforming a relationship of subordination of the media to political power which had lasted for more than seventy years. The new legal and regulatory framework also guaranteed editorial independence for journalists although, as in all countries where private ownership of the media is a feature, notional independence rarely overrules the wishes of a determined proprietor. But overall, and on balance, Yeltsin's government succeeded in establishing a regime of media freedom comparable with that which exists in many more mature capitalist countries, and which has survived determined efforts by reactionaries of both left and right to re-impose political control over the system.

In Russia, however, as elsewhere in the world, the media professional remains subject to various forms of governmental interference and pressure, such as the punitive use of libel law, and denial of access to information. According to one estimate, the Russian government brought some three hundred lawsuits against journalists in 1998.[1] Local government officials—more likely to be remnants of the old Soviet system and thus more conservative and instinctively censorial—are particularly fond of the use of the law as a defensive weapon against investigative journalism into their own and others' activities. Physical intimidation is also widely believed to have been used by politicians against the media, up to and including murder. In 1998, for example, the editor-in-chief of the regional newspaper *Sovetskaya Kalmykiya*, Larissa Yudina, was assassinated following several years of difficult relations with the government of Kalmykiya. The mystery of who was responsible for Yudina's murder, like most of the other twenty-five murders of journalists which occurred in 1997–8, had not been solved by early 2000 (see below).

■ The Press

If the post-1991 legal environment represents a definite improvement on the Soviet system of media censorship and regulation, the economic picture has been less obviously beneficial to media organizations and their employees. For newspapers, the cushion of state subsidy (an important mechanism of ideological control by the CPSU over the media) was abruptly withdrawn, forcing an unfamiliar reliance on sales and advertising revenues. The newly privatized press were also deprived of the state's traditional supporting roles in the organization of printing, distribution, and the collection of subscriptions from readers. Overnight, and with no previous experience, workers on newspapers and periodicals had to learn about marketing, competitive strategies, reader profiles, and all the other routine aspects of commercial publishing, but in conditions of hyperinflation and

---

1 Estimate supplied by Oleg Panfilov of the Glasnost Defence Fund, reported in *Post-Soviet Media Law and Policy Newsletter*, 56 (15 July 1999).

a collapsing rouble which put retooling and capital investment beyond the reach of most titles.

Some print media, like *Izvestia*, coped by entering into joint ventures with Western publications such as the *Financial Times*, producing in that case a Russian publication modelled on the latter, and which successfully targeted the rising business class. For the majority of publications, however, read by ordinary Russians languishing on poverty-level incomes, this solution to their problems was not available. Amidst the turmoil of transition, many publications went bust. As the co-founder of one of the more successful publications, the *Moscow Business News*, conceded in 1993:

> The suffocating practice of state control is over now. But it has been quite an unhappy surprise for Russian publishers to realise that the free market's demands could be even harder to come to terms with than the communist censorship of the past.[2]

But come to terms with the disciplines of the market many of them did. By the late 1990s a slimmed-down, but financially viable and undeniably 'free' press had been firmly established in Russia, servicing many of the same niche audiences as exist in more mature capitalist media markets. The Russian press had come to comprise a functioning public sphere, supporting the fragile Russian democracy by providing for competing views to be heard and discussed.

Then came the stock market crash of August 1998—'Russia's first ever market-based, capitalist crisis', as the chairwoman of the State Committee for the Support of Small Business put it in November that year.[3] The crash, and the associated collapse of the rouble's value from about seventeen US cents to one half of a cent, was a catastrophe for the entire Russian economy. For the media it meant a sudden decline, and in some cases the temporary disappearance of a key source of revenue—advertising. For the print media in particular it meant also that subscription revenues, determined by prices set well before the rouble's fall in value, plummeted.

The crash represented a further stage in the near-decade-long shaking out and downsizing of the Russian print media, forcing managerial and professional adaptations which some argued to be, in the longer run, beneficial for the sector. According to the National Press Institute, while the crash showed 'the serious obstacles' remaining in the path of the development of a healthy commercial press in Russia, its 'positive effects' included publishers' recognition of the need to cultivate diverse advertising bases, thus reducing their reliance on a few large clients. Moreover, 'publishers have begun to think actively about how they can make their newspapers essential to readers who now have even less disposable income than before'.[4] In a media variant of cultural Darwinism, hard-nosed Russian observers acknowledged that the crash would weed out the weak and

2 S. Panasenko, 'The Role of Newspapers and Magazines in Russian Economic Reform', unpubl. consultative report, co-authored with W. Dunkerley and A. Izyumov (Moscow, 1993).

3 Irina Khakamada, quoted in *Surviving the Crisis in Russia: Independent Newspapers Confront the Challenge* a report by the National Press Institute (Moscow: National Press Institute, 1998).

4 Ibid.

ensure the survival of only the fittest newspapers and periodicals. Fittest, in this context, meant 'those newspapers that have been most intensely exposed to modern newspaper management techniques'.

■ **Broadcasting**   For the broadcasters, state funding was no longer available in sufficient quantities after 1991 to support the large television and radio apparatus maintained by the Communist Party. As with the press, advertising and sponsorship were required to fill the gap, alongside a growing reliance on private investment which, by 1999, had reduced Russia's wholly state-funded broadcasting to two channels of network television (from five under the Soviet system) and one of network radio. The rest of the system, including the new cable and satellite services which were established after 1991, was wholly or largely owned by private interests (McNair 2000).

The privatization of the monolithic Soviet broadcasting apparatus was inevitable and, as in the case of the press, a necessary development in so far as it was the precondition for reform and restructuring of an unsustainable status quo. Though chaotically and corruptly managed from the outset (see below), the reforms had led by the end of the 1990s to a broadcasting system at least as professional (in terms of production and aesthetic values) as those of many more established systems. The austere, worthy, ideologically committed programming of the Soviet era had been replaced with all the generic diversity familiar to Western viewers: soap operas, game shows, documentaries, news and current affairs, youth programming, and late-night erotica were all present in the schedules. Some of this output was of dubious worth, of course, but much was of reasonable quality. The competition for audiences made necessary by privatization had encouraged innovation and risk-taking in programme production, especially from the younger generation of professionals unencumbered by the ideological baggage of the pre-1991 era. A substantial independent production sector had grown up, injecting the established apparatus with fresh talent and approaches. And despite the lack of state funding, there was even space for public service, educational programming on the Kultura channel,[5] set up by Yeltsin in 1996 as a response to concerns about the commercialization of the TV system.

The 1998 crash, when it came, impacted on the broadcasters as much as the press, and with the same results. All organizations, large and small, were thrown into crisis. But those organizations and companies able to survive a harsh economic environment in which advertising revenues declined or froze, and in which technical and software imports became dramatically more expensive overnight, benefited from it in as much as some of their competitors were forced from the marketplace. The chairman of Russia's biggest TV advertising sales company, Premier SV, argued that despite the obvious damage done by the collapse in advertising revenues, 'it's like a starvation diet for an obese man. I think that television will get healthier,

---

5   As someone who watched a great deal of TV as a student of Russian in the Soviet Union, my own preference is undoubtedly for the programming of a decade later, and I have little hesitation in speculating that the vast majority of Russians would agree with that.

and will seek out other reserves. I know many channels where there is a lot of dead weight. The crisis will only make television stronger'.[6]

■ **Broadcasting and the Corporate Clans**

To a far greater degree than the press, Russian TV and radio remained under the political control of government and the state in the 1990s. Although the old Soviet censorship laws were no longer in force, broadcasting, and TV in particular, remained under the close supervision of the government, either directly through the various federal committees set up for that purpose,[7] or indirectly, through the proxy control of the new generation of Russian media barons who took on ownership of much of the privatized apparatus. They, like their Soviet-era predecessors, managed broadcasting on the assumption that this was the key medium of influence in Russia, and far too important to be left to the professionals alone. Television became a political football in the constitutional struggles between the president and the parliament which characterized the decade (McNair 1996), and media professionals were encouraged to take sides.

Not that they needed much persuasion. Still lingering from the pre-1991 period, and effectively negating many of the formal freedoms put in place by the post-Soviet regime, is the 'Bolshevik psychology' of the Russian media professional—the belief, albeit sincerely held in many cases, that the role of the journalist is to be an ideological partisan of the politician, party, or organization to whom he or she 'belongs' (loyalty to the proletariat as a class is no longer required by the mainstream media, of course). As former prime minister Boris Nemtsov put it in a 1999 interview, referring to the tendency of media outlets to take sides and then impose a certain editorial position on their employees, 'there's competition between [media] groups. This is structural freedom. Inside one group, there is no freedom—it's *censura* [censorship]' (Nemtsov 1999: 8).

A recent example of the 'genetic memory' of the Russian journalist in practice is supplied by the figure of Sergei Dorenko, described in one Western newspaper report (before the rise of Vladimir Putin) as 'an unremitting propagandist for President Boris Yeltsin, and a close associate of the media mogul Boris Berezovsky'.[8] Mr Dorenko, it was reported in late 1999, was using his prime-time slot on ORT (channel 1) to attack Yeltsin's opponents in the forthcoming presidential election campaign. For Dorenko, 'using the media'—even a predominantly state-owned channel such as ORT—to promote a particular politician was quite normal. 'The state is the owner of this station and the state is Yeltsin,' he argued, adding that, although he was a journalist, 'I'm also a politician, a serious political operator'.

The title of the article from which these quotes are taken—'Biased and Proud of it'—neatly sums up the dominant professional ethic of Russian journalism, now as in the Soviet era, and explains why the issue of media

---

6 Sergei Lisovsky, interviewed on the *Chetvertaya Vlast* (Fourth Estate) programme, broadcast on REN-TV on 11 Oct. 1998.

7 Such as the Federal Service on TV and Radio Broadcasting, whose head is appointed by the president and overseen by a government minister.

8 I. Traynor, 'Biased and Proud of it—Yeltsin's Man at State TV', *Guardian*, 18 Oct. 1999.

freedom in Russia is much more complex and difficult to resolve than merely putting in place legal instruments to protect practitioners from state and government interference.[9]

One consequence of the close links between the media and politics in Russia is the routine use of the former to advance political causes and settle scores. Sometimes this is the result of a willing prostitution of the media's influence, as in the example of Sergei Dorenko referred to above; at other times it is an editorial requirement, to be obeyed or else, in the same way that Western media workers must often toe the editorial line. In Russia, to an extent unmatched even in Berlusconi's Italy, media power and political power are interlinked and mutually reinforcing, forming what I have called elsewhere a *media-ocracy* (McNair 2000). By media-ocracy I mean a media-industrial complex with huge influence on the machinery of government, and showing little hesitation in the public exercise of that influence to achieve its economic and political objectives.

In one respect at least, the late 1990s in-fighting between the corporate clans and the media which they controlled can be viewed as an improvement on the near-uniform pro-Yeltsin bias which characterized Russian broadcasting in the run-up to the 1996 election. In that campaign, when an unpopular and apparently unstable Yeltsin faced a credible Communist Party challenger (Gennady Zhuganov) as well as the extremist 'national patriot' Vladimir Zhirinovsky, the media barons (with the support of the majority of their employees, it should be noted, who had no desire to return to the authoritarian traditions of the Soviet Union) combined their resources and influence to back the president. Berezovsky, Gusinsky, and the other big media players formed what Yasen Zassoursky (1997) has called 'corporate clans' to defeat the Communists, imposing a uniformly pro-Yeltsin bias on the broadcast channels over which they had control. Even NTV's chairman Igor Malashenko—until that point a symbol of journalistic independence in Russia—joined the president's campaign team. By 1999, for better or worse, the clans had lost the tight cohesion evident in the mid- to late 1990s, in the context of a political environment which was more unpredictable and volatile than had been the case till then. As one report put it in August 1999:

> In some ways, the ferocious television war is a healthy sign of the political pluralism that is taking root in Russia. Only three years ago, most Russian journalists supported Mr Yeltsin's presidential campaign, fearing that they would be out of jobs if the Communist Party returned to power. The fact that newspapers and television are likely to support different candidates in next year's presidential elections is therefore a novel aspect of Russian political life.[10]

Shortly after the publication of this assessment, however, the relative unanimity of the corporate clans reasserted itself. Boris Yeltsin appointed the previously unknown Vladimir Putin as his prime minister, and his

9 See Davis, Hammond and Nizamova (1997) for a discussion of this problem in relation to regional journalism.

10 J. Thornhill, 'Broadcast and Be Damned', *Financial Times*, 1 Aug. 1999.

favoured successor in the forthcoming presidential election. As the election neared, and the war in Chechnya re-ignited (the two events not being unrelated), Putin played to the patriotism of the Russian electorate. The majority of the media swung behind his campaign, which he won comfortably in March 2000. As one observer noted, 'Putin owes a debt of gratitude to [Boris Berezovsky]. His presidential victory was effectively secured during campaigning for December's parliamentary elections, when a ferocious slur campaign run on Berezovsky's ORT TV channel eradicated his two main rivals'.[11]

The Media and Organized Crime

The power of Russia's media-ocracy is a unique feature of its political environment. Russia's media professionals are also distinctive, however, in the extent to which they must deal with the seductions and (if seduction fails) intimidations of the organized criminal community.

The arbitrary and chaotic manner of the dismantling of the Soviet media apparatus after 1991 allowed the Russian 'mafia' to become heavily involved in the privatization process (McNair 1996). Bribery, backhanders, and informal sponsorship deals became the means by which members of the organized criminal fraternity were able to buy into and exercise proprietorial influence on media organizations, especially those in the broadcasting sector. The building of media empires from scratch favoured the cash-rich and the brutally unscrupulous, many of whom moved into advertising and programme production, bringing their favoured business methods with them.

A number of media managers, editors, producers, and journalists were murdered in the 1990s, including Oleg Slabynko, former head of ORT and, at the time of his death, an independent producer working on an anti-corruption documentary; Vladislav Listev, who was killed just before he was due to become Director-General of ORT, and just after announcing his decision to suspend all advertising on the channel; Alexander Lyubimov, one of the best-known and most popular broadcasters in the country; and in late 1999, Christopher Rees, a British producer of youth programmes working for the STS regional network.[12] In the first half of 1999 sixteen murders of journalists were recorded in Russia, with many more non-fatal assaults recorded on media professionals at all levels of seniority (see above). In most cases the victims of these assaults were involved or implicated in investigative journalism, directed against either criminals or government officials (the difference between the two groups being blurred in contemporary Russia).[13]

---

11 A. Gentleman, 'The Means to an End', *Guardian*, 17 Apr. 2000.

12 STS links 150 regional companies across Russia.

13 For details of some recent examples of physical assaults against Russian media workers, see the *Post-Soviet Media Law and Policy Newsletter*, 56 (15 July 1999).

The Russian Media Today: Deficits and Difficulties

The Russian media ended the 1990s, then, having moved a considerable way along the road from Party-controlled propaganda apparatus towards a pluralistic media system. Some media—those that had survived the shocks and setbacks of the decade, that is—were producing content of an acceptable quality across the range of genres. Their problems were still considerable, however, particularly in the sphere of professional practice, where a combination of outside intimidation (official and criminal) and self-imposed partisanship continue to act as a constraint on the development of a fully functioning public sphere.

Remedying these problems will not be easy. A growing economy is clearly an essential prerequisite in the further development of high-quality media products and services, as is continuing legal reform, particularly in the area of broadcasting, which still lacks clear constitutional guarantees against political interference.

But remedying the deficits in professional practice described above will require more than economic health and good law alone, since these deficiencies are deeply rooted in Soviet and even pre-Soviet history and culture. They represent, as de Smaele rather euphemistically puts it, 'a specific Russian adaptation to the western model' (1999: 174) of free and independent media (to which, with all its limitations, the pro-reform Russians *have* signed up). It is, however, an adaptation which threatens to make the Russian media professional rather too vulnerable to, and complicit in, an authoritarian downturn in the political system, should one ever occur.

I will end, therefore, with reference to some attempts by external assistance agencies to inject such professional values as adversarialism (with regard to power elites), objectivity (with regard to reportage of news and current affairs), and neutrality (in coverage of partisan positions in debate) into the professional culture of the Russian media. Two schemes are especially notable.

■ The Marshall Plan of the Mind

The first, set up by the BBC in the early 1990s with funds provided by the UK government's Know How Fund, is the Marshall Plan of the Mind (MPM). MPM was established to encourage in Russia and other former Communist-dominated countries the construction of 'free and independent' media on the British public service model. To this end MPM supported Russian-language TV and radio production, using Russian staff and resources where possible. BBC staff were utilized where the necessary production and management skills were not available in Russia itself, and overall editorial control was retained in the London office of the BBC World Service, but as MPM developed in the 1990s greater and greater emphasis was placed on the employment and encouragement of indigenous Russian professionals at all levels of the production process. Series such as *How Business Works* and *The Media and Democracy* (both radio) and *Points of View* (TV) were made available to, and used extensively by, regional Russian broadcasters in dire need of quality programming. A radio soap opera, *House Number 7*, was also produced, on the model of socially aware soap operas familiar to British viewers of *Brookside* and *East Enders*.

In their production, and in the demonstration effect that might be produced by their transmission, these programmes were intended to strengthen the professionalism of Russia's media practitioners, providing an example of what public service broadcasting could be about, and practical training in how to produce it. The programmes were complemented by courses and seminars organized in Russia and the UK, internships, and other training schemes for transferring professional knowledge and technical skills from the BBC to the Russians.

Sensitive to charges of cultural imperialism in an atmosphere of growing 'national patriotism', however, and after seven years of operation, in April 1999 MPM transferred its assets to a new Foundation for Independent Radio Broadcasting. This organization, while retaining a link with the BBC in London, has been given the legal status of a Russian independent broadcaster, and will sink or swim on its ability to continue to supply good quality, and good value, public service-type radio programmes to regional stations.

■ **Internews** The Americans, meanwhile, through USAID and other agencies, funded their own media assistance projects in Russia during the 1990s. The Internews organization, for example, was established to encourage the development of independent news media in the regions of Russia. Internews produced its own news programmes in Moscow, for distribution by satellite across Russia, and provided professional training in production and media management. Internews provided professional training in a range of media skills and practices taken for granted in the USA but un- (or under-) developed in Russia. Internews continued its work in Russia, headed by the respected broadcaster Manana Aslamazyan.

Conclusion De Smaele is among those observers, inside and outside of Russia, who acknowledge that media workers have improved their professionalism in the post-Soviet era, at least in so far as they now 'show an openness to new, often western ideas and practices and demonstrate a growing recognition of the audience' (1999: 176). Responding perhaps better than might have been expected to the withdrawal of Soviet state funding as a comfortable, if deadening, cushion against the demands of the cultural market place, Russian media workers have struggled in the 1990s to throw off the 'genetic memory' of their traditional professional role as collective 'propagandists and agitators' for the Party, and to remake their role according to the normative standards of liberal democratic societies. While there have been many genuine achievements, and there are grounds for optimism that there will be more, it is too early to state with confidence that the transition has been successful.

There are still too many examples of interference with the media— emanating from both political and criminal elites—to allow for complacency. The Russian media professional remains in a fragile and vulnerable position, trying to play his or her role as part of an embryonic fourth estate in a political and economic landscape dominated by corruption, incompetence, and lingering authoritarianism. Foreign investment and assistance programmes such as those described above may help at the margins, but lasting solutions to the core problems must come from within the Russian media community, which remains subject to the impact of forces over which its members have little or no control. The future prospects of Russia's media professionals are bound up with uncertain political and economic futures.

References DAVIS, H., HAMMOND, P., and NIZAMOVA, L. (1997), 'Changing Identities and Practices in Post-Soviet Journalism', *European Journal of Communication*, 13: 1, 77–97.

DE SMAELE, H. (1999), 'The Applicability of Western Media Models to the Russian Media System', *European Journal of Communication*, 14: 2, 173–89.

MCNAIR, B. (1991), *Glasnost, Perestroika and the Soviet Media* (London: Routledge, 1991).

—— (1996), 'Television in a Post-Soviet Russia: From Monolith to Mafia', *Media, Culture and Society*, 18: 3, 489–99.

—— (2000), 'Power, Profit, Corruption and Lies: The Russian Media in the 1990s', in J. Curran and J. Son-Ming (eds.), *De-Westernising Media Studies* (London: Routledge, 2000), 79–94.

NEMTSOV, B. (1999), 'The Russian Oligarchs and the Press', *Press/Politics*, 4: 3, 5–11.

ZASSOURSKY, Y. (1997), 'Media and Politics in Transition: Three Models', *Post-Soviet Media Law and Policy Newsletter*, 35 (27 Feb. 1997), 11–15.

30

The Contradictions of Journalism in Germany

Hans J. Kleinsteuber and Siegfried Weischenberg

THE YEAR WAS 1908. For the first time German journalists realized what power they actually had. The catholic-centralist member of the national parliament Dr Adolf Gröber publicly called them, during a debate on colonial policy, 'Saubengel' (something like 'swine rogue'). All of them reacted spontaneously and decided to cease reporting on the Reichstag. Political communication came to a standstill until the chancellor intervened, because he was planning to give a crucial speech. Herr Gröber had to apologize and information about parliamentary affairs went out as usual.

The current state of journalism always reflects in one way or another the collective historical experiences of the culture in which journalists operate. The German experience is, of course, quite a mixed one. In terms of media technologies it has sometimes been on top; in terms of content it usually has lagged behind. Germany was shaped by its flourishing cities and the communication links they established across Europe. But its history also includes the tradition of a strong and authoritarian state that kept subdued freedom of expression and collapsed in the catastrophe of the Nazi era.

History

According to most descriptions, the success story of mass media was made possible by the invention of the art of printing as it was developed in the German city of Mainz around 1445, connected with the name of Johann Gutenberg. An investor had 'laid forward' (*verlegt*) the capital to produce the first printed version of the Bible. The money turned out to be insufficient and the project was taken away from Gutenberg. The capitalist later earned all the profits and a publisher is still called a *Verleger* in German.

The technology of printing quickly spread across Europe. Again, in German-speaking countries the periodical publication of printed papers began quite early. Newspapers started to appear at the beginning of the seventeenth century, first in places like Strasbourg, Wolfenbüttel,

Source: Not previously published. Hans J. Kleinsteuber is Professor of Political Science and Journalism at Hamburg University. Siegfried Weischenberg is Professor of Journalism at Münster University and President of the *Deutscher Journalisten Verband* (German Journalism Association).

Frankfurt, Berlin, and Hamburg. Early publishers often wrote for their own paper, acting as their own journalists. All these publications had to be licensed by the sovereign of the country, meaning that these 'privileged' papers could only be distributed after passing heavy censorship. In the early years, quite a few of the writers for these papers were so-called correspondents, meaning people who had a full-time position as diplomats, secretaries, or merchants and were working freelance and offering their reports to those involved in publication. The printers, on the other hand, were quite often postmasters. In the eighteenth century, the profession of journalist emerged. Many of them entered history as prominent literary figures; in fact many authors of books also worked as journalists. Their contributions often reached a high level of literary quality, whereas political messages were hidden or even absent, as all publications suffered under official censorship.

This was also the age when the up and coming, well-educated, and increasingly wealthy 'bourgeois' fought for its freedom and that of the press, attempting to create a kind of public that was (and is still called) *Öffentlichkeit* in Germany, made famous in the writings of (and somewhat romanticized by) Jürgen Habermas (Habermas 1962). The common English translation of this very German term is 'public sphere'. The term *Öffentlichkeit* carries the connotation that Germans discussed political events in depth (e.g. in the famous *Salons*, as Habermas describes them), but showed little interest in political participation. The traditions of political culture proved to be more 'subjective' than 'participatory', meaning that the quality of political communication and discourse was quite high but had little political significance. The notion of the press as a Fourth Estate was only adopted after the Second World War (Kleinsteuber 1997).

The first time the German press became a factor of importance in politics was during the failed revolution of 1848–9, when papers could be published free of state interference. Among others, the revolutionary Karl Marx (who had previously worked as a newspaper editor) established the *Neue Rheinische Zeitung* during those months of unrest and found other radical authors to work for his paper. After the intervention of the military the revolution was quickly crushed, sending Karl Marx and many other journalists into exile.

The German press became professional and commercial in the second half of the nineteenth century. The first Press Law of 1874 granted some limited press freedom and—even more important—offered a degree of stability to the emerging newspaper industry. Journalists now became fully employed workers in press offices, characterized by internal hierarchies and a high division of labour. This expansion created many new jobs in the fast-growing newspaper industry, although the new professionals often brought with them a rather low educational level (at least compared with the intellectuals of the eighteenth century) which contributed to their low social status (Max Weber calling them a 'pariah caste'). The formation of trade organizations for publishers and trade unions for journalists and print workers accompanied this process. As a reflection of the general political situation much of the press was closely affiliated with political parties and/ or social classes and embodied a specific *Weltanschauung*, a typical worldview.

At the end of the Kaiser era (1918), Germany had a fully developed media system with high-quality newspapers in Berlin and other centres in the country, a world news agency, Wolffs Telegraphisches Korrespondenz-bureau (WTB), and the beginnings of academic media research, with a journal called *Zeitungswissenschaft* (Newspaper Science). This well-established system carried over into the Weimar Republic of the 1920s, a time of sophisticated journalism (in Berlin there were as many as 140 dailies) and startling media concentration. This was the time when Max Weber proposed to do empirical research on journalists and demanded a systematic enquiry into their socio-economic situation. At the end of the Weimar Republic the newspaper group of the mogul Alfred Hugenberg, politically on the extreme right, paved the way for the Nazis; Hugenberg himself served in Adolf Hitler's first cabinet (1933) before he was isolated.

The Nazi era ended all promising developments in German media. Immediately after Hitler's seizure of power, the top personnel of the established radio system were forced to resign and were replaced by party propagandists. Journalists very soon experienced extreme repression, especially those on the political left and of Jewish origin. A *Reichs-pressekammer* (a chamber for media workers) with compulsory member-ship was established; Jews and opponents of the regime were barred from entering the *Kammer* and became jobless. As a consequence, Jews, who had featured strongly in German journalism, and many others were thrown out of the profession long before they ended up in concentration camps; many were forced into exile (Frei and Schmitz 1989). Journalists and publishers who remained in business demonstrated little courage and opportunism was the common behaviour. When the war ended (1945), the new occupation forces outlawed all media activities. Germany had the unique chance for an 'Hour Zero', for a completely new beginning in media and journalism.

The main object of the new military rulers of West Germany was to help establish a new, democratic press that would make disasters like the Nazi dictatorship impossible. It was no easy task to find journalists who had not disqualified themselves by what they had done before 1945. The Allies started by handing out licences to young journalists who knew the country but were not infected by Nazism (which, as it turned out later, was not always the case). Most of today's print media were started during the years before 1949, including *Der Spiegel*, *Die Zeit*, *Stern*, *Frankfurter Allgemeine Zeitung*, *Süddeutsche Zeitung*, and many others. After 1945 print journal-ism mostly continued the pattern of *Weltanschauunges*, of each paper having its own ideological profile. When British press officers came to Germany they realized that journalistic traditions were quite different (apart from the degeneracy of the Nazi years). For example, Germans were unfamiliar with the distinction between factual reporting and commen-tary. During those years, the model of Anglo-American journalism gained prominence; *Der Spiegel* still looks like *Time* magazine, and *Die Welt* even started out as the newspaper of the British occupation forces and only later was sold to a German publisher. All in all, the influences of those first years after the war were crucial determinants of the fundamental features of German journalism today.

**Journalism after
1945**

In broadcasting, the Allies introduced the public service system, mostly following the British BBC as a role model. A factor peculiar to the German style of public service was the centrality of the *Länder* (states) in broadcasting. At the time, when the Allies were beginning to relinquish control of the broadcasting organizations in their respective zones (1948–9), *Länder* authorities were firmly established, whereas the Federal Republic had just emerged during those months. Later the Federal Constitutional Court decided that domestic broadcasting is the ultimate responsibility of the *Länder*.

The *Länder* politicians wrote into their respective broadcasting laws—which constituted the broadcasting organizations—a strong role for political parties. This offered the respective *Länder* governments the possibility of exerting the leading influence, but usually the main opposition party was able to ensure some influence for itself. The result was a system of proportional representation in the broadcasting organizations, meaning that the *Intendant* (Director-General) of the *Anstalt* (broadcasting organization) was picked by the leading party, his representative (the Deputy Director-General) was selected by the second strongest party, and so on. This also meant that the *Intendant* was often selected for political reasons and had little prior experience in journalism. Basically public service broadcasting was seen as spoils to be shared between two large political formations, the conservative ('black') and the social-democratic ('red') party. The principle of proportional recruitment often pervaded the entire broadcasting hierarchy, from the heads of departments to the average journalist.

There were several implications of the principle of proportionality. First, it meant that a journalist in broadcasting had to think of his political party: he had to rally party support for his personal career at an early stage. The parties carefully monitored news and public events and would complain as soon as they felt that their political 'enemy' was being reported on more often or more favourably. It was (and still is) common for a politician to be interviewed by a journalist who is considered to represent the same party. As a result, news reporting tended to be balanced in every respect, which made it look like *Hofberichterstattung* (reporting from the 'political court') and also made it boring. A certain kind of criticism, however, was integrated into this 'corporatist' model of reporting. In particular, certain *Land* broadcasters published TV magazines with political background reports favouring their own side and continually attacking the other. Today, one successful TV magazine features an ironic form of balancing; it is based on two anchormen who continually criticize each other, reflecting the two major party lines (*Frontal*). Part of this binary system is that small parties have little influence on this variation of 'packaged' reporting. Matters are different during election campaigns, when parties are allotted free air time in relation to their most recent election results.

In principle, the policies of proportionality described above have not disappeared from public service broadcasting, but fierce competition from commercial radio and TV meant that news had to become livelier to be attractive to audiences. In consequence, elements of infotainment have entered news programming and viewers demand a faster pace and fewer 'talking heads'. As a result, politicians follow the American example and prefer to go straight into entertainment, a strategy for which Chancellor Gerhard Schröder (since 1998) is a good example. He has appeared in a soap opera, in TV films, and on the top Saturday evening quiz show.

Parties are not just important as political actors: their activities are closely interwoven with other organizations in society, such as trade associations, trade unions, civic associations, and churches. This has created the German brand of corporatism. In fact, the system of two dominant parties is also reflected in commercial broadcasting today, where nearly all TV channels of importance are controlled by two 'sender families'. One is headed by the media mogul Leo Kirch, who controls his 'family' of TV channels from the conservative *Land* of Bavaria (and is a member of Bavaria's conservative party, the CSU); the other is led by Bertelsmann and includes the CLT/Ufa channels, which operate out of the social-democratic *Land* of North Rhine-Westphalia. The two 'family companies' with their print affiliations constitute the two largest media companies in the country and enjoy close links with politics. Both employ former top politicians as well as journalists with party leanings; curiously enough, the present social-democratic president of North Rhine-Westphalia, the largest of all *Länder*, started his career as a journalist and office head of one of Bertelsmann's newspapers.

How to Become a Journalist?

Journalism training in Germany reflects the fact that everything had to start anew after 1945. During the Nazi years, journalists were forced into a framework of regulations controlled by the Fascists. The regime totally controlled access to the journalistic profession. Given this devastating example, there was only one option left after 1945. The profession of journalism is not protected, there are no entrance examinations and anybody may use the term 'journalism' to describe his profession. This fact has to be taken into consideration when statistics are presented about journalists working in Germany. Media professionals, of course, have found other ways of limiting access to their profession; for instance, the press card is issued by professional organizations to their members only to those that have proved that they earn at least half their income by writing for the media. This is a good example of the typical German practice of limiting state influence by leaving decision-making to subsidiary institutions.

Another element of the complete openness of the profession is reflected in training. Traditionally the path into journalism started with a *Volontariat*, an apprenticeship of 12 to 24 months as a member of a publishing office, based mainly on learning on the job. Some training is done outside the office in centres that are jointly run by the publishers and journalist organizations. One of these is the Akademie für Publizistik in Hamburg, which offers courses of intense training for *Volontäre* and has also moved into further education for practising journalists. The *Volontariat* used to be quite open, but admission has become more selective over the years as a result of joint agreements between journalists' organizations and media employers.

During the 1950s and 1960s quite a high proportion of journalists did not receive any formal training; at that time it was typical for a journalist to have begun a university education that was never finished. This has changed considerably during the last twenty years; today a career is rarely started without first acquiring a university degree (in German, and always at the Master's level). As a career in journalism is extremely popular, competition for the *Volontariat* is keen and working conditions have become tougher, especially for young journalists.

Over the years, a number of training institutions have been established. The oldest and most prestigious is the Deutsche Journalisten Schule in Munich. It was established in 1959 and closely co-operates with the local media as well as with the University of Munich. American journalism schools served as a model. Other journalism schools have followed, which are run by media organizations. Especially interesting are the schools that belong to large publishing houses, the best known being the Henry Nannen Schule of Gruner+Jahr (Bertelsmann) and the Axel Springer Schule of the Springer corporation. They both concentrate on training on the spot, offering experiences in different types of media, as they are run by diversified media conglomerates. Anyone may apply, but access is extremely competitive. Other organizations, such as churches and professional unions, are also involved in training (Fröhlich and Holtz-Bacha 1997).

In the universities after 1945, the field of *Publizistik*, a German version of media studies, evolved first with some roots going back before 1945. It offered a somewhat theoretical version of communication that had little relevance to journalists. Starting in the 1960s, universities offered journalism as an academic field. The current range of options is startling: it includes journalism as a major field, culminating in a diploma (e.g. Dortmund), journalism as part of communication studies (e.g. Munich), journalism as a minor field (e.g. Hamburg), and journalism as a post-graduate subject (e.g. Mainz) or as further education for practising journalists (e.g. Berlin). This mixture of different curricula reflects the political and cultural decentralization of Germany.

The Great Debate

It does not seem surprising that the central debate about journalists and their work more or less followed party lines. Traditionally the strongest party was the conservative CDU which had to go into opposition for the first time from 1969 until 1982, during which a social democratic–liberal coalition (SPD-FDP) was in power. The CDU soon began blaming the media for the situation. Basically two lines of arguments arose. First, public service broadcasters were accused of being very much under the control of the social democrats, who were using them to spread the leftish gospel (*Rotfunk*). This argument was clearly one-sided, as several of the public service broadcasters, especially in the South, and the Second Channel, ZDF, very much remained under the CDU control of their respective *Länder*.

The second argument was that a clear majority of journalists was supportive of the SPD and consciously—or perhaps sub-consciously—argued in favour of the party of their choice. They were able to create a 'spiral of silence', as it was called by Elisabeth Noelle-Neumann, a long-time adviser to the CDU and Chancellor Helmut Kohl (Noelle-Neumann 1993). This argument was primarily based on assumptions about public service, but also sometimes included the print media. It was a shaky argument, as most of the press clearly leaned towards conservative positions. The tabloid paper *Bild* was at that time (and still is) by far the most widely read paper (with a circulation of 4 million copies), produced in the offices of the largest printing company in Germany (and Europe), established by Axel Springer, an outspoken conservative.

The academic argument about German journalists went like this. In the ongoing tradition of *Weltanschauung* journalists behaved mainly as 'missionaries' who did not spend much time in investigative research; instead they preferred to preach their political opinions to their readership. The opposite could be found in the United Kingdom, it was claimed, where journalists see themselves much more as 'bloodhounds' (Köcher 1985,1986). (Studies critical of the activities of German journalists often came from the Communications Department of Mainz University, where Noelle-Neumann taught.) This argument was often repeated by the conservative party as well as by publishing organizations. The latter used it to defend themselves against demands from journalists' unions for 'press freedom' inside the media, i.e. for an increase in the personal leeway that a journalist could enjoy (the journalists were thoroughly defeated on this issue). Of course the journalists' organizations rejected the thesis of the 'missionaries', claiming it to be openly ideological. In terms of political outcomes, the argument is difficult to uphold. In 1982, still a time of an ongoing public service monopoly, a conservative–liberal coalition (CDU–FDP) took over and stayed in power until 1998.

The German Journalist: Empirical Evidence

The ongoing debate about the German journalist had led to several empirical studies of German journalism. The most extensive research thus far was conducted in 1993, based on a net sample of 1,500 respondents in the print and electronic media. Journalists were asked about socio-economic facts, individual motives, perceived system constraints and reflections on the structures of their work (Scholl and Weischenberg 1998).

These are some of the results. The 'typical German journalist' is male, has a university degree, and is 37 years old. For ten years, he has had a full-time job as a newspaper reporter in one of the traditional departments—politics, economics, culture, sports, or local news—and has been permanently employed for eight years. His monthly net income (in 1993) is about DM3,900. The highest incomes are in public service broadcasters and news agencies; sub-average salaries are paid by commercial radio stations. He is a member of a journalists' union or association. About 60 per cent of journalists entered the profession the traditional way and had practical training before they were permanently employed. One in ten journalists has no journalism-specific education at all; naturally the level of formal professional skill is higher among younger journalists. As it used to be fashionable to leave university without a degree, 18 per cent of journalists who spent some time at university did so. Comparative studies including journalists from the West and the East (the former German Democratic Republic) demonstrate that these two groups differ considerably, e.g. Eastern journalists are less familiar with advanced methods of investigative reporting.

There are also some cross-cultural differences if journalists are asked about their attitudes towards certain journalistic practices on the borderlines of legitimate behaviour. German journalists tend to give answers which suggest that they are less prepared to use controversial practices to gain relevant information. Here is one example. Asked if they would get a job in a company only to gain internal information, the reactions differ widely: 63 per cent of American journalists and 80 per cent of British journalists said 'yes', but only 22 per cent of journalists from Germany as a whole. If the question is asked only of those in the old West, then 46 per cent give the answer 'Yes' (Esser 1997, 1998). In a similar vein, German journalists generally say that they would not quote from secret government documents or pretend to be somebody else in order to gain information (only 19 per cent of Germans would do so as compared to 47 per cent in the UK).

Conclusion

If the thesis of the ideological journalist is tested empirically, it turns out to be a crude and poorly supported hypothesis and can be unequivocally rejected. As in other countries, the communication intentions of German journalists are based on permanent observation of their own professional aims and of their effects. The thesis of the 'missionary' proved to be academically unacceptable. The German journalist follows much more closely the mainstream of international journalism than the argument presumes. There is a vibrant tradition of investigative writing in Germany, including the Hamburg magazine *Der Spiegel* and TV magazines like *Panorama*, which have uncovered quite a number of political scandals and forced politicians to resign. One of the well-known 'heroes' of investigative reporting was author Günter Walraff, who was hired as a journalist and worked under cover at the office of *Bild* in 1977 to gather material for a book he wrote about their policy of faking stories.

If the figures on German journalists are compared to those of other countries, the German situation does not seem to be exceptional. One might claim that there is a tendency towards convergence among journalists and journalism in Western countries (Weaver 1998). Of course, national differences exist and German journalists have to carry a burden of a difficult past. If figures on investigative practices differ, the answers seem to reflect an ongoing orientation towards orderly behaviour in the authoritarian tradition. Nevertheless, journalists will engage in such practices, if necessary. Another reason for this might be that reflection on media ethics in Germany has only just started; journalists enjoy little popularity and are wary of talking about their professional practices (Thomaß 1998).

During the summer of 1998 the location of the German capital moved from the sleepy town of Bonn to the largest city in the country: Berlin. In Bonn, political communication was centred around a family of correspondents, reporting for papers with headquarters far away. Today the new government quarter in Berlin is dotted with newspaper offices and journalists follow the politicians' every step. The competitive struggle among newspapers to become the German *Washington Post* is still unresolved. If one takes the pulse of Berlin it does not seem to be accidental that at the end of 1999 journalists started to uncover the most serious scandal in Germany's post-war history. Details became public of an illegal web of 'black accounts' around leading figures of the CDU, and especially former Chancellor Kohl. Part of the leadership of the CDU had to be replaced. Reporting, it seems, is becoming much faster and more investigative with Berlin as the new capital. Most observers agree that during this far-reaching scandal, the media—regardless of their general political leaning—have been reporting in depth and have done an admirable job in terms of the media as a Fourth Estate. And that is what they are for.

References

ESSER, FRANK (1997), 'Journalistische Kultur in Großbritannien und Deutschland: Eine Analyse in vergleichender Perspektive', in Machill (1997), 111–36

—— (1998), *Die Kräfte hinter den Schlagzeilen: Englischer und deutscher Journalismus im Vergleich* (Freiburg: Alber Verlag).

FREI, NORBERT, and SCHMITZ, JOHANNES (1989), *Journalismus im Dritten Reich* (Munich: C. H.).

FRÖHLICH, ROMY, and HOLTZ-BACHA, CHRISTINA (1997), 'Journalistenausbildung in Europa', in Gerd Kopper (ed.), Europäische Öffentlichkeit: Entwicklung von Strukturen und Theorien (Berlin: Vistas), 149–82.

HABERMAS, JÜRGEN (1962), *Strukturwandel der Öffentlichkeit* (Neuwied: Luchterhand) (English-language edn. *The Structural Transformation of the Public Sphere*, Cambridge, MA: MIT Press, 1989).

KLEINSTEUBER, HANS J. (1997), '"Vierte Gewalt". Ein Schlüsselbegriff im Verhältnis Medien und Politik', *Gegenwartskunde*, no. 2, 159–74.

KÖCHER, RENATE (1985), 'Spürhund und Missionar: Eine vergleichende Untersuchung über Berufsethik und Aufgabenverständnis britischer und deutscher Journalisten' (Ph.D. diss., Munich)

—— (1986), 'Bloodhounds or Missionaries: Role Definitions of German and British Journalists' *European Journal of Communication*, 1, 43–64.

MACHILL, MARCEL (1997) (ed.), *Journalistische Kultur: Rahmenbedingungen im internationalen Vergleich* (Opladen: Westdeutscher Verlag).

NOELLE-NEUMANN, ELISABETH (1980), *Die Schweigespirale* (Munich: English-language edn. *The Spiral of Silence*, Chicago: 1993).

SCHOLL, ARMIN, and WEISCHENBERG, SIEGFRIED (1998), *Journalismus in der Gesellschaft: Theorie, Methodologie und Empirie* (Opladen: Westdeutscher Verlag).

THOMAß, BARBARA (1997), 'Diskurse über Ethik im Journalismus: Ein Vergleich zwischen Frankreich, Großbritannien und Deutschland', in Machill (1977), 95–109.

WEAVER, DAVID (1998), *The Global Journalist. News People around the World.* (Cresskill, NJ: Hampton Press).

Select Bibliography

ABBOTT, ANDREW, *The System of Professions* (Chicago: University of Chicago Press, 1988).

AKHAVAN-MAJID, ROYA, 'The Press as an Elite Power Group in Japan', *Journalism Quarterly*, 67:4 (1990), 1006–14.

ALLEY, ROBERT, S., *Television: Ethics for Hire?* (Nashville, Tenn: Abingdon, 1977).

ANDERSON, CHRISTOPHER, *Hollywood: The Studio System in the Fifties* (Austin, Tex.: University of Texas Press, 1994).

ARTHURS, JANE, 'Technology and Gender: Women and Television Production', *Screen*, 30 (1989), 40–59.

AUMENTE, JEROME, GROSS, PETER, HIEBERT, RAY, JOHNSON, OWEN V., and MILLS, DEAN, *Eastern European Journalism*, (Cresskill, NJ: Hampton Press, 1999).

BAKER, WAYNE E. and FAULKNER, ROBERT R., 'Role as Resource in the Hollywood Film Industry', *American Journal of Sociology*, 97: 2 (1991), 279–309.

BANKS, JACK, *Monopoly Television: MTV's Quest to Control the Music* (Boulder, Colo.: Westview Press, 1996).

BATSCHA, ROBERT M., *Foreign Affairs News and the Broadcast Journalist* (New York: Praeger, 1975).

BECKER, LEE B., FRUIT, JEFFREY W., and CAUDILL, SUSAN L., *The Training and Hiring of Journalists* (Norwood, NJ.: Ablex, 1987).

—— STONE, VERNON A. and GRAF, JOSEPH D., 'Journalism Labor Force Supply and Demand: Is Oversupply an Explanation for Low Wages?', *Journalism and Mass Communication Quarterly*, 73: 3 (1996), 519–33.

BERTRAND, CLAUDE-JEAN, 'Dissent: Media Accountability: The Case for Press Councils', *InterMedia*, 18 (Nov.–Dec. 1990), 10–14.

BIELBY, WILLIAM T., and BIELBY, DENISE D., 'Organizational Mediation of Project-based Labor Markets: Talent Agencies and the Careers of Screenwriters', *American Sociological Review*, 64 (1999), 64–85.

BIRD, S. ELIZABETH, *For Enquiring Minds: A Cultural Study of the Supermarket Tabloids* (Knoxville, Tenn.: University of Tennessee Press, 1992).

BORDEN, DIANE L. and HARVEY, KERRIE, (eds.), *The Electronic Grapevine: Rumor, Reputation, and Reporting in the New On-line Environment* (Mahwah, NJ: Lawrence Erlbaum, 1998).

BORDWELL, DAVID, STAIGER, JANET, and THOMPSON, KRISTIN, *The Classical Hollywood Cinema* (London: Routledge, 1985).

BOURGAULT, LOUISE, *Mass Media in Sub-Saharan Africa* (Bloomington, Ind.: Indiana University Press, 1995).

BOYD-BARRETT, OLIVER, *The International News Agencies* (London: Constable; Thousand Oaks, Calif.: Sage, 1980).

—— SEYMOUR-URE, COLIN, and TUNSTALL, JEREMY, *Studies on the Press* (London: Her Majesty's Stationery Office for the Royal Commission on the Press, 1977).

BROUGHTON, IRV, (ed.), *Producers on Producing: The Making of Film and Television* (Jefferson, NC: McFarland, 1986).

BURNS, TOM, *The BBC: Public Institution and Private World* (London: Macmillan, 1977).

BURRAGE, MICHAEL, and TORSTENDAHL, ROLF, (eds.), *Professions in Theory and History* (London: Sage, 1990).

CANTOR, MURIEL G., *The Hollywood TV Producer* (New York: Basic Books, 1971).

CARR-SAUNDERS, A. M. and WILSON, P. A., *The Professions* (Oxford: Clarendon Press, 1933).

CARTER, CYNTHIA, BRANSTON, GILL, and ALLAN, STUART, (eds.), *News, Gender and Power* (London: Routledge, 1998).

CLEVERLEY, GRAHAM, *The Fleet Street Disaster* (London: Constable, 1976).

COCKBURN, CYNTHIA, *Brothers: Male Dominance and Technological Change* (London: Pluto Press, 1983).

COHEN, YOEL, *Media Diplomacy* (London: Frank Cass, 1986).

COLERIDGE, NICHOLAS, *Paper Tigers* (London: Heinemann, 1993).

COTTLE, SIMON, *Television and Ethnic Minorities: Producer's Perspectives* (Aldershot: Avebury, 1997).

CURRAN, JAMES, 'Literary Editors, Social Networks and Cultural Tradition', in James Curran (ed.), *Media Organisations in Society* (London: Arnold, 2000), 215–39.

CURRY, JANE LEFTWICH, *Poland's Journalists: Professionalism and Politics* (Cambridge: Cambridge University Press, 1990).

DANNEN, FREDRIC, *Hit Men* (New York: Vintage Books, 1991).

DAVIS, RICHARD, and OWEN, DIANA, *New Media and American Politics* (New York: Oxford University Press, 1998).

DE LANGE, WILLIAM, *A History of Japanese Journalism* (Richmond: Curzon Press, 1998).

DICKEY, SARAH, *Cinema and the Urban Poor in India* (Cambridge: Cambridge University Press, 1993).

DOOLEY, PATRICIA, *Taking Their Place: Journalists and the Making of an Occupation* (Westport, Conn.: Greenwood Press, 1997).

EBERTS, JAKE, and ILOTT, TERRY, *My Indecision is Final: The Rise and Fall of Goldcrest Films* (London: Faber and Faber, 1990).

ELLIOTT, PHILIP, *The Making of a Television Series* (London: Constable, 1972).

—— *The Sociology of the Professions* (London: Macmillan, 1972).

EPSTEIN, EDWARD JAY, *News from Nowhere* (New York: Random House, 1973).

ETTEMA, JAMES S., and GLASSER, THEODORE L., *Custodians of Conscience: Investigative Journalism and Public Virtue* (New York: Columbia University Press, 1998).

—— and WHITNEY, D. CHARLES, (eds.), *Individuals in Mass Media Organizations* (Beverly Hills: Sage, 1982).

FAULKNER, ROBERT R., *Hollywood Studio Musicians* (Chicago: Aldine, Atherton, 1971).

—— *Music on Demand: Composers and Careers in the Hollywood Film Industry* (New Brunswick, NJ: Transaction Books, 1983).

FELSTEAD, ALAN, and JEWSON, NICK, (eds.), *Global Trends in Flexible Labour* (Basingstoke: Macmillan, 1999).

FOOTE, JOE S., (ed.), *Live from the Trenches* (Carbondale and Edwardsville, Ill.: Southern Illinois University Press, 1998).

FRANCKE, LIZZIE, *Script Girls: Women Screenwriters in Hollywood* (London: British Film Institute, 1994).

FREIBERG, J. W., *The French Press: Class, State and Ideology* (New York: Praeger, 1981).

FREIDSON, ELIOT *Professionalism Reborn: Theory, Prophecies and Policy* (Cambridge: Polity Press, 1994).

FRITH, SIMON, *Performing Rites: Evaluating Popular Music* (Oxford: Oxford University Press, 1998).

GAMSON, JOSHUA, *Freaks Talkback: Tabloid Talk Shows and Sexual Nonconformity* (Chicago: University of Chicago Press, 1998).

GANS, HERBERT J., *Deciding What's News* (New York: Pantheon, 1979; London: Constable, 1980).

GAUNT, PHILIP, *Choosing the News* (New York: Greenwood Press, 1990).

GERTH, H. H., and MILLS, C. WRIGHT, (eds.), *From Max Weber: Essays in Sociology* (London: Routledge, 1948).

GILLETT, CHARLIE, and FRITH, SIMON, (eds.), *The Beat Goes On: The Rock File Reader* (London: Pluto Press, 1996).

GITLIN, TODD, *Inside Prime Time* (New York: Pantheon, 1983).

GOLDING, PETER, and ELLIOTT, PHILIP, *Making the News* (London: Longman, 1979).

—— MURDOCK, GRAHAM, and SCHLESINGER, PHILIP (eds.), *Communicating Politics* (Leicester: Leicester University Press, 1986).

GOLDMAN, WILLIAM, *Adventures in the Screen Trade* (London: Macdonald, 1984).

HACKER, JONATHAN, and PRICE, DAVID, *Take Ten: Contemporary British Film Directors* (Oxford: Clarendon Press, 1991).

HARDT, HANNO, and BRENNEN, BONNIE, (eds.), *Newsworkers: Towards a History of the Rank and File* (Minneapolis: University of Minnesota Press, 1995).

HESS, STEPHEN, *International News and Foreign Correspondents* (Washington, DC: The Brookings Institution, 1996).

—— *Live from Capitol Hill!* (Washington, DC: The Brookings Institution, 1991).

—— *The Washington Reporters* (Washington, DC: The Brookings Institution, 1981).

HIGSON, ANDREW, (ed.), *Dissolving Views: Key Writings on British Cinema* (London: Cassell, 1996).

HIROSE, HIDEHIKO, 'The Press Club System in Japan: Its Past, Present and Future', *Keio Communication Review*, 16 (1994), 63–75.

JOHNSTONE, JOHN W. C., SLAWSKI, EDWARD J., and BOWMAN, WILLIAM W., *The News People* (Urbana/Champaign Ill.: University of Illinois Press, 1976).

KEIRSTEAD, PHILIP O., and KEIRSTEAD, S.-K., *Automating Television News: A Generation of Change* (Tallahassee, Fl.: Castle Garden Press, 1999).

KERR, PAUL, (ed.), *The Hollywood Film Industry: A Reader* (London: Routledge, 1986).

KIM, YOUNG C., *Japanese Journalists and their World* (Charlottesville, Va.: University of Virginia Press, 1981).

KIMBALL, PENN, *Downsizing the News* (Washington, DC: The Woodrow Wilson Center Press; Baltimore: Johns Hopkins University Press, 1994).

KNUDSON, JERRY W., 'Licensing Journalists in Latin America: An Appraisal', *Journalism and Mass Communication Quarterly*, 73: 4 (1996), 878–89.

KURTZ, HOWARD, *Hot Air: All Talk, All the Time* (New York: Basic Books, 1997).

LAIRD, PAMELA WALKER, *Advertising Progress: American Business and the Rise of Consumer Marketing* (Baltimore: Johns Hopkins University Press, 1998).

LAUZEN, MARTHA, M., and DOZIER, DAVID M., 'The Role of Women on Screen and Behind the Scenes in the Television and Film Industries', *Journal of Communication Inquiry*, 23 (Oct. 1999), 355–73.

LEAB, DAVID J., *A Union of Individuals: The Formation of the American Newspaper Guild, 1933–1936* (New York: Columbia University Press, 1970).

LEE, ALAN J., *The Origins of the Popular Press, 1855–1914* (London: Croom, Helm; Totowa, NJ: Rowman and Littlefield, 1976).

LEE, CHIN-CHUAN (ed.), *China's Media, Media's China* (Boulder, Colo.: Westview Press, 1994).

LEE, CHIN-CHUAN (ed.), *Money, Power and Media: Communication Patterns and Bureaucratic Control in Cultural China* (Evanston, Ill.: Northwestern University Press, 2000).

LEONARD, THOMAS C., *The Power of the Press: The Birth of American Political Reporting* (New York: Oxford University Press, 1986).

LIPSET, SEYMOUR MARTIN, TROW, MARTIN, and COLEMAN, JAMES, *Union Democracy* (New York: Free Press, 1956).

LOBRUTTO, VINCENT, *Principal Photography: Interviews with Feature Film Cinematographers* (Westport, Conn.: Praeger, 1999).

MACNAB, GEOFFREY, *J. Arthur Rank and the British Film Industry* (London: Routledge, 1993).

McNAIR, BRIAN, 'Television in a post-Soviet Russia: From Monolith to Mafia', *Media, Culture and Society*, 18: 3 (1996), 489–99.

McREYNOLDS, LOUISE, *The News under Russia's Old Regime* (Princeton, NJ: Princeton University Press, 1991).

MADGE, TIM, *Beyond the BBC: Broadcasters and the Public in the 1980s* (Basingstoke: Macmillan, 1989).

MAIER, THOMAS, *Newhouse* (New York: St Martin's Press, 1994).

MORGENSTERN, STEVE (ed.), *Inside the TV Business* (New York: Sterling Publishing, 1979).

MORRISON, DAVID E., and TUMBER, HOWARD, *Journalists at War* (London: Sage, 1988).

MYTTON, GRAHAM, *Mass Communication in Africa* (London: Arnold, 1983).

NEGUS, KEITH, *Producing Pop: Culture and Conflict in the Popular Music Industry* (London: Arnold, 1992).

NEWCOMB, HORACE, and ALLEY, ROBERT S. *The Producer's Medium: Conversations with Creators of American TV* (New York: Oxford University Press, 1983).

NIELSEN, MIKE, AND MAILES, GENE, *Hollywood's Other Blacklist: Union Struggles in the Studio System* (London: British Film Institute, 1995).

ORME, WILLIAM A. JR. (ed.), *A Culture of Collusion: An Inside Look at the Mexican Press* (Coral Cables, Fla.: North-South Center Press/University of Miami, 1997).

PAASILINNA, REINO, *Glasnost and Soviet Television* (Helsinki: YLE (Finnish Broadcasting Company), 1995).

PEDELTY, MARK, 'The Marginal Majority: Women War Correspondents in the Salvadoran Press Corps Association (SPCA)', *Critical Studies in Mass Communication*, 14 (1997), 49–76.

—— *War Stories: The Culture of Foreign Correspondents* (New York: Routledge, 1995).

PETERS, ANNE K., and CANTOR, MURIEL G., 'Screen Acting as Work', in Ettema and Whitney (eds.), *Individuals in Mass Media Organisations*, 53–68.

Political and Economic Planning, *Report on the British Press* (London: Political and Economic Planning, 1938).

POLLARD, GEORGE, 'The Impact of Social Attributes on Professionalism among Radio Announcers', *Gazette*, 56 (1995), 59–71.

POLLOCK, JOHN CROTHERS, *The Politics of Crisis Reporting* (New York: Praeger, 1981).

PORTER, WILLIAM E., *The Italian Journalist* (Ann Arbor, Mich.: University of Michigan Press, 1983).

POWDERMAKER, HORTENSE, *Hollywood, the Dream Factory* (London: Secker and Warburg, 1951).

READ, DONALD, *The Power of News: The History of Reuters*, 2nd edn. (Oxford University Press, 1999).

REEVES, RICHARD, *What the People Know: Freedom and the Press* (Cambridge, Mass.: Harvard University Press, 1998).

RILEY, SAM G., *The American Newspaper Columnist* (Westport, Conn.: Praeger, 1998).

ROBINSON, DEANNA CAMPBELL, BUCK, ELIZABETH B., and CUTHBERT, MARLENE, *Music at the Margins* (Newbury Park, Calif.: Sage, 1991).

ROSTEN, LEO, *Hollywood: The Movie Colony, the Movie Makers* (New York: Harcourt, Brace, 1941).

—— *The Washington Correspondents* (New York: Harcourt, Brace, 1937).

SCHLESINGER, PHILIP, *Putting Reality Together: BBC News* (London: Constable, 1978).

SCHUDSON, MICHAEL, *Discovering the News* (New York: Basic Books, 1978).

SEMETKO, HOLLI A., BLUMLER, JAY G., GUREVITCH, MICHAEL, and WEAVER, DAVID H., *The Formation of Campaign Agendas* (Hillsdale, NJ: Lawrence Erlbaum, 1991).

SERFATY, SIMON (ed.), *The Media and Foreign Policy* (Basingstoke: Macmillan, 1990).

SHAH, HEMANT, 'Factors Influencing Development News Production at Three Indian Dailies', *Journalism Quarterly*, 67: 4 (1990), 1034–41.

SHAW, DAVID, *Journalism Today* (New York: Harper's College Press, 1977).

SINGER, MICHAEL, *A Cut Above: 50 Film Directors Talk about their Craft* (Los Angeles: Lone Eagle, 1998).

SKLAR, ROBERT, and ZAGARRIO, VITO (eds.), *Frank Capra: Authorship and the Studio System* (Philadelphia: Temple University Press, 1998).

STEWART, PEARL, 'Women of Color as Newspaper Executives', in Pippa Norris (ed.), *Politics and the Press* (Boulder, Colo.: Lynne Rienner, 1997).

THOGMARTIN, CLYDE, *The National Daily Press in France* (Birmingham, Ala.: Summa Publications, 1998).

THOMPSON, ROBERT J., *Adventures in Prime Time* (New York: Praeger, 1990).

TIFFEN, RODNEY, *News and Power* (Sydney: Allen and Unwin, 1989).

—— *Scandals: Media, Politics and Corruption in Contemporary Australia* (Sydney: University of New South Wales Press, 1999).

TUCHMAN, GAYE (ed.), *The TV Establishment: Programming for Power and Profit* (Englewood Cliffs, NJ: Prentice-Hall, 1974).

TUMBER, HOWARD, (ed.), *Media Power, Professionals and Policies* (London: Routledge, 2000).

TUNSTALL, JEREMY, *The Westminster Lobby Correspondents* (London: Routledge, 1970).

—— *Journalists at Work* (London: Constable; Beverly Hills, Calif.: Sage, 1971).

—— *The Media are American* (London: Constable; New York: Columbia University Press, 1977).

—— *Television Producers* (London: Routledge, 1993).

—— *Newspaper Power* (Oxford: Clarendon Press, 1996).

—— and MACHIN, DAVID, *The Anglo-American Media Connection* (Oxford: Oxford University Press, 1999).

—— and PALMER, MICHAEL, *Media Moguls* (London: Routledge, 1991).

—— and WALKER, DAVID, *Media Made In California* (New York: Oxford University Press, 1981).

UNESCO, *The Training of Journalists: A World Wide Survey* (Paris: UNESCO, 1958).

WALLIS, ROGER, and MALM, KRISTEN, *Big Sounds from Small Peoples* (London: Constable, 1984).

WEAVER, DAVID H. *The Global Journalist: News People around the World* (Cresskill, NJ: Hampton Press, 1998).

WILLIS, JANET, and DEX, SHIRLEY, *Mothers Returning to TV Production Work: Equal Opportunities in a Flexible Labour Market*, Research Papers in Management Studies (Cambridge: The Judge Institute of Management Studies, 1999).

WILLS, GEOFF, and COOPER, CARY L., *Pressure Sensitive: Popular Musicians under Stress* (London: Sage, 1988).

WOLFSFELD, GADI, *Media and Political Conflict: News from the Middle East* (Cambridge: Cambridge University Press, 1997).

WYATT, JUSTIN, *High Concept: Movies and Marketing in Hollywood* (Austin, Tex.: University of Texas Press, 1994).

ZELIZER, BARBIE, 'Journalists as Interpretative Communities', *Critical Studies in Mass Communication*, 10 (1993), 219–37.

ZOOK, KRISTAL BRENT, *Color by Fox: The Fox Network and the Revolution in Black Television* (New York: Oxford University Press, 1999).

Index

AAP news agency 134
ABC (Australia Broadcasting Corporation) 155, 256
Abiola, Chief 235
ABS (Association of Broadcasting Staff) (formerly Staff Association) 190, 191–2
actors
  female 6, 102
  Hollywood salaries for 98
  moral division of labour 2, 6
  and television producers 186
  vertical occupation 16
ACTT (Association of Cinematograph Television and Allied Technicians) 189–90, 191
Adams, Noah 168
advertising
  African media 237
  in China 245, 246
  newspapers 38
  and radio talk show hosts 114
  in Russia 276
  vertical occupation 16
advertising agencies
  American 49–50, 51, 52, 54
  in pre-war Germany 81
Africa, sub-Saharan countries of 229–39
African Morning Post 230
Aga Khan 72
Agence France Presse 268, 271
Ahidjo, President 233–4
AJA (Australian Journalists Association) 255, 261
Aksyenov, A. N. 83, 86–7
All Quiet on the Western Front (film) 82
Allen, Fred 97
anchorpersons 154, 159
  in France 267
  in Germany 286
animation 19, 52
Annadurai, C. N. 101
Anti-rightist movement 240, 242
Apple, R. W. 173
Archer, William 35
Argentina 136
Arnault, Bernard 268
Arnett, Peter 168
Arnold, Arthur 30

Aslamazyan, Manana 281
Associated Press 11, 128–9, 133, 134
Astaire, Fred 97
audience(s) 4
  appeal 12
  political talk radio 114–15
  ratings 195
Audit Bureau of Circulations 54
Australia
  media moguls in 9, 67, 69, 72, 73, 75, 117, 258–9, 261
  media occupations in 253–62
  Warwick Fairfax episode 71
Australian, The 255
Australian Financial Review 255
auteurs 19
aviation correspondents 149
Awolowo, Chief 235
Azcarraga, Emilio 9
Azikiwe, Nnamdi 230

Baker, Russell 168
Barnouw, E., and Krishnaswamy, S. 100
Barton, Frank 230
Baxter, Warner 97
BBC (British Broadcasting Corporation)
  and ABC 256
  African Service of 238
  costume department 7
  Director-General of the 10, 11
  fast tracking in 5
  management at 192–3
  morale at 192–3, 211
  and MPM 280–1
  Producer Choice 196
  unionisation of the 189–93
Beery, Wallace 97
Beijing Youth Daily 246
Belair Jr., Felix 45
Benny, Jack 97
Bent, Silas 45
Berezovsky, Boris 277, 278
Bergen, Edgar 97
Berlin 291
Berlin, Irving 53
Berlusconi, Silvio 9, 66, 67
Bernard Shaw, George 35
Bernie, Ben 97
Berry, Don 118

Beuve-Méry, Hubert 270
Beveridge Committee 190–1
Beverly Hills, California 3
Bild 290
Biograph studio 50, 94
Birt, John 11
Bittermann, Jim 157
Black, Conrad 72, 73–4
Bloomberg L. P. 139
Bloomberg news agency 268
'Bollywood' 3
Bond, Alan 259
Bonnier, Albert 70
Boston Globe 163, 164
Boulder Dam 44
Bourdieu, Pierre 265, 266
Bourgault, Louise 234
Boyd-Barrett, Oliver 132, 138, 141
Boyer, Charles 94, 97
Bradshaw, Walter 130
Bragg, Melvyn 198
Brandon, Henry 151
Brazil, media moguls in 9
Brezhnev, Leonid 85–6, 88–9
Bridge Information Systems 139
broadcasting, *see* radio; television
broadsheets 122–3
Bronner, Ethan 163–4
Brooks, Geraldine 168
Brookside 281
Brown, Ashmun 47
BSkyB satellite television 10, 120
Buck, Edmund 129–30
Bulwer-Lytton, Edward George 263
bureau system 137–40
Burns, Bob 97
Burns, George and Allen, Gracie 97
Burns, John F. 168
business editors 37–8
bylines 255

cable television 15
call-in programmes 113–14
Cameroon 233–4
Canal Plus 268
career ladders
    media occupations 4–5
    television producers 180–2, 195
casual work, *see* freelance employment
CBS 8–9, 154, 156, 157, 165
CCTV (Central Television) 245–6, 248
CDU party 288–9, 291
celebrity television correspondents 161
censorship
    of African newspapers 232
    early French journalism 264

protection against 237
    in Soviet Union 85–6, 274
Central Africa 230
Cha, Louis 72
Chancellor, Christopher 131, 136
Chandler, Otis 76, 78
Chandler family 71, 73
Chandralekha (film) 101
Channel Four 196, 215, 223
Chaplin, Charlie 3, 13, 96
Chechnya 279
Chicago newspaper circulation war 52
Chicago Tribune 166
China 240–50
Chirac, Jacques 68
Chisholm, Sam 10
Chu Anping 240–1, 242, 247, 250
Citizen Kane 66
Civil Service 147
Clapper, Raymond 44
Clarion 45
class distinctions, in journalism 32, 33
Clifford, Alex 133
Clinton, President Bill 108, 109
CNN 15, 139, 157, 158
Cobbett, William 38
Cohn, Harry 53
Colbert, Claudette 94, 97
Cole, Tony 132, 134
Collins, Henry 120
colonialism 230, 231, 234–5
Columbia Pictures 53
Communism 248, 250
Communist Revolution (Chinese) 240
computerization
    in broadcasting 216–17, 221
    craft disputes over 18
    in French journalism 271
    and newspaper industry 120
    and television 225
    trade union resistance to 15, 218–19,
    224
Comtelburo 132
Confucian tradition 247
Conrad, Paul 78
Cook, Bert 255
Cooper, Kent 11, 134
corporatism
    in German media 286–7
    in Russian media 277–9
corruption, in China 247
Courier 30
Cox Chambers family 71
craft disputes 18–19
craft unionisation 13–16
Crawford, Joan 97

credits, screenwriters 61–2
crime correspondents 149
criticism
  and individual news sources
    152
  journalistic 20–1
Cromer, Lord 130
Crosby, Bing 13, 97
crossover careers 12, 13
cultural despotism 241
Cultural Revolution 242
Cuomo, Mario 107
Curran, James 20
cyberjournalism 161

Daily Chronicle 33
Daily Express 147–8
Daily Mail 8, 31, 71
Daily Mirror 120
Daily News 30
Daily Star 119
Daily Telegraph 118, 121–2
Daily Times 230, 234
Daily Variety 3
Dassoult, Serge 268
Davies, Marion 66
Davis, Bette 94
De Luca, Michael 9
de Smaele, H. 280, 281
Debray, Régis 266
Delane, John 4, 38
Delarue, Jean-Claude 271
Delporte, Christian 269
Deng Tuo 241, 247
Deng Xiaoping 242, 243–5, 249
Der Spiegel 285, 290
deregulation 15–16, 21, 239
Deutsche Journalisten Schule, Munich
  288
Diana, Princess of Wales 157
Dicey, Edward 33
Dickens, Charles 30
Dickinson, Frederic W. 130
Die Welt 67
Die Zeit 285
digital technology 216–17, 218, 236
Dionne, E. J. 168
directors
  Hollywood television 184–5
  occupational fragmentation
    19–20
  television 197
Directors Guild 185
Disney, Walt 52
distribution process 51
diversification 268–70

division of labour
  in media industry 53–4
  moral 2, 6, 152
DMK (Dravida Munnetra Kazhagam)
  party 101, 104, 105–6
Dobbs, Greg 112
Doctor Zhivago 19
Donald, Robert 33
Dorenko, Sergei 277, 278
Dorland advertising agency 81
Dostoyevsky, Fyodor 86
Douglas-Home, Charles 123
Dow-Jones news wires 139
downsizing
  foreign correspondents 168–9
  network television news 156–7, 161
  at RTE 217–18
dubbing 103
Dulles, John Foster 151
Dunne, Irene 97
Dunphy, Harry 163, 166
Durbin, Deanna 95

East Africa 230
Eastenders 281
Echo, The 30
Economic Daily 248
Eden, Anthony 151
Edinburgh Review 38
editors 30–1, 32, 33
  entrepreneurial 116–23
  Hollywood television 185
  and newspaper proprietors 74
Eisenhower, Dwight 151
El Salvador 170–8
Elders, Jocelyn 107
Elkabbach, Jean-Pierre 271
ENG/EFP equipment 218
engineering 218
Engländer, Sigismund 129
enterprise stories 158
entrepreneurs, *see* media moguls
Epstein, Edward 158
escapism
  in Indian cinema 101
  USSR television 86
ethnic minorities
  in media occupations 5–6
  television journalists 160
ETU (Electrical Trades Union) 191,
  192
Evans, Harold 119
Evening News 29
Evening Standard 121
executive producers 20, 159
exposés 120, 265–6, 267

factual television programmes 196,
197–8, 204
Fairbanks, Douglas 3, 13
Fairfax family 253, 258–9
Falklands War 136
fan clubs, Indian 100, 103–6
fast tracking 5
feedback information 150
Feist, Leo 53
Fiah, Erica 230
Fields, W. C. 97
Figaro, Le 8, 67
film industry 5
directors in 19
division of labour 54
in India 3, 12, 99–106
media barons in 10
moral division of labour 2
in New York 50, 51–2
occupational community 2–4
pre-war Germany 81
trade unions in 15, 17, *see also*
Hollywood; screenwriters; stars
film producers
and screenplays 61
and star personalities 94
Financial Times 275
Finney, Ruth 44
First National 96
First World War
and French journalists 264
Reuters correspondents in 135
FMLN (Farabundo Mart: National
Liberation Front) 173, 176, 177
Focus on Africa programme 238
football correspondents 147–8, 149, 150
Ford, Peter 163
foreign correspondents 31, 32
A/B teams 172–8
dangers faced by 167–8
generalists/specialists 166–7
hierarchy of 162–4
longevity in same position 164–5
for news agencies 128–42
in television 165
work arrangements 167
Foundation for Independent Radio
Broadcasting 281
Fox, William 53
France
journalists in 263–71
media moguls in 8, 66, 67–8, 69, 70,
268
France 2 (television channel) 267
Frankfurter Zeitung 82, 285
Freedman, Max 146

freedom of the press
in Africa 237
in China 240–1
in France 263–4
in Germany 284, 289
in Russia 274, 278
and Washington correspondents 43
freelance employment 21, 22, 33
foreign correspondents 162–3, 170
in France 265, 270
in Hollywood television 185
and staff correspondents 170–8
in television 6–7, 203, 204, 205, 206,
207–9, 210, 219
Frost, Thomas 32

Gable, Clark 94, 95, 97
gag writers 61
Gambia 230
Ganesan, Shivaji 100, 101, 102, 104
Garbo, Greta 97
Gauch, Sarah 163
Geiringer, Alfred 132
Gemini Studio, Madras 101
Germany
journalism in 283–91
and the *Länder* 286
media moguls 67, 68, 69, 70, 79–82
news agencies in 285
Ghana 236, 238
Ghandhi, Indira 72, 88
Ghandhi, Rajiv 72
ghost writers 150
Globe, The 30
Goebbels, Joseph 82
Goenka family 72
Gold Coast 230
Golden Globe awards 21
Goldwyn, Samuel 53
Gone with the Wind 95
gossip columns 46
Gosteleradio, chairmen of 83–7
government media policy
in Africa 232–4, 239
Australian television 256, 257, 259
in China 241
in post-war Germany 286
in Russia 274, 277–9
in Soviet Union 83–9
government studies into broadcasting
215–16
Graham, Donald 75
Graham, Kay 72, 75
Graham family 71, 72, 73
Grant, Cary 97
graphic design 218

Great Leap Forward policy 242
Greenpeace 265–6
Greenwood, Frederick 30
Greer, Germaine 253
Griffith, D. W. 13, 50
Guangming Daily 240
Guardian 116, 122–3
Guillermoprieto, Alma 163, 164
Gutenberg, Johann 283
Guttmann, Bernhard 82

Habermas, Jürgen 284
Hachette (media corporation) 268
Halberstam, David 164
Harmsworth, Alfred (*later* Lord
    Northcliffe) 4, 8, 31
Harmsworth family 71–2
Hastings, Max 118, 121–2, 123
Havas, Charles 129
Havas news agency 128, 134
Hearst, William R. 4, 8, 49, 66, 67, 69
Henie, Sonja 95
Henry Nannen Schule 288
Herald and Weekly Times 258, 259
Hersant, Robert 8, 66, 67–8, 69, 70, 72,
    268
Hess, Stephen 139
Hillenbrand, Barry 164–5
Hitler, Adolf 79, 81, 285
Hollywood 3
    anti-communist purges 18
    films in pre-war Germany 81, 82
    guilds in 15, 17
    small independent companies 5
    specialist journalists 21
    stars 12–13, 93–9
Hollywood Reporter (daily trade paper) 3
Holme, Christopher 133
Hope, Bob 97
horizontal occupations 1, 13–16
Horwitz, Tony 167
House of Commons 32
Howard, Roy H. 134
Hu Shi 250
Hu Yaobang 244
Hugenberg, Alfred 69, *79–82,* 285
Hughes, Charles E. 44
human interest stories 120
human rights 237
'Hundred Flowers' movement 240, 241–2
Hunt, Thornton 33

imported television programmes 256–7
independent television 223–5
    trade unions 189–91
India, film industry in 3, 12, 99–106

Ingersoll, Ralph 72, 75, 76–7
Institute of Journalists 34, 39–40
international news agencies, *see* news
    agencies
Internews organization 281
investigative journalism 265, 289, 290–1
investments in media 69, 280–2
Ireland, broadcasting in 214–25
Italy, media moguls in 9, 66, 67
Izvestia 275

Jain, Samir 72
Jeffrey, Lord Francis 38
Job, Peter 132
Johnson, Lyndon B. 146–7
Johnston, William 29
Jones, Kennedy 29, 35, 36
Jones, Roderick 11, 130, 133
Jones, Victoria 112
Jose, Babatunde 234–5
journalism/journalists
    'above the law' sanction 45–6
    in Africa 234–5, 236, 237
    anonymity 27, 30
    in Australia 255–6, 258, 260–1
    broadcast 5, 153–61
    and bureau system 138–40
    in China 247–50
    commercialism in 40–1
    competitive 46–7
    crime correspondents 149
    cross-cultural differences 290
    cultivating contacts 148–9
    during Cultural revolution 242–3
    cynicism of 46
    early low status of 29–30, 38
    foreign correspondents 128–42,
        162–78
    in France 263–71
    in Germany 283–91
    hierarchical aspect of 2
    high departure rates 260
    'muck-racking' 52, 267
    political 5, 20, 25–7, 42–8, 146–7
    professionalisation of 35–6
    and relationship with proprietors 77–8
    in Russia 274, 279
    salaries of 30–3, 39
    in Soviet Union 86
    specialist correspondents 144–52
    speed-up in 116–17
    sports 147–8, 149, 150
    star columnists 12–13, 77
    state recognition for 34
    trade unionism 28, 32, 34, 37, 39
    as vertical occupation 16, 20, 28

war correspondents 32, 135, 136, 168
widespread alcohol addiction 34
women in 6, 35

Kaftanov, S. V. 83, 84
Kamalhasan 102, 104
Kamphol (Vacharaphol) 72, 73
Karnow, Stanley 168
Karunanidhi, M. 101
Kaunda, Kenneth 238
Kennedy, Jim 75, 78
Kenya 230, 238
Kenyatta, Jomo 230
Kharlamov, M. A. 83, 84
Khrushchev, Nikita 84, 88
Kimball, Penn 159
King, Harold 131
King, Larry 108
Kirch, Leo 287
Kitchener, Sir Herbert 130
Knight, Robin 164
Koch, Ed 111
Kohl, Helmut 289, 291
Kouchner, Bernard 267
Kravchenko, L. N. 83, 87

labour correspondents 149–50
labour market, television 203–13
    restructuring of 217–23
Laemmle, Carl 53
Lagardère, Jean-Luc 268
Lagos Daily News 230
Lapin, Sergei 83, 84–6, 88–9
Las Vegas 13
Laski, Professor Harold 240
Lawrence, Lester 135
le Gendre, Bertrand 265
leader writers 31–2
League of Nations 44
Lean, David 19
Leeds Mercury 32
Lenin, Vladimir 86
Leninism 241, 247
Leykis, Tom 110
Liberation Army 242
Liberia 230
Liddy, G. Gordon 109
lighting 218
Limbaugh, Rush 107–9, 112, 113, 114
Lin Biao 243
Linnée, Susan 167
Lintas advertising agency 81
Lippmann, Walter 255
Listev, Vladislav 279
literary editors 20–1
Liu Shaoqi 242

live television 182
Lloyds Weekly News 30
location directors 197
Lockhart, John Gibson 38
Loew, Marcus 53
Long, Gerald 132
Longworth, Alice 44
Los Angeles 3
Los Angeles Times 71, 78, 166, 167
    foreign correspondents 164
lunching, source 147, 149, 150
Lytton, Lord 29, 33
Lyubimov, Alexander 279

Ma brothers 72
Macaulay, Herbert 230
McCann-Erickson advertising agency
    81
MacDonald, Jeanette 97
McKenzie, Kelvin 119–20, 121
McLaughlin, Ed 108
Madras film industry 99–106
magazine news programmes 156
Mallon, Paul 44
management, BBC 192–3
Manchester Guardian 4, 31
Manegold, Catherine S. 164
Mann, William C. 163
Mao Zedong 240, 241–2
Marinho, Roberto 72
market forces, and Chinese media
    249–50
market research 54
marketing, media 51–3, 237
Marks, Ed 53
Marx, Karl 284
mass campaigns, and the media 241–2
Massingham, H. W. 35
Mathews, Tom 169
Maxwell, Robert 72, 73
May, Clifford 164
Mayer, Louis B. 53
Mayhew, Henry 33
media
    assistance projects 280–1
    buying agencies 21
    conglomerates 246
    and economic reform in China 243–7,
        249
    ombudspersons 270
    production patterns 51–2
Media, Entertainment and Arts Alliance
    261
media barons 9–11, 65
    in Russia 277, 278
    in Soviet Union 83–7

media moguls 7–9
  in Australia 9, 67, 69, 72, 73, 75, 117, 258–9, 261
  European 65–70
  in France 268
  selling origins of 52–3
media-ocracy 278, 279
mediaklatura 265, 266–7
Médias 269
Mesetsev, N. N. 83, 84
Messier, Jean-Marie 268
Mexico, media moguls in 9
MGM Studio 95
Miami Herald 177
Mill, James 38
Miller, Keith 165
Monde, Le 265–6, 267, 268, 269
Montague, C. E. 31
moral division of labour 2, 6, 152
Moreau, Ron 165
Morley, John 29, 30, 31
Morning Advertiser 31
Morning Star 30
Morris, Nomi 163
Moscow Business News 275
Mosse newspaper group 79, 80, 82
Motion Picture and Television Producers Association 183, 185
motoring correspondents 149
Mozeley, Rev. 31
MPM (Marshall Plan of the Mind) 280–1
multi-skilling 22, 209–13, 217–18, 221, 225, 265, 268–9
Murdoch, Keith 67
Murdoch, Rupert 8, 9, 67, 69, 72, 73, 75, 258, 259
  and choice of editors 117, 119, 123
Murdoch, Sir Keith 258
Murphy, M. Farmer 44
Murray, E. C. G. 30
music industry 16, 50, 51, 53, 239
Myler, Colin 120

Nadir, Asil 72, 73, 76
National Concord 235
national news agencies, *see* news agencies
NATTKE (National Association of Theatrical, Television and Kine Employees) 191, 192
Nazis 285, 287
NBC 154, 157, 165
Neighbours 257
Neil, Andrew 119–20
Nelson, Anne 168
Nelson, Michael 132
Nemstov, Boris 277

Nenashev, M. F. 83, 87
nepotism 255
Network Africa programme 238
network television, and producer conflicts 186–8
network television (news)
  anchorpersons 154, 159
  correspondent visibility 160–1
  downsizing 156–7, 161
  prime time programming 156
  producer-driven 157–9
Neue Rheinische Zeitung 284
New York
  media occupations in 49–54
  network televison news 155, 159
New York Journal 49
New York Times 45, 71, 74
  foreign correspondents 162, 164, 166, 168, 173–4, 177
New York World 49
news agencies
  bureau system 137–40
  foreign correspondents 127, 163
  in France 268, 271
  in Germany 285
  media barons 10–11
  pre-war Germany 80, 81
  Reuters, *see* Reuters news agency
  in United States 268
News Corporation 258
News Industry Text Format 271
news programmes
  network television 153–61
  in Russia 281
Newspaper Benevolent Fund 34
newspaper industry
  and advertising revenue 38
  in Africa 230, 232–5, 236, 237
  in Australia 254–5, 258–9, 261
  in China 246, 248
  commercialization of 29
  coverage of television 195–6
  critics 20
  editors duties 117–19
  family empires 71–2
  French diversification 268–9
  in Germany 283–5
  media barons in 10–11
  media moguls in 8, 66–70
  New York 51
  print workers 1
  proprietors of 71–8, 257
  provincial 31, 32
  survival of post-Soviet 274–6
  young talent 4
Newsweek 169

Newton, Maxwell 258
nickelodeons 50
Nigeria 230, 234–5
Nixon, Richard M. 72
Noble, Kenneth 166
Noelle-Neumann, Elisabeth 289
North, Oliver 107, 110
Northern Echo 31
not-for-profit media barons 10, 11
    in Soviet Union 83–9
Nouvel Observateur, Le 267
NUJ (National Union of Journalists) 28,
    32, 34, 37, 39, 190–1
Nyerere, Julius 230, 234

O'Boyle, L. 29
occupational communities 2–3
occupational fragmentation 1, 16–20,
    20–2
Ockrent, Christine 267
Öffentlichkeit 284
Ohene, Elizabeth 238
O'Reilly, Tony 72
organized crime, and Russian media
    279
original series ideas 183–4, 187, 204
Oulahan, Richard V. 44
Ozal, Turgut 73

Packer, Kerry 9
Packer company 258, 259
Paley, William 8–9
Pall Mall Gazette 30, 31
Panos Institute 237, 238
Paramount Pictures 96
parliamentary reporters 31, 32
Péguy, Charles 266
People's Daily 241, 243, 245, 248
personality cults
    in China 242
    in Soviet Union 87–9
Peters, Anne 3
Philadelphia Inquirer 164, 167
photography 16
Pickford, Mary 3, 13, 50, 94, 96
pilot shows 182
Pinault, François 268
Pioneer Press 45
Plenel, Edwy 265–6
Poivre d'Arvor, Patrick 267
political journalists 5, 20, 25–7
    and name sources 146–7
    Washington correspondents 42–8
politicians 26, 34–5
politics
    and German media 284–7, 288–9, 291

and Indian cinema 101, 105–6
interference in journalism 248–9
and media barons 11
and media moguls 66–8, 69–70
newspaper proprietors and 72–4
and Russian media 277–9
star connections with 13
talk radio 107–15, *see also* government
    media policy
Pomfret, John 167
popular music
    in Africa 239
    in New York 50, 51, 53
possessory credit 19
presenters 198
Presley, Elvis 3
Preston, Julia 163, 164
Preston, Peter 116–17, 122
prime time news programming 155–6
Pringle, John Douglas 253
private interviews 146–7
privatization 15–16
    in Russia 276, 279
producers, *see* film producers; television
    producers
professional misconduct 270–1
professionalism 13–16, 261, 264
propaganda 249, *see also* personality cults
proportionality 286
PTI news agency 134
public service broadcasting 286, 288–9,
    see also BBC
publicity
    film 52
    media moguls and 66
    television 195–6
publishing houses 288
Pulitzer, Joseph 49, 51, 69
Putin, Vladimir 278–9

Quarterly Review 38

radio
    in Africa 231, 233, 236–8, 238–9
    in China 246
    ex-military personnel in 6
    ideological bias of 111–12
    media moguls in 8–9
    and occupational fragmentation 16
    political talk hosts 107–15
    in Russia 280–1
    as stepping stone to television 182
    technological changes in 216, 218
Radio France International 238
Rainbow Warrior 265–6
Rajnikanth, Tholipatti 104–5

Ramachandran, M. G.(MGR) 100, 101, 102, 104, 105–6
Randal, Jonathan 163, 165
Rather, Dan 154
Read, Donald 129, 132–3
Reagan, Michael 108, 110
Reagan, Ronald 78
Red Guards 242, 243
Rees, Christopher 279
Reference News 248
regulation 271
Reith, Lord 11, 191
Renfrew, Glen 132
reporters, *see* journalism/journalists
Reporters san frontières 237
Republican Party 109
Reupke, Michael 136
Reuter, Baron Herbert 130
Reuter, Julius 129
Reuters news agency 11, 81, 128, 163–4
  first correspondents 129–31
  guidelines for correspondents 140–1
  and partnerships 134
  post-war 131–3, 135–6, 142
  undermanning of 133
  and United States agencies 134
  war correspondents 135, 136
Richburg, Keith B. 166
Rieffel, Rémy 267
risk-taking 69–70
Robbins, Edward 34
Rocks, David 164
Romania 168
Roosevelt, Franklin D. 46, 47, 67
Rose, F. H. 33, 34
Rosenblum, Mort 163, 166, 173
Rothermere, Lord 71, 73, 74–5
Rowley, Sir Marmaduke 35
RTE (Radio Telefís Eireann) 215–25
Rusbridger, Alan 122–3
Russell, Herbert 135
Russia, media professionals in 273–82

Sala, George 33
salaries
  celebrity television correspondents 161
  freelance workers 163, 178
  Hollywood actors 98
  Hollywood stars 96–8
  Hollywood television producers 181
  journalists 30–3, 39
  media barons 10
  screenwriters 56
  television 206–7
  and vertical occupation 16
Sarkar, Aveek 72

Sarkar, Kobita 100
satellite television 15
satirical journalism 233
SBS (Special Broadcasting Channel) 256
Scherl newspaper group 79–80
Scherl Verlag (film trade paper) 82
Schneidermann, Daniel 266
Schröder, Gerhard 287
scientific media research 86, 215–16
Scott, C. P. 4
Screen Writers' Guild 56, 57
screenwriters 182, 183
  conflicts 18
  ex-journalists as 52, 58–9
  Hollywood 55–62
Second World War 285
Selig, Colonel William 53
Selznick, David O. 95
Selznick, Lewis J. 53
sensationalism 27
Sérillon, Claude 267
Sevareid, Eric 167–8
Sexton, Dave 147–8
Seydoux, Jérôme 268
Shearer, Norma 97
Sheean, Vincent 43
Sheepshanks, Dick 133
Shepherd's Bush, London 3–4
Shipler, David 164
short-term contracts 22, 207, 218
'shorts' agreement 189–90
Shuster, Alvin 166
Sian, Sally Aw 72
Sierra Leone 230
Simon, Bob 165
Sinclair, Anne 267
Singleton, Dean 72, 74, 76
Sixty Minutes 156
Slabynko, Oleg 279
soap operas 52
  in Australia 257
  in Russia 280–1
Society of Women Journalists 35
sources
  anonymous 147–8
  criticism and 152
  cultivating 148–9
  feedback 150
  and French journalists 265
  information exchange 150–1
  key individuals 144–6
  lunching 147, 149, 150
  motives for information 151–2
  private interviews 146–7
South Africa 230, 236, 237
South Bank Show, The 198

Southampton Southern Echo 32
Southern Weekend 248
Sovetskaya Kalmykiya 274
Soviet Union
  media barons 83–7
  news agency in 141, *see also* Russia
Spark, F. R. 32
SPD party 288–9
SPECA 171, 172, 175
specialist correspondents 144–52
Spender, Harold 32
Spender, J. A. 28
sports journalists 140, 147–8, 149
Springer, Axel 67, 68, 70, 289
Staff Association (BBC) 189–90, 191
Stalin, Joseph 86, 88
stars 8, 12–13
  average ages 95–6
  profitability of 95
  salaries 96–8
  and script consultation rights 185
Stead, W. T. 31
Stern 285
Stern, Joe 53
Stevens, Lord 72
story development
  Hollywood 60–1
  for television 182, 183–4
Stothard, Peter 123
Strauss-Kahn, Dominique 267
stringers, *see* freelance employment
studio directors 197
Su, Shaozhi 241
sub-editors 31, 32
Subbulakshmi, M. S. 100
Süddeutsche Zeitung 285
Suez crisis (1960) 136
Sulzberger, Punch 74, 75, 77–8
Sulzberger family 71, 72, 73
Sun, Lena H. 166
Sun, The 119–20
Sundarambal, K. B. 100
Sunday Times 119–20, 151
superstars 13
Suslov, Mikhail 84, 88
Sweden 70
Sydney Morning Herald 253
Syndicat National des Journalistes 264
syndication 12, 13
  political talk radio 108–10

tabloids 119–21
Tamils 101
Tanganyika 230
Tanzania 234
Tarde, Gabriel 263

TASS 84
Taylor, Paul 168
Telecine VTR 218
Telegraphen-Union 81
television
  in Africa 233, 236
  and associated printed material
    198
  attracting young audiences 4
  in Australia 256–7, 258–9
  changes in last two decades 212, 215,
    216–17, 223–5
  in China 245, 248
  creative work environment 211–12
  directors in 19–20, 184–5, 197
  ex-military personnel in 6
  foreign correspondents 165
  in France 267–8, 271
  in Germany 286–7
  Hollywood producers of 179–88
  labour market 203–13, 217–23
  media barons in 10–11
  media moguls in 8–9, 66
  network 153–61, 186–8
  occupational community 3–4
  and occupational fragmentation
    17
  press coverage of 195–6
  in Russia 276–80
  salaries 206–7
  short-term contracts in 207–8
  in Soviet Union 85
  stars of 12–13
  trade unions in 15, 189–93,
    218–19
  women in 6, 210–11
  working hours in 194, 205–6
television producers 19–20, 196,
    205
  additional responsibilities of 196
  autonomy levels of 197–8
  Hollywood 179–88
  network news 157–9
  and promotion 195–6
  specific genres of 194–5
  of televison news 157–9
television series 182, 197
Temple, Shirley 95, 97
TF1 (French television channel) 267
This Week (current affairs programme)
    189–90
Thogmartin, Clyde 266, 269
Thompson, H. B. 29, 34
Thompson, J. Walter 81
Thomson, Lord 189
Tiananmen crackdown 241, 245

Tighe, Desmond 135
Times, The 30, 31
  Delane as editor 4, 38
  entrepreneurial editors 123
  and Rupert Murdoch 67
Tin Pan Alley 50, 51, 53
Tisch, Lawrence 157
TnaG (Teilifís na Gaeilge) 215, 223
Tocqueville, Alexis de 47
Tolstoy, Leo 86
trade unions
  in Australian media 255, 261
  in BBC 189–93
  in France 264
  in Germany 284
  Hollywood television 183–4, 185
  in Irish broadcasting 216, 218–19
  and labour correspondents 149–50
  and new technology 15, 218–19, 224
  in newspaper industry 14–15, 28, 120,
    264
  NUJ 28, 32, 34, 37, 39
training, journalism 35, 40, 132
  in Africa 238
  in Germany 287–8
  vocational 5
Tucker, Ray 44
Turkey 73
Twentieth Century-Fox 95

Uganda 234
Ullstein newspaper group 79, 82
UNIP party 232
United Artists corporation 13, 96
United Press Associations (UP) 134
United Press International (UPI) 163,
  168
United States
  embassy in El Salvador 171–2
  and media assistance projects 281
  media moguls 8–9, 69
  news agencies 268
  newspaper-owning families 71
  newspaper trade unions in 15
  political talk radio in 107–15
  screenwriters in 18
  stars in 12
  Washington correspondents 42–8,
    see also Hollywood
Universal Studios 95
universities 5, 288
University of London 40

Vallée, Rudy 97
Vare 'slush fund' 44
Vasan, S. S. 101

Vera Verlagsanstalt 80
vertical occupations 1, 13–16
Vestnik news agency 141
Villalobos, Commander Jauquin 173
vocational training 5

Wall Street Journal 164, 167
Walraff, Günter 290
Walsh, Thomas J. 44
war correspondents 32, 135, 136,
  168
Ward, Bernie 110
Washington
  network news correspondents 155,
    158
  political correspondents 42–8
Washington Post 71, 75, 164, 166,
  167, 168, 177
Watanabe, Teresa 166
Watergate scandal 72, 109
Watts, W. N. 34
Weaver, David 6
Weber, Max 25, 42, 284, 285
Welles, Orson 66
West Africa 230, 236, 237
West African Pilot 230
West Germany 285
Westminster Review 38
Wiggins, J. R. 45
Williams, George Douglas 130
Winchell, Walter 97
WIPRO news agency 80
wire services, *see* news agencies
Wisker, John 35
Witmark, Isadore 53
Wolff, Bernhard 129
Wolffs Telegraphisches Korrespondez-
  bureau 82, 128, 285
women
  in French television 267
  increases in media numbers 22
  in Irish television 221–2
  in journalism 6, 35
  Reuters news agency 130
  in television 160, 207, 210–11
World Economic Herald 243
writers, *see* screenwriters
Writers' Guild of America, West
  (WGAW) 18, 55, 183–4

Xinmin Evening Daily 245

Yeltsin, Boris 277, 278
young industry syndrome 4–5, 206
Yudina, Larissa 274
Yugoslavia 168

Zambia 232, 233, 236, 238, 239
Zassoursky, Yasen 278
Zelnick, Robert 166
Zhao, Yuezhi 252
Zhao Ziyang 244

Zhirinovsky, Vladimir 278
Zhou Enlai 243
Zhuganov, Gennady 278
Zuckerman, Mortimer 72
Zukor, Adolph 53, 96

Printed in the United Kingdom
by Lightning Source UK Ltd.
110795UKS00001B/502-504